DESIGNING EDUCATION FOR THE FUTURE, NO. 2

Implications For Education Of Prospective Changes In Society

Edited by EDGAR L. MORPHET, *Director, and* CHARLES O. RYAN, *Associate Director, Designing Education for the Future: An Eight-State Project, Denver, Colorado*

Citation Press • New York • 1967

Library of Congress Catalog Card Number: 67-22888

1st printing, May 1967
Printed in the U.S.A.

PREFACE

At the close of the American Revolutionary War, the statement "Eternal vigilance is the price of liberty" became popular. After World War One, H. G. Wells expressed the same basic idea, with a modern application, when he said, "Human history becomes more and more a race between education and catastrophe."

During my many years in school teaching and administration, and more recently in educational publishing, these two statements, always vivid in my memory, never ceased giving me a deep sense of urgency in proceeding with the great task of vastly improving education and universalizing it in this country.

Seldom, if ever, has anyone given more meaning to the term "education" in so few words as did Mr. Wells. He was talking about the fast-moving accumulation of unprecedented power born of a technology never known to man in all history and capable of annihilating the slowly developed culture of the ages.

Against such a background of admonition and prophecy, it is indeed heartening to learn of the initiative taken by eight State Departments of Education in developing an Eight-State Project entitled "Designing Education for the Future" and supported generously by the U. S. Office of Education — a deliberate effort to keep education ahead in the race.

The initiators of the four-year project, launched in 1965, secured 16 carefully prepared papers by 24 authorities in various technical fields indicating what they believe will be the nature of many important facets of our society in 1980. These papers are published in *Prospective Changes in Society by 1980,* volume one in the "Designing Education for the Future" series.

The papers of the first volume were studied by 21 eminent educators who in turn prepared their respective statements of *Implications for Education of Prospective Changes in Society* for the second volume.

The third volume, entitled *Planning and Effecting Needed Changes in Education,* presents papers by other experts who have examined strategies and procedures for implementing changes in individual schools, school systems, and state educational agencies.

It should be stated that during the progress of the entire Project there were many conferences in which the writers thoroughly discussed the predictions and the implications.

JOHN W. STUDEBAKER
Chairman of the Editorial Boards
Scholastic Magazines, Inc.

DESIGNING EDUCATION FOR THE FUTURE:
An Eight-State Project

Policy Board and Project Staff

Sponsoring States	Chief State School Officers (Policy Board)	State Coordinators
ARIZONA	Sarah Folsom	Robert L. Pickering
COLORADO	Byron W. Hansford, *Chairman*	Russell B. Vlaanderen
IDAHO	D. F. Engelking	Robert S. Gibb
MONTANA	Harriet Miller	Earl B. Peterson
NEVADA	Burnell Larson	Lamar LeFevre
NEW MEXICO	Leonard J. De Layo	Thomas B. Bailey, Jr.
UTAH	Terrell H. Bell	Jay J. Campbell
WYOMING	Cecil M. Shaw	Paul G. Graves

Edgar L. Morphet, *Project Director*

Charles O. Ryan, *Associate Director*

Financed by funds provided under the
Elementary and Secondary Education Act of 1965
(Public Law 89-10, Title V, Sec. 505)
and
the Sponsoring States

Project Office:

1362 Lincoln Street
Denver, Colorado 80203

1

FOREWORD

The period in which we are living is an exciting and challenging one for anyone concerned with education. There is a growing recognition of the need to provide broadened and improved educational opportunities for all. In a highly complex technological society such as ours, a good education is essential for the welfare of the individual and for society.

(If our schools are to truly serve society as well as to help bring about desirable change, much improved advanced planning is needed) This project, "Designing Education for the Future", is an attempt to provide some of the needed long-range planning. The results to date have been very interesting and intellectually stimulating. We hope that they will be useful as well.

BYRON W. HANSFORD
Chairman, Policy Board

CONTENTS

INTRODUCTION

What changes *will* be made in education during the next ten to fifteen years? We know there *should*—and will—be many changes, but the nature and direction of those changes can only be determined by the people who live in each community, state and in the nation, and, to some extent, by international developments. The kind and quality of decisions reached— and of changes that *are* made—may have a significant bearing on the future of the nation and even of humanity.

While almost everyone knows that *changes must be made in education* for many reasons, there is so little agreement on many concepts and proposals that limited, if any, progress can be made in many areas. Such a situation—especially in these days of increasingly rapid and significant changes in society—is potentially dangerous for all of us.

This project constitutes an attempt on the part of the eight cooperating states to begin to resolve this important dilemma. The basic design and the general plans for the project are explained briefly in Chapter 1 of the first publication: *Prospective Changes in Society by 1980.* As pointed out in that chapter, there are two closely related aspects of the project that are being carried forward at the same time: (1) those planned and conducted *on an area basis* for the benefit of people living in the sponsoring states, and of others who may be interested, and (2) those being planned and conducted *in each state* to meet the needs of the people in that state. Since each state is primarily responsible for the program of education provided for all who live in the state, a major concern of the project is to assist the people in each sponsoring state to develop and implement an effective organization and procedure for planning and providing an adequate program of education, including changes that should be made during coming years.

The Area. The area aspects of the project include:

1. An attempt to identify some of the probable major changes in society during the next decade and a half. This constituted the basis for the *First Conference,* held in Denver, Colorado June 29-30 and July 1, 1966. The fifteen papers prepared by leading authorities are included in the publication: *Prospective Changes in Society by 1980 (Including Some Implications for Education).*

2. An effort to determine the major implications for education of prospective changes in society, which constituted the basis for the *Second Conference* held in Salt Lake City, Utah, October 24-26, 1966. The sixteen papers and four supplementary statements prepared by leading authorities are included in this publication: *Implications for Education of Prospective Changes in Society.*

3. An attempt to focus attention and provide information on the strategies and procedures in planning and effecting changes. The *Third Conference,* to be held at Scottsdale, Arizona, April 3-5, 1967, will be

devoted to *Strategies and Procedures for Planning and Effecting Needed Changes in Education.* The thirteen basic papers being prepared by leading authorities will be concerned with (1) basic strategies and procedures, (2) the application of these to individual schools, to local school systems, and to the state educational organization, leadership and functioning, and (3) research and development strategy, power structures in relationship to planning and change, and the politics of planning and change.

Each State. The policies, plans and procedures for the project in each state are developed by a coordinator (or director) and an advisory (or policy) committee comprised of leading lay citizens and educators—with the assistance of an out-of-state consultant and of the central staff. While the emphasis and procedures vary somewhat from state to state, the major attention during the current fiscal year in every state is devoted to:

1. Arranging for a substantial number of representatives (educators and lay citizens) to participate in each of the area conferences as a basis for improving their understanding of trends, problems and possibilities.

2. Encouraging and arranging for individuals and groups throughout the state to read and discuss each of the conference reports and other related materials and to attempt to agree upon important implications for the state.

3. Organizing study committees as needed to assemble and analyze pertinent information and develop proposals for long-range objectives and plans for effecting needed changes in their respective areas.

4. Arranging for the study committees concerned with various aspects of the *educational program* (such as: purposes, goals, scope and organization of education; educational needs of children, youth and adults; the curriculum or educational program; instructional procedures and the preparation of teachers and other professional personnel; supporting services essential for an adequate program of education; and evaluation of the educational program and of instructional effectiveness) to complete by the end of the current school year their studies, proposals for long-range goals and their plans and procedures for implementing them. Arrangements are also being made for study committees concerned with organization, finance, and other important aspects of education to be organized in time to identify problems and to develop plans for completing their studies during the following year.

5. Developing detailed plans for completing all major aspects of the study as soon as feasible, for disseminating and interpreting the findings, conclusions and recommendations, and for obtaining the cooperation of leaders in the state in beginning the process of implementation.

EDGAR L. MORPHET
Project Director

CHAPTER 1

Major Implications For Education
Of Prospective Changes In Society

One Perspective

PAUL A. MILLER*

The major implications for education of prospective changes in society should be a continuing concern of boards of education, superintendents of schools and staff members. Changes do not just happen. The causes are present today and more will emerge in the future. People are influenced by them. Pressures develop. Expression is given to these pressures. Schools and the school system feel these pressures almost as soon as they happen. Therefore, participation in the interpretation of changes is the inevitable responsibility of educators everywhere.

The problem becomes acute because in the schools the evidence—and the shape—of tomorrow rests in the lives of children and youth. Parents and the general citizenry see through the lives of the young into tomorrow; therefore, their interests in the influence of change upon the lives of the young become very deep-seated. Action is expected; results are desired; immediate programs are anticipated to produce the best of all possible futures for the boys and girls of today. Accordingly, this discussion is not a theoretical exercise without roots in day-to-day action in the natural laboratory provided by schools and their surroundings.

GENERAL ORIENTATION

The writer was born in a major war, proceeded through the formative years during the great depression, reached several milestones of formal education prior to another great war, and administered school systems during the emerging post-war period and the rapidly changing society of the 1960's. Men react differently, to be sure, to the same conditions. War, depression, and change have caused this writer to pursue through education the answers to three questions:

How do we prevent destruction and help men to begin to "beat their swords into plough-shares and their spears into pruning hooks"?

How do we avoid the stagnation, pessimism and cynicism resulting from depression, and other frustrating developments?

*Superintendent of Schools, Omaha, Nebraska. Dr. Miller is a native of Ohio and received his formal education at Wilmington College, Miami University, and The Ohio State University. He has served in many capacities from fourth grade teacher to chief administrator in districts with 400 to 60,000 pupils in Ohio, Iowa, New York, and Nebraska. In January 1967, he will become superintendent of the Cincinnati, Ohio, School Sytem.

1

How do we educate man to walk as confidently on Main Street as he now walks in space?

In this paper, important assumptions underlying any project concerned with planning or designing education for the future will be presented in order to establish the benchmarks for appropriate reflections by the reader. Basic consideration will be given to the individual, who is referred to as *the human constant in the midst of rapid change.* The relative position of the eight-state area will be examined as a region, as a part of the nation, and as an important part of global activity.

A projected tour of Education 1980 has been composed in narrative form to simulate the kind of hypothetical school-community that may be needed to answer the big questions that confront us. *The purpose here is to stimulate reflection and thought,* not to provide the answer; to challenge the reader to think of other alternatives, rather than to select any one solution as a pat answer.

Some major implications will be provided at the end of the paper, dealing with the student as he seeks his educational opportunity through education's line of responsibility at the local, state, national and international levels.

Now that the backdrop has been provided, let us look at some of the movement on stage. The viewpoints presented in *Prospective Changes in Society by 1980* tend to range themselves into several categories: description, values, communication, economic development, and government. The parallel with stated goals for education—namely, self-realization, human relations, economic efficiency, civic responsibility, and purpose priorities—seems apparent.

The authorities who prepared the papers on prospective changes in society indicate that the population will continue to expand dramatically and that the population explosion and its urban implosion are significant. Superintendents and others have been dealing with the *explosion* for a number of years. The *implosion* has been the phenomenon most difficult to manage during this decade.

The increased desire for individual choice and establishment of values is highlighted at the point that conservational art departs from progressive or "pop" art. For the educator, this involves the whole area of creativity.

Mobility of population and of ideas through quick communication and rapid transportation is a physical phenomenon that causes educators to attempt to design education to help people learn how to adapt to rapid changes in their environment. Since the technological picture is painted in vivid color, educators become devoted to the question of how to provide instant experience, instant knowledge, instant adjustment, and instant competency to meet the challenges that are inevitable in the world of tomorrow.

Economic sufficiency and its development have been fundamental from the beginning of time. It is interesting to note that education is equated with productivity, thus with basic wealth. The problem for educators becomes one of how school systems can share in the wealth they create in order to provide the regenerative power for national progress.

In a world of greatly increasing numbers, the organization of human resources through government and, as McConnell (chapter 7)* puts it, through "nongovernment" (organizations) is probably the greatest single issue confronting educators as well as lay citizens. At several points the need for greater social invention has been emphasized. Since education is a social invention, the greatest challenge would seem to be for us to learn how to use education to further needed social invention.

The basic emphasis of this presentation is directed to the question as to how education can best contribute to competent, responsive, and responsible citizenship.

IMPORTANT ASSUMPTIONS

The design for the eight-state project is based on several almost self-evident propositions including the following:

That change is inevitable;

That rapid change will continue;

That some changes will be beneficial to society, others may become harmful;

That to a marked extent man can plan and guide change;

That education is an important factor in the change process;

That education must also change rapidly to meet the challenge of change;

That planning rather than expediency should be the mode of operation in order to assure acceptable results;

That long-range planning is essential, particularly since time and distance have been reduced through improved technology;

That the geographic environment in which change, planning and education take place must be broader than a community, even a state, as large as a region, perhaps as expansive as the nation itself.

The writer believes the following propositions are also important:

That selective experience will continue to be the best teacher;

That simulated laboratory testing of selective experience is needed;

That the improvability of man through education is his hope for survival;

That learning is a fissionable process;

That the development of self-disciplined, free men is the ultimate purpose of education;

That instant, impact learning is essential to achievement;

That the classrooms constitute the basic regenerative cells for a free society.

---

*This and all similar references in this chapter are to authors and chapters in the first project publication: *Prospective Changes in Society by 1980* (Denver, Colo.: Designing Education for the Future, 1966).

BASIC CONSIDERATIONS

As one reflects upon the thought-provoking papers relating to probable changes, the impression is that of constant and dramatic change. One wonders if there will be anything left to be done by hand; yet with rapid change must go rapid adjustment.

At least one part of our environment will not change much in the foreseeable future. That element is the human being, the human constant. The infant has been field tested over a longer period of time than all of the exciting wonders reported by the authorities reflecting upon the important subject matter for 1980. The infant production period is still relatively constant, the result constant, and the growth and development from birth to death fairly constant. Therefore, an examination of this phenomenon appears pertinent.

This will be viewed from two vantage points: from that of society or the environment as it affects the individual and from that of the individual, looking upon himself as an identity, as an influencer, as well as one being influenced by environmental changes.

THE HUMAN CONSTANT

To bring into being responsible citizenship, five goals will still remain important for each of those six and one-half million babies expected to be born in 1980 as contrasted with the four million born during the past year: (1) to learn about self and seek self-realization; (2) to learn about others and the art of human relations; (3) to learn about economic life, so he may be fed, clothed, and sheltered; (4) to learn about organized man and his civic responsibility because organized resources— government, if you please—make it more certain that self-preservation becomes possible; and finally, (5) to learn to battle the elements with attendant successes and failures, and thus to become a philosopher to contemplate the purpose of things.

As a human constant, man's biology in the upcoming period may be tinkered with, hopefully for his benefit. However, along with Poor Richard, he will learn that "Dame Experience keeps a dear school, but a fool will learn in no other." His basic urges will be the same as those of his forebears as well as of his peers. He will need adventure, love, security, motivation, and success. He will be confronted, as have all of those who went before him, with three big decisions—marriage, jobs, and leisure.

In the present period, and particularly in the upcoming fifteen years, man will begin to appreciate and utilize the extensions to his perceptual apparatus, the availability of knowledge and the technical muscles provided him with which to do battle not only with earthly but with universal giants.

The most puzzling part of his experience may be the understanding of the Western ethic, particularly as it meets the Eastern in the battle of the ideologies. How to mesh his drive and motivation for success with that of others, will provide a puzzlement. How to bring unity with diversity will be his great frustration as it was his father's and his grandfather's.

His personal horizon will expand from himself to an interest in others and thence to the world of many nations. He will become interested in and acquainted with himself, his mate, his family and his neighbors, with many of those in his community, his state and his nation, and hopefully will seek to understand his world of several billion people. As this individual human constant reaches the cognitive stage with reference to global associates in 1980, the concepts expressed by the authorities will have brought him, as it must all men, to a point of humility. His oneness may seem insignificant among so many. Yet his basic urge will be to rise and be recognized.

ENVIRONMENTAL CHALLENGES

Looking through the infant's eyes out at the world of wonder (and hopefully a wonderful world), the trends indicated by Shetler (chapter 16) will certainly preoccupy much of his time and thought as he matures. The population explosion with its attendant implosion and urbanization will surround him because that is where he most likely will be living.

Automation will provide him with fewer work hours and more leisure. He will, as the Greeks, be able to devote himself to more education to expand his understanding through the arts. He may be awed, if not frustrated, when he realizes that he probably will have to develop competencies for three or four different careers in his lifetime to meet changes caused by technology.

The information revolution may stimulate man to the point of shock, with instant gossip, instant propaganda, instant decisions, instant adjustments. Instant families will not likely occur. Yet as Shetler indicates, he will "continue to aspire to a fuller, better, richer, and more comfortable life."

Interestingly enough, a recent publication of the American Association of School Administrators,[1] outlined the trends of society's goals in about the same manner as the authorities giving attention to the problems of 1980. In brief, the imperatives for today and tomorrow are listed as urbanization and its rewards, work and its preparation, creativity and its nurture, morality and its strengthening, tension and its tuning, democracy and its workability, resources and their conservation, leisure and its use-time budget, humanity and its improvability.

THE EDUCATION PRODUCT

Cutting through the information and concepts available for consideration, a global gap seems apparent. Dr. Walter Aley of the Industrial Information Institute, Youngstown, Ohio, once said: "As a social scientist, I must observe that in history nothing of significance ever happens that does not have its local expression; therefore, the study of history should start at home." It is important for a state to look to its neighbors in a region for cooperation in organizing all resources for the benefit of the region. These regions become the nation; and many nations become a world in which communication and transportation are expanding at a rapid rate. Our

---

[1] Shirley Cooper and others, *Imperatives in Education*. (Washington, D.C.: American Association of School Administrators, 1966).

next-door neighbor of tomorrow may be a Congolese native, a Tibetan chieftain, a friend in the local lodge, the Prime Minister of Great Britain— some one from another community, state or nation. The question here is: Are there not global as well as national ties for the eight-state area?

There has been much discussion concerning the need for more and better education. Productivity has been defined as the combination of education, research, and development. Thus, education is equated with productivity, hence with wealth. The old economic definition for wealth was the sum of goods and services. But goods and services must be produced. All of this requires productivity. As productivity increases, so does wealth; therefore, this rough syllogism makes productivity and education co-partners. If one result of education is to bring a product into being, could not one major product be education? Is not know-how a salable product in a world where it is sorely lacking? Boulding (chapter 12) points out that "the greatest product of society is people." Does it not follow that the greatest wealth is an educated people?

An examination of statistics reveals that only one-third of the world is enlightened and two-thirds are living in primitive conditions. Many are at the same level as their ancestors were ten thousand years ago. If all the goodness of the American system is to continue, further thought must be given to plans and provisions for the removal of the ignorance barrier.

This writer would like to see an extension of the population examination to the world at large to determine whether or not education is really running ahead of population and technology ahead of ignorance. The world of 1980 and beyond will bring our children and youth face to face with the answer as certainly as the Roman youth were confronted by Attila the Hun and his barbarians.

The admonition of almost two thousand years ago to "go forth and teach" may well be the best single goal for the individual as well as for the nation. Education truly may be our most important product.

MORE MUSCLE EQUIVALENTS

Although the basic human ingredients may be constant, the extension of man's physical equipment is almost beyond comprehension. His ability to sense extends to the quasars, billions of light-years away, as well as into the heart of the tiniest particle, millions of which could be placed on the point of a needle. He literally can stand on one heavenly body and use a lever and fulcrum to move another, as Galileo pointed out centuries ago. He can shoot an arrow into the air and not only know where it will land but can bring it back for the late show. He will be able to make Paul Bunyan appear as a pygmy. With one finger he could erase a city, move a mountain, or change the course of the ocean. He can even make his own clock and calendar run backward. With a little more practice in genetic roulette, he may be able to evolve even more super-supermen. His head, a formidable creation in itself with its three and one-half billion components multiplied by 25,000 reactions, has the capacity to tap and utilize for his own benefit (and hopefully for the benefit of others) a significant portion of the tenth to the fifteenth power bits (Knox, chapter 13) of nonredundant information compiled by all men in the previous ages and also to utilize an equal amount to be created by the time he graduates from high school. He must know how to ask, and find the best answers to, the right questions —a big question in itself. This will depend upon his value orientation. His fate will depend upon the direction his questions take.

Yes, his physical equipment capability makes man a new colossus that may stand astride the universe, with one foot on earth and the other foot in eternity. Yet this is not enough.

Man's Choices

The "not-enough" has to do with that something called "conscience," or what causes man to make his choices. As yet, science does not seem to have found its optimum location in human affairs. A tiny thread appears among the authorities relative to this point.

Boulding (chapter 12) seems to point in this direction when he says, "A failure to advance in the physical and biological sciences for the next twenty-five years would not present mankind with any serious problems, but the failure of knowledge to advance in the social sciences will be fatal." He goes on later to say, "We need social inventions to correct some of our problems."

Shinn (chapter 15) points to many problems of the conscience, such as human rights, undermining authority, affluence and poverty, choice of identity, responsible decisions in relation to things, man and integrity. He, too, says, "The world needs social inventions." Elazar (chapter 6), discussing government partnerships, points to the "need for better education in political processes." Wheaton (chapter 8), in his discussion of metropolitan problems, points out that we need "effective machinery for conflict resolution" and a "means of maintaining amenity among metro groups in a region."

The human constant with its big muscles must make choices to create human progress. How to prevent humanity's destruction raises some big questions of conscience. This is the province of the politician, the political scientist, and the philosopher. (Education is, or should be, the "mother" of such persons). The return to value premises and the big questions is necessary. The computer can only answer if asked the right questions.

Yet this can only happen when the human constant moves to his global horizons through his many billion world relationships. Again, this raises the question of how improvable is man.

The Time Line

Benjamin Franklin organized his life on a time basis and his day on a time schedule so that he assured himself of some improvement each day.

The individual, likewise, will move through such periods during his lifetime with certainty. His improvement will either be by accident or by design. In three score and ten years, man's course is run regardless of the expectancy improvements reported during the last sixty years. He is born;

he learns; he matures; he has a family; he works; he leads; he advises; and he retires.

Elazar (chapter 6) refers to the rhythm of change measured on a generational basis. Most of those devoting attention to problems and progress in the nation and in the eight-state area were certainly influenced by the great depression. This reflects itself in the leadership period thirty years later, which is now. Certainly, those entering their formative years during World War II will bring a particular flavor to the nation by 1980. The children and youth of the affluent sixties will be leading at the turn of the century; therefore, if significant influence is to be brought to bear, action must come promptly. The 1980's are with us now. Many of the leaders for the eighties entered the austere education of the forties, and are now in the early productive periods. This underscores *the need for continuing education now*.

The barking Sputnik scared everybody in the fifties. Some of the high school and college graduates of that early period and shortly thereafter will be rising to world leadership in the eighties.

Events on Main Street have scared people in the sixties. Most of those conscionable young men and women reacting to man's inhumanity to man on Main Street, U.S.A., will not reach the leadership control period until the 1980's.

Much dependence has been placed upon education for the hope of tomorrow, but the delayed action results must always be kept in mind. The little people of Head Start will be graduating from high school and entering the early years of college by 1980. Their leadership will not be felt significantly until the turn of the century. How few there are compared to the number of possibilities! How to educate the young is a formidable task, but how to teach the adults new concepts is equally so.

Every farmer has known from the beginning of time how important it is to select carefully the seed corn, to care for it, to plant it properly in meticulously prepared soil to bring it to a full, fruitful harvest. Yet man deals with his own improvability on a shotgun rather than a rifle basis.

As the human constant moves along the time line, it will be difficult for him to escape the educational influences brought by the developments in communication technology. Many Hottentots may view the magic tube, see their neighbors, hear Huntley and Brinkley; then their own big questions will be asked. Therefore, informal education the last fifty years of life may well be as important if not more so, than the first twenty of formal schooling.

As man does physiologically, he may also do educationally. In effect, he may shed his educational skin every few years to gain a new one.

ECONOMIC TECHNOLOGY IN EDUCATION

As the individual moves through time, inevitably self-preservation will be his first law; therefore, food, shelter, clothing, and the means leading thereto will be important early in life. Consequently, the individual must find a means of maintaining himself. This means a job. Changing technology and moving to the opportunity will be the two projected problems. A residual of free time will result from shorter work hours. Yet that leisure may well be the very opportunity to keep the individual in business, as it were, leading to the second, third, and fourth educational skins and a fuller life.

There may be a problem for a small segment of the world's society, that is, some of us may tend to "outsmart" ourselves. The informed may move too far away from the mass. Historically, the elite of France were sent to the guillotine from which France has never recovered.[2] This may have happened to the German nation who drove the elite to other shores. Therefore, our most salable product in tomorrow's world market may well be know-how. If we are to survive as a first-rate nation, closing the gap between the elite and the mass through education appears essential. Tactically, in the military, extending the supply lines too far without means of bringing up the main forces may result in defeat. If the avant garde of technology moves too far out from the bulk of humanity, by sheer numbers the ignorant may cut off the very force upon which their own survival depends.

How to educate an individual for jobs that do not exist becomes another big question for education. How do we organize to get that job done?

Along with the individual's time line and his geographic expansion, he soon learns the lesson of grandfather and the hornets. When grandfather was asked by his grandson why he did not pick off the hornets' nest with his rifle, he replied, "They's organized." Therefore, the meshing of the various governments, both formal and informal, becomes an even more important problem with growing urbanization, rapid communication, rapid transit, and instant everything.

This brings us to what probably is the most important aspect of this presentation.

SOCIAL INVENTION

As Hilleboe (chapter 4) points out, "Loss of identity, fight for privacy, and general tensions impinge upon the individual." All of these exist in varying degrees among the several incorporated or nonincorporated sovereignties found especially in any urban complex. Elazar (chapter 6) has commented extensively on the United States government (the new junior partner in education), admonishing those who are critical of its overt interests in education, pointing out that the balance of power still rests in the hands of the people under our Constitutional system if they work at it. It always has. Governments may come and governments may go, but people seem to survive in spite of them. How to relate the several autonomies from the local through the state, regional, federal, and international structures becomes the problem. Therefore, the observation that the world needs social invention is a most pertinent point.

Ironically, the laboratory has yet to contribute to the social sciences as effectively as it has to the physical side of things. As Kuhns (chapter 14)

---

[2] Nathaniel Weyl and Stefan T. Possony, *The Geography of the Intellect*. (Henry Regnery Company, 1963).

points out for the arts, political science is at the conservational rather than at the progressive end of development. A half-billion-ton thrust lifts man gently into the sky. Thousands guard his safety. Yet along Main Street clubs are still used. Few feel safe. Many may watch, detached, while one perishes below in the street.

No industrial firm would think of hiring a chemist who has merely read the books. We certainly would not want a surgeon who had only taught anatomy; we would insist upon demonstrated laboratory competence and performance. Yet in nongovernmental and governmental organization, it is generally assumed that if we know the right answers our performance should be commensurate with the correctness of our recapitulated knowledge.

The chief implication for education is to design a laboratory for testing citizenship rights and responsibilities. We must develop the creativity necessary to lead to social invention and to send the individual forth with the same assurance of civic performance as polio vaccine is sent off the end of the assembly line of the industrial laboratory with confidence for prevention of a dread disease.

In the accomplishment of such a task, technology can play a great role. Everyone has been greatly impressed by the procedures used in solving the polio problem.[3] All of the bits of information were placed into the grader in order to sift out the kernels of most probable worth. Research was pinpointed on those few kernels. The solution was quickly forthcoming. The results speak for themselves.

In education today, many old wives' tales exist. From time to time the cycle turns around and the same old problems, the same old solutions, and the same old failures keep cropping up. Of course, there are many successes. The individual with his ingenuity to survive succeeds in spite of problems. Even the frog in the well, when he jumps three feet and slides back two eventually gets out of the well. A hundred years of effort with a three percent acceptance of a good idea is, at best, a chance relationship. This seems to discredit the power of intelligence which may have had very little to do with it. This lag can be ill-afforded in this day.

Today we are enamored of the word innovation—what's new? Newness, without exhaustive testing, is hardly goodness. The many variables and probabilities have been almost beyond the ken of man until now. The computer with its experimental aspects has great promise. Tied in with the research and development centers and their satellites, and with appropriate tie-lines among the several centers, the hardware will make possible a giant step to man's real time improvement.

Roberts[4] of the Atmospheric Research Center gives hope of ultimate accomplishment. By 1975, a system may be devised and the hardware fitted to handle bits of information from each hundred square miles of the earth's surface every ten minutes to bring the weather within predictability and projection. The program has been written to use the hardware to

---

[3] George Gallup, The Miracle Ahead. (Harper and Row, 1964).
[4] Walter Orr Roberts, Science Frontiers. (American Association of School Administrators Conference, Washington, D.C.: October 1965).

handle the many variables. Thus, we may be able to do more than talk about the weather.

Education is much like the weather. Everybody talks about it. This is inevitable. Now we are beginning to do something about it. Education, like the weather with its many variables, has the technology to help solve its complex problems. Such a program is needed for the improvability of man beyond chance relationships.

With this kind of ability and its application, perhaps a new Darwin will write the origin of behavior and the laws of naturally being human. How do we start in education? Perhaps a theory of social relativity will be written and laboratory tested. In any case, man's education cannot be left to chance.

FOCUS UPON THE EIGHT-STATE AREA

Where does the eight-state (mountain) area fit into the total scheme of things, not only for the benefit of the area and the people in the individual states but for the nation and the world? In brief, it appears that it has all of the requirements for a testing laboratory needed to create the kinds of social inventions so sorely needed.

The expansive geography, sparsity as well as the density of population, the climate from the deserts to the mountains, and the determination of people are certainly important ingredients. The very fact that this eight-state project exists is evidence of foresight not only for regional determination but national leadership and world influence.

THE POPULATION

In general, during the past five years the area has gained population more rapidly than the nation as a whole, which gained 8.1 percent in this period. At the same time, percentage increases among the eight states were bimodal. Four ranged from 11 to 54 percent, and four varied from three to eight percent.

Inasmuch as urbanization is a national phenomenon, the eight-state area is rather typical of the nation as a whole in this regard. Four of the states are above the national average of 70.4 percent of the people who live in or near a central city. In four others, the population is about 50-50 in this respect. It has become significant as we look forward to 1980, because central city is where most people will be living—half in the central core and the other half in the ring of suburbs. In the future, as Wheaton (chapter 8) points out, 80 percent of the population growth may be expected in such metropolitan centers. In this region there are many such centers undergoing dramatic expansion.

By way of contrast, in the eight-state area the sparsity factor is equally significant. In this vast land area, the average of only nine persons per square mile compares with the national average of 55. Transportation, communication, and concentration of resources become important, particularly to the educational task.

Looking into the future, which exists in the classrooms of today, the children really tell the story. In each of the eight states with the exception of one the gain was more than the 25.8 percent reported as the national average. Therefore, with the high birth rate and relatively low infant mortality figure compared with the nation as a whole, these population gains may be expected to continue as previous observers have indicated.

QUALITY OF THE PEOPLE

More important than number is the kind of people found in the region. Since practically all authorities have emphasized the importance of education as a contributing factor to the growth and development of any particular place, it is important to review some of the indicators which point the direction of the momentum for education in the eight-state area. Hughes and Lancelot[5] ranked many of the states of this area high in educational performance in terms of their standards. This speaks well for the region.

The willingness of most of the people to support education is evident. In 1959, the Committee for Economic Development[6] reported that the effort of the people in the area to provide good education was at a high level. Figures show that the people devoted almost four percent of their income to education while the nation averaged 3.11 percent. More recent data[7] indicate a similar continued high regard for education. The six percent average for the area is well above the 5.3 percent for the United States as a whole. It seems significant that the region has been generally high in effort but below the national average in personal income figures.

It is difficult to determine which is cause and which is effect relative to educational expenditures. It is interesting to find that the quality of people determined through various criteria relating to education is also relatively high. The National Education Association report reveals that the region spends significantly lower amounts for public welfare, requires less for police protection, and has a higher educational level of adults twenty-five years of age or older. The illiteracy levels are well below the national average. Other favorable characteristics may be noted. For example, more of the people go to the polls; the region attracts more professional and technical people; the crime rate is increasing at a lesser degree; there are fewer people proportionately on public assistance; fewer are rejected by the Armed Services; and the proportion of seniors graduating from high school is increasing faster than for the nation at large.

This is not to say that difficult problems do not exist. A large proportion of the existing population lives in metropolitan centers; yet the density of population is low. Therefore, this high urbanization sharply contrasts with the sparsity factor, making the provision of quality education to the isolated students very difficult.

There are wide variances among the eight states and within several of the states. The accomplishments and the quality of the people indicate commendable levels; therefore, the basic ingredients exist to take the steps

[5] Raymond M. Hughes and William H. Lancelot, *Education, America's Magic*. (The Iowa State College Press, 1946).

[6] Committee for Economic Development. *Paying for Better Public Schools*. A statement on national policy by the Research and Policy Committee for Economic Development. (1959).

[7] National Education Association, Research Division. *Rankings of the States*. (January 1966).

that must logically result from the eight-state project, "Designing Education for the Future."

IMPLICATIONS FOR THE EIGHT-STATE AREA

First of all, the basic quality of population with its great interest and demonstrated performance relative to education and development of the area is a good starting point for any effort. Secondly, both density and sparsity factors of great proportions exist to challenge the best in educational management. The expansive geography provides many of the variables that can be found any place in the world. Thirdly, limited resources make it necessary to look to the human being as the real source of wealth to unlock the treasures of any land for the benefit of its people. Fourthly, the area is in a position to learn from the mistakes made by others. Crowded conditions on either coast do not yet exist except in a few places.

Therefore as a regional field laboratory the eight-state project may well set an example and a pattern for moving seemingly immovable objects by the irresistible force of education. Such a regional laboratory means the careful gathering of all the bits of nonredundant information relevant to the eight states, to "shake them down," as it were, to discover the kernels of most worth for the development of a master plan by and for each of the states.

Interaction could be organized in such a manner as to provide a social generator within the population, cycling between the grass roots and leadership. The power of knowledge could pour through the university laboratory penstocks into the elementary and seconday classroom turbines out along the "world of work" power lines to serve human productivity. The lines could be grounded in demonstrated every-day performance, thus completing the cycle from master control to the performance level and completing the leadership-producer circuit.

This could assure continuous upgrading of the plan in light of the natural testing in daily performance. Maintaining individual identity is important; mustering the political forces is paramount; keeping those who occupy the Mount Olympus of thinking and research in touch with those who develop the working parts and also with those who serve the common good along Main Street, is vital.

This means for education that organized research, development, and application are essential. Such an example now exists in the chemical industry. All of the Research and Development Centers of the region together with their satellites as generative units in the several states could be tied together not only for the development of master plans but for the implementation and field testing of the action taken.

The eight-state area has an advantage in this regard because of its long-standing work with the federal government as a continuous partner in its development; therefore, the tieline from the region to the national capital is a natural one. The benefits could accrue to other contemplated regional developments. The region as a total laboratory might well be a simulator not only for other regions in this nation but for similar projects throughout the world.

PROJECTED TOUR FOR EDUCATION 1980

Here an attempt is made to paint a word picture of a hypothetical solution to some of the educational problems, then to take a look at some of the results by 1980. Of course, many other approaches may be developed.

The visitation to the learning center is both hypothetical and real. Some schools have begun to appear that have developed along the lines described.

The teacher and the student—as has always been the case—are the human constants; yet the increasing usage of communication, and of technology in particular, will be evident in a rapidly changing environment.

Attention is given to urbanization because most of the population will be living in standard metropolitan statistical areas (SMSA's) or metropolitan centers.

It is evident that not all people will live in such centers. About ten percent or less will be living on farms and ranches and another 20 percent in much smaller hamlets and villages than the metropolitan centers with 50,000 or more population. Therefore, the tour continues out through the countryside at this point to see what has happened in terms of projected programming for those somewhat removed from the center of activity.

SMSA IS THE PLACE

Since most of the present and future population is projected to live within metropolitan centers, the eight-state region has one advantage. SMSA, or the Standard Metropolitan Statistical Area, identifies such centers. The various urban centers are relatively isolated one from the other. The overlapping problems similar to those found along the East and West Coast strips are few. SMSA in this region is not without its present problems. Small sovereignties are forming iron rings around their mother cities. This tends to handicap reasonable, fluid, satisfactory development not only of the central city but also of the smaller sovereign suburbs. Many of these already have developed almost to the point of no return. Many will be left in the middle of central city to be swallowed by the inevitable outward movement of population growth.

The new SMSA field-test of this region now being researched should prove not only helpful to cities of the area but to others confronted with similar problems. The application of miniaturization in the urban planning sciences could be used to advantage to find the effect of given changes within a simulated urban complex. The computer with its ability to handle multiple variables as in experimental science has possibilities in this regard.

Here as elsewhere one problem will be how to maintain the proper mix in the population to prevent cultural crystallization or stratification, yet maintain reasonable intercultural pride as well as its identity. For education as a portion of the total planning in some situations this may mean organizing schools into a school-city within the total city or upon a sectional basis should SMSA grow beyond a predetermined critical population point.

New SMSA's can be planned much more easily than those that are now in existence. If our political scientists are correct in their observation that the melting-pot influence in America has made it strong, then SMSA planning should be directed to its continuation through education. Concurrent rapid transit and communication could make distance less of an obstacle not only for SMSA but for those in isolated spots throughout the region.

According to many reports, cities of 250,000 to 500,000 population (Wheaton, chapter 8) are considered of ideal size for SMSA. Such a population could be accommodated within a hundred square miles, a territory ten miles by ten miles. This would pose no particular problem either for communication or transit, point to point, under present or projected technological conditions.

In any SMSA of this size range there probably would be from sixty to a hundred thousand or more students. These could be accommodated in some one hundred elementary school centers, twenty-five junior high schools, and six senior high schools. The normal acreage now required would amount to a minimum of a thousand and a maximum of two thousand acres. Roughly, this would be two or three square miles or about three percent of the total land area. In Omaha, a city of 360,000 population, the land presently used for public schools amounts to 854 acres, with 94 school centers for 60,000 pupils. For new SMSA and its surrounding communities such a school campus, or campuses, could be planned and built somewhat as some university campuses are today.

In present SMSA, old school buildings will soon become obsolete. A critical path could be plotted in the planning, to trade the old sites to create an adequate new central campus or several smaller ones to accommodate children, youth and adults. With such an arrangement as the nucleus, related health, recreation, and park developments could be interspersed among the several units. Such deployment of land, building, and services could provide an economic advantage. Superb service achievement certainly could result. Urban renewal via the education route could be accomplished. The resultant balancing of the educational scales could provide an appropriate intercultural mix and prevent the blisters that are developing today. Probably the horny bunions caused by social conflict could be treated successfully.

This veritable Youth Town could field test a young citizen's performance before his entrance into the adult world market. For that matter, adults could be re-educated to meet modern social and economic needs and changes.

Perhaps rather than Youth Town the reference should be the Youth Quarter(s) of the city, a kind of educational shopping center. What a beauty spot it could be. The author believes that it could be produced and operated with a lesser drain upon total resources than occurs under present austerity levels.

A LEARNING CENTER IN THE YOUTH QUARTER

Let us move our calendar up to 1980, then drive to the Youth Quarter. Shall we select a learning center for older youth to see what it might be like almost two decades hence?

As we stop after our meandering drive through the Quarter, we are inspired by the artful relationships of the several units dotted around the green and beautifully landscaped terrain. One might get the impression that education's influence upon art would be similar to the contribution made by the Greek Forum to the Athenians. As we stroll toward the reception center, the individual freedom of youth to come and go reminds us of some college campuses in decades past. Upon reflection, this should not be surprising when it is remembered that these youth are coming from homes with a much higher level of sophistication than those of the 1960's.

Upon entering the learning center, we are immediately impressed with the attention given to environmental control as part of the total learning experience. Even the freshness of the air is noticeable. Upon inquiry we find that this is due to an ionization process developed for climate control by a graduate of a high school remembered twenty years previously. In fact, our host relates to us that the students practically live at the school, coming early in the morning and leaving, reluctantly, at night because of the congenial environmental atmosphere. We muse, as we check in at the reception center, that this is an amazing change from our remembered "good old days." At the reception center we find that the chief administrator is in Area 3 working with teachers on a new course of study for space health.

The administrator's inability to join us causes no concern. A student host identifies himself as our companion for our period of visitation. He takes us to the Town Square for a bit of conversation and refreshment. Again, we muse at the similarity between this area and the many small town squares that we remember so well across the country. How well it reminds us of our American heritage.

Upon inquiry we find many students conducting tours, tending the store, publishing the "Space Gazette" in two languages, supervising student hearings on Youth Quarter, as well as discussing student learning center problems and reviewing disciplinary cases. This living laboratory is simulating the adult world of the future with success and failure repeated as important to the learning process. We meet the student mayor and center government staff. We then remember discussing the need for social invention at a mountain region conference years ago. We note that at last the citizen laboratory has come of age for the educational and political sciences. Upon reflection we conclude that this should bring politics back to the Jeffersonian, Washingtonian and Franklinian status to help man walk Main Street with confidence equal to that demonstrated by his achievement in space. Perhaps this will move humanity ahead of technology.

Our student host makes up a tour. He explains that this learning center is really made up of several units—the business community, with its own Junior Chamber of Commerce; the scientific society, with its

Academy of Science; the industrial area, with its Futures Unlimited; the fine arts colony, with its Exhibition Center; the home arts area, with its Hospitality Suite; food service, with its Restaurant Association; drama, with its Playhouse; music, with its Choral-Symphony Association; engineering arts, with its Craftsmen, Inc. All are well advertised around the Square.

Here we pause to think about the formal education breaking out, as it were, throughout the school into laboratory participation and field-test units. This provides a sense of satisfaction that education for all American youth is finally being realized.

On the tour we find that the desks are different from those in the "good old days." As we enter a mathematics room we find oscillogized instruction boards replacing the old chalkboards. The instructor is using an electronic pen. As we pause by one student, we find the material on the board appearing at the student console. Some of the students are making reprints, no doubt for their homework. Looking more closely at the student carrel, we find a small computer about the size of the old transistor radio. We find another student penciling an answer to a question posed by the teacher which he later supplemented with a reprinted page from a book retrieved from the IMC by what appeared to be the old airline computer card system. The instructor and the student use the oscillograph not only to plot the formula but also to test relationships among the data with which they are dealing. We remember the New Math of twenty years ago. Here we find it rooted in the scientific principle of discovery and learning by the same means.

Continuing the tour we find small groups of 10, large groups of 150, as well as many individuals pursuing learning tasks throughout the center. We find that the emphasis is changed from one of the passive learner to one of an active participant in the learning process. In many cases, the question is more important than the answer. Action upon knowledge is more important than the quantity of right answers.

Peering into the viewscope of one room marked "taping in process" we find a teacher on camera conducting a delicate dissection. Upon examination of some of the schedules we find that this same material is being relayed to another Youth Quarter many miles away in an isolated community near a mountain camp site. A mental note is made to inquire about services to sparsely populated areas. Later, on our tour, we find a student in his carrel at the instructional center reviewing that same tape on Replay 1143.

The IMC—or, as we remember it, the library—is really a communication center with tapes (video as well as audio), microfilm thermoplastic retrievable storage, programmed learning units, and information recall systems. These materials are available not only here but to individuals at home and in areas far away. Yes, we find that books are still there, too. Many of them are coordinated with sight and sound.

Musing about the perceptual extension available to students, we remember what Smith (chapter 10) said about each individual at an eight-state conference years ago. He had reported that the home in the future would accommodate a private telecommunications center with television, audio and video recorders, a two-way picture phone, and an electronic printer, as well as a small computer and display unit.

We asked the student host about his schedule. He reported that it varies from day to day in accordance with his own personal needs. Upon further inquiry we find the student spends much of his time at his own carrel center at home which is "wired in" with the school programming as well as to other units of the Youth Quarter and on occasion throughout the region.

We puzzle about such scheduling, and then remember that the computer makes possible the vast amount of work required for such variable processing. Our conclusion is that the modular experiments of two decades ago appear to have become common practice.

Our only regret as we left was our lack of opportunity to follow up these students into their tests in real life which inevitably will come after they leave such a center. We take comfort that the careful thought and planning evolved twenty years previously has been placed in competent hands.

THE TEACHER AT THE LEARNING CENTER

As we strolled toward our car we engaged one of the teachers in conversation. We asked whether the warm, personal touch had disappeared with the increased use of "gadgets." She assured us that it was even more of a factor than when she began teaching back in the sixties. Now she had been relieved of the drudgery of repetition in the classroom because she was on tape and on call, literally, by each of her charges night and day. She indicated that her preparation was much more efficient due to the rapid availability of experiences through the instructional materials center. She felt more confident of results because of the constant testing and re-testing of materials against results. Upon our inquiry about the console she enthusiastically indicated that instant experience was fast becoming commonplace. She said this was brought about by the fact that even though knowledge had been piling up so fast, retrieval had caught up. She further reflected that, as a beginning teacher, she resorted to repetition, reinforcement, and drill to be sure the student had learned. Now she could select the experiences, singly or in combination, which could have such an impact that once over was enough. Furthermore, she said she could prove it. Such impact learning through selectivity and timing was made possible by her console. Now she could, by the simple pushing of a button, make the stars appear, bring forth a world map or for that matter the other side of the moon, cause an electron to perform on the oscillograph, unfold the life span of the oak or the amoeba, introduce in near-life many of the great figures in times gone by, bring a Satchmo or a Bernstein to life and up front for recitation, select an obscure reference from a remote library as readily as she made a plane reservation in the early days, engage her students in multi-language class discussion via short-wave available to the center, keep up with the class through sensory perception, and get rid of administrivia by electronic accounting, or bring everything to dead silence. The teacher has finally risen to the point of real freedom. The shackles of "things" have been broken. They no longer bind the teacher. This releases the creativeness of the free spirit to devote more time for determining the appropriate direction for the right questions.

THE STUDENT AND HIS LEARNING

Self-reliance and independence are evident. Dependence and co-operation are included when it takes more than one to accomplish a given task. The development of self-support through demonstrated skills is present on every hand among the several laboratories. Each student not only tests himself but is tested in terms of how much he knows and how well he performs in terms of what he knows. When a student is placed in such a life simulator, the real-life test should prove more than adequate. Yet as the student travels along his time line his successes and failures are fed back into research and development centers for the benefit of the learning center, and to the individual in the field for his own benefit.

We hope that he not only knows *why* but knows *how* and puts his heart into the doing.

BEYOND THE YOUTH QUARTER

After leaving the learning center at the Youth Quarter, the mental note about the effect of such an arrangement upon much smaller places and isolated population units was remembered. Therefore, we started out through the countryside to find that camp-community enjoyed many years previously.

"Sweet Grass" was not too difficult to find. We located the school facilities. They looked much the same from the outside as we had recalled them. On the inside, we found a link to the classroom observed in the Youth Quarter. Actually, the few pupils could participate directly in many of the learning activities at the center via either short wave or telecommunication. Periodically, students went directly to the center via air buses. Likewise, caravans from the Quarter set up educational camps as an extension of the learning center under conditions not found in the central complex.

As we think about this, it is not far removed from the correspondence courses except more instant, more personal and more meaningful, both from the student's as well as the teacher's standpoint.

Upon inquiry we find that all of the educational units have reciprocal ties on a kind of educational REA basis. This completes our circuit of the eight-state regional laboratory arrangement described earlier for the eight-state project back in the 1960's.

RESOURCES FOR THE YOUTH QUARTER AND BEYOND

Human resources are the most important ingredient of any successful endeavor because people make up society. A productive person is both the means to and the end product of education; therefore, the start must be made with the individual himself identifying his role in relation to that of others in the eight states, in the nation and in the world.

Sooner or later we must get around to a consideration of money as an essential second ingredient—to stored resources that come as the result of love's labor won. Permeating the thinking of the last half of the twentieth century is the dawning realization that without superb education there cannot be a superb nation. Hence it follows that education must have an adequate share of that which it produces in order to regenerate itself in an ever-improving fashion. The implied issue here is not how little will suffice but where does the law of diminishing return set in for the financial input?. This, too, must be tested in the economics laboratory, beyond the question of a doubt, so that the dollar added may demonstrate its worth in acceptable results.

Here, again, the eight states may be fortunate since they have established a precedent of giving children and youth relatively high priority in terms of money provided for education. Yet how do we know when enough is enough? Perhaps that time will have arrived only when men actually begin to "beat their swords into plough-shares, and their spears into pruning hooks."

SOME MAJOR IMPLICATIONS

In the foregoing pages, many significant changes that will affect education have been noted. By 1980 our population will have increased by about 25 percent. Most of this increase will occur in metropolitan areas in which nearly 80 percent of the nation's population will reside.

Implication: Social inventiveness will be taxed to keep pace with expanding urbanization and to assure adequate living conditions, services, and programs of education. New arrangements will be needed to meet the implosion in order to prevent the strangulation of the central city, yet maintain reasonable autonomy among the several units through more appropriate annexation procedures or through local compacts to enhance the use of resources.

Knowledge will continue to increase and probably will double in many areas.

Implication: Greatly improved storage and retrieval systems will be needed, especially for education, in order to avoid the waste in duplicating experiments and studies due to the inability to find what is known and to activate learning.

Instant communication will be available at the home level.

Implication: The organization of various telecommunication devices into a coordinated console arrangement is pertinent to the teacher's task, the student's self-learning efforts, and the adult's continuing education.

Transportation will move up to the Mach III level in the air and will be greatly improved on the surface.

Implication: Increasing mobility of population is already evident. Meeting the problems of adjustment in local schools and communities throughout the nation will necessitate the development and transfer of adequate individual records and of effective provisions in local school systems for determining and meeting the needs of individual students.

Economists indicate that the gross national product may increase by more than 50 percent of present levels.

Implication: The proportion or amount needed for education must be established at local, state, and federal levels and made available on a basis that will assure the maintenance of relative autonomy in relationship to the responsibility at all levels.

The work force will increase by about one third, and many new kinds of occupations will develop.

Implication: People must be prepared to meet vocational as well as other citizenship needs. Continuing education for all to meet job changes will be paramount.

The productivity of each individual and the effectiveness of the organizational and operational procedures will determine the economic level of any community in the nation. This is anticipated to increase by a third.

Implication: The know-how of education will become a product in itself. This further highlights mobility as a strength of national as well as international stability.

Many ideas have been and will be increasingly in conflict. This will be influenced particularly by the greater proportion of the young, while leadership control still will be in the hands of the older population. The struggle between the conservational and the progressive approach will further complicate value choices.

Implication: For education this will require careful selection on tested bases of the best from the past and the present and the equally careful use of progressive inventions which have been proven under simulated conditions. Procedures will need to be discovered to improve the rationality of decisions and choices.

The human constant will bring to man's life the same pattern of development and basic urges as in the past. The environment into which the child is brought will be vastly different from that of the individual who is responsible for his birth.

Implication: Due recognition of the ever-widening environmental gap between child and parent must be recognized and education brought to bear to close that developing chasm.

Government at all levels will be much closer to the individual yet will seem farther away in means of influencing its decisions. A developing schism between the new establishment and the old is chronic now and may develop into an acute problem.

Implication: Social invention must be provided to assure that the leadership elite does not lose touch with the masses. Conversely, education for the masses must develop ways and means of keeping all persons abreast and a part of the local, state, and national goals and developments.

Nongovernment organizations over the years have been a stabilizing influence and will play an ever more important role in maintaining the balance of ideas, progress, and local, state, and national achievement.

Implication: Through education, students need to learn to understand better the strengths and weaknesses of organizations. For the educational profession this will mean change in associational relationships, perhaps through the creation of an American Association for the Advancement of Education, including all of the influential nongovernmental educational groups. Such an organization would be of such size and influence as to be looked to as a source of sound authoritative education.

The above are positive changes. There are negative ones, such as war, the race issue, a depression, or a national catastrophe.

Implication: In the teaching process, children and youth need to understand the human processes and ways of preventing, when possible, or dealing effectively with unfavorable developments.

Education itself is a social invention. The major premise of this paper has been devoted to the question: How can education provide the social inventions necessary to solve society's problems concerned with the further improvability of man and his institutions? A synopsis of previous emphases regarding *Major Implications* follows:

For the Federal Government: Since the Federal Government is the largest and most effective tax collector and since lay autonomy in education is a tested principle in our national tradition, then an acceptable formula for sharing in the resources of the nation is paramount. The U.S. Office of Education could properly and more adequately tap the lode of state and local educational expertise rather than develop a new administrative hierarchy. Furthermore the Office of Education could properly devote its major attention to the greatest need in education—adequate research, application, and development—to provide the pertinent facts for the solution of educational problems and the enhancement of its traditional role.

For the State Government: Bona fide state leadership and unitary professional administration of education with the same prerogatives and responsibilities now held by many local administrators and their boards of education, particularly in urban centers, are essential; the encouragement of arrangements among states of a region for the more adequate pooling of resources is necessary.

For the Local School District: Since communication and transportation have shrunk the state geography to the relative size of a judicial district, most states should look to as few school units as there are judicial districts, as administrative entities directly related to the state superintendent and board.

For the Curriculum: Arrangements for the further individualization of instruction on a self-learning as well as a directed teaching basis are required. Mastery of retrieval technology is important to achieve a more valid means of assuring selectivity in materials. To reduce repetition and to achieve impact learning is a necessary goal.

For the Teacher: The mastery of the tools of technology is essential in order to bring at least simulated experience of all kinds and varieties into the classroom; furthermore, the art of administering learning will cause the redeployment of teachers in many varying teaching tasks.

For the Student: Self-learning on a continuous basis will be the goal. How to maintain individual identity either in isolation or in groups will be the end. The student will need the ability to measure continuously his own improvement, particularly his ability to behave not only in terms of what he knows but in relationship to what appears to be desirable and acceptable behavior.

For the School Facility: The school facility as such will need to be designed as a total citizen laboratory in itself, a place for self-learning and continuing education tied into the home workshop units as well as with other related facilities distributed in the community.

For Business: Direct participation in the improvement of the educative process must continue. This should lead to the development of knowledge retrieval utilities for education similar to those that now exist in many large corporations for their own benefit.

For Finance: A much larger percentage of the personal income will be needed for elementary and secondary education and research, and at least a comparable percentage increase for all other kinds of continuing learning including higher education.

For the Law: A renewed emphasis upon a government by law rather than by men is essential. Metropolitan areas will need to develop new legal authorities, similar to the Metropolitan Authority of Toronto, Canada, in order to prevent central city strangulation and at the same time to gain better usage of metropolitan resources in planning and providing for improvements in education. Each state will need to develop and refine its "conceptual design" for education and take steps to assure that its legal structure is consistent with the design. Federal laws must be designed to stimulate states and (through the states) the local communities to higher achievement to meet individual as well as national goals through expansion of a comprehensive rather than a categorical grants-in-aid program.

For the Eight-State Project: A social invention in itself, the careful planning now going on must lead to action, demonstrated accomplishment, and a higher personal benefit for each member of the population. All of the necessary ingredients are present. How to create the social generator is the problem.

For the World: Know-how and its teaching inference may well be our most important product until such time as other nations reach the self-regenerative point.

Another Perspective

LAURENCE D. HASKEW *

Implications seldom emerge independently from a given body of data. They are, instead, extracted therefrom. In this process, the stance and perceptual background of the person who does the extracting are significant. In the companion paper giving one perspective on this topic, Paul Miller makes this point quite clearly. The differences between the two papers arise from differing vantage points, from differing manifestations of the same concerns, and from individualized views of what it is important to stress.

This author will extract implications and organize his paper by assuming three separate stances from which to view prospective changes in society. The first stance is that of a person concerned with the basic structures for conducting—in all ramifications of that term—the education enterprise. The second is that of one whose professional engagement is with planning. The third stance is that of an educationist inquiring into what all this says or implies about the intent and content of schooling.

IMPLICATIONS FOR STRUCTURE

The part of the education enterprise which conducts schools has— as its predominant structural element—a local school district which is the prime (but not completely autonomous) executor of what needs to be done. All other structure seeks to feed the local district the resources with which to accomplish a complete job in its geographical bailiwick. State and federal school finance systems, for example, concentrate on assuring or providing funds needed for the effective operation of local districts. In many of the states involved in this project, the local district is the prime structural element in deriving tax support for schools. Ninety-five percent or more of all the staffing for schools occurs as a local district phenomenon. While many structural devices for inter-district collaboration have come into existence, almost all of them rest upon federated pooling of resources which are delivered first to a local district. "If schooling is to be accomplished, local districts must accomplish it" is the presently pervading rationale of our structural design.

LOCAL STRUCTURES AND RESPONSIBILITIES

However, the forecasts of what is to become possible for schooling even through the applications thereto of technology, portend some serious challenges to this rationale. Let us take, as an example, computer-assisted instruction. To devise, refine, execute, and constantly modify even one system of this character requires a mammoth dedication of talent and energy, and its installation necessitates capital investment and operational

* Vice Chancellor, University of Texas; Dean, College of Education, University of Texas (1947-62); Director, Teacher Education, Emory University and Agnes Scott College (1941-47); President, Commission on High Education (1947); Consultant, Gilmer-Aikin Committee on Education, Texas (1947-48); Author of This is Teaching, and contributor to numerous educational periodicals.

support in great magnitude. A structure which depends upon hundreds or thousands of local school districts for the essential financial provisions and for the execution of such accomplishments seems manifestly inefficient and perhaps ineffective. This is only one of many pertinent illustrations of what apparently will become a multiform demand generated by large-cost technology for units-of-execution—and hence units-for-expenditure of foundation program dollars—which will transcend the traditional local school district.

Several other portents of change raise similar questions about our present design for making the execution of education primarily a localistic enterprise. Burgeoning urbanism, for example, does not fit the largely accidental and historic geographic boundaries established for local school districts. The pressing needs of the emerging society can neither be perceived nor be served by dilatory or uninformed provincialism. The power or ability to deal effectively with the projected 57 percent increase by 1980 in the 18- to 34-year-old group is not likely to arise from thousands of autonomous decisions by thousands of operating units. The approaching society will produce crisis after crisis in the human rights field; crises which should—and almost must—be met by universal and rapid responses. Yet, the programmatic autonomy of local districts is a device with built-in deterrents to rapid and socially-significant reactions to emergency. Fewer than 10 percent of the local school districts in this country have the resources—even if they have the disposition—to overcome our scandalous insulation of children from the kinds of materials and experiences that are so essential to education in the modern sense. Such illustrations could continue almost indefinitely. In the opinion of this author, *such evidence does not imply that we should scrap local districts or local execution as a feature of our structure for public schooling.* It does, however, justify extraction of an important implication.

Implication One. The local school district structure is in need of prompt and sharp revision—in function, in scope of programmatic control, in authority relations to other units of execution, in methods of operation and governance, in geographic definition, and in the roles expected of it in financing schools and in purchasing school services.

NATIONAL INTEREST RELATED TO STRUCTURE

A second implication for structure is explicit in several papers included in *Prospective Changes in Society by 1980,* and is implicit in all. Nationalization—and to a large extent internationalization—of the environment (both ideational and ecological) for education is the revolution in whose aftermath education will be conducted between now and 1980. This means that national interest will be a powerful influence in shaping the response of public schooling to present and impending social change. But, at present, we have only a series of tacked-on improvisations as structure for expressing and executing the national interest. For example, our present structure of "quickie" federal grants—programmed on a year-to-year crash basis—is woefully inefficient in producing execution of the national interest in improved schooling for those disadvantaged by defects in our national culture. The objects in view for most nationalized interventions are of such importance that they may warrant risking great initial miscarriages of resources and intent. But if we must—and I am afraid we must—live constantly in a state of war between educational advance and institutional obsolescence, we must structure the nation to conduct that war with something more efficient than guerrilla raiding parties. To open up the problem of what that national structure should be is not the province of this particular paper. It is its province, however, to extract an implication.

Implication Two. For proper and effective expression of the national interest in the direction and execution of public schooling, our whole basic structure has to be re-cast to expedite efficient, prophetically prudential, and economical applications of that interest. Implied here is not one more "establishment"-spawned overhaul of the machinery and policies of the federal government and other national agencies. The re-casting apparently called for is one which makes nationalized action by chartered role and procedures *a member in the* structural organization for public schooling, not a charismatic sideline signal-caller.

STATE TAX AND FINANCE STRUCTURE

The implications of social change for the structures for discharging the responsibilities of each state for public education are not clear. It *is* clear that providing the money to pay for the schooling needed between now and 1980 is not an insuperable task with the prospective Gross National Product as a base. But to provide the major portion of that money from within-state taxes looms as a serious problem for most of the states involved in this project as well as for most other states. Certainly present taxation bases and structures will not suffice. They will become even more inadequate in view of the emerging dimensions of what will be considered an absolutely minimum program of schooling. The economic forecasts augur well for the presence of economic well-being sufficient for most states to devote sharply-increased sums to the support of education. Nevertheless, we must not forget that in very few of these states have the people yet decided to use tax sources adequately congruent with economic activity. Neither can we forget the tremendous new load to be shouldered by all states in providing opportunities for higher education. Nor can planners disregard the preemption of almost all forms of growth taxation by the federal government. "Where there is the will, there is a way" may not be as true as we would wish if we rest our hope primarily on a state structure to produce the money for schools.

As indicated earlier, the structure for application and distribution of the tax money which states collect for public education is presently out of tune with the needed responses to social, ecological, and technical change. That structure may soon be actually discordant. Fifty years ago we were much interested in stimulative, incentive usage of what was then called "state aid" for education. The equalization principle—properly, I believe—has largely superseded the original stimulative strategy. When one looks at the new responses to social need—imperative but not mandated—which open before us, he finds himself thinking once more of the stimulative power of money upon program. The foundation program approach to support for local school systems is certainly not outdated by prospective changes in society. However, we may once more look with real favor upon proposals to supplement an adequately financed foundation program by using a significant proportion of state funds for incentive or stimulation purposes.

More disrupting discordance, however, begins to appear from another feature of our present structure for allocation of state-collected funds. Very small portions of these are now allocated to entrepreneurs other than local school districts. In the future we shall have to use many additional entrepreneurs, such as the state department of education, multi-district service centers, major specialized production enterprises and repositories of technical expertise, interchange arrangements for personnel and equipment, and concentrations of evaluation and planning services. This means that local districts may receive directly much smaller proportions of the state-fund dollars, and thus a new rationale for allocation of state funds is almost mandated.

Implication Three. Modernization of state tax and finance structures needs to be undertaken immediately. The emphasis here is upon "immediately"; the chance to be effective is rapidly contracting.

The State Education Agency

And, what of the state department of education in the stream of impending social change? Will the few metropolitan centers in the states so outrun the functions performable and performed by the central education agency that the latter will become largely ancillary? Will the state education agency come to bear the same responsibility and authority for oversight of expenditures of federal funds used within the state as it now bears for state-produced funds? Will it be a prime source of creative leadership for school responses to society's needs—or will it function chiefly as a repeater-adapter station in the transmission of nationally-conceived responses? The pertinence of these questions to the prospective changes in society is obvious. The answers, unfortunately, are far from obvious. By training and predilection I am disposed to champion a powerful and strategic role-structure for the central state education agency. But the facts of impending social change in themselves fail to dictate—or to negate—such structure. The answers can be found only in what we do *for* and *with* the structural designs adopted. We must confess that we have not done too well by, or with, many state departments of education thus far.

Implication Four. The state-level structure for executing public education apparently faces decisive re-tooling. The choice is still open as to whether it will, or can, be effectively and meaningfully restructured—or will face a declining significance.

POSSIBLE NEW STRUCTURAL ELEMENTS

The evidence available to us demonstrates rather conclusively that three features of the school enterprise must enter upon a period of unprecedented expansion. One of these is *research* (used here to include derivation and use of management data as well as search for fundamental guidance for a science and art of education). A second is *development*, with special emphasis upon planning. The third is *provision of technical adequacy and expertise in execution.*

While students of structure in education can see many ways in which necessary expansions can be accommodated within the three traditional units of structure—nation, state, and locality—many find themselves almost compelled to envision an additional kind of unit (or units). It is difficult to name and to locate this unit, although it is already present with us in many forms. The *Eight-State Project* is one such unit; Regional Educational Laboratories form another example. Within each state there are scores of organized entities now executing supplementary-, ancillary- or specialized-service projects—another example of the move toward a different kind of unit. Seldom do the "new" units have much kinship with the "intermediate units" described by textbooks in school administration. Instead, they are free-floating, non-geographic, non-uniform entities with no particular home but with important jobs to get done.

My question is whether these new forms are with us to stay—as *basic* elements in our structure for conducting education. Note that this egregious unit is a mechanism for response to the sort of societal change with which *this project* is pre-occupied—responses implemented in this form largely because former structures were not sufficient. But, these units—by and large—*are improvisations upon structure,* and *not elements in a re-organized structure.* Their future serviceability may be as irregular as their present relationships to traditional units, but no realist can consider educational structure between now and 1980 without envisioning their presence, if not their proliferation. Societal change is obviously calling for educational response which transcends our classic structural elements, and hence gives rise to another implication.

Implication Five. The task of re-ordering our basic nation-state-local structure to comprehend and coordinate transcending operational entities, and to make them truly effective parts-of-a-whole, is high on the agenda for innovators in education.

IMPLICATIONS FOR PLANNING

Two risks are always run by focusing attention upon changes in society as the starting place for changes in education. On one hand is the risk of inducing a sort of fatalistic paralysis in the face of overwhelming challenge. At the other extreme is the risk of triggering frenetic, shallow reactions based upon unanalyzed inspiration. This project seeks to damper such risks by concentrating attention upon *planning* as its prime outcome.

CONTINUOUS PLANNING FUNCTION

The title of this project is *"Designing* Education for the Future," not "A Design for Education in the Future." The difference is an important one. "Designing" is a constant process, never completed. It does produce some designs, but only as temporary artifacts of the designing process and in a context where design is always followed by re-design. In this rationale, any particular "solution" to a problem serves chiefly as a point of departure for further planning. Operators of the educational enterprise often deliberately depart from past plans in the light of current circumstance and insight, but the planning process makes it possible to know what we are departing from and why we are making the departure. It is planning—and not plans—which is the essence of living toward the future. Prospective changes in society identified in 1966 will not inevitably be those identified in 1970, but the machinery, attitudes, and planning skills now developed will stand educational management in great stead as it addresses the impending future.

Implication Six. All states definitely need to provide for the establishment and support of ways and means to conduct continuously the planning function as a vital element in their organization for education.

PROFESSIONAL LEVEL COMPETENCE IN PLANNING

However, one must grant that the best way to develop *expertise* in planning, and to acquire an habitual posture toward movement according to plan, is to develop plans and become committed to them. A plan is not so much represented by a final design as by a series of steps heading toward an apparently fitting solution to a problem. For example, there is convincing evidence that ways must be found to meet the approaching demands of industry for personnel with a wide range of technical skills. It is necessary, and relatively easy, to produce a master design for institutions, both new and old, to provide the volume of educational training envisioned as essential. But this is only the first increment of labor for planners. There then comes the more exacting labor of sketching out the serial steps required to get from where we are to actual execution of the complete design over a period of several years. These steps must be possible ones, not dreams of what ought to transpire. Thus, planning becomes an exercise in pragmatic strategy and not just a foray into imaginative projections.

To be sure, the presentation of a "revolutionary" new design for some part of the educational enterprise and its almost immediate adoption by a state or a school district is not a rare phenomenon. But, a design is still merely a device for tackling a problem and not, in itself, a solution to a problem. We may set up new vocational-technical schools almost overnight, but still confronting us are most portions of the problem of turning out personnel to meet the needs of industry. Arduous, step-by-step planning is still required to make the design produce what it was intended to produce. A design is, at best, only a small corner in the domain of planning. Planning keeps its eyes upon the needs to be met and upon the comprehensive set of actions which must transpire to meet those needs.

Planning certainly searches for plans, and sets down plans. These plans, tentative though they may be, seek to reflect the imperatives foreseen. To produce such plans is not easy; inertia is great in each planning unit. It is difficult to break away from mere extension of what we have. Hence, when faced with both imperatives and inertia, planners are tempted to adopt devices worked out by others as if those devices are "solutions" in themselves. American education has a long history of moving according to "Plan," spelled with a capital P—the Winnetka Plan, the Three-Track Plan, the California Plan, and so on and on. A current illustration is the so-called "School Park Plan," and I shall use that to make the point in mind. This is a device largely untried in its present formulation but with appealing features. It may turn out to be an excellent device in some situations, but it is still that—a device and not a solution to the problems it addresses. Used by local planners as an element in a master strategy for educational modernization, it may make desirable contributions. But, its wholesale adoption as an end in itself is hardly warranted by the evidence at hand, and substitution of such mail-order innovations for the exercise of thoughtful indigenous planning has seldom in the past produced rich dividends. In other words, the "School Park Plan" deserves consideration by planners, but several alternative routes toward the same ends are also deserving of consideration. Planning at its most productive level is not *adopting* plans but *producing* them.

To summarize the analyses just presented requires the statement of another implication.

Implication Seven. Prospective changes in society reinforce the necessity of developing—for the management of education—professional-level competence in the discipline of planning. By now it should be clear that education must come abreast of, if not outstrip, the industrial sector of our society in its utilization of planning technology. But it must transcend technology because in a professional sense this is what planning is all about. And it certainly is not all about *plans*—static artifacts; but about an active, strategic, continuous, and indigenous undertaking.

IMPLICATIONS FOR THE INTENT AND CONTENT OF SCHOOLING

Pondering the totality presented by the reports in *Prospective Changes in Society by 1980,* I am struck with great force by three implications for the intent and content of schooling. In this concluding section an attempt is made to direct attention to them. This is done humbly because other papers in the present series deal in depth with programming educational endeavor in the light of what portends. From them will doubtless emerge insights which far transcend the particular generalizations extracted here. My present purpose is simply to place three, among many, derivable implications in the limelight.

PREPARING THE INDIVIDUAL FOR SOCIAL CHANGE

The source for the first of these implications is the picture of the possibility that individual man may be at the mercy of social changes but not understand what goes on. Two things are wrong with this picture. The individual resembles a puppet when he should resemble a playwright; thus, social change is king, man is subject. And, in effect, man is an illiterate in a world which does not exist for him.

As a projection from the past intent of schooling, this picture is realistic. Schools have *professed* the desire to equip young people to cope with a changing society. But seldom, if ever, have they manifested genuine intent by matching this profession with determination and implementation. To be specific through illustrations, students in my hometown high schools know a great deal more about nuclear fusion than they know about population explosion. They study communism but not urbanism. They project themselves backward into the Constitutional Convention but not forward into the future of Austin as a center for the convening of people to live together under conditions now foreseen. They are involved in vocational choice but seldom involved in choice of total style of life in view of what can be made to happen in society. In effect, we are saying "Give us (the school directors) full credit for our professions which we do not really intend to do anything about. We promise you a highly-finished, attractive product, namely, pawns to decorate the chessboard of life in a game to be played by social forces."

The above statement is intentionally more harsh than the facts justify. Many schools are trying to make young people habitual, informed participants in the community, the nation and the world of now and the near future. More should be seriously trying to do this, it appears to me. I make no pretense of being able to state how the intent to identify the individual with changing society and with changes in society can be expressed more viably. Certainly we can attack plain ignorance with more zeal. (I wish fifth-graders knew half as much about the present life of American ghetto-dwellers as they know about the past life of American Indians, for example). We should have wit and wisdom sufficient to focus more potent attacks upon other elements of the disengagement syndrome. This is no new appeal, of course. But the picture now faced adds a new imperative to old professions of objectives, an imperative which should transform a mere *profession* into a much more tangible *intent*.

Implication Eight. Schooling should viably implement an intent to identify the individual with social change, as a force therein, as an informed student thereof, and as a sapient reactor thereto.

IMPROVING THE COMMUNITY—PRODUCING CONTENT OF CURRICULA

The next implication is extracted from contemplation of all those social changes which apparently head toward mass rootlessness of people— a society of dwellers rather than a society of communities. One of the paradoxes of megapolitan civilization is that, as aggregations of people grow larger, the need for small communities of social action and social control increases tremendously. These communities of face-to-face intercommunication—designing and executing pressures upon the total body politic as well as providing essential experiences for their members and others—may no longer be defined geographically but they must abound and proliferate if society stays healthy. Such communities come into existence and achieve potency through the phenomenon of leadership—an arrangement in which the ideas and actions of a person or an institution serve to catalyze the making of common cause and shared life-concerns by many.

It appears that the content of *what is provided as schooling must include community-producing leadership*. Some of this content would be revealed in what the school, as an institutional person, does in the midst of its surrounding dwellers. The dramatic conceptions of Litchfield Park— where school is seen as a well-spring of community nurture—give fresh re-statement of the community-school idea. But these conceptions are applicable in significant degree to existing dwelling-places as well as to a brand-new city in Arizona. *Almost every school can be community-producing*. That is, it can exert leadership to bring people-in-families together for common actions, for identification with each other, for developing a sense of belonging to a body and belonging in this world. This does not propose that the school is the proper and logical center around which to organize communal life in megapolitan America. It does propose that the school, as a school, contain a strong echelon of direct effort with adults aimed at producing community in the new sense of that term.

The desired content would also be revealed in what the school offers to children and youth. Obviously, there is a heavy cognitive factor at work when individuals commit themselves to the exercise of leadership in fostering face-to-face relations between people. That includes knowledge that the needs of people-in-society extend far beyond the need for food, clothing, and shelter; knowledge of how human personality is shaped by need-frustration; knowledge of the symptoms and consequences of alienation; knowledge of how community and commonalty are developed, and of how such processes can be made to work. There is also a heavy affective factor at work—the attitudinal and valuational equipment of the committed individual. Content of the school's educational program should be able to do much to develop each of these factors. But opportunity extends even beyond that. In school, much can be done to develop the leadership capacities and predilections of young people, At present, some of this is being done, but with entirely too restricted coverage and with largely incidental attention. Overlooked particularly in our leader-preparing programs are those large segments of our student bodies drawn from the plain people of our attendance areas. It seems to me that schools will miss one of their greatest opportunities to become creators of a new age if they fail to plan for content designed to produce large numbers of graduates trained in the skills of community-forming leadership.

Implication Nine. The programs and curriculums of schools should be decidedly improved and expanded in the provisions they make for content which is community-producing.

DEVELOPING HUMANISTIC TALENTS

In 1980, we are told, an appreciable segment of our population will be working longer hours than ever before in attempts at social activism, endeavoring to correct by collective action the ills of society. Another large segment of our people will be working shorter hours but, with the aid of automated devices, producing two or three times the present volume of recreational and entertainment goods and services for the private market. Some unknown but large percentage of our people will have thirty, forty or fifty hours a week to fill with something while they are not on the job. In the face of these and similar parallel projections, it is highly fitting that *Prospective Changes in Society by 1980* closes by asking, in effect: And who shall speak for man? Speak for him and to him as an individual, a human individual with capacity for becoming humane?

The prime object of education is not to equip Tom Tucker to find his way with minimum pain and maximum pleasure through the labyrinthine maze of society, nor is it to enable him to build a "better" society. The prime object of education is to help Tom Tucker construct for himself a humane, humanistic self. No matter how we gild him with civilization, enable him to acquire materialistic accoutrements for pleasurable existence, and equip him to survive in the fierce jungle of competition for scarce commodities, we have played him false if educators have undernourished his essential humanistic talents and drives.

The academic disciplines known as the humanities may not be the best content for humanization of the individual. So far, however, no one has come up with more pregnant content. The problem is to connect—really join—practically all students with that content in such ways that permanent liaisons result. This is perhaps the greatest single curriculum problem schools need to face and try to solve. In fact, the attention and determination devoted to progress in the humanities may well be the *best measure of whether educators are creatures or creators in society*. The tangible, powerful pressures from organized society upon schools in the next fifteen years will be chiefly aimed at producing progress in technological and social outcomes from education. Achievements in satisfying the wants of employers for skilled technicians will bring recognition and rewards for the educator. Progressive steps toward mitigating social unrest will be hailed. Educators are, and should be, creatures of society in satisfying such demands. But *they can be creators also if they become stewards of education for humaneness* in a society relatively oblivious to the importance of such education. They can become such stewards by working indefatigably to substitute concern in the place of obliviousness; by teaching the humanities as they have seldom, if ever, been taught before.

Implication Ten. The individualizing humanistic content of schooling should be demonstrated to be the most important reason for keeping schools in operation.

CHAPTER 2

Purposes, Scope And Organization
Of Education

RALPH W. TYLER*

The papers prepared for the Conference on *Prospective Changes in Society by 1980* suggest a number of significant implications for changes in the purposes, scope and organization of public school programs. Several, however, are especially significant.

IMPLICATIONS OF CHANGES IN SOCIETY

Since 1925, and particularly since World War II, the rapid rate of technological development in agriculture, industry and defense has so changed the occupational distribution of the total labor force that the chance for a youth or young adult without high school education to obtain employment is increasingly small. Farmers and farm laborers who made up 38 percent of the labor force at the turn of the century now comprise only 7 percent and the proportion continues to decrease. Unskilled labor in other fields represented more than 20 percent of the labor force in 1900 and now only 6 percent. Gerhard Colm, in chapter 5† on "Prospective Economic Developments," states that:

> One expert on automation has said that 15 years from now, 2 or 3 per-
> cent of the population could do all the work that has to be done to satisfy the
> material needs of our society. (p. 90).

However, Colm goes on to say:

> I believe that the modern technology will make it feasible to meet many
> more needs and provide many more services rather than replacing virtually
> all labor. For the next 10 to 20 years, I believe so much needs to be done
> in the fight against poverty here and abroad, in rebuilding our cities, improv-
> ing our transportation systems, that even with the use of all feasible tech-
> nology, we can make full and effective use of those who are able and willing
> to work.
> Increased productivity leads to greater affluence, which in turn means
> that the greatest increases in demand are for recreation, entertainment and
> recreation services . . . and the highly individualized artistic work by handi-
> craft methods. (p. 91).

Furthermore, he points out that:

> There is less need for unskilled labor . . . and for skills which require
> years of apprenticeship and training. Instead we need a highly alert labor
> force equipped with basic human skills and adjustability to new tasks.
> There will also be a demand for more people with professional training in
> humanities and sciences. (p. 92).

* *Director, Center for Advanced Study in the Behavioral Sciences, Stanford, California;* Vice-Chairman, National Science Board; President, National Academy of Education. Formerly, Chairman Department of Education and Dean of Social Sciences, University of Chicago; Director of Evaluation for Eight Year Study of Secondary Schools, and of the Cooperative Study in General Education in Colleges.

† All references to chapters by title or number relate to chapters in *Prospective Changes in Society by 1980* (Denver, Colo.: Designing Education for the Future, 1966).

These prospects as viewed by Colm are in accord with longtime trends. As a smaller proportion of the labor force has been employed in agriculture, mining and manufacturing, an increased percentage is working to meet the demands for non-material services such as education, health, recreation and social services. The National Bureau of Economic Research reported that already by 1960 only 45 percent of the U. S. Labor Force was employed in the production and distribution of material goods, while 55 percent was engaged in supplying demands for non-material services.

The opportunities for employment as an unskilled laborer are very limited. The percentage of the labor force employed in the skilled trades is not likely to increase. But there are large increases in the percentage of people employed in the health services, recreation, the social services, science, engineering, administration, accounting and controlling. As opportunities have become very small for those with limited education, the demands have greatly increased in those occupations requiring a considerable degree of education. Later in this chapter the significance of these facts for the objectives and the scope of educational programs will be examined in more detail.

Joseph Fisher, in chapter 2 on "Natural Resource Trends", not only reminds us of the increasing economic importance to this region of outdoor recreation, with its corresponding implications for vocational education, but also of the developing problems of water use, environmental pollution, and conservation of natural resources, and the need for a more adequate understanding of the issues involved in order that each person may play a constructive role as an individual and a citizen.

Daniel Elazar, writing on "The American Partnership", (Chapter 6) shows that the prevailing notions of governmental relations and processes are largely mistaken. In urging the need for an effective political education that is relevant to the real partnership that exists among the several levels of government, and the role of the party-system he states:

> Finally . . . the increasing complexity of American government means that better education in the political processes of this country—what we have called in the past 'civics'—is absolutely necessary. Schools at all levels must develop means to convey some sense of the functioning of the American system to their students, not along the simplistic lines of the past, nor for reformist purposes as so frequently has been the case in recent years, but to give them an understanding of a very complex system of government so that they may function as intelligent citizens in it. (p. 118).

There are implications in Grant McConnell's chapter 7 on "Non-Government Organizations in American Political Life" that this, too, is an area in which there is much misunderstanding and that citizens need to learn more about the role of the private organizations in our society. The discussion in Chapter 9 "The Industrial Relations System" indicates another area where better understanding is necessary.

In William Wheaton's Chapter 8 on "Urban and Metropolitan Development", after outlining the rapid urban growth of recent years, he suggests an educational objective when he states:

> Growth also requires a willingness to accept change—change in the social order; change in business activity; change in public services; change in political values. To the extent that the public does not believe in the future and is unwilling to accept change and its costs, we face serious impediments to growth. (p. 142).

This statement implies an educational program oriented to the future as well as using the past in helping students to develop greater understanding of present problems and possibilities for the future. Wheaton also indicates serious urban problems which people need to work on: control of air and water pollution, providing adequate housing and community facilities and improvement of transportation. These are indicated as areas for study in school and college.

Most of the papers in *Prospective Changes in Society by 1980* stress the importance of people expecting change and being able to deal with new problems and new opportunities. Kenneth Boulding in Chapter 12, "Expecting the Unexpected," puts this quite simply:

> One thing we can say about a man's future with a good deal of confidence is that it will be more or less surprising. This phenomenon of surprise is not something which arises merely out of man's ignorance, though ignorance can contribute to what might be called unnecessary surprises. There is, however, something fundamental in the nature of an evolutionary system which makes exact foreknowledge about it impossible, and as social systems are in a large measure evolutionary in character, they participate in the property of containing uneradicable surprise. (p. 199).

The goals of education for a predictable, relatively unchanging future are much easier to identify and the education they imply can strongly emphasize fixed habits, memorization of important facts, and the development of specific skills. *The goals of education appropriate for a future that will include many surprises will include strong emphasis upon problem-solving, upon learning how to meet new situations, upon the skills of observation, analysis and communication, and upon the development of attitudes appropriate to change.*

There are other educational implications in Boulding's paper. He points out:

> The growth of knowledge is one of the most persistent and significant movements in the history of man. . . . In many fields of science, new knowledge seems to double about every fifteen years. It is this enormous increase in the rate of growth of knowledge which has dominated the history of the last two or three hundred years, in all aspects of human life, politically, economically, and in all forms of human organization. (p. 203-4).

It is this so-called "knowledge explosion" that has made unattainable the earlier efforts of educators to provide students with a comprehensive knowledge of the major fields of study. Probably three-fourths of the knowledge now available to man was not known at the close of World War II. Hence, *if giving students specific knowledge while in school is a major objective, each student's supply as received while in school, will be largely obsolete by the time he is 35.* For this reason, a better goal is the objective of developing students who know how to study and learn and who become actively engaged in life-long learning.

Another new task of the schools is suggested by Boulding:

The American educational system in the past has been quite successful in preparing people to be middle class, to the point indeed where middle class values permeate perhaps 80 percent of our population. The system has not succeeded in preparing people to live useful and cheerful lives at the lower end of the income scale . . . (p. 212).

Richard Kuhns, in his chapter 14 on "The Future of the Humanities", and Roger Shinn, in his treatment of "Human Responsibility in the Emerging Society" (Chapter 15), join Boulding in calling attention to the problem of education in relation to moral and aesthetic values. In Boulding's words:

The final problem is subtle and hard to put one's finger on; nevertheless it may be the most important problem of all. This is the problem of the role of the educational system in creating what might be called a moral identity. The obsolescence of older moral identities in the face of enormous technological change is a problem which underlies almost all others in the social system . . . In its solution the educational system would play an absolutely crucial role. It would be precisely indeed in the things which our conservatives despise as "frills" that the development of satisfying human identities may have to be found. It must never be forgotten that the ultimate thing which any society is producing is people . . . If this principle is stamped firmly in the minds of those who guide and operate our educational system, we can afford to make a great many mistakes, we can afford to be surprised by the future, we can even afford to make some bad educational investments, because we will be protected against the ultimate mistake, which would be to make the educational system a means, not an end, serving purposes other than man himself. (p. 213).

These three chapters help in maintaining a focus for the schools that is concerned with education for the full development of boys and girls, men and women, and will not distort its objectives through undue emphasis on certain aspects of educational development. Furthermore, Philip Hauser's Chapter 3 on "Population Trends" provides an additional consideration that should balance local or regional provincialism. The population of the United States and of the eight-state area is a very mobile one. Many children grow up in rural and small town areas but live and work as adults in urban centers. Most families move from place to place, intrastate and interstate. Within an area, new industries develop as others disappear. The education of children and youth must not be limited by local or regional perspectives lest they suffer serious disadvantage in later life because of limited occupational, civic, social or personal competence.

NEW TASKS FOR THE SCHOOLS

This brief review of the papers in *Prospective Changes in Society by 1980* suggests certain new tasks which now confront the schools. Four of these are readily recognized.

We have seen that, with the increasing use of technology in agriculture, industry and defense, the demand for unskilled labor has sharply diminished and is continuing to drop. At present, as noted, the unskilled comprise only about 6 percent of our labor force. Yet in the United States, and in other advanced nations, between 15 and 20 percent of the population have not acquired sufficient skill and general literacy to qualify for skilled or higher levels of employment. The fact that more than 80 percent of our

children have achieved an educational level above the minimum requirements for modern literacy and employment is a tribute to the determination of our people and the efforts of our schools. But this is not
enough either in terms of percentage or educational level. As of today,
about 95 percent of our children should be effectively reached by our
educational efforts, and even this percentage must be increased. We know
how to stimulate and guide the learning of children who come from
homes where education is valued and where the basis for it has been
laid in the home experiences. We do not have widely accepted means for
reaching children whose background has given them little or no basis for
school work. *To reach all or nearly all of these children is a new educational task of our schools.*

A second new task is also partly a result of modern technology. As
automation has sharply reduced the demand for unskilled labor, the occupations in which there is increasing demand are those requiring a fairly
high level of education. These are in engineering, science, the health services, education, the social services, the recreational fields, accounting, and
administration. Hence, to provide employment opportunities for all of our
people and to keep our economy fully productive will require a much
larger proportion of our youth to complete high school and many more
than in the past to gain professional, semi-professional or technical competence. *To provide adequate educational opportunities for all in order
to keep our economy fully productive, and to ensure effective learning
for youth from varied backgrounds of training, experience, and outlook,
is another new and important educational task which we now face.* Neither
we, nor any other country has previously attempted it.

*Technological change is producing a third new task, the re-education
of those whose jobs have been eliminated by automation or have been
greatly changed by the development of new techniques, materials, or
devices.* Until very recently, technological change moved slowly enough
that the members of each new generation could take the new jobs and
acquire the new knowledge and skills, and the members of the older
generation were able to stay in the old jobs until their work careers were
ended. Thus, although the coal miner's children are not in the mines, most
of the coal miners of the 20's finished out their working years without
moving into a new occupation. This is no longer possible in most fields.
Many people now are, and will be, changing occupations during their
working career, and many of these changes require education and training to obtain the necessary understanding and skills for the new jobs.
This is another educational task for which we have meager experience
and no tested doctrine to guide us.

Because these three tasks—educating the children who have not heretofore been reached, affording effective post-high school education for
many youth with limited educational backgrounds, and providing for
the re-education of adults—have come to our attention as a result of
occupational changes, we are in danger of thinking of these tasks as
devoted solely to occupational education. This would be a mistake. The
requirements for effective functioning as citizen, neighbor, and family

member also demand more adequate education. Even the use by the individual of the many avenues for his self-realization can be greatly enhanced by learning. Without spelling this out again in detail, it should be obvious from the many statements about prospective changes in society, that the political, economic, and social problems we confront today are not adequately understood by the citizen whose education is limited either by amount or by concentration on occupational preparation. Hence, these new tasks must include the elements of a comprehensive educational program.

Finally, attention should be directed to *a fourth new task faced by our schools and colleges: the attainment of certain new ends or objectives.* One of these is to teach students how to learn. With the rapid acquisition of new knowledge, it is no longer possible to give the student in school an adequate command of the facts in each major subject which will serve him throughout the balance of his life. The school can only start him on a lifelong career of continued learning. Hence, *an important aim today is to teach students to learn and to develop in them a strong interest in continued study together with the motivation and skills required to keep on with their learning after graduation.* This objective has not generally been accepted by schools and colleges in the past, although some teachers here and there have given it major attention.

Another new educational aim has arisen from the recent involvement of outstanding scholars in the development of courses and curricula. In each of the major fields of learning, the scholars are emphasizing the contribution that can be made by learning to use the intellectual apparatus of the field as well as to become familiar with the results of scholarship. In mathematics, for example, the new courses teach the student to think in mathematical terms so that he can deal with new mathematical ideas and problems, as well as learning the techniques of arithmetic, algebra, geometry, trigonometry, and the like. In history, as another example, the new courses teach the student to think in historical terms about the development of cultural, economic, and political institutions, as well as learning some of the significant facts and interpretations of previous historical work. *To help the student acquire and use the important intellectual tools is a new educational aim* which has not been widely attempted in the past. This is another illustration of the fact that one of the new tasks of our schools is to aim at certain new objectives.

CHANGING OBJECTIVES

Scholars, scientists, and educational leaders generally are busily engaged in reviewing the educational requirements that are emerging from the current changes in American life. From these reviews, some significant new objectives are being formulated and in other cases new emphases are recommended. In this section, some of these will be discussed in greater detail.

THE LANGUAGE ARTS

The language arts—reading, writing, speaking and listening (communicating)—will continue to be an important part of the basic core of the schools' efforts. However, even for the seriously disadvantaged children, reading and writing cannot be treated simply as useful skills to be acquired. In the world we now confront, reading and writing as well as speaking and listening are essential parts of our way of life. Employment, civic responsibilities and personal enjoyment and development involve continuing use of the language arts. Not only in the primary grades, but throughout the period of schooling there needs to be emphasis on the variety of ways in which language serves the student's purposes, provides satisfactions and contributes to his effectiveness. The objectives of the language arts are to increase the student's interest in reading and writing, help him develop discrimination in his choices of reading materials, develop increasing skill in the use of the language arts and acquire as part of his way of life effective language habits. The current importance of TV and oral recordings makes the development of habits and skills of critical listening more important.

MATHEMATICS

Mathematics will also continue to be an important part of the basic core of the school's efforts. But much more attention will be given to developing an understanding of mathematics as a way of thinking about many kinds of phenomena. Commonly, today, mathematics is viewed by most children, and the public, as a set of rules for dealing with quantitative problems. Those whose occupations or avocations require computations become and remain facile in calculations and solving the common quantitative problems with which they deal. Others show little interest in mathematics and their computational skills are often erratic.

In the world of today, and even more in the world of the 1970's, many features of our lives cannot well be understood without the use of concepts, like the binary number system, sets and subsets, systems, cost-benefit analyses, that are essentially mathematical. Hence, as with the language arts, the objectives of mathematics will be those that help the student think about many facets of his life and the world in mathematical terms, understanding basic mathematical concepts and using mathematical logic and other modes of thought when they are appropriate. To accomplish these goals, mathematics, in its various branches, will need to be part of the emphasis through the period of schooling.

THE NATURAL SCIENCES

Science has been limited in most schools of the past to the junior and senior high schools. This field was often viewed as one to impart the basic facts of biology, physics and chemistry. The problem of the so-called knowledge explosion has been briefly discussed. Since the facts of science are accumulating so rapidly it is not possible for the student to learn those that are now known. In fifteen years, what is known will have doubled. If coverage of a subject is our goal it is an impossible one. Textbooks cannot be expanded indefinitely. Learning takes time. For young people to gain an understanding of ideas, of principles and facts, requires an active participation on their part in expressing these ideas, principles and facts in their own words, in using them to explain phe-

nomena and to guide their actions. Effective learning is not passively re-
calling what is presented. It is an active endeavor on the part of the
learner, and what becomes part of him is what he has actively formulated,
responded to, or used in some way that is relevant. With these considerations in mind, the new courses being constructed in science include as
their goals comprehending the kinds of problems with which the scientist
deals in seeking to understand natural phenomena and seeking to gain
some control over them, the methods he uses for studying these problems,
the major concepts that have evolved for helping to understand the
phenomena and some of the generalizations that have been developed
for relating factors and helping in their explanation. The courses also
seek to arouse the student's curiosity and interest in understanding the
natural world and help him to acquire skills and habits useful in carrying
on continuing inquiry about scientific matters.

These objectives can best be attained by beginning early as the child
observes phenomena and starts to question: *"What* is this? *Why* is this?"
Turning curiosity into constructive and illuminating inquiry should be the
concern throughout the period of schooling and will be part of the basic
core of the school's efforts.

THE SOCIAL SCIENCES

The social sciences, or social studies, have special responsibility for
dealing with systematic inquiry and knowledge about how man behaves
as a social being and about the political, economic and social institutions
he has developed. This field also has a part to play in other areas of the
student's experience and in his development of social ideals, values, habits
and practices.

In the schools of the 1970's and 1980's, much greater attention will
be given to systematic inquiry in the social sciences. This is due both to
the greater need of our citizens for understanding a wide range of social
problems and constructive social actions, and to the rapidly expanding
knowledge in the various fields of the social sciences. Many authorities
have emphasized the need for a more realistic understanding of such
developing social problems as urban and rural slums, depletion of natural
resources, environmental pollution, traffic congestion, crime and delinquency and civil rights. They also have stressed the need for dispelling
the myths and misunderstandings about our political, economic and social
systems and for developing more adequate ability to examine the issues
and appraise the promise of proposed solutions. These objectives call for
a massive reconstruction of the courses in social studies and social sciences.
Fortunately, with private and governmental support, there are now a dozen
or more curriculum projects under way in this field that are somewhat
parallel to those now being completed in mathematics and the natural
sciences. Work is going on in anthropology, economics, geography, history,
political science, psychology and sociology and in some areas that will
draw upon several of these subject fields. Such reoriented courses and the
materials being developed should be useful in the effort to attain these
important goals.

EDUCATION FOR CITIZENSHIP

Education for citizenship includes not only the acquisition of intellectual understanding and skills but also the development of social ideals, values, habits and practices. The social studies or social sciences have a part to play in achieving these objectives but other fields also have their roles and the social life of the school as a community can make a very considerable contribution.

The basic values of our democratic way of life include respect for the dignity and worth of every individual human being without reference to his race, religion, national origin or financial circumstance. A second value is the sharing by all members of the community in the common life, including the making of decisions, the carrying out of plans and the rewards of productive efforts. A third basic value is an appreciation of the contributions of diversity in social groups, including tolerance for widely different individual characteristics and behavior. A fourth is respect for law, an appreciation of the importance of living up to rules and principles for group life that have been adopted by due process. A fifth is respect for justice, or fair play. These values are interpreted and refined through reflection, reading and discussion but they become vital in the lives of children and youth through direct first-hand experiences where their impact is felt and observed and where habits of justice, considerateness and obedience to law can be developed in connection with constructive group activities in school and community.

The importance of these values requires no elaboration, but their development calls for increasing attention by the schools as the opportunities for constructive work and community service outside the school are narrowing. Furthermore, when housing neighborhoods become more segregated it is increasingly difficult for the home or neighborhood to provide experiences in common work and play that are shared by children of widely different backgrounds. Hence, without conscious effort by the schools, the opportunity to know and appreciate persons of various races, religions, national backgrounds and financial circumstances are missing and, with this void, essential democratic values are likely to be lost for many children and youth.

THE FINE ARTS

The fine arts will have a larger place in the school program in the future than they have at present. Earlier in this chapter, I quoted Boulding's comment on the possible role of art, music, literature and drama in helping us to find meaning in life and a sense of our own identity. Like other fields emphasized in the schools, the fine arts must be treated as an important part of life—not a glass to cover up essentially ugly lives, or something acquired for social prestige. The objectives of education in the arts include not only the development of skills as creators or producers and interest as consumers, but also the development of supplementary resources for expressing ideas and feelings, for finding aesthetic values and satisfactions, for exploring and inquiring into experiences and things that seem complex or baffling but are important. The arts can in this way become personal resources for living more vitally and questioning more deeply, rather than simply providing an escape from the world, pleasurable sensations, or a way to while away hours that would otherwise be boring. Products of art, music and literature are available from many cultures and from many parts of the world. Thus, they are important sources for gaining appreciation of the contributions made by other peoples and other nations and serve to emphasize values in diversity.

HEALTH EDUCATION

The maintenance of good physical health is an important goal in modern life. Its attainment depends on a variety of conditions only some of which represent the possible contributions of education and the schools. The child's early diet and physical regimen, the sanitary conditions in the home and community are significant factors over which the schools have little control. However, the development of understanding of the way in which the body operates and of the conditions for effective body functioning, together with an appreciation of the values of hygienic living are clearly objectives of the schools. Furthermore, the provision of opportunities for satisfying physical activities and the development of interest in and habits of daily exercise are increasingly important responsibilities of the schools as the children find little chance for these activities elsewhere in the community.

FOREIGN LANGUAGES

Education in foreign languages has become a subject of considerable debate. The increasing international connections of this nation, modern transportation, the ease of foreign travel and other developments are bringing several million U. S. citizens more closely in touch with peoples of other nations than was feasible a generation ago. More Americans have opportunity and need for using foreign languages than ever before. This situation raises questions about whom should be taught a foreign language, what languages should be taught, and when the instruction should begin. Many schools and some states have answered these questions by providing a foreign language program for all children beginning at some point in the elementary grades. A review of the situation, however, raises serious doubts about such sweeping action.

If the schools teach skills which the child has little or no opportunity to practice outside the classroom, the time required to maintain the skills is very great. Hence, in general, an important consideration in selecting what skills are to be learned and when they are to be taught is that they shall be skills which the learner can begin to use almost immediately and that he should be taught when he has opportunity for a great deal of outside practice.

There are children in many communities who have opportunities to use a foreign language and there are some communities in which most of the children have such opportunities. But taking the nation as a whole, less than 10 percent of the children have these opportunities. Thus, it is a very inefficient use of resources for every school to offer foreign language instruction to all the children. On a selected basis, foreign languages have a place in the schools but they are not likely to be part of the central core even by 1980.

VOCATIONAL EDUCATION

Another educational area which is currently undergoing serious re-examination because of the changing conditions of American life is that of vocational education. As pointed out earlier, only a very small number of people today can find employment in unskilled occupations. Education has become a prerequisite for almost all jobs, but many of our former definitions of vocational education are inadequate to cover the world of work as it is now developing. The traditional vocational education programs of the high school involved agriculture, trade and industry, business and office occupations, distributive occupations and vocational home economics. Only about one-seventh of the high school students were enrolled in such programs as of 1960 and less than half of those found employment in the fields in which they were enrolled.

The education required for occupational competence involves much more than training in specific vocational skills. It begins in early childhood and continues throughout active occupational life. Its objectives include: increasing understanding of the world of work, knowledge of vocational opportunities, development of basic literacy and work habits, development of ability to plan for a career, development of the abilities required in the general field of an occupation, and development of specific occupational skills as needed. Occupational education is a core responsibility of the schools when viewed in this larger context, but as such it should emphasize individual flexibility, broad general education, competence in career planning and in developing more specific skills as needed. It involves not only experiences in the elementary and secondary schools but also in colleges and other post-high school institutions. Opportunities should not be limited by age or previous schooling if the student can be substantially aided in his educational development by further school experiences.

NEED FOR NEW ORGANIZATION

Earlier in this chapter, the need for the schools to reach the 15 to 20 percent of the children who are not now actively engaged in school learning was stressed. Seriously disadvantaged children do not have many opportunities and encouragement to learn at home when they are very young. Typically, they are one year behind the intellectual performance of the average child when they enter school between 5 and 6 years of age, and by the time they become 12 years old they are more than 2 years behind. Bloom [1] reviewed a large number of longitudinal studies of children and concluded that the environment has its greatest influence on children's development in the first five years of life; thereafter development

---

[1] Benjamin S. Bloom, *Stability and Change in Human Characteristics*, (John Wiley & Sons, 1964).

is relatively stable and quite predictable. It seems likely from these studies and from the preliminary results being obtained from current experimental work with young children, that efforts made to improve the learning environment of disadvantaged children during the preschool years will be more effective than waiting until they have reached the usual school age. Hence, it is recommended that the schools provide educational programs designed for selected younger children and their parents. The organization of such preschool and parent programs should be focused on the 15 to 20 percent of children whose environment for learning is very limited.

Authorities have commented on the separation in an urbanized society of the various institutions that serve it. The separation of the school from the world of work and from the world of community service results in several unfortunate consequences. For many students, school learning seems irrelevant because it is not seen as closely related to their future lives in the community. This is one of the factors that causes many to drop out of school. For many students who do not drop out, the apparent lack of relevance of their school work results in low interest and effort in their studies. From the standpoint of society, the separation of school life from many aspects of community life makes more difficult the transition from school to work and from school to constructive community membership. Foreseeing the increased isolation of the schools as the urban and metropolitan areas develop, the educational authorities with the cooperation of others, *should be planning now and instituting as rapidly as possible, school-community organizations* to provide cooperative education (work-study programs), community service programs and other means by which school youth can be actively involved in work experiences, in community services, in joint civic participation with adults and the like. These programs will be of benefit both to the educational development of the individual and to the community's advancement.

Other organizational innovations should be considered. In some cases there may be need to devise new institutions and new institutional arrangements. For example, in attacking the problem of helping children from limited home backgrounds, several new forms of learning centers are now in operation. Some are extensions of the public schools, some are laboratory centers under the direction of university departments, some are cooperative agencies of community or neighborhood groups, some are projects of churches, some are new, non-profit corporations, and there are several other forms of institutions. Not all of these are likely to be successful, but the encouragement of innovations in institutions and institutional arrangements increases the likelihood of getting more varied ideas tried, of involving a wider range of people who might contribute to the program and of escaping some of the restrictions which commonly develop in older institutions because of the rigidity of traditional attitudes and practices. The Elementary and Secondary Education Act of 1965 authorizes federal assistance in the support of supplementary education centers and these should make a constructive contribution to developing new and needed institutional arrangements.

IN SUMMARY

Education has been a powerful factor in the development of our people since the founding of this country. With the changes now taking place in our society, education has an even more important role to play. Furthermore, the schools face certain new tasks: reaching all the children, encouraging a much larger number to finish high school and continue their education, aiding in the further education and re-education of adults, and attaining some new objectives. To accomplish these heavy responsibilities, most curriculum areas need careful review. The reconstruction and the organization of the schools must also be more fully adapted to their expanded role. This is a large order, but not an impossible one. These eight states should begin now to plan and take the steps required to develop educational systems that are appropriate and effective for the 1970's and the 1980's.

CHAPTER 3

The Educational Program

To 1980 and Beyond

JOHN I. GOODLAD *

The most important task for our schools during the next few years—and for many generations to come—is their daily practice and demonstration of those qualities of compassion, sensitivity, sound judgment, flexibility, adaptability, humility, self-renewal—and many more that we have long claimed to be seeking in the human products of education. In effect, *this task is to infuse the means of education with the values we have hitherto espoused in defining the ends.*

This does not sound like a very exciting charge. Certainly it does not seem as dramatic as conversation about computer-based instruction, modular scheduling, flexible school buildings, private telecommunications centers, and all the rest. We will have and use this educational technology, just as we now have and use supersonic airplanes, atomic-powered submarines, and remote-controlled space ships. But there is soberingly less assurance that the revolution now beginning to tear at the edges of schooling will reach to the inner core.

SOME BASIC CONSIDERATIONS

The inner core is where the school and all it stands for reaches the human client. Does it respect him somewhat more than the typical salesman respects his client? Does it give him more experience with success than with failure? Does the school involve its client in the decisions from which flow consequences the client will relish or regret? Does it recognize the client's time for the precious thing it is? Does the school's program really reach and grip the student?

Examples to the contrary are legion. Just a few suffice to make my point. Some 25 percent of the students in elementary and secondary schools receive 75 percent of the failing grades. Call it wholesome competition, if you will. But a significant proportion of this 25 percent drops out of school as early as the law allows, if not sooner. The year 1980 has little to offer them, nor they it. There are few second chances.

Or this example: An educator in a position of considerable influence recently rejected the concept of involvement in educational decision-mak-

*Professor of Education and Director, the University Elementary School, University of California, Los Angeles; also Director, Research and Development Division, Institute for Development of Educational Activities; President-elect, American Educational Research Association; Formerly Professor and Director, Center for Teacher Education, University of Chicago. Publications include: Planning and Organizing for Teaching (1963), School Curriculum Reform in the United States (1964), The Development of a Conceptual System for Dealing with Problems of Curriculum and Instruction (1966), The Changing School Curriculum (1966), and numerous professional articles and monographs.

47

ing with the concluding comment, "I was a school administrator once and had to give a little lip-service to democracy now and again." Do we know what education is? Are schools really democratic institutions?

And a third: The studies of my colleague, Professor C. Robert Pace,[1] reveal that a substantial number of students in higher education, especially in large universities, feel that the program does not reach them in any deep and significant way, that they do not participate in its planning, and that it is not planned with their lives in mind.

Then there are the many instances of sheer idiocy, as when students who are too ill to "suit up" for vigorous physical activity—but not too ill to read—are left to twiddle their thumbs during the so-called physical education period. Or when school system regulations restrict inter-class and inter-school visitation to teachers who are in probationary status. Or when opportunities to read "story" books, paint, or experiment with various "goodies" are open only to students who finish assignments early.

We do not need to look far in most communities to find thrilling examples of enlightened school practice, too. Clearly, an impassioned exchange of favorites, pro and con, does little or nothing to clarify or enhance the condition of our schools. But a careful appraisal of where we are would provide a baseline and a better awareness, perhaps, of unfinished business which must occupy at least part of our time to 1980 and beyond.

I shall now attempt to do the following: (1) summarize on the basis of evidence some realities in the present conduct of American schooling. (Here, I shall draw heavily from the recent studies of my colleagues and myself, simply because the data are highly relevant and fresh before me); (2) describe and analyze briefly the promise of some forms and substances being proposed—and sometimes widely hailed—to deal with these realities; (3) set forth some emphases for educational programs designed to cope with certain societal realities projected for 1980; and (4) recommend some possible self-renewing mechanisms for an educational system that would seek to shape the future as well as to adapt wisely. These purposes are advanced here concurrently as well as serially.

I am eschewing for two reasons the intoxicating temptation to summarize the provocative review of anticipated changes in society set forth in an earlier conference[2] and from this, in turn, to project what education should do. First, Paul Miller, in chapter 1, has described engagingly a visit to the school milieu of 1980 and drawn educational implications from emerging societal conditions. Second, I simply am unable to prescribe with any useful precision the school programs that will markedly alleviate the conditions mankind faces and probably will continue to face: tidal waves of knowledge and people, abject poverty, pollution, social disorganization, the sheer magnitude of grasping and shaping the culture, changing values and mores, alienation among members of all age groups, and failure to devel-

---

[1] C. Robert Pace, "Perspectives on the Student and His College," *The College and the Student,* edited by Lawrence Dennis and Joseph Kaufman (Washington, D.C.: American Council on Education, 1966), pp. 76-100.

[2] *Prospective Changes in Society by 1980* (Denver, Colorado: Designing Education for Future, July, 1966).

op a feeling of personal worth. My own inadequacies in this regard would depress me less if I could see around me more plans that approximate in imagination and clarity our brilliant analyses of the conditions we face.

The fact that the Rocky Mountain area states will not encounter seriously in the near future many of the conditions to be overcome elsewhere does not remove their responsibility to their own population and to mankind. The schools of these states share with schools everywhere the task of increasingly humanizing the ends and means of education.

REALITIES OF THE PRESENT

There is heady talk and enlightened action in education today. It is a wonderful time to be an educator. And it is great fun to light the fires of innovation.

But there is also the more sobering business of determining where we are, assessing what needs doing and why, projecting plans, and working long and hard enough to carry them out and, as a result, making a real difference. Let us then take inventory.

First, there appears to be little relationship between the earmarks of success in school and subsequent demonstration of those virtues inherent in many statements of educational aims. Marks in school subjects are virtually useless as predictors of creativity, inventiveness, leadership, good citizenship, personal and social maturity, family happiness, and honest workmanship.[3] Either we are not rewarding or we are not providing adequately (or both) for development of qualities so frequently set forth in statements of educational goals.

Second, there is an unwillingness or an inability (or both) to state— at any level of responsibility or authority—what purposes are to be served by education, schools, or specific programs of instruction. States are confused as to their freedom and responsibilities in this regard and do not define adequately the role of their departments of education, as any cursory examination of state courses of study quickly reveals. Local school boards are assiduous in their avoidance of the issues involved,[4] failing to take advantage of American pluralism. When the prospect of determining educational goals at the federal level of responsibility looms, we cry local autonomy—failing to realize that we have a vacuum here into which spill the wares of remote curriculum builders. There should be small wonder that many educators have little stomach for the determination of educational objectives.

Third, the common expectation and demonstrated function of our schools are to cover tasks and materials that have been predetermined for specific grades and periods of time.[5] This condition appears not to have a

---

[3] Pace, *op. cit.*

[4] Margaret P. Ammons, "Educational Objectives: The Relation between the Process Used in Their Development and Their Quality", (Unpublished doctoral dissertation, University of Chicago, 1961).

[5] This and several subsequent observations are based on data from a report by John I. Goodlad and Associates, *A Study of Childhood Schooling* (typed manuscript; report as yet unpublished). Study conducted under a grant from the Fund for the Advancement of Education of the Ford Foundation.

sound pedagogical base. It denies our growing awareness of individual differences in learning and of the probability that *what children learn* has more to do with whether or not they are *exposed* to it, than to our genius in the grade placement of children and content.

Fourth, a substantial portion of the curriculum has not been justified on criteria other than habit or tradition. This is particularly true in the social studies where too many insignificant historical events are learned by rote, where homogenized community studies predominate in the lower years, and where a "mankind" approach is largely lacking.

Fifth, the separate-subject pattern of curriculum organization that has predominated during the past decade of curriculum reform has placed profound problems of choice upon local school districts.[6] There simply cannot be thirty or more academic disciplines in the kindergarten. Further, the strengthening of subjects already in the curriculum through massive federal grants (largely from the National Science Foundation) has not enhanced the status of relatively new but nonetheless important disciplines.

Sixth, the much-heralded pedagogical revolution is still largely in the cumulo-nimbus clouds of educational reform that roll back and forth across this vast and varied land. These clouds have not yet enveloped the millions of teachers who make up the working force of our elementary and secondary schools to anything like the high degree claimed by many innovators and popular magazines. To be specific, teaching is still largely a "telling" procedure, with exchanges being primarily between teacher and child rather than among groups of children. The processes of "discovery" and "inquiry"—so lauded by curriculum reformers—seem not to be well understood and tend to be used mechanically, if at all. The textbook dominates instruction. Films, when used, more often than not are supplementary and are not woven into the fabric of the program. It is difficult to detect in the classroom common use of such psychological concepts as goal setting, motivation, positive reinforcement, evaluative checking, and so on. The class usually is instructed as a whole, except for the common practice of achievement grouping for reading in the primary grades and of some grouping in mathematics. The technological revolution has scarcely ruffled most classrooms; the computer is used for routine data processing in large school systems and for instructional purposes in only a handful of experimental laboratories.[7]

Paralleling this picture is the observation that teachers appear to be genuinely concerned about and interested in children. In general, the atmosphere of the classroom is warm and positive; activities tend to proceed at a comfortable, relaxed pace. The supply of interesting and varied instructional materials, particularly books, is surprisingly below what one would expect to find in an affluent society. Teachers in secondary schools are confronted with a bewildering array of faces in the course of a day; teachers in elementary schools are seldom out of sight and sound of children. There are few provisions and opportunties for the exchange of peda-

---

6 See John I. Goodlad and Associates, *The Changing School Curriculum* (New York: Fund for the Advancement of Education, 1966).
7 See John I. Goodlad, John F. O'Toole, Jr., and Louise L. Tyler, *Computers and Information Systems in Education* (New York: Harcourt, Brace and World, Inc., 1966).

gogical views and for the long-term planning that we would like to associate with educational institutions. Are we expecting too much and giving too little to our teachers?

Seventh, innovations which, in concept, are designed to unshackle the restrictive, monolithic structure of schools appear often to be tacked on. Nongrading is supposed to raise the ceilings and lower the floors of expectancy for the class group, reduce the importance of age as a factor in determining the student's program, encourage greater flexibility in grouping practices, and so on. But a study of the supposed nongraded elementary schools in the United States found little movement in these directions.[8] Nongrading, team teaching, and other innovations of potential power are far from simple in concept and implementation. Are we expecting too much in attempting them apart from simulation, demonstration, and the kind of in-service teacher education that has characterized recent curriculum reform?

Eighth, there is precious little experimentation with the school as an educational instrument. A recent poll suggests that the lay public is at least as ready for change as the educators.[9] But there always seems to be enough resistance on the part of vocal parents and entrenched professionals to cause undue caution on the part of administrators. At least one highly visible school principal is convinced that his administrative colleagues are not now giving the leadership that we need—and that is possible, even within the existing structure of American education.[10] De we need schools whose very reason for existence is experimentation and innovation?

Ninth, teacher education (and I refer to the whole of the program— not just to the education courses), which should be the fountainhead, too often is a drainage ditch. There is no point in entering now into the problems and issues of what James B. Conant has called "that can of worms." They have been well documented elsewhere.[11] It seems apparent that *nothing short of a complete overhaul will bring to our teacher education programs, both preservice and inservice, the vitality they must have if teachers are to effect the rapid educational evolution we want.*

Tenth, there is an assumption abroad in the land that the task before us now is to implement a host of educational innovations which already have been amply demonstrated and proved worthy. This is, to a degree, accompanied by the assumption that federal intervention has created a self-renewing mechanism of supplementary and regional laboratories that will provide the new forms and substances we need for 1980 and beyond. I am uneasy with respect to both assumptions.

Regarding the first assumption, we have had but a handful of potent, imaginative, educational innovations during the past decade or so. Further, we have had very little detailed development and demonstration of

---

[8] Maria T. Delgado-Marcano, "The Operation of Curriculum and Instruction in Twenty Nongraded Elementary Schools" (Submitted in partial fulfillment of the requirements for the Doctor of Education degree in the School of Education, Indiana University, September, 1965).

[9] "Parents Are Ready; a Report of a Gallup Poll Measuring Public Reactions," *The Instructor,* 76 (October, 1966), pp. 149, 154.

[10] B. Frank Brown, *The Nongraded High School* (Englewood Cliffs, N. J.: Prentice-Hall, Inc., 1963).

[11] See, for example, James B. Conant, *The Education of American Teachers* (New York: McGraw-Hill, 1963).

these and very little interpretation or testing of the assumptions underlying them. Widespread dissemination of what we rather dimly perceive will occupy much time and energy, but whether it will profoundly change or improve education is questionable.

Regarding the second assumption, we need, in addition to our action-oriented enterprises, a much greater commitment to protected, funded, and superbly staffed, long-term inquiry of a sort that neither the federal government nor the private foundation is now providing.

Ten is a good round number, so I conclude my discussion of present realities here. Lest you judge me too dyspeptic, however, I must remind you that these observations are drawn from studies which—although not satisfying all the purists with respect to scientific rigor—are far from casual in nature. Further, they are not far, I believe, from what other observers[12] of the educational scene have concluded and from the views of educators in the vineyards. But they do give us pain. As one who could scarcely be described as riding the white horse of leadership but who has been in the midst of the change effort, I, too, am pained. Nonetheless, if we are to fight the battle well, we should be apprised of the nature and condition of the enemy.

SOME EVIDENCES OF PROGRESS

Conditions of our schools, summarized here, have motivated to some extent the major educational reforms of the past 10 to 15 years. But these reforms have been motivated, also, and certainly defended in their rationales, by changing conditions in society—many of which will accelerate through 1980.[13] We are now very sensitive to the possible educational implications of bewildering increases in knowledge, changing conceptions of knowledge, eroding and shifting values, anonymity and alienation, technology, and of the three "p's": population, poverty, and pollution. Let us turn, then, to the solutions that are being offered, against the background both of school conditions and of the kind of world in which we live and will live. Four clusters of these are particularly relevant to the form and substance of school programs: curriculum changes, new patterns of organizing classes and personnel, instructional materials, and technology in the conduct of school affairs.

CURRICULUM CHANGES

Current curriculum reform is designed primarily to update the content of instruction; to provide structured approaches to otherwise unmanageable accumulations of knowledge; and to bring the student into processes of the scholar, into reasoning for himself. The words "structure" and "intuition" are the pedagogical catchwords of the new era, just as "readiness" and "the whole child" characterized an earlier one. Bothered by apparent submergence of the disciplines in broad fields and fused types of curriculum

---

[12] Such as Martin Mayer, *The Schools.*

[13] For a review of recent school changes and their rationales, see *The Changing American School.* Sixty-fifth Yearbook, Part II, National Society for the Study of Education (Chicago: University of Chicago Press, 1966).

organization, current reformers have *begun with* and *held to* separate subjects, merging them only with great care.

The gains from this movement—beginning about 1951 and expanding rapidly after 1957—are now fairly clear: first-rate scholars have become active in precollegiate curriculum planning; man's approaches to understanding phenomena have been organized for teaching and learning purposes; many teachers have been rejuvenated in their work; the flagging interest of some students has been restimulated; curtains of mystique surrounding the work of scholars have been thrust aside. The learning fare simply is not what it was a decade ago. *Any new cycle of curriculum change certainly should build upon progress of the last fifteen years.*

But *any new cycle should examine also some shortcomings, omissions, and problems.* We have tended to ignore or, at least, to give only lip-service to the more learner-centered concepts, such as stages of human development, affective concomitants of learning, developmental tasks, and so on. In our flush of pleasure over the learning capabilities of young children especially, *we have given too little attention to what knowledge might be of most worth to them and have neglected the question of what kinds of human beings we should seek to develop.*

As with most movements that receive substantial financial backing and commitment of human resources, this one has swept through all levels of education. We have not asked ourselves the question as to whether or not a separate-discipline approach is equally appropriate for all levels of education. Nor have we seriously considered the possibility of organizing parts of the curriculum around present problems of young people or pressing problems of mankind. These were the approaches of previous eras that have been temporarily discredited.

Two complex problems of social engineering have emerged. First, the processes of induction or discovery that supposedly are to be developed in the students are not compatible with the modes of teaching long used by many teachers. Teachers have been conditioned to "coverage" and to "telling," as my earlier summary of conditions in the schools suggests. It is not surprising, then, that many teachers cover the topics of the new curricula much as they covered the topics of the old.

Second, curriculum reformers have experienced difficulty with the lock-step structure of the schools and—they say—with the cautious, traditional approaches of school administrators. They have had to conform to what often appear to be rigid and unreasonable time and grade demands. Their sequences of content are naturally continuous and nongraded, but the schools are not.

We do not change easily the established, patterned ways of human beings. Social engineering, with its technique of persuasion and appeals to reason, with its requirement that people forego immediate gratification for long-term social gain, is necessarily slow. Technological change is not. Is it possible that some of the roadblocks to the improvement of school programs are more amenable to technological engineering than we think?

NEW PATTERNS OF ORGANIZING CLASSES AND PERSONNEL

New patterns of organizing classes and personnel are designed to widen the range of educational expectancy for an age group; eliminate the stops and starts of pupil nonpromotion practices; encourage attention to individual differences; break down monolithic concepts of class size; encourage flexible grouping; and broaden the range of instructional personnel brought into the schools. Two innovations that seek, in tandem, to facilitate attainment of these purposes, and that have received widespread attention, are nongrading and team teaching.

Both innovations were resisted at first by large segments of the teaching profession. But, in 1961, the Department of Elementary School Principals issued a yearbook favoring them;[14] in 1963, the Project on Instruction of the National Education Association recommended their serious consideration;[15] and, in 1966, the National Commission on Teacher Education and Professional Standards recommended the desirability of alternatives to the self-contained classroom.[16] Although there have been demands for a thorough research justification of both patterns, there has been no serious questioning of their logical justification. There seems to be at present rather general acceptance of the usefulness of these plans and widespread interest in implementing them.

But, as noted earlier, many efforts at implementation have faltered— the results often looking more like the rigidity of homogeneous, inter-class grouping and departmentalization than the expected flexibility of nongrading and team teaching. Why is this so? Let me suggest two hypotheses. First, comprehensive operating models have been virtually non-existent. It is not surprising, therefore, that educators have fallen back on inappropriate but familiar models of the recent past. Second, and closely related, there have been neither tools nor concepts available for use following the first efforts at restructuring. To take away the teacher-per-class-per-grade structure is not necessarily to provide alternatives. Teachers are left to seek new criteria for pupil placement, content selection, teacher assignment, and so on. These criteria are not easy to come by.

Once again, is it possible that we should have moved in behind the restructuring effort with appropriate technological assistance? For example, might we have determined the new kinds of data needed for the new decisions and then arranged to gather and store them electronically for automated retrieval? Electronic data processing would be of enormous help in complex team-teaching environments, it seems to me. In our large cities we use computers for mundane operations like meeting payrolls but do not consider using spare computer time for educational operations like these.

INSTRUCTIONAL MATERIALS

A third area of progress in seeking to cope with school problems is that of instructional materials. *The most promising materials are those which are designed to be responsive to the explorations of the student; enable the*

---

[14] *Elementary School Organization* (Washington, D.C.: National Education Association, 1961).
[15] *Schools for the 60's* (New York: McGraw-Hill Book Co., 1963).
[16] *The Year of the Non-Conference* (Washington, D.C.: National Commission on Teacher Education and Professional Standards, 1967).

student to be self-propelling; extend the range of stimuli to several senses; provide alternative means to common ends; and free the teacher from burdens of routine correcting and testing. Few countries of the world serve their schools as well in the quantity and variety of materials produced for them. The picture of textbook domination in the classroom is, therefore, all the more surprising and distressing.

Films, film strips, records, taped lessons, and other developments of many kinds still lie outside the ken of a large segment of our teachers. Publishers are perplexed. Encyclopaedia Britannica Films, in its Project Discovery, virtually designed and financed a substantial part of its concerted attack on the problem in several large cities. To introduce alternatives to textbooks and workbooks as a process of social engineering seems not to be convincingly effective. Perhaps the bottleneck can be broken simply by bringing to the student a system of media and materials not requiring extensive mediation by the teacher. It would then not be necessary for innovations in materials to await re-education of the teacher. There need not be anything undemocratic about this. As Weinberg has so well pointed out, we must provide safer automobiles quickly while necessarily continuing the slow process of driver education.[17] Similarly, we may be able to bring the student directly to rich learning opportunities while engaging ceaselessly in teacher education.

INTRODUCING AND UTILIZING TECHNOLOGY

We hear much these days about our technological society: the promises of a better tomorrow featuring increased leisure, inevitable dislocations, dangers of alienation, and so on. The schools are admonished to do something about it, but that "something" rarely is made clear. Perhaps one of the things they should do is introduce technology seriously into their affairs. *By living daily with automation, students and teachers might well come to terms with it and learn to bend it to their will.*

SELF-RENEWING MECHANISMS FOR THE FUTURE

I now find myself in the uneasy role of the analyst who has observed the ways of the enemy but not yet planned the battle. In view of the charge given to me, to remember that analysis of the problem brings one at least half-way to its solution, is no consolation. Something more is expected. Let me attempt a few suggestions regarding form and substance of the school program and conclude with some recommendations for self-renewal.

THE SCHOOL AS THE BASIC UNIT FOR CHANGE

The *first* proposition: *In seeking to effect whatever educational changes are deemed desirable, we should bring them about in the school as a single, comprehensive unit.* The school with its principal, staff, pupil population, parents, and surrounding cultural milieu, is the largest organic unit for change. For most people this *is* the educational system. It is visible, man-

---

[17] Alvin M. Weinberg, "Can Technology Replace Social Engineering?" *University of Chicago Magazine,* LIX (October, 1966), pp. 6-10.

ageable, and concrete. Move beyond the single school and you have an abstraction or, at best, a supporting structure.

To have goals for education is not enough; *the school must have a sense of purpose.* To have cycles of curriculum reform is not enough; *they must be brought into the school by deliberate design.* To propose nongrading and team teaching is not enough; *we must bring them to full fruition in the school.* Whatever values motivate change must surround all that takes place in the school—ends and means alike.

We have not often thought of educational improvement in this way. Usually, we think of the whole school system as the mechanism for change. Consequently, principals have felt—and have tended to be—impotent. Teachers have seen themselves as anonymous cells in an incomprehensible whole. There has been little opportunity for the teacher or principal on the firing line to get hold of a handle and to shake the system with it. The idea of the "lighthouse school" is catching on across the country but this is in spite of—rather than because of—encouragement by the formal unit of the school district. It is my belief that *we would see profound changes taking place in our schools if we really believed and acted on the premise that the central office and school district mechanisms exist only to be supportive of the local school.*

My *second* suggestion pertains to the general absence of specific goals and objectives for our schools and the fact that any major curriculum reform tends to be considered good for all levels of education. These two conditions are related. Because goals are lacking, there are no criteria for determining the validity of a given curriculum approach. Consequently, we tend to swing from emphasis to emphasis in cycles of twenty years or more. The '30's and '40's emphasized breadth; the current cycle stresses depth. Both have much to commend them. *It is most unfortunate that prevailing fashions tend to deny a generation of students whatever is currently out of fashion.*

Let us assume, now, that my suggestion regarding the single school as the unit of change has been taken seriously by 1980, and that each faculty has before it a reasonably *behavioral* set of objectives: a basic orientation toward *self,* characterized by self-appraisal, self-reliance, and self-control; proficiency in fundamental movement skills; ability to communicate effectively and aesthetically; facility in higher cognitive behaviors such as application of knowledge, analysis of relationships, judgment in terms of external criteria; and so on. But these, while providing a general sense of direction, are still too vague to guide the daily activities of teachers and students.

And so, let me recommend what I have been calling the "overlapping phases" approach to school programs. It involves planning for a relatively short period of schooling that corresponds to a phase of development in a child's life. Thus, there is a period, of from about ages 3 to 5 or 6, during which the child is making a series of adjustments to things, others and self. Often, we do not help him but, instead, throw blocks in his way, such as trying to get him ready for college. Let us regard this period as the first phase of schooling, early childhood education, a phase which probably will be an organized part of formal schooling by 1980.

At the University Elementary School, UCLA, we have spelled out specific goals for this phase which, we think, contribute to adjustments to things, peers, adults, and self. These are achieved at different rates of speed in children and, therefore, the *early childhood program simply has to be nongraded*. Increasing maturity involves broadening the range of exposure to more peers and more adults and so team teaching is essential to providing this experience. Nongrading and team teaching are not tacked on; it is impossible to conduct the program adequately without them.

Reading and arithmetic are not denied to children of this age but nor are they mandatory. There is nothing pre-school about any of this; *it is school*. The children are not "getting ready" for anything apart from the extent to which progressing well right now is preparation for what follows. Life *right now* is just as important as life three, ten, or thirty years from now.

The second phase of schooling is lower elementary, beginning at 5 or 6 years of age, and concluding at 7, 8, or 9 years of age. The rough overlapping edges are necessary because of individual differences among children. During this phase, the function is to teach reading and other fundamental learning skills and to do it thoroughly. To make learning to read a goal of elementary education is sloppy; *reading can and should be taught in a period of three or four years*. To argue over phonics or no phonics is specious. The truth is that teachers are not really well prepared in any method. How can they be when their teacher education program provides only an average of 2.5 semester hours in the teaching of reading? We need diagnosis of the individual and a prescription drawn from a repertoire of techniques. We need differentiated methods, periods of time, and grouping procedures based on analysis of need rather than achievement. Once again, nongrading and team teaching are essential.

Space and time prevent further elaboration. We begin to see how the character of a phase of schooling can be defined in comprehensive fashion and how the emphasis of one phase might be counter-cyclical to the emphasis of another. Concern for shaking up the program every three or four years outweighs concern for a nice, smooth progression from phase to phase of schooling. Who knows—with this kind of thinking, we might be able to identify distinctive functions for the junior high school instead of arguing over whether it should be an upward extension of elementary education or a downward extension of secondary. To define the role of the junior high school by 1980 would, indeed, be an accomplishment.

A *third* suggestion for re-aligning our schools can be set forth more precisely: *Get into the curriculum the problems likely to be facing young adults in 1980*. These persons currently are in the primary years of schooling. If we were to begin now, we could plan for them a junior high school curriculum organized around problems of population, poverty, pollution, and many more. Such a counter-cyclical program would not be organized around subjects at all but might well reach these young people in ways that present school fare seem not to do.

Fourth, school guidance should be taking cognizance of the fact that promising job opportunities for the future appear to be in public health, community service and planning, recreation, conservation, and education.

Fifth, since the time available for non-remunerative pursuits is likely to increase, it is necessary that we examine immediately the imbalances in the curriculum. In spite of an assumed "culture explosion", we continue in the schools to neglect art, music, drama, dance, sculpture, and, in fact, almost everything that smacks of being non-utilitarian. Ironically, we may discover not long after 1980 that, in the 1960's and 1970's we had an upside-down curriculum, with what was considered then to be of most worth proving to be of little value to masses of the people. Let us at least hedge our bets by assuring a reasonable balance among the several realms of human inquiry.

The *sixth* suggestion I have implied at several points. *It is that we back up the teacher with every possible technological aid.* The purpose is not to place the teacher in the role of a manager and manipulator of gadgets. Slow progress to date with audio-visual media in the classroom suggests the folly of this approach. What is needed is systematic analysis of the entire range of decisions that must be made by principals and teachers—especially in using new curricula, patterns of school organization, and flexible scheduling and grouping plans. Perhaps many such decisions can be automated so that innovations are effected without placing immediate demands for change on harried school personnel. For example, expecting the physical education teacher to have available several appropriate alternatives for students who cannot "suit up" may be expecting too much. Instead, the student who has been excused by the school nurse is held responsible for "calling up" one of the instructional alternatives that has been programmed for such emergencies. Similarly, the weekly plans prepared for an instructional group of 150 children are programmed in such a way that printouts occur automatically, leaving the teaching team completely free from the otherwise bewildering array of managerial tasks.

To date, *we have tended to think of educational technology as a supplement*—as something "added on." Such thinking is likely to lead to complicating, rather than to easing, the crushing burdens now carried by many teachers. Let us pretend for a while that there are no human teachers at all. My guess is that we will end up automating what should be automated and will leave to the human teacher what should not and cannot be automated. We might find, too, that the conduct of education is markedly changed and improved without suddenly requiring profound behavioral changes on the part of teachers.

SELF-RENEWING MECHANISMS

Specific proposals for improving school programs are of much less value than are mechanisms for continuing self-renewal. The self-renewing mechanisms I am about to recommend could be mounted and maintained by large states such as New York and California. But they probably are beyond the resources of small states. Further, there are certain strategic advantages in change mechanisms that cut across political entities. The eight-state, mountain complex seems to me to be a superb unit for what I have in mind.

First, there should be a center permanently and continuously engaged in the kinds of societal projections and educational extrapolations sought in the present eight-state study. The techniques of this project are so clear and sensible that I need not dwell on details. The core of my recommendation is that the process be made continuous and that the center be independent of any single state or of direct federal sponsorship.

Second, this center, or another one should engage in an array of simulation activities designed to reveal alternative school programs and the consequences of introducing any combination of changes into a school. In this way, the stresses and strains likely to occur in a real school would be anticipated to a degree. Plans for relieving problems through technological intervention, for example, could be formulated in advance.

Third, there should be several experimental schools existing apart from the requirements of any state or local school system. Pupil admission would be by application only, thus placing selection of the student body in the hands of the staff. To effect this requirement, each such school would be located so as to provide parents with at least one alternative school for their children.

Each school would serve different kinds of populations; seeking a cross-section is futile. And each school would experiment and innovate along different lines. There should be no effort to make these schools prototypes of schools everywhere. In fact, such an effort would be self-defeating.

Fourth, there should be a network of demonstration schools linked communicatively with the several experimental schools. These should be selected carefully to represent the complete range of schools and school problems found generally in America. It is to these schools that educators would turn in seeking models of what might be attempted in schools throughout the region.[18]

One of the functions assumed by the study center proposed in the first recommendation should be determination of the respective roles of state and local school districts, universities, and industries in developing the experimental-demonstration system recommended in the other three. The need for cooperative involvement is particularly clear in teacher education. The moribund condition of this important enterprise is in large part due to continued separation of these components.

SUMMARY

If any single theme can be drawn from my observations, conclusions, and recommendations, it is that the change effort in education is still disparate and unmanaged. Proposals for improving the curriculum, school

---

[18] A rough prototype for what is recommended here, now exists in Southern California. See John I. Goodlad, "The League of Cooperating Schools," to be published in *California Journal for Instructional Improvement.*

organization, pupil personnel policies, instruction, and all the rest tend to emerge as discrete entities, usually far removed from the inner core of schooling—where teachers, students, and what is to be learned all come together. The meteors of change, however bright and shining, too often lose their impetus long before they reach this inner core, fizzling out into scattered piles of ashes.

The change thesis to be tested is that *our high-sounding aims and proposals for education must be brought down to the single school, permeating its daily goals and all the means for their attainment.* Unless this occurs, there is not likely to be much productive communication or interchange between the world and the schools of 1980 and beyond.

CHAPTER 4

Conditions of Learning

B. OTHANEL SMITH*

Classroom learning is conditioned by the socioeconomic conditions of pupils. This fact is to be seen in the social status of boys and girls who drop out of school.

SOCIAL CONDITIONS AND THE HOLDING POWER OF SCHOOLS

In the fall of 1966, approximately 43 million boys and girls enrolled in our public elementary and secondary schools. If the future is like the past (which it should not be) approximately 27 percent of these young students will not complete high school and some of them will not even enter it.[1] In other words, a little more than one out of every four of these young people will receive little or no high school education, and in consequence, will be ill-prepared for the vocational and civic responsibilities they must face in the specialized and interdependent society of today and the future.

When this gross figure of 27 percent is broken down, we find that approximately 25 percent of urban youth will drop out of school before completing the twelfth grade. The chances of a rural boy or girl remaining in school are even less. Approximately 29 percent of farm youth will receive less than a high school education, while a little over 33 percent—or one out of every three boys and girls who live in small rural towns—will forfeit their chances of a high school education. The present picture for the nonwhite rural youth is considerably worse. If one is nonwhite and lives in a rural area, he has only one chance out of two of completing high school. The chances for the corresponding white youth are about two out of three.

It can be seen from what has just been said that if a youth is nonwhite, or lives in a small village or on a farm, he is considerably less apt to complete elementary and high school than if he is white and lives in an urban region. But even more telling are the conditions of his family. If a youth's parents have little or no education, and the family income is low or the father is unemployed, the chances that he will remain in school through the elementary and high school years are very low indeed regardless of his race, his station in life, or the locality in which he lives.

* *Professor of Education, University of Illinois;* Past President of the National Society of College Teachers of Education and of the Philosophy of Education Society; Formerly editor of *Progressive Education,* and a member of the editorial board of the *Journal of Teacher Education.* Currently a member of the editorial board of the *Encyclopedia of Educational Research.* Author of *Logical Aspects of Educational Measurement* and numerous articles; Co-author of *Fundamentals of Curriculum Development, Social Foundations of Education* and *Improvement of Practical Intelligence,* and co-editor of *Language and Concepts in Education.*

[1] Taken from *Agricultural Economic Report* No. 65. "Characteristics of School Drop-outs and High School Graduates, Farm and Non-Farm, 1960." (U. S. Department of Agriculture, Economic and Statistical Analysis Division, Economic Research Service).

This alarming rate of elimination is not new. Over 50 years ago in a classic study, Leonard P. Ayres called attention to the high rate of retardation and elimination. "The general tendency of city school systems," he said, "is to keep all the children to the fifth grade, to drop half of them by the time the eighth grade is reached, and to carry one in ten to the fourth year of the high school."[2] In comparison, the urban schools of today look much better. A change in holding power from one in ten to three out of four in approximately 50 years is no mean achievement.

Ayres attributed the high elimination rate in the first decade of the current century to the fact that the schools had not adjusted the instructional program to the average pupil. The prevailing view at that time, according to Ayres, was that retardation and high elimination rates were earmarks of a good school—that to promote few pupils was a sign that the work was of such high quality that only the best could do it. To reduce the dropout rate and the frequency and severity of retardation, Ayres recommended an adjustment of the curriculum to the pupil. In addition, he stressed the need for pupil accounting, flexible grading, special classes, identification of physical defects, and a revision of promotion policies. Most of these measures have been taken, and it is largely to these developments that we attribute the increased holding power of the schools today.

Yet we are not satisfied with the present capacity of schools to retain the youth. The loss of one in four is still a distressing ratio. By what means can this ratio be further reduced? Ayres was quite right in pointing to school programs and procedures as the primary source of the trouble. And there is still reason to believe that inadequate curriculum adjustment, grouping and promotion policies, and ineffective teaching procedures, account for much of the disenchantment of youth with the schools of today. Nevertheless, the problem of retaining youth in school is much broader than Ayres took it to be. For, as we have noted, the socioeconomic conditions from which a boy or a girl comes must be taken into account in assessing his chances of getting an adequate education. In spite of this fact, there is a tendency to believe that the schools alone, by improving the educational program, could retain and educate all of the children of all of the people regardless of the social conditions from which they come. This view is open to question. There appears to be some critical level of social existence below which schooling—however well planned and carried on—becomes almost meaningless for youth, and above which a well-conceived program can succeed with them. In short, it appears that *the education of all the children of all the people is a socioeconomic and political matter as well as a pedagogical one.*

Thus, there are two sets of conditions that influence the growth and development of boys and girls: those within the control of the schools and those that lie largely beyond the reach of schools in the broader community. While these two sets of conditions tend to shade into each other so no hard and fast line can be drawn between them, the distinction will nevertheless hold as a matter of emphasis.

---

[2] Leonard P. Ayres, *Laggards in Our Schools* (New York: Charities Publication Committee, 1909), p. 65.

Social Influences on Motives and Learning

The teacher's efforts to encourage learning are not made in a social vacuum. What he does is hedged about by all sorts of forces and conditions that have their roots in the home, in the way children and youth are treated by community agencies, and in the impersonal character of community life.

Impersonal Relationships

Life in the modern community is becoming more and more impersonal. The individual has only to go a few blocks from his home to become a total stranger—seeing only people he does not know and who do not know him. When he does anything, even if he does it out of his deepest sentiments, its effects seem to be lost in space and time. For example, charity has become impersonal. An individual gives money to an agency which in turn gives it to those in need. But the donor is unaware, save in an abstract sense, of the consequences of his giving. This example of the impersonal and abstract character of the effects of what an individual does can be multiplied a hundredfold by instances from daily activities. Under these circumstances, the young grow up in a network of impersonal relationships in which the chance of identifying with activities permeated with human warmth is almost zero. Even models of "the good life" have all but vanished in this impersonal network of human association; at best they are abstractions.

Isolation of Youth

For another thing, children and youth are no longer integrated into our pattern of life. As everyone knows, the family pattern has gone through profound changes in the last few decades, and only in relatively few families does the child now enjoy the performance of important duties. This is because the family is no longer a productive unit but one in which the father or mother, or both, are extramural breadwinners. At the same time the children have a surplus of time that is consumed in no way by responsibilities in the family or community.

The child's association with adults tends to be superficial and divested of social meaning. This isolation from the family and adult community is driving youth to their own kind. We speak today of child interest and peer groups that in my youth were unheard of and that my father would not have understood at all. These peer groups have their own standards of conduct that are often at odds with those of the community. To be popular with one's peer group is thus to be "in wrong" with the adult. To make low grades, to be sloven, to be aggressive and violent are all too often approved ways of the peer group. For a boy or girl to go against these ways of his group is to alienate himself from the only persons with whom he has some identity. This picture of youth's plight may seem extreme, and, in a sense, it can be said that there are some small communities in which it is not entirely true. But by and large it is an accurate description of what is happening in our industrialized and urbanized world where an entire generation of people is being uprooted.

Those Who Withdraw. From depressed economic conditions plus the impersonal character of society and the isolation of youth—yes, from these conditions emerge certain social types of children and youth that make up at least a third of our school population. The first group is made up of those who have withdrawn from life. These children suffer from severe deprivation, ending in hopelessness. The conditions for learning are all but destroyed. In school they sit, silent and inacting. The immediate and pressing problem is one of how to restore communication with these children who have fled from the scene. They can be reached, if at all, not by instruction but by individual and group therapy aimed at the restoration of communication and activity.

Once this normal condition of human existence has been restored, school learning once again becomes possible. To accomplish this much requires more than a sensitive and devoted teacher. It will require also a clinical psychologist who can rise above the dogmas of his training and grasp the significance of social depression among children of migrant farm workers, of families in depressed city areas, and of original Americans who have been disposed and assigned a barren existence on reservations. The task here is one in which both teacher and clinician work together to restore hope, trust, self-confidence, and communication. These children must learn to hope again before they can learn anything else. We have grown accustomed to the belief that such children are somewhere else—that they are not here—not in our community, not in our school. But this is blindness, for they are in every community, varying only in number and severity of depression. One of the major tasks of community education broadly conceived is to identify these children and to work out ways of helping them.

The Aggressive. Another group is comprised of children and youth who react to deprivation and isolation with aggression. They attack the school, the teachers, fellow pupils, and the community and its people. They have not lost hope amid deprivation and chaos. They still can communicate but they do so on their own terms. They still have aspirations, but they do not see the regular channels of social achievement and elevation as open to them. So they go down other pathways and run afoul of the folkways and mores as incorporated in laws and institutions. They do not respond positively to the school. In large communities these children and youth number in the thousands. In the great cities, special schools staffed with selected teachers are being set up to rehabilitate these children who have turned against the established order. The problem of helping them in the smaller communities and rural areas has hardly been formulated let alone attacked through the public schools.

OTHER SIGNIFICANT INFLUENCES

It is well that we remind ourselves also that the formative influence of the home, church, commercial and industrial establishments, police and the courts, television and movie houses, magazines and paperbacks is no less potent than that of the school. We too easily forget that *the burden of bringing up the next generation does not fall wholly on the shoulders of the home and school.* We are not accustomed to thinking of the police as having an educative influence. But the fact that they do is being driven home to us daily by reports of encounters by youth with the police and the courts. Nor do we ordinarily think of business and industry as being educative. But they are great formative agencies. These enterprises are not only involved in extensive training programs but also their concepts, values, and social practices permeate the climate of opinion. Typically they give youth their first contact with the world of adult responsibility. Here the youth learn duties and how to perform them. But equally important is the fact that they learn—depending upon how they are treated—to like or to dislike the establishment, to think that they are given a fair deal or a run-around, to feel that they are respected as human beings or that they count for little or nothing. Similar observations can be made about what is learned from the agencies and instruments of communication. There is little reason to doubt that attitudes toward sex and crime as well as the basic norms of society are profoundly influenced by the screen and the press. *What a youth learns from agencies and institutions of the community shapes his character and his future no less than what he learns from his teachers.* All this is so well known and so often remarked upon that it seems needless to say it again. Yet its significance continues to haunt us. But we hesitate to do any thing about it. To gear all of these formative agencies to a common goal entails so many conflicting interests and social forces that we find it easier to concentrate our attention upon the schools.

The point of what has been said is simple but important. *Education of the young does not occur in a vacuum. It is socially developed, sustained, and expanded.* Just as it is socially built, it can also be socially destroyed. It can be reduced, and pushed in evil directions. For the young, it is well to remember that the social context of their lives is the crucial factor that shapes what they will seek to do. *Schools in which children are highly motivated, and the dropouts consequently low, will be found in a community that mobilizes its social resources and directs them to the creation of an environment that gives significance to the lives of children and youth.*

PSYCHOLOGICAL ASPECTS OF MOTIVATION

While motives are shaped in large part by social conditions, it is important to remember that motives are also rooted in psychological realities. "Motivation" refers to the conditions that induce an individual to perform activities. To motivate a person is to manipulate these conditions. They may be external or internal to the individual or both. For example, a person may be moved to work on a puzzle in which he has no interest by telling him that he may win a free vacation if he solves it. From working at the puzzle, he learns. The motivation is related to, or consists in, what was said or done to induce him to attack the puzzle, or he may work on the puzzle out of curiosity. In the latter case, to motivate him is to bring the puzzle to his attention. As a teacher comes to know the various elements of the environment that will move a pupil to act and also how to manipulate these elements in teaching, he becomes competent in the art of motivation.

INTRINSIC MOTIVES

There is widespread belief that the individual likes to learn. But this is not so. Learning, like digestion, is a natural process. The individual neither likes nor dislikes to learn any more than he likes or dislikes to digest food. Rather, he likes to be active—to be exploring, to be contriving, constructing, and manipulating things. These are natural impulses and they move an individual to engage in activities if let alone.[3] From these activities he learns. Basically he does not intend to learn but rather to engage in activities after the fashion of his liking.

This is the fundamental fact upon which the program of instruction through activities has long been based, especially in the elementary schools. In the early years of schooling, the teacher appeals to the individual's natural inclinations to manipulate, to contrive and construct, and to explore his surroundings. As the child engages in activities induced by such intrinsic motives, he acquires manual and symbolic skills, concepts, and the ways of working with fellow pupils and adults. These learnings constitute the means with which he copes with the more complex tasks that confront him as he advances through the educational program. But as the learning tasks become more complex and more taxing, the influence of these intrinsic motives becomes relatively less. This is certain to be the case if the pupil is required to work on tasks that he cannot do. His efforts are then met with failure and frustration, and in consequence his tendency to explore and to manipulate as well as to engage in contriving and constructing activities is depressed and often turned in directions that are not conducive to his further growth and development. In any event, it has become clear in recent years that *an educational program cannot be operated successfully on intrinsic motives alone.* So, the job of engineering the behavior of students is one that must necessarily be expanded beyond the appeal to natural inclinations.

POWER AND MOTIVATION

The teacher has at least two other modes of influence which he can use to trigger the energy of the pupil. The teacher is in a position of authority and can exercise various forms of power. He can disapprove of a student's efforts when the latter has done less than he is able to do. Or the teacher can approve of the student's behavior when he has come up to or exceeded the teacher's expectations. Such power is to be used with caution. If a teacher disapproves when a student has done his best, the outcome is apt to be a reduction of incentive and a consequent lowering of the level of performance. On the other hand, when the rewards are in keeping with the quality of the performance, the result is likely to be an increased effort on the part of the student. It seems to be clear from these few facts that the teacher is in a position either to stimulate a student to do his best or to reduce his incentives—depending upon how the teacher's power is used.

This is an important insight into teaching behavior, for it reveals the fact that the schoolroom is a power system and that the relationship between teacher and student is necessarily involved in the power structure. From a

---

[3] Bernard Berelson and Gary A. Steiner, *Human Behavior* (New York: Harcourt, Brace and World, 1964), p. 244ff.

sociological and political standpoint, the power relations in the classroom are important. As Dewey pointed out many years ago, the school ought to be an embryonic typical community. In power terms, this means that the *teacher's behavior should represent a refined, legitimate, and effective use of power.* In this way, an optimum amount of learning may take place and at the same time preparation may be given for living in and dealing with power relations outside of school.

ACHIEVEMENT MOTIVES

The teacher can also appeal to achievement motives; that is, to the desire to meet standards of excellence.[4] Unlike the motivations that come from the use of power or intrinsic motives such as the desire to contrive and manipulate, the achievement motive seems to be dependent upon prior learnings. *A sense of level of performance in an activity is acquired.* Many students become imbued with a desire for better performance even though it may include only certain activities. A student may be easily appealed to with respect to accuracy in mathematical processes, but be heedless when standards of neatness are appealed to in his written work. Nevertheless, each individual has some sense of a level of performance that satisfies him, and the teacher can use this level when he is appealing to the individual to perform at his best.

The sociological aspects of the achievement motive must be considered in pedagogical work. There is a difference in the sense of achievement for an individual in an open society from that of an individual in a closed one.[5] In a closed system, the individual's sense of achievement will be set in terms of what is becoming to him in his station. The notion of achievement in the sense of achieving more for the purpose of promoting oneself in the social scale is seldom found in a closed system. The motivation in such a system seems to be that of the satisfaction derived from doing a job extremely well and consistently so. A gardener who strives to be nothing more than a gardener and who takes pride in doing the best job of gardening of which he is capable is moved by a sense of achievement foreign to that of an individual who is doing his best for the purpose of stepping to something more rewarding in money and prestige. Booker Washington tells us in his autobiography that his entrance examination at Hampton Institute consisted of the thorough cleaning of a room, a task assigned to him by a member of the institute staff. He tells us with what meticulous care he cleaned the room and of the approval which came to him from a staff member who inspected his work. Booker Washington was motivated here not primarily by a sense of satisfaction that comes from having done a job with one's utmost ability but from the satisfaction of the opportunities thereby opened up to him in the competitive struggle of a social system.

When we think of achievement motive as being one of the primary conditions a teacher can manipulate to enhance the possibilities of learning, it must be kept in mind that such motivation is ultimately rooted in the

---

[4] David C. McClelland, *et al. The Achievement Motive* (New York: Appleton-Century-Crofts, 1953). See also David C. McClelland *The Achieving Society* (New York: Van Nostrand, 1961).

[5] Bernard Berelson and Gary Steiner, *Human Behavior* (New York: Harcourt, Brace and World, 1964), p. 463ff.

social milieu. In our society we like to think that the criterion of social success is neither blood nor property but achievement. While these criteria are somewhat mixed in actual practice, the achievement motive tends to become the dominant criterion of social success in an open society. What an individual becomes is in considerable measure contingent upon his own efforts. Achievement is then a means of upward mobility and not an end in itself. Perhaps, in an open society, it is in an idividual's later years when he has made some sort of compromise with his ambitions that achievement, as such, is apt to be its own reward. In the early years an individual is on the move and full of hopes and dreams. And the use of the achievement motive in the sense of doing the task well for its own sake is likely to get little or no buoyancy from the currents of social mobility.

INFLUENCE OF THE ENVIRONMENT

But neither achievement motives nor intrinsic motives—or for that matter the motives aroused through the use of power—can induce every boy and girl from impoverished surroundings to do the work expected in the schools. Mostly for this reason, over 25 percent of our youth are dropping out before completing high school.

Why these means of motivation are inadequate is not far to seek. For one thing, *what an individual will aspire to do is dependent upon what he sees as possible.* He will not undertake something which seems to him impossible to accomplish, or if he does so, he will not long attempt to do it. For what is out of reach is very soon out of mind. This is the case because the individual does not long tolerate the pangs of disappointment and frustration. From attempting to do tasks that are—to him—impossible, the individual soon learns that it does not pay to try. So if the schools offer him a program in preparation for a life which is to him unattainable, he will do little to succeed in its tasks.

Boys and girls who come from social backgrounds that are weighted with poverty and hopelessness will see little opportunity for success in those activities of life that are open to the more privileged elements of the population. This is the case because young people are realistic about what is possible for them. If the life they see out of school offers little or no opportunity to advance in the social scale, they will conclude very quickly that it does not pay to try. They then sink to the level of whatever is perceived by them to be possible in their social environment, and under conditions of dire poverty and racial prejudice little will be visible to them. When they come to school, they will have little incentive to succeed in an educational program that is geared to those who readily see opportunities for themselves in the broader society.

Moreover, the ability as well as the will to learn are contingent upon what one has already learned. The preschool child in an impoverished culture fails to take on the mental processes, concepts, and attitudes by which he can profit from the school environment. The impoverished child is thus retarded before he enters school. The appeal to intrinsic motives such as the desire to explore and manipulate will stir him much less when he is in the first grade than the child who comes from a life of rich experience.

While a school or school system can adjust its program to the needs of culturally impoverished youth, it can do so only to a limited extent. But no matter what adjustments may be made, the solution is less than the problem requires. For the problem is as broad as poverty and its elements cannot be squeezed into a pedagogical formula. The program of the schools must be accompanied by socioeconomic policies and political actions designed to upgrade the social conditions in which the lower third of the population now lives. When the work of the schools is synchronized with an adequate program of social remediation, the teacher can manipulate the conditions of motivation with greater promise of success with those pupils who now make up the bulk of our dropouts. *Until the political forces push back the social and economic barriers that today deny countless thousands of potentially capable boys and girls an opportunity to advance in an open society, the schools are not likely to succeed in their efforts to interest all children in a more adequate education.*

LEARNING THEORY AND TEACHING BEHAVIOR

Assuming that the social and psychological conditions of motivation are taken care of, the task of schooling is then one of directing the learning process. Learning is the process by which individuals profit from past experience and is typically initiated by some sort of motivation. This process has been interpreted in various ways, but three interpretations have played significant roles in educational developments.

CONCEPTIONS OF LEARNING

The first of these interpretations is that learning is a *process of conditioning.* By "conditioning" is meant nothing more than that learning occurs under a specified set of circumstances which hold from one learning situation to another. The prototype of this conception of learning is that put forward by Pavlov. It involves the substitution of one stimulus for another where the response remains the same.

The second view of learning is that of *trial and error* and is associated with the name of Thorndike. It consists in the individual trying at random one response after another, as he deals with a situation for which he has no adequate way of behaving. The unsuccessful responses are eliminated as the successful ones are retained.

A third conception of learning is that which comes from German psychology, particularly the works of Kohler. This view is that learning occurs neither by trial and error, nor by conditioning, but rather by *insight.* If an individual is traveling by automobile and finds himself off of his route, he may stop his car and imagine where he is and by looking at the map of the region come to see the relations among the various streets and highways. From these relations he sees the path which he should take to set himself on the right course again. This would be learning by insight. But were the motorist to go first one way and then another, more or less at random, and finally work himself back to the highway he had lost, he would be learning by trial and error.

IMPLICATIONS FOR TEACHING

What do these conceptions of learning have to do with teaching? If one looks at what psychologists do when they perform learning experiments, he will see that their behavior may be taken as a form of teaching. This important fact can be noted in the work of both Thorndike and Skinner. One phase of Thorndike's early experiments was a puzzle box into which a hungry cat was placed. Food was visible outside the box. To get to the food the cat had to manipulate a mechanism that opened the door. In any such situation, the cat sniffs, looks around, and tries first one way of getting out and then another. In the course of his random acts the cat accidentally hits upon the mechanism and is released. When this same situation is repeated time and time again, the random movements are reduced so that the time finally comes when the cat is able to get out of the box immediately.

In this experiment, Thorndike might have been called a teacher. He set the situation and placed the cat in it. He arranged the reward for successful efforts. But he neither told nor showed the cat anything. He gave the cat no instruction and it learned nothing from him.

The essential difference between Thorndike and Skinner with respect to their role as teachers is this: Instead of permitting the cat to escape from the box by accident, Skinner's procedure would reward the cat when its actions were *in the direction of* the behavior required to escape. When the cat makes a move toward the releasing mechanism it is immediately rewarded. For each further move in that direction it is rewarded again. In this way the correct response is built up step by step instead of waiting for it to develop by trial and error.

Skinner's mode of teaching is that of responding to the behavior of the learner. He worked out a number of schedules for rewarding the learner. These constitute the types of performance that a teacher is supposed to understand and execute as he teaches.

In the case of learning by insight, it is expected that the teacher will put within the view of the learner all of the essential elements required for the solution of a given problem. It is then the task of the learner to put these elements together in a combination that enables him to succeed in reaching the object of his need. The teacher's task is primarily to arrange the stimulus situation so as to provide an opportunity for the learner to contrive the appropriate response.

The point of this information about learning is rather simple. If we wish to get at the heart of what the experimental psychologist has to tell us about teaching, we would do well to pay attention to *what the experimenter does rather than to what he says about learning.* For, as he carries on experiments, the psychologist does precisely the things that the teacher must do if he is to make use of what the psychologist has to teach.

Pedagogically, these theories of learning suffer from two defects. For one thing, they are not general theories, holding good for any and all types of learning, but apply only to special cases involving special subjects and special materials. For another thing, they provide no means for eliciting from the learner the sorts of responses desired by the teacher. The most that any of these theories has to say on that question is simply to give the trivial answer that the learner should be put in problem situations. *The job of teaching is one that requires the teacher to elicit from students the sorts of behavior that the educational program calls for.* And a theory of learning that has no systematic formulation of this problem, nor ways of handling it, can be of little more than passing interest to the teacher.

TEACHING BEHAVIOR AND THE LEARNING OF IDEAS

The question of how pupil behavior is to be initiated and guided is one that has been of major concern in educational research during the last decade, and will continue to be for some time to come.

Teaching behavior, like any other phenomenon, can be looked at from a number of angles. We can view it from the standpoint of emotion and feeling and ask what the teacher does to ingratiate pupils. We can look at teaching behavior as modes of involving pupils, somewhat as we did when we were discussing motivation. It can be studied as a system of questions, answers, and discussion. And it can be looked at in still other ways. What we prefer to do first is to consider teaching behavior from the standpoint of how ideas and concepts are taught and to ask what sorts of acts make up the bulk of teaching behavior so conceived.

FORMS AND STRUCTURES OF SUBJECT MATTER

The teacher handles different forms of subject matter and behaves differently from one form of subject matter to another. What we mean by "the form of subject matter" is the kind of knowledge—concepts, causes, values, rules, etc.—that make up the content of instruction. *Each of these forms has a structure* and *to know its structure is to know something about how to teach it.*

Perhaps the first study of the structure of subject matter was made by Thorndike in the first part of this century when he analyzed the sequence of elements in the performance of mathematical operations.[6] Today there is a return to this approach to the study of teaching and learning. This is to be seen in task analysis[7] and in programmed instruction where the detailed elements of content and their sequences are taken into account. In both task analysis and programming we find an attempt to analyze the content of instruction and to arrange it into a sequence conducive to optimal learning. It has been suggested by some research students that most subject matter can be divided into rules and examples, and that these components can be arranged in an optimal sequence for instruction.[8] But this reduction of subject matter to two forms—rules and examples—is intuitive and appears to be naive when compared to the complexity of either knowledge or teaching behavior.

---

[6] Edward L. Thorndike, *The New Methods in Arithmetic* (Chicago: Rand McNally and Company, 1921).

[7] R. M. Gagne, *et al.* "Factors in Acquiring Knowledge of a Mathematical Task," *Psychological Monograph*, No. 7 (Whole No. 526), 1962.

[8] J. L. Evans, *et al.* "The Rule System for the Construction of Programmed Learning Sequences," *Journal of Educational Research*, 55:515-520 (1962).

Other investigators have approached the problem through observation and analysis of teaching behavior.[9] From my own studies it appears that there are several forms of content. Among these are concepts, causes, reasons, rules, procedures, valuations, and particulars. Each of these forms is characterized, as noted, by a structure. For example, a *concept* consists in a group of objects, either concrete or abstract, possessing features that characterize them in common and meeting certain criteria by virtue of these features. A *cause* is a set of empirical conditions invariably associated with another set of conditions said to be the "consequent." A *procedure* consists of a sequence of steps by which a specified end is reached.

The behavior of the teacher will vary in significant ways as he deals with first one and then another of these forms of instructional content. In guiding the pupil's behavior as he is taught a concept such as the "nervous system," the teacher will do one or more of the following—or will elicit these behaviors from his pupils. He will give the functions of the nervous system, tell what it is like, or name its parts and their functions. In contrast, to guide pupil learning with respect to rules is to state the rule, analyze a situation to show how the rule applies, give the meaning of terms in the rule, tell the range of cases covered by the rule, and give practice in the use of the rule.

To repeat, the way information is fed into the learning process—whether it be by a student or by the teacher—is seen to vary with the form of the content. To teach a concept, as we have just noted, is in part to give characteristics and functions, to name parts as well as to give instances, and to make comparisons. But a teacher will never do these when he is teaching causes or rules, for example, because the form of the content does not allow them. Thus, a teacher of physics may refer to and discuss the molecular theory of matter as a general proposition used to explain the gas laws by which a particular phenomenon—the firmness of an inflated tire—is in turn explained. But this sort of reference to the use of generalizations is never found in the teaching of concepts, for the structure of concepts precludes this possibility. In a similar way, it can be shown that each of the forms of content requires its own unique set of teaching operations by which its elements are fed into the learning process and the pupil's behavior thus directed.

Teaching behavior also shifts from one level of thinking to another. At one point a teacher may be dealing with particular bits of content. A moment later he may shift to a conceptual level and from there move on to reasons. He may then shift to valuation. Suppose that the object of discussion in a history class is Andrew Jackson's veto of the Maysville Road Bill. As the issue is being discussed, the amount of the proposed federal appropriation and Calhoun's support of it may be introduced as factual information. At an appropriate point, Jackson's reasons for opposing the

[9] B. Othanel Smith, *et al. A Tentative Report on the Strategies of Teaching.* (Urbana: Bureau of Educational Research, University of Illinois, 1964). See also Graham A. Nuthall and P. J. Laurence, *Thinking in the Classroom* (Christchurch: Whitcombe and Tombs, Ltd., 1965); Arno Bellack, J. R. Davitz, *et al. The Language of the Classroom.* (New York: Institute of Psychological Research, Teachers College, Columbia University, 1964); and Hilda Taba, *et al. Thinking in Elementary School Children* (San Francisco State College, 1964).

measure—strict construction of the Constitution, personal feelings toward Calhoun, and expediency—are brought in. Then the concept of strict construction may be dealt with by way of explicating the reasons and, finally, the question of whether or not Jackson's veto was justifiable. Now as the teaching behavior shifts from one of these content forms to another there is a corresponding shift in the level and type of student thinking."[10]

Teaching behavior also embraces other sorts of activities. For example, the teacher structures the learning situation by focusing attention on topics, issues, etc., that evoke verbal exchanges among members of the classroom group. Then there are soliciting activities that call out responses and typically are expressed in question form.[11] Teaching activities of this type together with those that mediate the content of instruction largely constitute the sorts of conditions that evoke student behavior and sustain and shape it to learning outcomes. As the teacher engages in these activities—or involves students in them, student reaction (behavior) is under constant scrutiny by the teacher. He analyzes student behavior from moment to moment to detect where and how it fails to measure up to what is required by the forms of knowledge. In the light of his analysis the teacher modifies his own behavior.

Now the point of this discussion is that learning in the classroom is largely a result of the teacher's behavior in initiating and guiding student activities, in reinforcing student responses, and in accentuating student involvement in the learning process.

To study these aspects of teaching behavior, and, on the basis of experimental evidence, to select teaching operations and their sequences in terms of their effectiveness in guiding student learning, and then to synchronize them with motivating conditions and reinforcement schedules, is to put teaching behavior on a sound footing. Research workers have already taken effective steps in that direction—steps that are leading to constructive changes in teacher training programs. When we understand the psychology of our instructional content as well as the behavior and motives of our students there will be less reason for any student to fail in his work.

AFFECTIVE DIMENSIONS OF TEACHING BEHAVIOR

On theoretical grounds it appears that there is still another set of conditions that influence classroom learning; namely, those that bear upon affective relations between teacher and student. These conditions are now being disentangled from the old doctrine that personality is what makes the difference between teachers that are effective and those that are not. In other words, we are getting over the personality cult in classroom research. Instead of thinking in terms of personality as constitutional or

---

[10] Hilda Taba has provided ample evidence of this point. See her *Thinking in Elementary School Children* (San Francisco: San Francisco State College, 1964).

[11] H. Bellock, and J. R. Davitz, *et al. The Language of the Classroom* (New York: Institute of Psychological Research, Teachers College, Columbia University, 1964).

temperamental characteristics—such as outgoing or withdrawn, tough or sensitive, enthusiastic or apathetic—we are beginning to analyze teaching behavior into operations, verbal and nonverbal, that have affective import.[12]

Studies of this dimension of teaching behavior, like other investigations of teaching, are hardly beyond the exploratory stage. Their findings are a first approximation at best and will be corrected and refined as further studies come along. In fact, the claim that indirect teaching behavior, involving a high degree of permissiveness, is more conducive to learning than direct behavior is having to be revised under the impact of more recent studies. It now appears that when the teacher's behavior is business-like and direct, achievement is apt to be relatively greater than we had been led to think by early research.[13] But when other relevant factors such as grade level, socioeconomic status, ways of mediating content, and so on are taken into account and their influence determined, it will probably be necessary to make further modification in these early conclusions. Perhaps the most that can be said at this stage of classroom research is that *if the teacher evokes strong negative feelings, the amount of learning will be reduced.* A student does not have to like the classroom in order to learn, but he is not apt to learn optimally if he is negative in attitude.

What we have been saying about the affective aspect of teaching behavior is similar to what we said about the teaching of ideas; namely, that research in psychology has had little to say about ways of initiating and directing pupil behavior. Nowhere is this lack more evident than in the domain of classroom management, or if you wish, control of pupil conduct. Psychology has been rather helpful in redirecting the teacher's perspective about conduct. From psychology the *teacher has learned to view misconduct as a phenomenon to be understood* and to interpret it in terms of a system of psychological categories such as "frustration," "aggression," "withdrawal," "projection," "rationalization," and so on. But psychological research has not been nearly so productive in finding ways of dealing with behaviors so interpreted. So, the teacher often finds himself in the position of understanding pupil conduct but possessing no tested means of dealing with it.

This deficiency is now being recognized and a number of research studies are being directed to the task of testing out the effects of certain teacher behaviors on classroom conduct. Perhaps the most impressive of

---

[12] Among the references on this aspect of teaching behavior may be mentioned the following: H. H. Anderson, Helen M. Brewer, "Studies of Teachers' Classroom Personalities. I. Dominative and Socially Integrative Behavior of Kindergarten Teachers." *Applied Psychology Monograph,* No. 6, 1945. See also H. H. Anderson, and J. E. Brewer, "Studies of Teachers' Classroom Personalities." II. "Effects of Teachers' Dominative and Integrative Contacts on Children's Classroom Behavior." *Applied Psychology Monograph,* No. 8, 1946; H. H. Anderson, J. E. Brewer, and Mary F. Reed, "Studies of Teachers' Classroom Personalities." III. "Follow-up Studies of the Effects of Dominative and Integrative Contacts on Children's Behavior." *Applied Psychology Monograph,* No. 11, 1946. See also N. A. Flanders, *Teacher Influence, Pupil Attitudes, and Achievement.* Minneapolis: University of Minnesota (U. S. Office of Education Cooperative Research Project No. 397), 1960, and Robert L. Spaulding, *Achievement, Creativity, and Self-Concept Correlates of Teacher-Pupil Transactions in Elementary Schools* (Urbana: College of Education, University of Illinois, 1963).
[13] Robert S. Soar, "Teacher-Pupil Interaction and Pupil Growth." (Philadelphia: Temple University, February, 1966). (Mimeographed) The analysis of Oliver and Shavers shows that the same conclusion can be reached from an interpretation of Flanders' data. See Donald Oliver and James Shaver, *The Analysis of Public Controversy,* Vol. 2 (Cambridge: Graduate School of Education, Harvard University, 1962).

these studies is to be found in the works of Kounin and his associates.[14] They have identified some of the points in teaching at which disorder is apt to occur and have tested out some of the ways of handling these sources of difficulty. They have studied the "desist behavior" of teachers and have described some of the conditions under which it is effective in directing pupil behavior. They have described the spread of effects over the class as the teacher's behavior becomes disciplinary and also how the effects vary with the type of disciplinary move. And they have found some evidence that teachers who are effective in managing groups of normal pupils are also apt to be successful with emotionally disturbed pupils.

LOOKING TO THE FUTURE

We are now in the middle of the sixties and there is reason for optimism. At last we have come to grips with our phenomenon; namely, teaching behavior, and have begun to deal with it on its own terms. We now understand our problems and are beginning to define them in ways that promise practical dividends as they are solved. We are developing techniques of observation and analysis that uncover more basic variables than our earlier naive concepts could reveal. We are taking our research to the classroom and the school setting without losing the precision that our practical solutions require. As our knowledge of teaching behavior accumulates, the *day will come when no child will fail to learn in keeping with his capacity if his socioeconomic status (existence) is at an adequate level.* This hoped-for day is, I believe, closer than we think.

Research on the problems of teaching and learning is advancing rapidly. It is time that we face realistically the question of how the findings of such research can be fed into programs of teacher education and into the channels of in-service training. There is no ready answer to this question. But two suggestions are made here for consideration. For one thing, state and regional centers for in-service training of teachers might be established. These centers would serve to bring teachers into contact with new developments—new techniques of diagnosis, new modes of teaching, new materials of instruction, and new evaluation techniques—all at a practical level. These training centers should be staffed with the most competent practitioners to be found, persons who can demonstrate the best practices as well as talk about them and who can also train others. The training of a practitioner is the job of the competent practitioner. But he must not be the kind of person Disraeli referred to when he said "a practical man is the one who repeats the errors of his forefathers."

For another thing, *programs of pre-service training should be brought into line with the new knowledge and techniques.* Perhaps the best place to begin here is with a statewide program for the faculty complex responsible for student teaching. The hub of preservice training is student teaching.

---

[14] Jacob S. Kounin, Wallace V. Friessen, and A. Evangeline Norton. "Managing Emotionally Disturbed Children in Regular Classrooms," *Journal of Educational Psychology*, Vol. 57, No. 1, (1966), pp. 1-13. See also Jacob S. Kounin, and P. V. Gump, "The Ripple Effect in Discipline." *Elementary School Journal*, Vol. 62, (1958), pp. 158-162; Paul V. Gump, and Jacob S. Kounin, "Effects of Teachers' Methods of Controlling Misconduct Upon Kindergarten Children." *American Psychologist*, Vol. 12, (1957), p. 396ff.

To put new life into it is ultimately to influence the total program of training. In some states, the higher institutions can take the initiative; in others the state departments can. It all depends upon where suitable persons with drive and energy are located.

We are becoming more keenly aware of the educative effects of the economic and social conditions of life and of the influence of social agencies and institutions upon the development of youth. The time is upon us when *we must contrive the social mehanisms by which all of these influences can be coordinated and directed to a common end. There must be a unified approach to the education of youth.* We can no longer afford to let business and industry, agencies of government, schools, and other institutions and groups go their separate ways where the development of youth is concerned. *In every community there is need for some sort of council through which the work of every agency that comes into functional contact with youth can be considered in terms of a total program.* Perhaps the first step to be taken in this direction is for each state to make an extensive study to identify the agencies and institutions that influence the development of youth in both rural and urban areas and to determine the pattern of these influences.

We are beyond the day when the personnel that deals with youth can operate by common sense alone. *Persons who work with youth must be trained for the task* whether they be in industry, in the police force, or in other community agencies. They need to know those elements of psychology, social work, counseling and the basic social sciences relevant to their jobs. We must begin to think of a program of training—not for teachers alone, not for policemen alone, not for personnel managers alone, not for scout leaders alone, not for church workers alone, but—for personnel to deal with the problems of youth on a community-wide basis. *There is need for a basic program of training to give a common perspective and a sense of a common task to those whose differentiated responsibilities are concerned with special aspects of the problems of youth.*

The task of guiding the growth of the young from birth to adulthood is, in the final analysis, a function of the total community. It is as broad as the complex of social forces that plays upon human nature. It requires the resources of the state and nation and the cooperative planning and work of every responsible agency. We have come a long way toward creating an environment conducive to physical health. Community hygiene and public health measures have freed us of many diseases that only a few decades ago were common ills. We are approaching the time when *similar measures must be taken to create a social and psychological environment to protect our children and ourselves against ignorance and the ravages of social and personal abnormalities.*

CHAPTER 5

Early Childhood and Compensatory Education

A. HARRY PASSOW*

Predicting the shape of early childhood and compensatory education is difficult primarily because of one great unknown: the fate of programs currently being developed and implemented. Success may breed success. But will failure today blight tomorrow's innovations for the educationally deprived? Rarely have American schools been so directly in the line of fire as they are today. The war on poverty, the struggle for equal opportunity and civil rights, the efforts to enlarge experience with the humanities and the cultural arts: all of these summon the public schools to a leadership role. What will issue from such historic legislation as the Economic Opportunity Act of 1964 or the Elementary and Secondary Education Act of 1965? What can we expect from the so-called "curriculum revolution," especially from those projects designed for younger children in science, economics, mathematics and the social sciences? What is the potential out-reach of the technological developments in educational media, such as computer-assisted instructional systems? How will efforts to desegregate schools succeed? We can only speculate on how the cultural patterns and life styles of the minority groups in the mountain area (and other) states— Spanish-Americans, American Indians, Negroes, migrants, orientals and others—will be affected by these programs.

Hopefully, some progress will emerge from the violence over equal opportunities in education, housing, employment, political and civic power. There is murkiness to these and other aspects of the cultural, economic and social mainstreams of American life which could profoundly influence the growing years of those whom today we call "disadvantaged"—or the "culturally different". Presumably, some of the innovations and inventions now being tested and disseminated, and some of the research and experimentation under way, will be incorporated into early childhood programs, altering the nature of those programs, the curriculum and the instruction patterns for the population we serve. Yet the decade to come will pose a jungle of questions obscuring the roads ahead.

Of some things, we can be reasonably sure. There will be many more pupils—perhaps a 20 to 30 percent increase over present enrollments.

* Professor of Education, Teachers College, Columbia University and Chairman, Committee on Urban Education; Director, Study of the Washington, D. C. Public Schools (1966-67); Research Associate and Director of Talented Youth Project, Horace Mann—Lincoln Institute of School Experimentation (1952-65); Kappa Delta Pi Fellow in International Education (1958-59); Publications include: Education in Depressed Areas; Intellectual Development; Another Look (1964); and (co-author) The Effects of Ability Grouping and Bright Underachievers (1966).

These pupils will enter school at an earlier age and will continue for a longer period. A larger portion of this population will reside in metropolitan areas, many in cities which will face some, if not all, of the problems that bedevil the depressed areas of our larger cities. It will continue to be a highly mobile and transient population. It is possible, but highly unlikely, that the need for "compensatory education" as now conceived—that is, schooling to compensate for the disabilities suffered through experience and environment—could all but disappear and be replaced by that older notion: differentiating experiences to satisfy individual needs.

THE CRUCIAL EARLY YEARS

The past few years have abounded in early childhood programs, particularly at the "pre-school" levels of nursery and kindergarten. Aside from sheer growth in numbers, changes have multiplied in content and procedures for educating younger children. One of the basic ideas guiding the direction of program development has been the impact of cognitive learnings and language development during the first five years on later personality and intellect. Bloom's analysis of hundreds of studies (dealing with intelligence, achievement, physical traits, interests, attitudes and personality) points up the early stabilization of many characteristics. With respect to general intelligence measured at age 17, for example, Bloom concludes that the individual develops about 50 percent of his mature intelligence between conception and age 4, another 30 percent from ages 4 to 8 and the remaining 20 percent from ages 8 to 17. Other characteristics follow a similar pattern, suggesting that *the early environment is of crucial importance in laying the base for further development*. The central thesis which emerges from Bloom's analysis is that:

> . . . change in many human characteristics becomes more and more difficult as the characteristics become more fully developed. Although there may be some change in a particular characteristic at almost any point in the individual's history the amount of change possible is a declining function as the characteristic becomes increasingly stabilized.[1]*

It is these studies of early cognitive development, of langauge learning, of concept formation, of affective development, that have provided the impetus for re-examination of early childhood programs generally and of compensatory programs for the disadvantaged in particular. Incidentally, the term *disadvantaged* is one of several applied to a diverse and heterogeneous population—often of minority racial or ethnic status—whose members suffer from economic and cultural deprivation. In school, the disadvantaged population exhibits severe academic retardation, an alarmingly high dropout rate, and little participation in higher education. In the end, youth in these groups leave school, as one panel put it, "ill-prepared to lead a satisfying, useful life or to participate in the community."

During the past half-dozen years or so efforts have intensified to reach a population which has failed in school and which the school has failed. Academic retardation and early school withdrawal are, of course, not new phenomena. In fact, progress toward improvement of these conditions has

---

* Numbers refer to footnote references at end of chapter.

been regular. However, there is still a substantial, although not clearly determined, population which continues to force schools to face the question of whether they are up to the "weighty task of giving life to the great ideal of educational opportunity for the varied children of a heterogeneous people." There is no question that the problems of the disadvantaged stem from poverty and unemployment, from segregation by race or sub-culture, from discrimination, and from lack of equal opportunity. As recent data have shown, *adequate education alone—without parallel gains in overcoming barriers to opportunity in employment, housing and political participation—will not, in and of itself, guarantee to end the vicious cycle of poverty.* But these some data indicate that proper education is a necessary pre-condition to breaking that cycle.

THE DISADVANTAGED PUPIL

The efforts to apprehend the *why* behind the inferior educational records of the disadvantaged—especially the phenomenon of cumulative academic retardation and its consequences—have centered on understanding the pupil, the program and their interactions. There are those who blame this pupil failure on ineffective teaching by a rejecting staff—a deliberate "programmed retardation." Clark, for instance, asks to what extent this population does "not learn because those who are charged with the responsibility of teaching them do not believe they can learn, do not expect that they can learn, and do not act toward them in ways which help them to learn?"[2] In his view, schools have become the scene of educational atrophy and class struggle and only as educators change their own attitudes and expectations will children of poverty and the ghetto achieve.

Thirty years ago the schools were being condemned for similar behavior. The alleged targets then were lower class pupils with race a less significant factor. Angrily, the studies of the 1930's declared that schools were middle-class institutions with curricula and materials which reflected middle-class culture; that staff was inhibited by a value orientation which was middle-class; that modes of discipline and control were middle-class; and that the general climate rewarded and reinforced the behaviorial patterns sanctioned by the middle class, as it punished or denigrated lower-class behavior. As Burton put it, "the school has generally been geared to the aims, ambitions, moral or ethical standards of the white, prosperous, middle-class, Protestant, Anglo-Saxon population."[3] It is a judgment which has forced new perspectives on teacher education and re-orientation, on curriculum modifications and development of better teaching strategies, on systematic improvement of instructional materials. Implied in these changes is *respect for our heterogeneous population, whose needs demand alteration of the environment for effective learning.*

Much of the literature on the disadvantaged zeroes in on the largest minority group—the Negro of the inner-city ghetto and the impoverished rural South. However, studies indicate that poverty—economic poverty with its related social, cultural and psychological concomitants—is the common denominator for the disadvantaged, be they Spanish-Americans of the Southwest, Appalachian Whites or Alaskan Eskimoes. Manuel's study of Spanish-speaking children in five southwestern states details the particular difficulties of these pupils. Entering school, they have more to learn than their Anglo classmates: a second language and other knowledges and skills foreign to their homes. He points out:

> They cannot start their schooling at the level already reached by English speaking children. Starting behind and facing greater handicaps, the Spanish-speaking children tend to fall farther and farther behind with advance in grade. The progress of many is hindered by poor attendance resulting from the poverty of the home and the ignorance of their parents. Many find the going too hard, in part because the school program is not adapted to their needs, and drop out when age permits them to do so.[4]

It is not only problems of language that Spanish-speaking children face, Manuel contends, but those of emotional and social adjustment and the hazards of mental health that fester in a conflict of two groups and two cultures. Literature on the American Indian, both on the reservation and in the city, describes similar problems of acculturation in a technological society.[5]

What has now been added to the mix of staff and program is the recognition that *educators can design pre-school and early childhood experiences to counteract the experiential deficits children suffer in poverty.* Awareness that such children enter school with a background which handicaps their ability to cope is the impetus for creating compensatory programs as early as possible. Ausubel describes the learning environment of the disadvantaged child as both generally inferior and specifically inappropriate:

> His cumulative intellectual deficit, therefore, almost invariably reflects, in part, the cumulative impact of a continuing and consistently deficient learning environment, as well as his emotional and motivational reaction to this environment. Thus, much of the lower-class child's alienation from the school is not so much a reflection of discriminatory or rejecting attitudes on the part of teachers and other school personnel—although the importance of this factor should not be underestimated; it is in greater measure a reflection of the cumulative effects of a curriculum that is too demanding of him, and of the resulting load of frustration, confusion, demoralization, and impaired self-confidence that he must bear.[6]

By blending studies, this composite character portrait of the disadvantaged groups emerges:

Language inadequacies, including limited vocabulary and syntactical structure; inability to handle abstract symbols and complex language forms to interpret and communicate; difficulties in developing and maintaining thought sequences verbally; restricted verbal comprehension.

Unfamiliarity with formal speech patterns; dialects which set them apart from the mainstream, with English as a second language.

Visual and perceptual deficiences, including problems of spatial organization and lateral orientation.

A mode of expression which tends to be more motorial and concrete, rather than conceptual and idea symbol-focused.

An orientation to life which seeks immediate gratification in the here-and-now rather than ability to delay for future advantage.

A low self-image, denigrating one's potential both as a person and as a learner.

Modest aspirations and low motivation to achieve those academic goals which the school rewards; apathy and detachment from formal educational goals and processes.

Limited role-behavior skills and inadequate or inappropriate adult models.

Restricted attention span and general inability to cope with the demands and expectations of the school programs and personnel.

Obviously, not all poor children share this blighted sketch. Such a portrait of gloom omits the highlights and qualities which enable many poor children to bestride their world and overcome difficulties with a marvelous poise. But for the purposes of educational reform, it is the shortcomings that matter.

The consequence of these deficiencies is evident from the time that many disadvantaged children enter school: a self-feeding cycle of failure and frustration is born. Whiteman shows how this process of early failure leads to impaired self-confidence:

> The lowered achievement level may even feed back on the slower development of the originally lowered cognitive skills. A series of interactions between underlying abilities, overt achievement, and inward self-confidence may take place—lower abilities producing lowered achievements, lowered achievements inducing diminished self-confidence, which in turn feeds back upon achievement, and so on. If one adds the devaluations brought about by race-prejudice superimposed on poverty-prejudice, these processes may be accelerated.[7]

The disadvantaged child does bring certain "strengths" to school: ways of sizing up and handling a difficult environment; a set of values which lock him into his particular culture, such as freedom from family overprotection. Such resources tend to win respect from the school which can comfortably incorporate them into its instructional and socializing practices. Teachers must bypass the generalities trap, remembering that individual children will vary considerably in the nature and the extent of their cognitive development, value orientation, motivation and other intellectual, personal and social characteristics. Any composite portrait of deficits suggests the outline of a group—never a single real child.

INFLUENCE OF CHILD-REARING PRACTICES

Due to conditions related to social class and/or minority group membership, the disadvantaged child enters school with prior socializing experiences different from those of his middle-class counterpart. These are differences—not defects. They should be accepted as the bases for developing strategies and structures in "compensatory education."

Observing that the disadvantaged child manifests greatest retardation in the area of language development and verbal functioning, Ausubel attributes this to the home environment and to parent-child interaction:

> The culturally deprived home . . . lacks the large variety of objects, utensils, toys, pictures, etc., that require labeling and serve as referents for language acquisition in the middle-class home. The culturally deprived child is also not spoken to or read to very much by adults. Hence his auditory discrimina-

tion tends to be poor and he receives little corrective feedback regarding his enunciation, pronunciation, and grammar . . . Furthermore, the syntactical model provided him by his parents is typically faulty.[8]

Hess and Shipman trace the differences in mental ability and cognitive styles among lower- and middle-class groups to the ways parents speak to children and to their modes of transmitting information processing strategies. Their studies suggest that cognitive development is influenced by interactions between mother and young child; that the family's position in the community social structure and the choice of life style available to the parents, influence the nature of these interactions; and that the mother's behavior directly affects the development of the child's cognitive style and his orientation to authority. These interactions between child and parent—all part of the acculturating or socializing process—can either raise or block the young child's ability to adopt the role of pupil when he enters the formality of the school classroom.

A significant relationship has been found by Olim, Hess and Shipman between the mother's language elaboration, (or lack thereof) and the child's cognitive style and its development. How the mother feels about education and public schools and how she feels about her own ability to deal with the school system are clearly related to the child's cognitive abilities as well as to his behavior in the school setting. The image that lower-class mothers seem to hold of the school—and which they transmit to their children—is essentially one of "a distant and formidable institution with which they have very little interaction and over which they exercise very little control." They depict the school as a place where the child must follow rules and obey the teacher, not as an opportunity for learning:

> Thus, the initial relationship between the child and the teacher is posed in terms of authority rather than interaction and in terms of rules of obedience rather than inquiry and exploration. This early attitude supports and reinforces the passivity of many working class children who come into contact with middle-class institutions. It represents an orientation toward authority and toward learning which has indeed been taught by the mother and by the community environment and which needs to be modified through experience with teachers.[9]

Hess and his associates suggest that motivational and affective factors in the home are as significant as cognitive factors in promoting academic achievement in school-like situations. As with other studies, the importance of non-intellective factors looms large in the child's academic attainment.

Wolf studied the relation between home and environment and general intelligence. Thirteen variables were classified under three major categories: (a) *Press for Achievement Motivation*—intellectual expectations and aspirations for the child, information concerning the child's intellectual development and rewards for intellectual development; (b) *Press for Language Development*—emphasis on language use in varied situations, opportunities for enlarging vocabulary, stress on correctness of language usage and quality of available language models; and (c) *Provision for General Learning*—opportunities for learning in home and neighborhood, easy access to books and other learning supplies, nature and amount of help with difficulties in learning. Studying 60 fifth-graders, Wolf found a multiple correlation between Henmon Nelson I.Q. scores and ratings of home environment higher than the usual ratio between general intelligence and socioeconomic status. This underscores the significance of parental expectations of success in school as the thrust behind intellectual attainment.[10]

The training and disciplining techniques used by lower-class parents differ from the middle-class tactics, Bernstein found.[11] The lower-class parent tends to discipline children by exercising arbitrary authority and making categorical demands without providing explanations or permitting questioning. Thus, children grow up with little or no experience in exploring options of verbal behavior. They can not begin to build a repertoire of choices founded on conceptualization and reasoning. Strodtbeck found that "dependent poor" mothers (those receiving funds under the Aid to Dependent Children Program) discipline their children primarily through physical punishment—seldom in terms of language symbols, reasoning or positive models. Consequently, the children are not helped to understand the connection between what they do and how their mothers react. Further, these youngsters remain unequipped to ponder or to practice alternative ways of behaving.[12]

Contrasting expectations in values and in child-adult interactions and relationships were evident in the energy ADC mothers expended in admonishing their children to "be good." In the context of over-crowded living quarters and the family's general vulnerability to serious and unpredictable threat, Strodtbeck notes that being "good" means being quiet, physically inactive, and non-observant. Carried into the classroom by lower-class youngsters, the idea of being good means staying out of trouble with school authorities. For the middle-class child, the same admonition to "be good" means far more than avoiding disciplinary problems. Instead, it means to achieve, to do well academically and, especially in the beginning, to learn to read and write.

Events of the past few years have laid the basis, psychological as well as physical, for programs and strategies to help disadvantaged children. *The key is to intervene as early as possible to understand the nature of deficits in specific children and to compensate for these through planned, sequential experiences and activities.*

The psychological basis for early intervention programs grows from research that cites early childhood as the optimum time when preventive and remedial procedures can be applied to eliminate or ameliorate the negative effects of the discontinuities between home and school milieus of the disadvantaged.

PROGRAMS FOR THE DISADVANTAGED

There has been a proliferation of these early childhood and pre-school programs the past half-dozen years. Some thrive in essentially middle-class nursery schools, which now admit some disadvantaged children; others move to blighted neighborhoods but hesitate to modify their programs. Some schemes are simply public kindergarten programs offered free to children in certain states or communities for the first time. A good many are school-based—but early childhood and pre-school programs crop up in churches, store-fronts, apartment houses and elsewhere. Some are short-term summer projects; others operate year-round. *Operation: Head Start* and Title I of the Elementary and Secondary Education Act have probably provided the major stimuli for hundreds of programs.

Guiding most program planning, explicitly or implicitly, are two major goals—language development and acculturation or socialization of the child. Both of these objectives, in turn, aim at improving the chances of the disadvantaged child for success in school. In most instances there is some recognition that the current school program for which the child is "being prepared" is not necessarily an ideal one and that changes are essential at all other levels in addition to the pre-school. Generally, the planners adopt the notion of "readiness," but reject the old attitude of passive waiting, preferring to sponsor planned experiences and creative environmental conditions. Underlying most of these early intervention or compensatory efforts, Deutsch points out, are four assumptions to be tested empirically:

1. Earlier intervention is always superior to later.
2. Any intervention program is better than none.
3. If a rich, structured program is begun for children when they are three or four years of age, it will ignite growth potential which up to then has been dormant in the child.
4. Where there has been limitation of environmental encounters the child should be exposed to as much compensatory stimulation as possible.[13]

The intense pressure to provide programs for the thousands of known disadvantaged children complicates thoughtful research. Yet, experimentation is needed to test these four persuasive assumptions, logical as they may be. Neither time, funds nor patience have existed for research into the crucial elements of environment, instruction, resources and relationships in compensatory programs. The consequence is that project planners develop a program or "treatment" for entire populations, when individual diagnosis and study might indicate that only certain aspects of the treatment are appropriate to help a particular child. The intent of these observations is not to ignore the considerable body of research and experience. The point is, rather, that planners need to be more sensitive and alert in adapting these into their programming.

Experimental Programs

New insights are emerging from carefully designed experimental programs. Some examples of these programs follow, illustrating promising approaches to curriculum development for the disadvantaged young child.

Enrichment Program of the Institute for Developmental Studies. One of the earliest research and development programs (circa 1958), is that of the Institute for Developmental Studies (IDS) under the direction of Martin Deutsch. IDS combines analytic studies of cultural and social deprivation with experimental development of curricula and techniques for overcoming or ameliorating these deficits. The six specific purposes of the IDS Enrichment Program are:

1. To develop a "therapeutic curriculum" in language, math, science, reading skills, and concept formation.
2. To determine whether children with specific ability patterns are particularly responsive—or unresponsive—to the enrichment program itself, and whether

these ability patterns are in turn related to patterns of environmental deprivation . . .

3. To determine how such a preschool program will influence and modify the intellectual performance and eventual academic achievement of disadvantaged children, especially when they are enrolled in ordinary public school classes.

4. To determine whether the increased "success" experience provided by this program will promote positive attitudes toward society and self and raise aspirations.

5. To develop a teacher-training program based on an educational and psychological understanding of the disadvantaged child.

6. To promote an early and meaningful parent-school interaction so that formerly uninvolved parents may be assisted to supplement and reinforce school goals and values.[14]

Philosophically, IDS emphasizes the development of language and verbal skills, concept formation, visual and auditory discrimination, general environmental orientation, self concepts—and the ways to relate them to school performance. The approach is essentially an eclectic one, combining relevant developmental and educational research and theory. For instance, the Piaget-based development model underlying many procedures and materials is a three-step learning sequence: (a) a sensorimotor stage stressing perceptual discrimination, basically through concrete materials; (b) a perceptual stage involving finer discriminations thorugh contrasting stimuli of colors, shapes, sizes and sounds; and (c) an ideational-representational stage in which the child learns to relate things on a verbal and conceptual level with a minimum of concrete and perceptual aid.

Technically, the IDS enrichment program tests the relation of strategies and techniques, equipment, and environmental factors to specific learnings. Their research shows, for example, the coupling of socioeconomic class and linguistic codes, with side effects such as specific deficiencies in linguistic and conceptual abilities, rather than uniformly poor language ability. Their program development is based on these findings. They have experimented with auto-instructional devices such as the Edison Responsive Environment (ERE)—a "computerized typewriter . . . offering tactile, visual, and verbal feedback and reinforcement in reading acquisition"; a Language Master which combines visual and auditory stimuli; a Listening Center which enables the child to have a "dialogue" with a taped story teller. Other manipulative and symbolic materials have aimed at enhancing conceptual as well as language development and at upgrading self-concept and motivation for achievement. Deutsch argues that there is neither explanation nor justification for any child with an "intact brain"—other than those severely disturbed—to fail to acquire basic scholastic skills. "The failure of such children to learn is the failure of the school to develop curricula consistent with the environmental experiences of the children and their subsequent initial abilities and disabilities," he declares.[15]

Thus, the IDS curriculum is founded on sound research into child development. Stressing language, concept formation and perceptual discrimination, it clearly specifies structural aspects of the curriculum—such as room arrangements and routines—to crystallize concepts of order and space. It attempts to develop a positive self-image, using techniques and procedures which enable Negro children, especially, to see themselves in ways which will help to overcome any feelings of inferiority. Compensatory in theme and in working elements, the IDS enrichment program aims at preventing further disabilities while providing remediation for existing deficiencies. The curriculum is designed to offer teaching techniques and strategies, materials and devices, and environmental structures directly related to learning. On the assumption that continuity is essential to lasting, positive results, the program continues beyond the pre-school years.

In assessing the effects of its enrichment program, the Institute has fashioned evaluation techniques to: (a) delineate the disadvantaged child's specific patterns of cognitive, verbal, perceptual and motivational abilities; (b) measure the effects of enrichment techniques in compensating for specific deficit patterns; (c) assess the consequences of teacher behavior; and (d) index relevant factors in the child's environment and relate these to patterns of teaching and learning.[16]

An Academically Oriented Pre-School Program. Bereiter and Engelmann are presently testing a program which they describe as academically oriented.[17] They reject the typical nursery school program "based upon mimicry of those aspects of the culturally privileged home environment which are deemed significant for intellectual and personality growth." Instead, they propose to select "specific and significant educational objectives and teach them in the most direct manner possible, as is done in the intermediate and secondary school grades."

Their nucleus is verbal skills and language training. Language, they believe, is the medium for accomplishing almost every task required by the school, for offering every explanation, for exploring every concept. Not only must the child understand various words used by the teacher but the general semantic assumptions underlying these words. Consequently, they operate from two premises: enrichment of experiences alone will not provide the skills essential for later academic success; training in the formal, structural aspects of language will be more valuable than simply enabling the disadvantaged child to "get along" linguistically. Beyond this, they argue that while a child can learn other skills on the basis of verbal concepts, the reverse is not true.

The Bereiter-Englemann curriculum is based on an analysis of the formal characteristics of language, reading, arithmetic—the elemental information processes required for thinking. These analyses are translated into instructional goals. "Subjects," which they perceive as different areas of application of the same basic information processes, are taught in three daily 20-minute periods, interspersed with a half-hour for refreshments and singing and a shorter period for unstructured play. The children are grouped for instruction on the basis of their over-all rate of progress, with frequent shifts as individual achievement levels change. Language instruction seeks to implant grammatical statement patterns and a grasp of the logical organization of these patterns. Arithmetic is taught through language operations, much as a foreign language might be taught. Reading is taught as a logical process with children being given a maximum amount of experience in handling six sets of rules. Beyond this, they describe the program as follows:

> The school as a whole is run in a highly task-oriented, no-nonsense manner. Full participation of all children in the learning tasks is treated as a requirement to which the children must conform (much like the hand washing requirement in the conventional nursery school) rather than as a developmental goal toward which the children are allowed to progress at their own rate. Emphasis is placed upon effort, attention, and mastery, but not upon competition, as is so damagingly done in many of our more achievement-oriented elementary schools.[18]

Because Bereiter and his associates are carefully studying and evaluating the consequences of their approach, it should be possible (once the findings are reported) to judge the effectiveness of a pre-school program which concentrates on language skills as the prime essential for academic success.

A Diagnostically-Based Language Curriculum. The Experimental Preschool Project at Indiana University bases a language development program on diagnostic information from psycho-socially deprived children.[19] Hodges and his associates assume that "elaborative representational language is necessary to the development of symbolic thought, to verbal mediation skills and to school success." Therefore, every classroom activity is a chance to elicit elaborative language and to reinforce its use. Their efforts focus on production of daily language lessons whose goal is elaborative, flexible usage. Each lesson is short, has a specific content core, and integrates the children's levels of language skill, as diagnosed by such measures as the Illinois Test of Psycholinguistics Ability. The lessons call for: making discriminating selections from a range of adjectives and adverbs; clarifying grammatical order and syntax; lengthening sentences and increasing their complexity; qualifying statements through conjunctions and subordinate clauses; categorizing by differentiating among words and objects and generalizing about common characteristics of objects and actions. The lessons move in a sequence from "restricted" to "elaborative" language. The three-step sequence involves: (a) learning labels and names for objects which the child experiences through sight, sound, touch, smell and taste; (b) eliciting the salient features of properly labeled objects; and (c) making discriminations among similar objects on the basis of structural characteristics. The language lessons are the spine of the program, control living curriculum and offer opportunities for testing and subsequently modifying both the techniques and the content.

The Perry Preschool Project. This experiment was designed to assess the effects of a two-year preschool program for disadvantaged children in Ypsilanti, Michigan.[20] The schedule combined a cognitively oriented morning program with afternoon home visits to involve mothers in the educative process. Weikert and his associates developed a permissive but teacher-governed syllabus geared to deepen the awareness of preschoolers to the world about them. Prime emphasis was on verbal stimulation, dramatic play and field trips, rather than on social behavior.

To vary the instruction, the school-based morning sessions use structured *group teaching* and organized *area teaching*. Group instruction, lasting from 10 to 20 minutes daily, sought to overcome a particular skill deficit or to present a pre-academic concept of foundation importance. Cognitive skills served to divide the preschoolers—with the more advanced group undertaking units for language usage, auditory discrimination and complex dramatic play, while the less advanced group spent time in basic skill training, simple pre-math concepts and orientation to group activities. During area teaching, an hour each day, children were free to select from four activity centers—the housekeeping area, the clock area, the art area, and the pre-academic (quiet) area—or to work with attractive equipment and toys. Each of the areas stimulated cognitive development as well as socialization. Tied into these areas were numerous field trips. Besides giving direct experiences with the outer world, the trips were sequential, and emphasized a single aspect of one of the "areas."

Teachers went to homes in the afternoons—seeking to involve the mother in the education of her child, to demonstrate the process of teaching, and to tutor the child on a one-to-one basis. Sessions provided for cognitive skill and training (visual, fine motor, auditory, pre-math and science) and field trips. What the teacher had observed of a child's understanding on one trip led to later trips. Mothers were invited to join the teacher and child on these field trips. Fathers and mothers, meeting separately in small monthly groups, proved a vital element. According to evaluations, this exchange of views and perceptions helped shift child-rearing attitudes, even among the so-called "hard-to-reach" mothers. Follow-up of an experimental group after a year of kindergarten indicated that they had out-distanced the controls on nearly all variables studied: achievement, school motivation, attendance and relationship with adults.

Head-Start Child Development Programs. The Head-Start Child Development Centers take many forms, such as follow-through programs for children who participated during the summer, full-year programs for pre-school children three years old or older, and short-term summer programs. Guidelines for developing Head Start programs indicate that: parent participation must be solicited for all phases of planning and operation; qualified professionals are needed to direct health, educational, social welfare and psychological services; and widespread community support is required from local voluntary and governmental agencies, groups and individuals. Since the programs fall into the Office of Economic Opportunity's Community Action Program, applications funnel through local community Action Agencies. Actual operation may be delegated to a group with the capacity to organize and run such a program—a public agency, a private non-profit group, or institution of higher education.

While local centers are urged to tailor their programs to the needs of the families they serve, certain broad goals prevail generally. These include:

Improving the child's health.
Helping the child's emotional and social development by encouraging self-confidence, self-expression, self-discipline and curiosity.
Improving and expanding the child's ability to think, reason and speak clearly.
Helping children to get wider and more varied experiences which will broaden their horizons, increase their ease of conversation and improve their understanding of the world in which they live.

Giving the child frequent chances to succeed. Such chances may thus erase patterns of frustration and failure and especially, fear of failure.

Developing a climate of confidence for the child which will make him want to learn.

Increasing the child's ability to get along with others in his family and, at the same time, helping the family to understand him and his problems, thus strengthening family ties.

Developing in the child and his family a responsible attitude toward society and fostering feelings of belonging to a community.

Planning activities which allow groups from every social, ethnic and economic level in a community to join together with the poor in solving problems.

Offering a chance for the child to meet and see teachers, policemen, health and welfare officers—all figures of authority—in situations which will bring respect and not fear.

Giving the child a chance to meet with older children, teenagers, and adults, who will serve as "models" in manners, behavior, and speech.

Helping both the child and his family to a greater confidence, self-respect and dignity.[21]

To what extent Head Start Centers achieved or even attempted to achieve some or all of these broad purposes is speculative. The early "evaluations" from the summer of 1965 (561,000 children in 2,398 communities —one out of every two eligible, according to OEO) seem to rate Head Start an unqualified success—until one realizes that crash programs leave no time for the kind of evaluation design and assessment techniques that justify valid conclusions. Most observers accept the basic idea of Head Start as worthy. As the program now settles down and as communities take time to reflect—even as they ready another round of applications—undoubtedly some of the hard analytic study will take place. The data and insights from such analyses could provide direction for some major changes in preschool education as the foundation stage for learning.

Whatever its shortcomings (and these show plainly), Head Start Centers have already "loosened up" the thinking and planning of professional educators. It has front-paged early intervention and compensatory programs in newspapers across the country, even in communities where public kindergartens were not supported. The program has combined professional health and welfare services with education, ensuring young children of medical examinations at an age where preventive care is feasible. By drawing parents and community organizations into planning as well as operating the Centers, Head Start may be a new instrument to mesh home and school, and school and other community agencies. It has uncorked questions about appropriate staffing—creating new and significant roles for the volunteer and the paraprofessional. And, by aiming at a class of 15 children with an experienced teacher and several aides plus parental involvement, Head Start made possible the kind of cheek-by-jowl relationship which will, say its advocates, make or break compensatory education.

There are, of course, many reservations about the Head Start program. These generally hint that enthusiasm of do-gooders has been substituted for hard know-how of early childhood specialists; that there are good intentions but no program other than custodial care; that medical and dental check-ups barely touch the health problems which exist; and that the "wrong" population is being reached. Finally, comes the charge that by limiting the program to children of the poor (90 percent must come from such families), centers tend to be *de facto* segregated with the consequent perpetuation of the consequences of ghettoization. Unfair or not, this last criticism may be one of the most telling, counteracting some other positive results of the program.

In these illustrative programs, one finds different approaches to the development of compensatory education for disadvantaged children. There is not yet a prototype for compensatory and early childhood education but only some leads to fundamental changes in structure and process.

EARLY CHILDHOOD EDUCATION IN THE FUTURE

What seems clear from the current concern with developing early intervention and compensatory programs for the disadvantaged is that *planners should change the structure of the educational enterprise as a whole.* Simply readying the disadvantaged child for a curriculum and an educational program which, at bottom, is weak, can only delay and compound the disappointments. Fantini has argued that:

> . . . given an outdated educational system *all learners are thus viewed as disadvantaged.* One need only examine the drop-out rate in college, the performance of most citizens in the wider social arena, the apathy toward social injustice, to highlight this issue. It appears that if Sputnik rendered the educational system inadequate for the privileged, it certainly will be inadequate for those who are underprivileged.[22]

Thus, *the task educators face is* not simply that of bringing the lower-class child to the point where he is "equal" to his middle class counterpart when he enters the primary grades, but rather *one of unlocking cognitive and motivation potential.* He requires the training to profit from educative experiences which will speed him into the stream of continuing life-long education and growth so essential in today's world. Just as concern for the education of the gifted a dozen years ago revived consideration of the needs of individual students—and for appropriate instruction—the present experiments with compensatory early intervention programs promise to clarify our insights into education for the youngest children of every social milieu.

The case for early childhood education has been urged ever more strongly over the past few years; the possibilities of such education are just introducing themselves. The potential for using the preschool years for cognitive education, Fowler believes, has hardly been realized. The advantages, he suggests, are many:

> Most obvious, is the availability of more years of childhood to absorb the increasingly complex technology of modern society, a technology already requiring many of the more productive years of development to acquire. A second is the less evident but more crucial possibility that conceptual learning sets, habit patterns, and interest areas, may well be more favorably established at early than later stages of the development cycle.[23]

Predictably, early childhood education in the years ahead will practice improved techniques for diagnosing and understanding the particular patterns of intellectual and cognitive abilities of specific children; better strategies for direct instruction for cognitive and language development; selection of content aimed at providing what Hunt calls "the proper match" between the child's developmental level and the materials and activities provided him; clearer appreciation of the effects of environmental stimulation and their contributions to the learning environment; more knowing tactics for nurturing a child's healthy self-image, motivational development and abilities in "learning how to learn"; and smoother articulation with primary education, which will have undergone salutary surgery by the same time.

Three progressive, though overlapping, goals for planning intervention programs can be defined, Deutsch suggests. *The first goal* is "preventing or arresting the cumulative deficit, so that disadvantaged children will not continue to lose ground." *The second goal* is to reverse the effects of deprivation so that disadvantaged children will achieve at national norms. *The third goal* is to facilitate maximum growth and utilization of potential. This latter goal involves "devising environments, strategies, and techniques to make it possible for more children to 'learn to learn' and to be more self-initiating and self-propelled in the learning process." This third goal, suitable for all children, represents the blending of developmental goals for all early childhood programs with the special efforts for the disadvantaged.[24]

SPECIAL DEMANDS ON SCHOOLS WITH DISADVANTAGED

Education in the school with disadvantaged has dimensions which matter far less for the privileged children in more favored schools. The disadvantaged learner must obtain superior education to ensure development of his potential. It must heighten his ego development and yield a positive self-image, preparing him for taking his place in the mainstream of society. A curriculum for the disadvantaged must first of all seek ways for "reversing the spiral of futility"—the corroding belief that the American dream is not for the disadvantaged but for others, and that one really cannot break out of the ghetto or surpass poverty and discrimination. Education needs to treat such symptoms of that spiral as (a) a deprecatory self-image, (b) cognitive deficiencies which have stemmed from limited environmental stimulation and experiences, and (c) ignorance of the learning-how-to-learn skill. In sum, *schools must develop general education which will nurture individual potential in a population where it has incubated for generations.*

Analyses of learners' needs are the prerequisite to developing and applying strategies for upgrading scholastic attainment. Real understanding of the world from which the disadvantaged child comes, the specific kinds of deficiencies he brings with him, and the dissonances between self-expectations and school tasks, is essential. The particular teaching strategies and methods which will reach the disadvantaged are probably not strikingly different from those normally used—only their application differs. Sometimes, they are developmental strategies, other times remedial. To a large extent, they are really continual strivings toward understanding and improving know-how for individualizing instruction, and for working with

numbers of learners with a wide range of abilities, attainments and aspirations in such a way that each is reached at his own level.

Three "types" of instructional content must be considered in planning.
One is basically *compensatory* in the sense of overcoming deficits in experience and knowledge. Here, activities and experiences are furnished in
such areas as visual and auditory discrimination, concept formation, ego-
development, motivation, and general urban acculturation and orientation.
A second kind of instructional content is *developmental* in the sense that it
incorporates the basic, indispensable skills. There is a third class of content,
urban acculturation, which derives from today's urban world—its vast and
complex problems as well as its opulent resources. All students—not only
the disadvantaged—must learn to live with some composure in a baffling
society; they must come to terms with urbanization, automation, mass communication and all of the interrelated problems which impinge on modern
living. The foundation for this urban acculturation is built in the early
childhood programs. Beilin has observed that our efforts to provide compensatory education are designed to "compensate for resources never developed through a kind of education ostensibly never received." To the
extent that the particular patterning of intellectual and cognitive abilities
is understood, it becomes possible to plan strategies for overcoming deficits
in experience and knowledge.[25]

Planning of compensatory procedures, Deutsch suggests, must start
from diagnosis and evaluation of the resources missing from the child's
background and go on to estimate the lost contribution of these missing
parts. He argues against a belated transfusion of these early learnings,
suggesting instead that the present experiences must be structured to serve
the child in terms of his current developmental level. This level must be
ascertained, then "cognitive deficits which may be present can be analyzed,
and this would be followed by the devising of compensatory educational
procedures to ameliorate them."

Hess and Shipman suggest "the meaning of deprivation is a deprivation of meaning." The lower-class environment is one in which behavior
is not mediated by verbal cues nor by the kind of teaching which relates one
event to another or the present to the future. The meaning of behavior is not
made clear to the child. Hess and Shipman indicate:

> . . . that enrichment for the sake of enrichment may miss the point—that
> it is not additional, or even more varied, stimulation that is needed, but ex-
> perience which gives stimuli a pattern of sequential meaning. It argues that
> such programs must not merely teach the child new words, but must show the
> child how ideas and events are related to one another. And it argues that the
> transition that a child must make from a cognitive style of immediate re-
> activity to one of problem-solving must be made by experiences with authority,
> not with machines.[26]

A number of curriculum projects are under way which will have an
impact on the early childhood programs. For instance, in his Science Curriculum Improvement Study which begins with first graders, Karplus has
stated that a principal objective is the development of "scientific literacy
by which students are enabled to interpret scientific information as though
they had obtained it themselves."[27] For him, the starting point of the

scientific endeavor is an observation interpreted in the light of the scientific point of view or the synthesis of past experience. Karplus places great stress on nurturing in each child a strong feeling of the integrity of his own observations. This stress on sharpening individual observations of environmental phenomena, reinforcing the child's growing awareness of objects and their properties, and checking his own animistic interpretations, may well double as a learning-how-to-learn skill for the disadvantaged child—in addition to opening a door to science. Comparing and sorting collections of objects according to particular properties (shape, size, color and composition) and attaching verbal labels may lead to the development of the concept of classes and, eventually, to more significant abstractions. Basic physical ideas such as *interaction, equilibrium, reversibility* and *irreversibility, relativity* and *motion* are probably more significant for the disadvantaged than is the pseudo-science of many present programs. To what extent basic concepts and abstracts can be taught in an intuitive fashion—especially if one were to begin early enough to nurture and develop concept formation—is not yet clear.

Robinson and Spodek have reported on their studies in kindergarten in which the learning of certain key concepts from such disciplines as geography, history, economics, social sciences, mathematics and science was demonstrated. The learning of key concepts, they demonstrated, "could become the intellectual goals of the grade, supplementing physical, social and emotional goals" which are common in kindergarten. They have interpreted research concerning children's cognitive abilities and needs as firmly supporting the young child's appetite for intellectual content in his school program.[28]

Wann's study of young children's cognitive development and their intellectual interests led him to conclude:

> The readiness and need for young children to organize and see relationships among their observations of the world around them points to concept development as a key element in selection [of educational content]. Key ideas from the subject matter disciplines can furnish the base for choosing experiences and a focus for guiding children's thinking about their experiences . . . Properly nurtured the concepts can grow and bring real meaning to subsequent experiences.[29]

The dozens of projects in disciplines—ranging from anthropology and astronomy to economics and political science, and from physics and geometry to sociology and geography—sketch the range of testing of new content and procedures in early childhood education. How the disadvantaged can be matched with this content is still being explored by researchers. If there are indeed values in these discipline-centered curricula, then effective ways must be found for interpreting them to children—all children. Some curriculum projects are concerned with so-called meta-learnings: learning how to learn, productive inquiry, curiosity and creative thinking. These are important kinds of learnings for disadvantaged youngsters who are lacking in their development.

Goldberg has set forth eight propositions which, from psychological and pedagogical evidence, seem to characterize approaches which have been relatively successful with disadvantaged pupils:

1. Each pupil's status in each learning area has to be ascertained. Teaching must begin where the pupil is, regardless of grade level; age differential and materials must be appropriate to his present level. No assumptions can be made about the child's prior knowledge derived from home or neighborhood experiences.

2. Each pupil merits respect as a person, appreciation of his efforts and understanding of his problems. The teacher must not show by word, look, gesture that the child's inability to perform adequately or his lack of comprehension of even the most rudimentary concepts is shocking or disturbing.

3. All procedures need to be placed in accordance with the pupil's speed of learning. No assumptions should be made that a child has grasped what has been taught until he is able to demonstrate his grasp over and over again in a variety of contexts.

4. The learning situation needs to have a high degree of structure and consistency so that the child knows what is expected of him at all times and is neither confused nor tempted to test the limits through inappropriate behavior.

5. The learning situation should provide a maximum of positive reinforcement and a minimum of negative reinforcement. Self-teaching materials, as well as the teacher, should confront the learner with as few tasks as possible in which there is a high probability of error.

6. The classroom as well as afterschool learning activities should provide as much one-to-one teacher-pupil learning contact as possible.

7. Materials should be related to the world of the learner but not limited to his immediate environment. Stories about cowboys and rockets may prove more exciting and thus, a better learning medium than those about the local firehouse or sanitation truck.

8. One additional proposition needs to be stated, derived not from evidence but from the basic values underlying education in a democracy: although the school must start with the learner where he is, its responsibility is to enable him to move as far as he can go—which is often much further than he himself regards as his limits.[30]

Early childhood programs of the future will have to give far more attention to the learning environment as it affects the ego-development and self-concept of disadvantaged children, especially those from racial and ethnic minority groups. *Attitudes and biases of teachers*—conscious or not—*shape behavioral patterns in children.* The consequences of discrimination and segregation on ego-development, motivation and personality traits of minority group children have been well documented, though not appreciated fully. Increasingly, educators are beginning to understand the meaning of this background which the Negro child (and his counterpart in every other minority group, with gross or slight variations) brings into the classroom from the time he enters. Young children are fully aware of racial differences long before they enter school and much of what goes on in the classroom extends and reinforces their feelings of inferiority.

Examining children's perceptions of their teacher's feelings toward them and their self-concepts, scholastic achievement, and behavior—Helen Davidson and Gerhard Lang found a direct relationship between children's social class and teachers' ratings. Also, they found that children clearly sensed their teachers' attitudes toward them; those who felt their teachers ranked them low seemed to have lower self-perceptions, achieved less well and behaved less well in the classroom than did more favored classmates.[31]

Teacher training programs for those working with disadvantaged pupils are concerned with both curriculum and climate—with insights into teaching strategies and content adaptations as well as with understandings of cultural differences. Involvement of sub-professionals, teacher aides, and indigenous residents in programs designed to help children from depressed areas the school serves, has opened up new training programs and opportunities. Some of these have been as helpful for the trainers as for the trainees in altering attitudes toward the culturally different.

Early childhood programs of the future will have to provide far more parent education and involvement than schools presently make available and it will differ in nature. For example, Olim and his associates' findings concerning the influence of mothers' language styles and attitudes toward education and schooling in helping or blocking their children's cognitive development, lead to this recommendation: when structuring pre-school intervention programs, involve mothers directly in the educational programs for their own children. They suggest:

> . . . decreasing the separation of lower-class mothers from the reality of the school system by encouraging them to attend their children's classes, discussing their hopes and expectations for their child, within the context of their attitudes toward and beliefs about the public school system; offering them the opportunity of interacting with teachers, of experiencing success in expressing their feelings and ideas to an authority; and engaging them more actively in their children's learning should help in forming more positive attitudes on the mother's part and, through them, more adaptive behaviors on the part of the child.[32]

IN SUMMARY

The downward extension of schooling seems assured in the years ahead. *What is now considered pre-school will become a basic component of America's "common school."* Having recognized the crucial importance of the formative childhood years on intellectual, personal and social growth, *educators and laymen are beginning to program instruction to constitute a sound foundation for all children, whatever their origins.* The experiences and environment of the early years are critical for continued learnings.

The early childhood program will not feature one-time primary grade activities moved down. Rather, it will provide experiences, activities and materials specifically designed for cognitive and motivational growth of young children. Its curriculum will apply the findings of continuing diagnosis of each child's developmental progress. It will seek deliberately to compensate for environment and experiential deficits, tailoring its units to unlock potential which is latent. The program will be highly individualized, using technological aids when appropriate. While many elements of today's nursery and kindergarten programs will be apparent, far more attention will be given to structuring the environment for learning.

In critical areas, instruction will be direct, specific, and still informal. With a core of language development, in its broadest dimensions, *the curriculum will be aimed at cognitive growth, concept formation, abstract reasoning, values and perceptual refinement.* "Reading readiness" will assume a different meaning—the subtle difference of "learning readiness." Within the framework of key concepts from basic subject disciplines, children will be helped to think about experiences and to interpret the world about them. The curriculum perimeters will include understandings, processes, concepts, attitudes, values and feelings.

To the staff will come the new (or renewed) professionals, strengthened by insights into the diverse cultures which send their pupils to them. Appreciative of how these backgrounds and differences in life styles can widen and season the climate for learning, such teachers can guide pupils to creative understanding and acceptance of individuals as individuals. Paraprofessionals of many kinds, volunteers and aides, will be assigned to enhance the possibilities of one-to-one relationships between the young child and the adult and to affect the attitudes and understandings of the adults as well. Consequently, *parent education and involvement will be transformed to an integral part of the early childhood program.*

Tomorrow's school will concern itself with attitudes, values and commitment. Accepting racial awareness and other differences, planners will develop instructions for understanding others and for developing healthy pride of self. *The school will catalyze essential health, social and welfare services, working closely with private as well as public agencies.* Once again, the school will adopt an acculturation role—this time, for improving the quality of living in the urban setting. Its "classroom" will breach the walls of the school building, expanding into the community. Tomorrow's school will breathe life into the nation's goal of equal opportunity for all.

Those who write of a "renaissance in early childhood education" are thinking partly of the live possibilities for capitalizing on the support and enthusiasm which applaud and subsidize our concern for the disadvantaged. Out of this can grow the pace-setting new perspectives on early childhood programs for all children. Yet, lest idealism cloud our senses, we must admit that at present—without effective early childhood education—large numbers of children are doomed to the failure and frustration which come with academic retardation and the continued misery of poverty. What may be in embryo could be the germ of a true system of universal education—meaningful, life-equipping and lifelong, for all who value or can be helped to value this gift. The courage, intelligence and leadership of educators with the active cooperation of lay citizens, can win this quiet revolution for generations to come.

FOOTNOTE REFERENCES

1. Benjamin S. Bloom, *Stability and Change in Human Characteristics* (New York: John Wiley and Sons, 1964), p. 218.
2. Kenneth B. Clark, *Dark Ghetto: Dilemmas of Social Power* (New York: Harper and Row, 1965), p. 131.
3. William H. Burton, "Education and Social Class in the United States," *Harvard Educational Review,* 33:248-249, (Fall 1953).
4. Herschel T. Manuel, *Spanish-Speaking Children of the Southwest* (Austin: University of Texas Press, 1965), p. 188.
5. Norman C. Greenberg and Gilda M. Greenberg, *Education of the American Indian in Today's World* (Dubuque, Iowa: Wm. C. Brown Book Co., 1964); Charles K. Ray, Joan Ryan, and Seymour Parker, *Alaskan Native Secondary School Dropouts: A Research Report* (College: University of Alaska, 1962).
6. David P. Ausubel, "A Teaching Strategy for Culturally Deprived Pupils: Cognitive and Motivational Consideration," *School Review,* 71:454, (Winter 1963).
7. Martin Whiteman, "Developmental Theory and Enrichment Programs," in *Environmental Deprivation and Enrichment,* (New York: Ferkhauf Graduate School of Education, Yeshiva University, 1965), p. 56.
8. David P. Ausubel, "How Reversible are the Cognitive and Motivational Effects of Cultural Deprivation? Implications for Teaching the Culturally Deprived Child," *Urban Education,* 1:23-24, (Summer 1964).
9. Robert D. Hess and Virginia C. Shipman, "Maternal Attitude Toward the School and the Role of Pupil: Some Social Class Comparison. " (Paper prepared for the Fifth Work Conference on Curriculum and Teaching in Depressed Urban Areas, Teachers College, Columbia University, 1966).

10. Richard M. Wolf, "The Measurement of Environments," in *Proceedings of the 1964 Invitational Conference on Testing Problems*, (Princeton, N. J.: Educational Testing Services, 1965), pp. 93-106.

11. Basil Bernstein, "Social Structure, Language and Learning," *Educational Research*, 3: 163-176, (June 1961).

12. Fred L. Strodtbeck, "The Hidden Curriculum of the Middle Class Home," in *Urban Education and Cultural Deprivation*, edited by C. W. Hunnicutt, (Syracuse: Syracuse University Press, 1964), pp. 15-31.

13. Martin Deutsch, *Social Intervention and the Malleability of the Child* (Ithaca: Cornell University School of Education, 1965), pp. 5-9.

14. Institute for Developmental Studies, *Annual Report 1965* (New York: Institute for Developmental studies, Department of Psychiatry, New York Medical College, 1966), p. 57.

15. Martin Deutsch, "Facilitating Development in the Pre-School Child: Social and Psychological Perspectives," *Merrill-Palmer Quarterly*, 10:258, (July 1964).

16. Institute for Developmental Studies, op. cit., p. 82 ff.

17. Carl Bereiter, Jean Osborn, Siegfried Engelmann, and Philip A. Reidford, "An Academically-Oriented Preschool for Culturally Deprived Children, (Paper presented at the American Educational Research Convention, February 1965). See also, Bereiter, Carl and Engelmann, Siegfried, *Teaching Culturally Deprived Children in the Preschool* (Englewood Cliffs, N. J.: Prentice-Hall, 1966).

18. *Ibid.*, p. 4.

19. Walter Hodges, Howard Spickel, and Keith Stearns, "Interim Report: A Diagnostically-Based Language Curriculum for Psycho-Socially Deprived Preschool Children." (Paper presented at the American Educational Research Association Convention, February 1966).

20. David P. Weikert, Constance K. Kamii, and Norma L. Radin, "Perry Preschool Project: Progress Report." (Ypsilanti, Mich.: Ypsilanti Public Schools, June 1964).

21. Project *Head Start, Head Start Child Development Programs*. (Washington, D.C.: Community Action Program, Office of Economic Opportunity, 1966), pp. 10-11.

22. Mario D. Fantini, "How Can We Best Educate the Economically Disadvantaged Student." (Paper prepared for the Governor's Conference on Education, State of New Jersey, April 2, 1966).

23. William Fowler, "Cognitive Learning in Infancy and Early Childhood," *Psychological Bulletin*, 59:146 (1962).

24. Deutsch, 1965, *op. cit.*, p. 16.

25. Harry Beilin, "A Cognitive Strategy for Curriculum Development." (Paper presented at the Fifth Work Conference on Curriculum and Teaching in Depressed Urban Areas, Teachers College, Columbia University, 1966).

26. Robert D. Hess and Virginia Shipman, "Early Blocks to Children's Learning." *Children* (September-October 1965).

27. Robert Karplus, "One Physicist Looks at Science Education," in *Intellectual Development: Another Look*, edited by A. Harry Passow and Robert Leeper, (Washington: Association for Supervision and Curriculum Development, 1964), pp. 17-98.

28. Helen F. Robison and Bernard Spodek, *New Directions in the Kindergarten* (New York: Teachers College Press, 1965).

29. Kenneth D. Wann, Miriam S. Dorn and Elizabeth A. Liddle, *Fostering Intellectual Development in Young Children* (New York: Teachers College Press, 1962), p. 117.

30. Miriam L. Goldberg, "Methods and Materials for Educationally Disadvantaged Youth." (Paper prepared for Post-Doctoral Seminar of the College of Education, The Ohio State University, October 1964).

31. Helen H. Davidson and Gerhard Lang, "Children's Perceptions of Their Teachers' Feelings Toward Them Related to Self-Perception, School Achievement, and Behavior," *Journal of Experimental Education*, 29:107-118 (December 1960).

32. Ellis G. Olim, Robert D. Hess and Virginia C. Shipman, "Role of Mothers' Language Styles in Mediating Their Children's Cognitive Development." (Paper prepared for American Educational Research Association Convention, 1966).

CHAPTER 6

Education for the World of Work

GORDON I. SWANSON*

Education, like business, has certain cyclical characteristics. During these cycles there has been a greater or lesser amount of attention to patterns of school organization, considerations of subject content within the curriculum, and various interpretations of excellence. Educational historians have chronicled these cycles and have attempted to interpret their meaning within a context of educational objectives and values. Education for work has always been a part of this cyclical emphasis and de-emphasis. In recent years, such interest has appeared to be more sustained and more intense. Never before has this nation been as concerned with the relationships between the educational system and the full range of its manpower needs.

The current emphasis appears to be more than a cyclical phenomenon. Perhaps the sustained interest has grown out of a refinement of analytical tools for educational planning, or it may be an acceptance of economic policy commitments for achieving both growth and full employment. The reasons may be elusive but they no longer appear to be transitory. Education for work now has a continuous claim on educational priorities.

PRESENT STATUS

As a starting point for discussing this type of education, it is necessary to begin by describing some of the forces which are already at work; the forces which—taken together—provide a kind of natural dynamics within the educational setting. It is from this setting that further planning will need to emerge.

THE INHERENT VALUE OF WORK

In our society, work is central to our interpretation of progress. Often it is thought that our price system is the only operating mechanism for rationing goods and services. Another mechanism, and perhaps a more important one, is work. It is work that rations money in the first place and allows other rationing systems to work. It is a man's work, for example, which is the major determiner of his eligibility for credit. Few will disagree that the process of assigning future income has an important role in the distribution of economic goods.

Work is also a determiner of man's social acceptance within his community. As a worker he is a contributor to the flow of public services which

* *Professor of Education and Coordinator of International Education, University of Minnesota.* Member, UNESCO Advisory Committee on the Role of Science and Technology in Development, NEA Commission on International Relations, and Phi Delta Kappa Commission on Education, Manpower and Economic Growth; Chairman, American Vocational Association Committee on International Education; Formerly, Associate Director, Division of Vocational and Technical Education, UNESCO (1959-60), and consultant, Ford Foundation—Vocational Education in Brazil (1964).

he helps to consume. The work ethic is the framework for social acceptability as well as an important avenue for the achievement of independence
and freedom. It is likely that the most important values in work are also the
most difficult to measure and the most dimly visible to those who are employed. Professionals in vocational rehabilitation may be in the best position
to assess the relationship of work to self-respect, personal adjustment and
social acceptability. They are in daily contact with the severe problems
which arise from inability to work.

Work continues to have intrinsic merit within the acceptable scheme
of personal and social values. It is also essential to the preferred schemes
of national economic planning.

THE FULL EMPLOYMENT OBJECTIVE

This paper is not the place to discuss the "new economics"—which
is not new at all, except perhaps in its latest refinements and in its successful and dramatic implementation as illustrated by the massive tax reductions
in the early 1960's. It rests on some early formulations by John Maynard
Keynes. These have since been refined and elaborated by other economists
for more than three decades. It now constitutes a part of the natural dynamics of the economy and also of the combination of forces affecting
education.

Crucial to this concept of economic planning is its commitment to full
employment. This concept had early beginnings in this country in 1946
with the passage of the Employment Act—a controversial piece of legislation about which the debate hinged on the role of government in price
stability and compensatory spending. This legislation was not a manifestation of limited or parochial views. It was paralleled in other industrialized
countries by similar legislation with similar commitments to full employment. Even the United Nations charter subscribed to full employment as an
economic and social goal.

This Employment Act was essentially a commitment to a principle—
the principle that government must assume responsibility for the level of
employment through action available to it at the federal level. It is quite
possible that this principle has never had a complete and adequate test.
The Korean and the Vietnam conflicts may have overshadowed the effort to
provide such a test.

Moreover, the "new" elements of the "new economics" may not describe the field of economics at all. They may only describe the extent to
which leaders of government and business can now agree to speak a mutually acceptable language as they discuss economic planning and, also, the
degree of sophistication which characterizes this conversation. These discussions have now broken out of professional circles. This is both fortunate
and essential. The implementation of economic plans requires the support
of public opinion.

Even though the commitment to full employment may not have undergone an adequate test, the commitment is present, nevertheless, as an
essential part of the strategy for national planning. The 1966 Report of the

Council of Economic Advisers[1] reiterates the policy concepts which relate to high employment levels, price stability and balanced growth.

What are the educational implications in this commitment to full employment? *First* of all, they reaffirm our natural preference for a work ethic. Even though there is argument about the appropriate definition of full employment, any definition assumes both the social and economic value of work. In his early formulations, Keynes predicted that, by the end of this century, the work week would be reduced to 15 hours. Whether this prediction is close to—or far from—its target is secondary to our main consideration here: that work for everyone, as interpreted by full employment, is a national goal with importance for education.

Second, the fiscal and monetary manipulation needed to achieve growth, high employment and price stability is necessarily accompanied by an orientation toward national goals and a "goals consciousness." Except for periods of national emergency, a system of national goals is new to the field of education. Since education is a state responsibility, the federal government has been conspicuously non-hierarchical in its relationship to state governments. The educational system has been oriented toward a more limited geography and toward more individual needs and aspirations. A "goals consciousness" at the federal level provides a new framework for educational planning. It also signals a new basis upon which the effectiveness of education will be measured.

Third, the fact of full employment has its own effect on education for work. Full employment carries with it the nominal assumption that labor will be in a seller's market. Once full employment is reached, the demand for labor will have largely absorbed the unskilled into the labor market and further demands for labor will compete even more for the less skilled as labor force participation rates continue to rise. The usual effect is a narrowing of wage differentials between the skilled and the unskilled, and the personal incentive to engage in training tends to decline. Since the wage differential between the skilled and the unskilled represents a return on the investment in training, this narrowing of wage differentials has a direct effect on education. This has been a part of the phenomenon which has resulted in a rise in the enrollment of both vocational schools and junior colleges during periods of unemployment and a relative decline in periods of high employment. If full employment is an attainable and sustainable goal in the future—and if higher qualitative standards are to be achieved—education for work may require incentives which exceed those that are available as wage rates in the labor market. It may be necessary to provide the incentive in the form of fellowships and scholarships to those enrolled in vocational education in the same way that these have been available to students in other forms of higher education for a long time.

Fourth, economic planning requires orderly and intensive educational planning as one of its concomitants. Education has not been regarded as a mechanism for assuring full employment. It is crucial, however, in any economy undergoing rapid changes in technology and rapid transformation

---

[1] *Annual Report of the Council of Economic Advisers,* (January, 1966), p. 180.

in occupational structure. Educational planning will also be important for many other reasons, but the value of planning to meet the needs of education for work is sufficient to highlight its importance here.

There are many educational implications to be drawn from a national goal of full employment and a set of policy objectives for economic growth. The ones mentioned here are as incomplete as they are imperfect. The few mentioned may serve as indicators of some of the forces now at work.

THE ROLE OF THE COMPREHENSIVE SCHOOL

In any consideration of education for work, sooner or later, the comprehensive elementary and secondary school becomes a focal point of interest. It involves school districts—the basic units of our educational structure —and it contains the form of common education which we have accepted as the American pattern. The comprehensive school has been criticized, subjected to various unequal pressures, and required to accept some obligations which are not educational. Yet it remains as almost a unanimous choice for achieving the purposes which have been interpreted as educational. It provides the institutional framework for compulsory school attendance. For most students, the secondary school is their last and only contact with formalized education.

The American comprehensive school has some unique features which have been found worthy of emulation in many of the other advanced countries of the world. It is the institutional framework which encompasses the entire pool of young talent until the age of approximately 18. Its compelling purpose is to enable its students to develop and fully realize their capacities. It also attempts to operate somewhat as a selective school by endeavoring to provide opportunity while recognizing individual differences in endowment, interest and purpose. This is accomplished through its approach to teaching, guidance, and a differentiated curricula. It is a socializing institution that deals with codes, values, concepts of individualism, conformity and a sense of community. Further it is unique in that it provides a large share of the formalized adult education that is available.

These are among the unique features which characterize the nature of the comprehensive school and add to its comprehensiveness. In the future, as in the past, where wisdom at the top is insufficient to solve our problems and where resources at the bottom are insufficient to undertake them, the comprehensive school is likely to get the problems—or perhaps the blame for not having already solved them.

The comprehensive school is in a position to make a crucial contribution to education for work. It has not risen to the magnitude of the challenge, although it is in one of the best positions to do so.

SPECIAL FORMAL SCHOOL TRAINING AND ON-THE-JOB TRAINING

In addition to comprehensive schools, there are a variety of schools which give special emphasis to vocational and technical education. Many of these are junior and community colleges with a vocational emphasis. Even more are post-high school vocational schools or technical institutes. Some states have developed schools to which they refer as "Industrial Training

Centers." Perhaps the most rapidly expanding pattern is that of the "Area Vocational and Technical School"—a type of institution encouraged by the National Defense Education Act of 1958 and by further vocational legislation in 1963. During 1966, construction began on 238 new area vocational and technical schools.

Most of these schools are post-high school institutions. All attempt a measure of comprehensiveness as well as skill training. They represent formalized education for work as contrasted with the more popular informal approach, namely, on-the-job training. On-the-job training is widespread in industry and in the armed forces.

There are basic and fundamental differences between the more formalized training of vocational schools and the less formal pattern of on-the-job training. These differences are important to manpower policy. First of all, formalized training—as conducted in vocational schools—attempts, as a rule, to prepare students for a category of jobs rather than for a single job. Thus it supports a fundamental purpose of education—to widen choice and to improve its quality. On-the-job training, on the other hand, has the effect of narrowing the choice to the specific task, and often to the specific location where the task must be performed.

Moreover, on-the-job training is carried on for a single purpose—job filling. Formalized vocational education includes multiple purposes. Included among these are the possibilities that its students may create, as well as fill, jobs. Most vocational schools include some entrepreneurial skills in their curricula and most vocational educators dwell on the hope that becoming an employer will not be an excessive aspiration for students whose entry job begins as an employee.

The oldest and perhaps the most durable form of on-the-job training is the trades-apprenticeship. Changes in the nature and amount of skill needed for job performance have caused a steady decline in the importance of the apprenticeship system to the skilled labor market. At the present time, apprenticeships provide less than five percent of the skilled workers added to the labor force. These are highly concentrated in only a few trades.

AN INCREASE IN THE SCHOOL-LEAVING AGE

One of the most visible of the present educational phenomena is the rise in school-leaving age. This is also a world-wide trend. In the underdeveloped countries, it exists as an increasing demand for secondary education. In this country, it is shown as a growing demand for post-high school education. Education now has almost a unanimous vote. The growing importance assigned to education has had its own effect on job requirements. Employers demand higher educational qualifications even when the added educational component is not essential to the job. Education has begun to affect job requirements in the same way that job requirements have had an effect on education. As the school-leaving age rises, employers find it easy to regard education as a screening mechanism for their available jobs. The educational system thus enters the uncomfortable role of a gatekeeper for the labor market. It places excessive value on the high school diploma and it severely penalizes those who do not have the diploma.

The problem of dropouts is not new in American education. However the proportion of dropouts is lower today than ever before in history. What is new is the degree of economic penalty suffered by the dropout and the extent of increase in this penalty as the average school-leaving age rises.

The plea to remain in school is difficult for many young people to accept. More than anything else, young people want to be treated as adults, to be independent, and to have the freedom associated with remunerative employment. Yet they are asked to remain in school and be regarded as unprepared for the roles which were available to their parents at an earlier age and with less education.

INCREASED DEMAND FOR TECHNOLOGICAL MANPOWER

The rise in the school-leaving age and the increased appeal for education may be an early-warning signal as well as a rather comfortable beginning step toward the necessity to accommodate a sharply accelerating demand for technological manpower. A great deal has been heard about the trend of technological change and the extent to which it will penetrate every aspect of life including the structure of the society in which we live. Less has been heard about the manpower requirements needed to assist the change and to adjust to it.

The purpose here is not to catalog the nature of these changes but to identify forces at work which affect the rate and the direction of change. Among the most important of these is the stimulation provided by expenditures in research and development. In the decade from 1953 to 1963, these expenditures more than tripled. By 1975, it is expected that they will rise to about 40 billion dollars. In the earlier decade most of the expenditure supported developments in space, atomic energy and defense. By 1975 expenditures are expected to shift more toward the civilian sector with research and development (R & D) expenditures expanding in education, environmental research, health, and the social sciences. Thus one can expect a change in the direction as well as in the degree of technological advance. Research and development expenditures are good indications of the rate and the direction of technological advance and are also good indicators of the future demand for technological manpower. Other indicators include the national goals which have been outlined for the future. These are not necessarily good indicators of the specific kind of labor that will be required, although it seems certain that there will be more division of labor, a greater range of needed skills, and more attention to the role of education in developing both general and special skills.

THE PRESTIGE PATTERNS OF EDUCATION

Whether the educational system can respond to the expected demand of the manpower market is still open to conjecture. *This may depend on the prestige patterns in education, especially at its lower levels.* In the past, neither the prestige hierarchy within the educational system at the secondary level nor the incentive and reward system which supports it, has given more than a modest priority to education for work.

The educational system is highly preoccupied with organizing various categories of knowledge. In any plan for organizing knowledge there is a tendency to include some information at the expense of other information —to emphasize some categories of knowledge at the expense of others. The secondary school tends to deal with highly conventionalized forms of knowledge and with highly conventional approaches to scheduling, providing units of credit, and measuring progress. It can be expected to reflect patterns of inclusion and exclusion, emphasis and subordination, which support its conventions. *To the extent that such patterns tend to diminish the stature of education for work, it can be expected that the secondary school exercises significant control over the way in which great numbers of people judge the importance of work in society or in the educational system itself.*

Problems of manpower supply can be created within the secondary school as well as solved within it. To the degree that the non-vocational curriculum minimizes its commitment to education for work and to the degree that the vocational curriculum exists mainly to placate thwarted aspirations—especially among the disadvantaged—a secondary school may be adding to the employment problems of its students rather than to the solution of them. Worse, it could be encouraging a kind of occupational snobbery which could leave its graduates—especially those in academic curricula—unprepared for the technological age in which they will live and for the work roles they will later occupy.

These are some of the forces which prescribe the current status of education for work. Their momentum is influenced by tradition and also by modernizing trends. We can now turn to the changes on the horizon and to unmet needs.

CHANGES ON THE HORIZON AND UNMET NEEDS

One cannot begin to observe reality on the educational scene, or in any economic or social setting, without confronting the variety of ways in which the problems of the disadvantaged must be viewed. Indeed, one is led to believe that these problems have no easily identified boundaries and that the discovery of these boundaries is the first task—and the most difficult one—in examining these problems.

ACCEPTANCE OF THE DISADVANTAGED

Some have argued that the disadvantaged may be victims of their cultural origin—that they are people whose cultural orientation demands a prior commitment to their family, community, race, ethnic group, or social class. These commitments are an expression of loyalty to a type of group cohesion which is threatened by education. For this group, it is argued, education becomes too costly if it dispossesses them from their prior commitments.

Others have cautioned[2] that the boundaries of the problem of the disadvantaged should draw attention to its consequences as well as to its

---
[2] Leonard A. Lecht, "Manpower Needs, National Goals and Educational Policy in the 1970's." *Phi Delta Kappa Symposium on Education Manpower and Economic Growth.* (University of Illinois, March 27-30, 1966).

causes. If present tendencies persist, the net effect would be to divide the entire labor force into two groups. One group would have limited schooling and limited occupational skills. This group would suffer unemployment and underemployment. The other group would consist of well educated technical and professional people whose employment rate would be high and whose services would be in growing demand.

If this caution is appropriate, large scale changes should be anticipated in educational institutions, social structure and in government policies. The former group might be the first to be recipients of guaranteed income schemes or they may be heavily represented in public employment. The latter group would always appear more favored.

There is a third view[3] which regards the disadvantaged as members of a group with an unwillingness to play the game or who have not acquired the skills which allow them to play it. According to this view, the march toward technological progress will inevitably produce casualties and the disadvantaged are these casualties. Civil-rights efforts, poverty programs, and rehabilitation programs are only holding operations, according to this view.

There is a fourth view which interprets equality of opportunity as an unbalancing ideal unless it gives preferential treatment to the disadvantaged. The differential between the advantaged and the disadvantaged will get wider, it is argued, unless preferential treatment is provided.

From the standpoint of the schools, the disadvantaged student should be regarded as a select group when viewed from the environment from which he comes. He is almost always labeled a "slow learner" even though his slowness may not be related to his genetic endowment. He often suffers neglect, shallow contacts, and rejection. He has little experience with reading, travel or friends who are intellectually stimulating. His questions and problems are brought only to his equally inexperienced peers.

The greatest danger faced by the slow-learner is that he may accept the prevailing judgment of his worth and that worthlessness becomes an acceptable self-definition.

There are also risks for the educational system. If its efficiency is determined by the way education becomes a prerequisite for the favored positions in the social structure, then it will appear increasingly difficult for the disadvantaged students to view education as a mechanism for achieving higher aspirations. From the viewpoint of the disadvantaged student, the school may not appear to be an instrument for diminishing inequality, It may appear to be an instrument for reinforcing it. This threatens the educational function of the school.

The other risk is that the vocational or technical curriculum might be thought to be the appropriate one for the disadvantaged student. The chances are that he is no better prepared for this curriculum, nor will it do a better job of removing his deficiencies. *It is a serious mistake to expect that the educational solution to the problem of the disadvantaged is*

---

[3] Solon T. Kimball, "American Education and the Future" *Phi Delta Kappa Symposium on Education, Manpower, and Economic Growth.* (University of Illinois, March 27-30, 1966).

assignment to vocation education. This also threatens the educational function of the schools and it may compound the inequities felt by the disadvantaged student.

A good general education which is the prerequisite of successful vocational adjustment is also the preparation which is likely to enrich personal lives and help people become effective members of their community. Whether future needs for technicians, craftsmen, and paraprofessionals are to be met, will depend on progress made in the field of education. Much of this progress will depend on how much is learned about educating the disadvantaged. Some of the current programs—like Project Head Start, Youth Opportunity Programs, and the literacy programs of the Manpower Development and Training Act—may provide good laboratories for this progress.

SOME CHOICES TO BE MADE BY VOCATIONAL SCHOOLS AND COMMUNITY COLLEGES

The growth in demand for post-high school education intensifies the problem of disadvantaged and marginal students. The popularization of higher education has resulted in an influx of marginal students who increasingly view the community or junior college as a logical extension of the secondary schools. When a high school education was not a prerequisite for gainful employment, and before the time of widespread concern about dropouts, this group could more easily be absorbed into the labor market. Public pressure now creates a situation where this group also seeks accomodation in post-high school educational institutions.

The distinguishing feature of the community (junior) college and most post-high school vocational schools has been their open-door admissions policy. It is probable that as many as one-third of the students who enter can be described as high risk or marginal students. As many as two-thirds begin with the hope of transferring to a senior college, although only about one-third actually transfer.

The community colleges and the vocational schools are torn between the necessity of maintaining the standards which will guarantee transferability and employability of their graduates and the knowledge that a certain amount of post-high school education may be better than none.

The increasing numbers of marginal students may be viewed as an overwhelming problem—or as an enormous opportunity. From either point of view, the post-high school institution faces a serious challenge. The form and the degree of educational opportunity provided will determine the future of the post-high school institution. Moreover, the future of millions of students will be shaped by the kind of response given by this institution.

There are three directions that the community college might take as it faces this challenge. The first emphasizes the possibility of transfer; it follows the model of careful selections and high attrition. The implicit thought behind such policies is that the responsibility of the institution may be fulfilled by providing the opportunity for learning without concern for the opportunities for employment available to those who are not retained. The second direction follows the policy of choosing retention as the basic objective. The diploma (or the degree) in a highly generalized curriculum is the end product. Neither rigor nor relevance is emphasized and persistence rather than performance is the measure of the graduate's qualifications. A third direction is one that is not based on institutional convenience. It is based on a knowledge of student needs, previous experiences and a continuous assessment of the employment market. It recognizes that students who could not profit from traditional approaches in the secondary school may not profit from them in post-high school education. It requires a new type of education with more variation in its exit requirements, more experimentation in the incremental ways in which instruction cumulates, and more sensitivity to the need for adaptability among its graduates.

The three directions are not exclusive. In one way or another they will confront every community college or post-high school technical institution. The lay public may not understand why the problem cannot be solved merely by improving the quality of education at the elementary and secondary level. Quite obviously, there is need for this, but the mere fact of the popularization of post-high school education is shifting many of the problems of secondary education to the higher level. It also re-emphasizes the importance of education for work and for vocational counseling at both levels.

VOCATIONAL COUNSELING AND "RITES OF PASSAGE"

Occupational choice can no longer be viewed as a simple decision process or as a single decision. It may be a series of decisions throughout the lifetime of most individuals involved. When these decisions are made by people who aspire to jobs which match their interest and their capacity, the decisions are likely to be happy and productive. Vocational counseling should start at least as early as the beginning years of secondary education and should continue throughout the working life of individuals.

There is another important possibility which could be closely related to vocational counseling. In other countries it has been effectively demonstrated through an effort to reduce the excessive unemployment rates for teenagers and people under 25 years of age. It has been referred to as "rites of passage,"[4] or opportunities to move more slowly into the competition of the labor market.

Why are unemployment rates among the 16 to 24 age group more than double those of the mature age group? Should this be taken for granted as a natural phenomenon? Why should young people compete with experienced people for the same jobs and the same rates of pay?

In Japan and in many European countries, special arrangements are available to link schools and work. Young persons are given special protection and guidance in a number of entry jobs which constitute the "rites of passage" to later opportunities. In the United States, this approach has had limited use—mainly in the field of vocational rehabilitation. Here "rites of passage" exist as sheltered employment and often at lower wage rates than the legal minimums.

---

4 Arthur Ross, "The Role of Government in Promoting Full Employment." *Phi Delta Kappa Symposium on Education Manpower and Economic Growth.* (University of Illinois, March 27-30, 1966).

In this country, many young people get a chance for further formal training only because they can earn while they learn or because they can rely upon previous vocational training to obtain income support for further education. A significant amount of the demand for further education is thus a demand for vocational preparation providing appropriate stepping stones.

There is need for vocational counseling to support this process; there is also need to institutionalize the "rites of passage" for young people to achieve the satisfactions which attend work at the same time they acquire more knowledge about the subsequent occupational decisions they will make.

ADULT EDUCATION

In discussing education for work, it always seems convenient to concentrate on the young, on keeping people in school, and on the unemployed. Direct federal involvement in recent years has been concentrated in these areas. Yet the burden of insufficient education weighs more heavily on the older workers than it does on the young.

At the present time, about 10 million workers in the labor force have not completed elementary school. According to U.S. Department of Labor estimates,[5] 60 percent of the persons in the civilian labor force will have completed four or more years of high school by 1975. For persons in the 25-34 age group, this percentage is estimated to be about 70. Older workers who obtained inadequate schooling, or who had little opportunity for retraining, may find extreme difficulty in finding jobs or getting promoted. The economic penalty associated with inadequate education is likely to be much greater in the 1970's than in the 1960's.

Manpower retraining is likely to be one of the most difficult problems within the next several decades. Other advanced countries with well-integrated manpower policies endeavor to retrain about one percent of their labor force each year. In this country, the Manpower Development and Training Act of 1962 aspires to this one percent goal. To achieve this goal, a training program would have to be mounted to train approximately 800,000 workers per year. In the eight states included in this project, a retraining program involving one percent of the labor force each year would require a present enrollment of about 32,000 adults. This would rise to about 44,000 by 1980. The obvious difficulty is that—for older workers who need retraining or who received inadequate education in their youth— neither the nation nor this area has developed an adequate educational system. It would seem that the establishment of such a system might become an early imperative in educational planning.

IMMEDIATE AND FUTURE PROGRAM EMPHASES

In considering the nature of programs to be provided in the future, it is necessary to begin once more with the common or comprehensive school. In any form of educational planning this institution is pivotal. It illuminates the access routes available to its students and it endeavors to

---

[5] *Manpower Report to the President,* (1966), Table E-7, p. 218.

let them examine the extent to which their aspirations are realistic. This institution determines the quality and the relevance of the general education available to each generation of students.

COMPREHENSIVE SCHOOL PROGRAMS

In the comprehensive school, education for work, as present in the various formulations for occupational education, is as important for our industrial-technological age as the liberal arts were during the period when the Renaissance was the major cultural antecedent. Both occupational education and the liberal arts have matured. *They need each other and no education can be regarded as comprehensive unless it finds ways of fitting them together.* If this is not done, it is difficult to avoid the conclusion that C. P. Snow's cultures—all three of them—will be limited to a very small fraction of the population. As mentioned previously, education for work is relevant in both the vocational and the non-vocational curriculum. These curricula can mutually support this goal. The vocational curriculum has always been a useful vehicle for learning a variety of important quantitative relationships and problem solving processes. For some students it has been the most important vehicle to achieve these purposes. Conversely, the non-vocational curriculum can provide instruction that will satisfy many of the requisites of adaptability in the world of work.

Recent studies have shown that there are categories or families of occupational skills whose inclusion in curricula may add to the adaptability of those who graduate in vocational fields. Also there is a demand for more vocational specificity as a response to the need for training in newer occupations and for those for which there has been no program in the comprehensive school.

The importance of education for work in the secondary school has been emphasized by an increasing number of studies. In a recent study by the American Institute for Research sponsored by the Ford Foundation, Altman and Gayne concluded:

> There is a definable and well-structured domain of vocational capabilities which has not previously been systematically taught by our educational institutions. This domain is compatible with and intimately related to existing academic disciplines and specialized vocational training. It can be a focal point for developing vocational awareness, vocational choice, and career planning. If properly exploited, it also promises to enhance the flexibility with which students can apply the results of their educational experiences.[6]

In other research involving project TALENT data, the American Institute of Research has reported that:

1. Vocational graduates get their first full-time job after graduation much sooner than other graduates who do not go on to College
2. Vocational graduates enjoy more employment security
3. Vocational graduates have greater accumulated earning (over the eleven year period of the study) than academic graduates without a college education.

While these studies reemphasize the value of vocational programs at the secondary level, there is likely to be a continuing trend toward later

---

[6] James Altman, and Robert M. Gayné, *Research on General Vocational Capabilities (Skills and Knowledges).* (American Institute for Research, Pittsburgh, Pa. March 1966).

entry of young people into the full-time work force. This trend is affected by unemployment levels and also by an increasing demand for technological competence requiring more formal education. Even though these trends are apparent, there is likely to be a continuing demand for skills which can be learned in the vocational programs of secondary schools. In the same way that mathematical skills are now taught at lower grade-levels, job skills demanded by industry can be mastered by more, not fewer, students of high school age.

In meeting their responsibilities to students and to the changing character of the employment market, comprehensive schools may find at least four emphases which will repay their planning efforts: (1) There is need to increase the range of occupations and also the capacity of the existing programs in vocational education. (This includes the field of agriculture which, until recently, was thought to be declining in importance)[7]; (2) There is need to add an occupational relevance to the general secondary curriculum. (This is needed to understand the advancing role of technology and the need for adaptability); (3) There is need for continuous, up-to-date, vocational counseling including opportunities for work experience and "rites of passage"; and (4) There is need for planning to fill a large void which now exists in adult education: updating, and retraining.

POST-HIGH SCHOOL VOCATIONAL AND TECHNICAL EDUCATION

At the post-high school level, there are many patterns of organization for occupational education. In some states, the community college is the prevailing type of institution. In others the area vocational and technical institute is the common pattern. Many states have both types of organization. Earlier in this discussion, mention was made of the problems facing such institutions, particularly as they deal with marginal and disadvantaged students.

In spite of such problems, the post-high institutions for occupational education are rapidly increasing in number and in diversity of offerings. They are demonstrating unusual adaptability and flexibility. A significant part of this growth has resulted from the availability of financial assistance through federal legislation and also from an urgent public demand for the kind of educational programs offered in such institutions.

There seems to be no normative or expected pattern of growth for this category of institution. They appear to respond to a variety of political, economic, and other community forces. Often they respond solely to the pressure of matriculants and accept all students who wish to enter. Some respond largely to the pressures of exit; they concentrate on a number of specializations in demand in the employment market or through which students may transfer to other institutions for further education. To the extent that such institutions draw upon state and federal financial support it is desirable that their programs be coordinated as a balanced system rather than as an aggregation of independent efforts.

Important to such coordination are the following:

Equality of Opportunity. For post-high school education, equality of opportunity has a close relationship to its geographic availability. Costs of travel and

---

[7] For additional argument on this point, see pages 15 and 21 in *Prospective Changes in Society by 1980,* (Denver, Colo.: Designing Education for the Future: An Eight-State Project, July 1966).

maintenance become large items of additional cost for students who live great distances from school. This inequality can be reduced only through a system of scholarships and fellowships.

Economy. The pre-student costs of technical education are very high. This is a reflection of the high cost of equipment, high operational costs and rapid rates of obsolescence. To minimize these costs per student, it is often necessary to affect certain economies of scale by encouraging institutional specialization and inter-regional cooperation among institutions.

Relevance. Relevance in a technical training program is a measure of its quality and its alertness to the demands of the labor market for its graduates. Scientific and technical specializations often change quickly in their skill requirements. Changes also occur in their basic educational background requirements. Relevance is a serious and immediate challenge to all post-high school technical programs. *Relevance* is invariably juxtaposed with *rigor*. If a program is sufficiently relevant, it often includes rigor as a fringe benefit. But the relationship is not reversible. By becoming more rigorous, an educational program does not necessarily accrue relevance as a fringe benefit.

These are essentially problems of program and its coordination. There are also important questions of organization and administration. Who should coordinate occupational education within a state or region? How should the location of institutions be determined? How shall adult education and retraining efforts become a part of the total plan? In what ways should the formal training in educational institutions and industry relate to various kinds of informal training? In the light of the magnitude and the urgency of these questions, it seems clear that formal machinery is needed for research, development and planning of this level of occupational education.

COLLEGE AND UNIVERSITY PROGRAMS

The role of colleges and universities is often underestimated in education for work. Their contribution is to the advanced training of manpower —scientists, engineers, business executives, educators, and research workers in many fields. They exist as pools of talent whose services can be utilized professionally and technically in agriculture, business, labor, industry, and government. They maintain a human resource balance within an area and provide an intellectual community for stimulating research, development, and economic growth. Their educational output involves higher costs but with minimum risks.

The work of the Upper Midwest Research and Development Council provides a good example of the way in which education is identified as an important instrument for economic growth. Their studies are within the Ninth Federal Reserve District and deal with numerous aspects of growth within the Region. In considering the educational priorities for future planning, higher education has been awarded the highest position.[8] Second priority is awarded to vocational and technical education. Other priorities follow in appropriate order.

A CONTEXT FOR PLANNING

A recurring and persistent theme throughout the Eight-State Project has also been the need for education and for planning. Complex sets of problems face education decision-makers at every level of education. The

⁸ Robert J. Keller, et al. *Education and Economic Growth—The Next Steps.* (Upper Midwest Research and Development Council and the University of Minnesota, August 1965), p. 40.

educational system in each state will be the key factor in determining the future quality of the labor force. The capacity of the educational system to respond to changing conditions and needs will determine the distribution of students, programs, and relationships among institutions. The allocation of functions and funds should meet the needs of students and employers, as well as of other human resource requisites of economic growth including research and the need for raising qualitative standards. The efficiency of this process will rely on deliberate planning efforts which combine the talents and interests of leaders in education, government, business, industry, and labor.

A context and numerous guidelines for this planning effort are already available. They are available as forces, trends, goals and aspirations at national, regional, and state levels.

A NATIONAL CONTEXT

Earlier in this paper, mention was made of national goals and a growing "goals consciousness." Illustrations of these are the national goals in vocational rehabilitation established by the President and endorsed by Congress in 1954, and the work of the Commission on National Goals appointed by President Eisenhower. Space goals involving a lunar landing later became a part of a national commitment and the national goals orientation continues to expand.

The Goals Project of the National Planning Association's Center for Priority Analysis has made a study of the estimated dollar costs of achieving sixteen national goals by 1975.[9] The identified goals and their percentage increases in expenditure between 1962 and 1975 are as follows:

Goal Area	Percentage Increase (1962 to 1975)
Consumer Expenditure	86
Private Plant and Equipment	210
Urban Development	102
Social Welfare	144
Health	164
Education	170
Transportation	115
National Defense	31
Housing	110
Research and Development	112
Natural Resources	183
International Aid	158
Space	188
Agriculture	28
Manpower Retraining	2750
Area Redevelopment	171

This mere listing of the goals identified in the Goals Project is wholly inadequate as a summary. It deserves careful study by educational plan-

[9] Leonard A. Lecht, *The Dollar Costs of Our National Goals*, (Washington, D.C.: National Planning Association, 1965).

ners. It is also likely that more national goals will be added in the years ahead and the impact of existing goals will become more clear.

Some of the guidelines provided by the pattern of national goals are now clear. Most obvious is the extent to which *the goals require that added value be provided more and more by human resources and decreasingly by natural resources.* Many of the goals depend almost wholly on the development of human resources. This is coupled with a striking emphasis on the need for selectivity and quality in the labor force. The national goals require a growing stock of specialized skills and a rising educational level.

The emphasis on national goals helps to describe shifts in occupational structure. For example, it reinforces other estimates of the growing demand for service industries and service trades. It helps to identify an increased spread in the range of technical skills needed. Finally, there is an obvious claim on adaptability. At least 20 percent of the goals in a similar list would not have appeared two decades ago. In the next two decades, similar changes are likely. It will be necessary for the labor force to be capable of adapting to new goals and to changes within existing goals. This need for adaptability is highly emphasized in the large increases planned for manpower retraining.

The guidelines provided by national goals are extremely useful in educational planning. The fact should also be emphasized that they are not remote in either time or space. In their accomplishment they require individual decisions and institutional decisions as well as government decisions at every level.

THE REGIONAL CONTEXT

The regional context for planning is well illustrated by the Eight-State Project. The organization for regional planning effort begins to assemble background data and identifies common elements of concern within the area. This effort is well documented in this Project.

In planning education for work, a number of issues became of special significance to the area and these begin to denominate the planning process. From population projections, it is clear, for example, that the growth of the labor force will exceed the growth of the total population. This is also true nationally as post World War II babies enter the labor force. About one-third of the labor force in 1980 will consist of those who entered it after 1965. This turnover will be accompanied by an increase in the demand for highly skilled and trained employees.

The present occupational structure tells a great deal about the present educational system and the educational attainments within the area. The future occupational structure will rely largely on the educational attainment available within the region. Although the area now has a net-in-migration, the distribution of manpower skills will depend mainly on the training available within the region. It will also determine the mobility and thus the employability of skilled workers.

THE STATE AND INSTITUTIONAL CONTEXT

The crucial elements of planning will be left to states and to educational institutions within states. The most visible adjustment will be that of accommodating a higher education enrollment (college, university, and post-high school) that will approximately double within the next 15 years. The rise of expenditures along with enrollments will easily identify this problem in every state.

A *second* element of planning of importance at the state level will be the need to increase educational quality. States which merely endeavor to maintain present levels of quality will fall behind in the national trend toward higher qualitative standards. Rough measures of quality are reflected in professional salaries and in teacher certification requirements. Other measures are reflected in the extent of curriculum improvement, moves toward efficiency in school district organization, and similar developments.

A *third* category of planning effort is represented by the entire field of vocational and technical education. This should include an examination of present vocational offerings, new specializations which may be added and the appropriate "mix" of occupational education at all levels. The need for this kind of planning at the state level can hardly be overestimated. In the past, an absence of such effort has resulted in a variety of federal programs with a remedial emphasis. These programs can become normative training programs rather than *ad hoc* or emergency programs. A special effort will undoubtedly be essential to establish the necessary institutional commitment to manpower retraining and adult education.

A *fourth* category of planning effort can be viewed in a rather negative sense. Such inquiry would ask how deficiencies in education, training, or rehabilitation would be related to costs associated with welfare appropriations, delinquency, underemployment, or lack of vocational rehabilitation.

For this approach to planning there are dramatic examples from the field of vocational rehabilitation. This field has existed for many years on inadequate resources and with a justification that was largely humane rather than economic. Yet it has been demonstrated that each dollar expended by rehabilitation agencies has provided a yield of future outputs worth from 10 to 17 dollars.[10] It seems clear that an efficient referral system, a sufficient number of qualified rehabilitation counselors, adequate facilities, and sufficient funds for vocational rehabilitation would be easily seen as an important area for state planning. In addition to economic rewards, there are other and perhaps larger benefits which accrue to individuals who achieve the self-reliance which accompanies rehabilitation.

A *fifth* category of state effort involves the establishment of machinery for research, development, and long-range planning. As mentioned earlier, this is particularly important for occupational education. Such an agency should engage in programmatic study of questions relating to human resources, manpower requirements, organizational structure, and the development of vocational and technical programs.

Neither states nor regions can do much about levels of unemployment in the entire economy but *they can do a great deal about underemployment and about employability. What they can do will result from their efforts in planning education for work.*

---

[10] Ronald W. Conley, *The Economics of Vocational Rehabilitation.* (Johns Hopkins Press, 1965), p. 81.

CHAPTER 7

Community Colleges And Other Education Programs Beyond The Twelfth Grade

A Look To The Future

LELAND L. MEDSKER*

"I hold that man is in the right who is most closely in league with the future." So said Henrik Ibsen in 1882.

In less than a decade and a half—fourteen years hence—clanging bells and festive balloons will herald the year 1980. Experts have predicted the social, cultural, and scientific changes that will have occurred by then and even the most conservative individual concedes that life at that time will be different from that of today. However, it is one thing to speculate on the nature of changes to come and quite another to consider what these changes imply for individual human beings—men, women, and children from all segments of the population—as they celebrate New Year's Eve in 1979. Two facts are startling. First, the date is not far away. Looking back to 1950—approximately the same distance in the past—one can put time in perspective. Second, people in 1980 will be the same as they are now. Those who will be served by the community college and like institutions, namely, older youth and adults, will have, along with other characteristics, the same hopes and ambitions for themselves and their children, the same drive toward upward mobility, the same need to earn a livelihood, the same curiosity about the meaning of life, and the same need for skills in communication and in performing other functions of everyday living that people have today. Indeed, many of them will be the same people, grown older. It is true, of course, that some of their needs will have become more acute. Many individuals may feel insecure in a world that has become infinitely more complex during their lifetime. Many may face the necessity for changing occupations periodically. Most will have an unparalleled amount of leisure time at their disposal. The great majority of them will live in urban centers with space about them becoming increasingly limited. It is in this setting that the role of educational programs becomes an exceedingly important matter.

It is important at the outset to consider briefly the nature of the institutions falling within the purview of this topic. The term community college will be used to denote the public, comprehensive institution that

* Professor of Education and Acting Director, Center for the Study of Higher Education, University of California, Berkeley; Past President, American Association of Junior Colleges; Member, Board of Trustees, College Entrance Examination Board; Coordinator, University of California, Berkeley, Junior College Leadership Program, and of Ford Foundation Program of Assistance to Junior Colleges in Chile; Author of numerous publications, including The Junior College: Progress and Prospect (1960).

has its derivation in the junior college. To date, it has been regarded primarily as a two-year college designed to serve a diversity of purposes in a community setting. The phrase "other educational programs beyond the twelfth grade" will cover the services of technical institutes, vocational schools, adult education centers, and university extension centers which offer in whole or in part programs similar to those found in community colleges. The most important criterion in describing all such institutions is that they do not award the baccalaureate degree. The length of their program is not highly relevant because, as will be discussed later, there are reasons why the concept of the two-year span may have to be changed.

There are innumerable reasons why these types of institutions must be given special attention by individual states as they evaluate the total impact which societal changes will have on education. While most of these reasons are implicit in the discussion which follows, one point is worth noting now. It is that the age groups most profoundly affected by social change—namely, (1) youths just emerging from high school and (2) older youths and adults who must adapt to new conditions—are the very ones that these institutions are designed to serve. There are naturally other types of institutions to serve them but it is expected that the community type school, by whatever name, will bear an increasing responsibility for providing opportunities to these two segments of the population.

In approaching this topic a brief review will first be made of the community college today and of the social forces which are shaping it. The principal burden of the discussion, of course, will be to project future developments at this level of education in view of some of the predicted social changes to come. Finally, a few implications for immediate action on the part of planning groups will be suggested, particularly in view of certain problems likely to be encountered.

THE COMMUNITY COLLEGE—A TWENTIETH CENTURY PHENOMENON

Long ago Lord Byron declared, "the best of prophets of the future is the past." Thus, in a prognosis of any social institution's future there is undoubtedly something to be gained by a review of its development to date. The idea of the junior college is traced to the latter half of the last century when certain university presidents advocated that the freshman and sophomore years should be turned over to the secondary schools and that the university should begin its work with the junior year. However, it was not until after 1900 that the public schools began to assume any such obligation. The movement in this direction grew slowly at the outset. The first comprehensive study of the junior college made by Koos [1] in 1925 reported that between 1900 and 1921 junior colleges grew in number from 8 to almost 200 with an enrollment of some 16,000 students. By 1950 the number of institutions had increased to almost 650 and the total enrollment to nearly 466,000. Fifteen years later—in 1965—there were, according to the 1966 Directory of the American Association of Junior Colleges, 771 junior colleges in the country with a total enroll-

---

[1] Leonard V. Koos, *The Junior College Movement* (Ginn and Co.: Boston, New York, 1925).

ment of 1,292,753 students. Of these institutions 268 were private and 503 public. The public institutions enroll 82 percent of the full time students and since they tend to be comprehensive in nature, as well as closely integrated with their communities, they are the primary concern of this discussion.

Today one out of every four students entering college does so in a junior college, most of them in what would be classified as a community college. The dynamic nature of the movement is shown by recent developments. Fifty new community colleges first admitted students in 1965. Enrollments in community colleges reported in 1965 were materially greater in many states than they were in 1964. Many states which until only a short time ago had no community colleges are now moving ahead with a plan for them. These include Ohio, Pennsylvania, Hawaii, New Jersey, Louisiana, and Alabama. States that have had such colleges in limited number are now greatly expanding and strengthening them. Among these states are Illinois, Michigan, Kansas, Missouri, New York, North Carolina, Iowa, Oregon, Arizona, Florida, Texas, and California. Colorado and Washington are struggling with the problem of how to implement a system of such institutions. The growth and importance of community colleges in urban areas is spectacular. Among the cities in which a network of community colleges has been or soon will be established are Los Angeles, New York, Miami, Chicago, Cleveland, St. Louis, Philadelphia, and Detroit.

The functions normally assigned to the community college are many and varied. *In the first place,* it presumably serves as a democratizing agent by making education available to all high school graduates as well as to older youth and adults who can profit from its services. This is accomplished largely because it is located close to the homes of its students, it usually charges either a minimum tuition or none at all, and it normally accepts all high school graduates or older individuals regardless of their ability level or interest pattern. *In the second place,* it offers a multiplicity of programs so that students can either be prepared for an occupation or to transfer and pursue their baccalaureate degree in a four-year institution. Likewise, it presumes to offer many opportunities to adults and to perform a variety of community services. *In the third place,* much has been said about the community college as an institution committed to student development, particularly by means of a good program of student personnel services including counseling and guidance. *Finally,* as an overriding characteristic, the community college is presumed to have developed an identity—in some ways unique—as an "in between" institution with the secondary school on the one side and both the world of work and the four-year college on the other.

How well the community college discharges all these responsibilities is a subject of some concern since various studies have shown an unevenness among institutions in this regard. Many are truly comprehensive, whereas others tend to limit their efforts to the transfer function. There is, however, increasing concern among the community colleges themselves and the state agencies responsible for them about how they may improve their multiple services. Thus it is expected that the future will bring a better matching of what is expected of the community college and what it actually does.

Enabling legislation for the establishment and maintenance of community colleges now exists in most of the states. In more than twenty states these colleges are under some type of local control—either within local school systems or in separate districts established for junior college purposes only. Within the last five years there has been a decided nationwide trend toward the establishment of separate districts. In the states where local control prevails, the community colleges are ordinarily supported by a combination of local and state effort. A few states, including Minnesota, Massachusetts, Oklahoma, and Georgia, have established systems of state community colleges in which both the control and the support lie with the state.

As the community colleges have been developing, other related institutions at the post-high-school level have also come into being. Of these, the university extension center is numerically the most important. Several states, including Wisconsin, Indiana, Pennsylvania, Ohio, and Kentucky, make extensive use of such centers in decentralizing undergraduate higher education. In general, these centers are restricted to normal academic freshman and sophomore programs, although exceptions to this are found in some of the states. As an example, in Wisconsin vocational schools have been established to provide occupational training and thus a system of dual institutions exists. In other instances a system of technical institutes has been authorized as the principal means of extending non-baccalaureate education beyond the high school. With recent federal legislation providing funds for vocational education has come an impetus for such training and there has been much discussion about the merit of area vocational schools as still another type of institution in the category considered here. Also of increasing importance is the adult education center, found predominantly in urban areas, which offers programs at all levels, including work normally considered beyond high school in nature and rigor.

It would be an oversimplification to say that the community colleges, as well as the programs offered by similar institutions, are the result of social forces which have created and shaped these institutions. This is true of any organization. It seems clear, however, that certain forces have played an important role in bringing about the phenomenal rise in midlevel institutions in the United States. Such factors as the shift from a rural to an urban society, the rapid scientific and technological developments, the trend toward an egalitarian society, the increasing complexity of social and political issues at home and abroad, and the changing nature of the nation's population have all combined to force an examination of the educational system beyond the high school.

Such factors have led not only to the necessity for more education for more people, but also to a belief on the part of an increasing proportion of the people that various types of post high school education are a necessity for them and their children. This in turn has resulted in a demand for a broader base for higher education and for easier access to it. Much of what is included as part of higher education today would have been excluded a decade or so ago. Further, there is the growing belief that educational opportunity beyond the high school must be equalized. Thus it is that institutions with multiple purposes and programs have been established in many communities to offer service to young high school graduates as well as their elders at a cost they can all afford.

While these new institutions, with the community college predominating, have taken their place on the educational scene, their direction is not entirely clear. That they are to increase in number and importance is hardly questionable. But there are already indications of considerable diversity in types of institutions as well as in the manner in which they are to be controlled and supported. The matter of what institutions, for what purposes, and under what organizational plan, is a question for the future. Even so, the manner in which the community college in particular has already responded to social forces is indicative that it and similar institutions can and will react realistically to the impending social changes ahead. It is to the manner in which this is likely to happen that this discussion now turns.

A Look to the Future

It is not the purpose of this paper to discuss the predicted nature of social and technological change. Experts have done this in an earlier conference. Their forceful presentations on pending developments and problems in such areas as urbanization, technology, transportation, government, economics, population, and natural resources are as sobering as they are exciting. They could be combined with other developing problems such as social integration and world interdependence to make the picture still more complex.

The impact of the projected changes on education at the immediate post-high-school level can perhaps best be considered in view of their effect on the world of work, the problems of increased leisure time for most people, the problems of the individual in an urban society, and the number of people to be educated. An attempt to relate cause and effect in any minute way so as to predict the impact of each social change on this level of education would be much too difficult and time-consuming for this presentation. The alternative is to consider the probable impact in a general way and simply, when necessary, to refer to certain societal changes which appear clearly to point the course to the future of community-college-level education. It seems certain that the impact of the changes will be great and that their long-term influence on this level of education will be in the following directions:

1. *The significance of community-college-level and type of education will become materially greater in the future than it has been in the past.* Although the future need for community-centered institutions should not be argued merely on pragmatic grounds, population data alone suggest

that the present trend toward the decentralization of education beyond the high school must continue. Not only will there continue to be more people in the college-age group but an increasing percentage of them will feel the necessity for continuing their formal education. Already each of the various states is seeking means of accommodating its college population and, as noted earlier, most of them are relying more and more on a system of community colleges to carry a substantial part of the load. Presumably, enrollment in these colleges could be projected to 1980 by a mathematical formula based both on the expected number of high school graduates and the variation in the percentage of them likely to go beyond high school. There seems little point, however, in attempting to compile projected enrollment data, not only because they are hardly needed for this discussion, but also because the people to be served by institutions at this level will by no means come only from the college-age group. Thus accurate projections would be impossible.

It is noteworthy that many national commissions have advocated the extension of educational opportunity through the community college. The Commission on National Goals said in 1960 that states should expect community colleges to take care of perhaps 50 percent of students entering college for the first time. In 1964 the Educational Policies Commission stated that ". . . the nation's goal of universal educational opportunity must be expanded to include at least two further years of education, open to any high school graduate, and designed to move each student toward intellectual freedom." [2]

At an address to the Association for Higher Education in 1963, Alvin Eurich, then the Vice President for the Fund for the Advancement of Education, asked his audience to assume that they were living in the year 2000 A.D., and from that vantage point to view the development of higher education in the U. S. during the last 37 years of the twentieth century. The following statements, among others that Dr. Eurich made, are relative to this topic:

> During the second half [of the twentieth century] we made higher education universal through the junior college. In the process we reconstructed our educational system.
> During the quarter century following World War II, teachers colleges disappeared completely from the American scene. Their place has been taken by multipurpose institutions which, together with the strong liberal arts colleges and the universities, have discontinued the first two years, since these now come almost wholly within the province of the junior colleges. The transition took place with surprising smoothness . . . . These new institutions now admit qualified graduates from the junior colleges and offer three-year programs culminating in the master's degree.[3]

Obviously, if Dr. Eurich's dream should be only partially correct, it has grave implications for the community college. Undoubtedly, American higher education does face reorganization. Already, many four-year col-

[2] The Educational Policies Commission of the National Education Association of the United States and the American Association of School Administrators. *Universal Opportunity for Education Beyond the High School* (Washington, D. C.: National Education Association of the United States, 1964).

[3] Alvin C. Eurich, "A Twenty-first Century Look at Higher Education," *1963 Current Issues in Higher Education: Critical Decisions in Higher Education.* The Proceedings of the Eighteenth Annual National Conference on Higher Education. Washington, D. C.: (March, 1963). Association for Higher Education, a Department of the National Education Association.

leges and universities are becoming selective and at the same time are deliberately reducing the proportion of lower division students to those in upper division and graduate status. Under these circumstances the need for an open-door, mid-level institution to perform the distributive function grows greater.

As implied earlier, however, the future potential of the community college does not rest alone on the conventional pattern of higher education. By 1980 most individuals will feel the necessity for either continuous or at least periodic identification with some type of educational institution on either a formal or informal basis. This will be so, both because of the amount of leisure time at their disposal and the complexity of the world about them. Obviously, they will not be able to turn to institutions far from their homes and, even if there are conventional colleges within reach, it does not follow that with their concentration on degree programs these colleges could perform all the services desired by the general public. Thus, in the final analysis there will be some type of community-centered educational agency with sufficient flexibility to enable it to organize programs of an unconventional character.

The needs of individuals for such programs will be no greater than the need for them on the part of society in general. Donald M. Michael in his report, *Cybernation: The Silent Conquest,* voiced some exceedingly sobering thoughts concerning the impact which automation and computers will have on people. After making the point that even the service industries will be automated, he moves to the problem of middle level management and says:

> As cybernation moves into the areas now dominated by middle management in government and in business—and this move is already beginning—growing numbers of middle managers will find themselves displaced.
>
> Middle management is the group in the society with the most intensive emotional drive for success and status. Their family and social life is molded by these needs, as the endless literature on life in suburbia and exurbia demonstrate. They stand to be deeply disturbed by the threat and fact of their replacement by machines. One wonders what the threat will do to the ambitions of those who will still be students and who, as followers of one of the pervasive American dreams, will have aspired to the role of middle manager 'on the way up'.[4]

The author then moves to the employment of adolescents and predicts that by the end of this decade three million youngsters will be starting their quests for jobs each year, as against two million at the time of his writing. The prospect of unemployment and a significant proportion of idleness among teenage workers gives rise to the question of how the time of these young people is to be spent after they are out of high school and before they are employed.

Related to the matter of increased leisure time stemming from both the shorter work week and the decreased life employment span, the report includes the following alarming statement concerning the great masses of

[4] Donald N. Michael, *Cybernation: The Silent Conquest,* (Santa Barbara, California: Center for the Study of Democratic Institutions, 1962).

lower and middle class people who are not prepared for so much leisure
time, either psychologically or sociologically:

> Some of the remaining population will be productively engaged in human-to-
> human or human-to-machine activities requiring judgment and a high level
> of intelligence and training. But the rest, whose innate intelligence or train-
> ing is not of the highest, what will they do? We can foresee a nation with
> a large portion of its people doing, directly or indirectly, the endless public
> tasks that the welfare state needs and that the government will not allow
> to be cybernated because of the serious unemployment that would result.
> These people will work short hours, with much time for the pursuit of
> leisure activities.

> Even with a college education, what will they do all their long lives, day after
> day, four-day week-end after week-end, vacation after vacation, in a more
> and more crowded world? (There is a population explosion to face in another
> ten to thirty years.) What will they believe in and aspire to as they work their
> shorter hours and on the outside, pursue their "self-fulfilling" activities, what-
> ever they may be? No one has ever seriously envisioned what characteristics
> these activities might have in order to be able to engross most men and
> women most of their adult lives. What will be the relationship of these people
> to government to the "upper intellectuals," to the rest of the world, to
> themselves?[4]

Conditions will be such as to mandate community centers which will
provide constructive activities for postadolescents: for attention to the
recreational and cultural problems of adults, including the development
of new, non-vocational interests; for the reorientation of people of all
ages in intercultural relations; and for anticipating the shifts in manpower
needs and their implications for workers at all levels. When societal needs
become sufficiently acute, forces tend to converge to bring into being a
mechanism for meeting these needs. The problems here identified are so
real that they almost inevitably point the way to a community centered
institution as a focal point for service to and for redirection of an untold
number of individuals.

2. *The multidimensional nature of educational institutions at the
immediate post-high-school level will be enhanced.* Implicit in the foregoing statements is the prediction that institutions of the type considered
here will operate informal as well as formal programs. In essence, they
will by necessity become education centers in their respective communities,
responsible for much of the formal education in the two years immediately
beyond high school but responsible also for a variety of noncredit programs, including cultural, civic, and recreational activities and various
special services to the community. While many community colleges fit
this description today, they probably are mere prototypes of the institutions that must function in 1980.

It is relatively easy to visualize the role of the community education
center in suburbia or in more isolated centers of population where in both
instances there is likely to be both a felt need for help on the part of the
citizens and a reasonably high degree of local visibility as far as the center
is concerned. It is less easy to project the idea of the education center in
the central city with its problems of a mobile population, urban renewal,
and a concentration of culturally different families. Yet it is here where
this level of education may have its greatest impact. A recent study of the

---

[4] *ibid.*

role of the community college in the urban setting conducted by Dorothy Knoell for the State University of New York [5] portrays well the need for assistance in such settings. Untold numbers of youths will continue to flow from the city's high schools either as dropouts or graduates, or to migrate to the city, unable to find employment or to find satisfaction in life. They will grow older in this environment. True, the problem of helping them become useful, productive citizens is not a problem of education alone but where, if at all, is this segment of the population to be upgraded unless it is in some type of school or college that is geared to their backgrounds and that has a genuine concern for their welfare?

The education centers of the variety here described will have certain well defined responsibilities. Included among them will be the following:

Occupational Training at a Variety of Levels. The nature of the world of work and preparation for it is the subject of another paper in this publication (Chapter 6), hence no attempt is made here to assess the full character of vocational education for the future.

It is assumed, however, that despite the advance of technology, it will still be necessary to prepare people at levels lower than the professional for positions in at least the clerical, sales, technical, and service fields. Further, it is assumed that most of the pre-employment training will, in the future, be given at the post-high-school level. This will place an exceedingly heavy burden on those who plan educational programs in a period when cybernation is likely to be accelerated, lest young people be prepared for jobs that do not exist. In this connection there will also be the responsibility for determining the need for various levels of training. It is assumed that there will continue to be a demand for well prepared high level technicians, but it must still be recognized that many young people will not have the ability to pursue the onerous programs leading to such positions. This problem is acute now but it will be much more so by 1980. Thus community colleges and other institutions will have to contrive programs which build on students' general interests and native abilities and strive to make them employable in a general way without attempting to develop a skill that itself is not marketable. It may well be realized eventually that for many types of lower level positions, the development of a personally effective individual with breadth of view and good communication skills is the most important aspect of vocational education. Even at higher levels of vocational training it is probable that the emphasis will turn increasingly to general education.

With the years ahead will come an even greater responsibility for vocational upgrading and retraining, much of which will be borne by community colleges and similar institutions. They will be the likely agencies for this service because even displaced workers can remain in their home community while re-preparing or "retreading" themselves for another line of work. It is probable that retraining and upgrading will be needed in all fields, including what is often referred to as maddle level managerial jobs.

5 Dorothy M. Knoell, *Towards Educational Opportunity for All* (Albany, N. Y.: State University of New York, 1966).

Basic Lower Division Work. As suggested in an earlier section of this report, the community college is likely to assume an ever increasing responsibility for lower division work. Its record to date in this regard is good and there is no reason to believe that it cannot continue to prepare students well for advanced work in another institution. The problems of articulation with the other colleges will increase and adequate formal as well as informal devices for planning and communication with other segments will be necessary. It is likely that by 1980 each state will have a strong coordinating agency for higher education and that at least the formal college programs in the community colleges will be subject to coordination by such an agency.

Community Counseling. The drastic changes predicted for society in general foretell a need for continuous educational and occupational guidance on the part of most people. The necessity for the community college to counsel its regular students will increase materially but, if it is also to serve as an education center, there will be need for the community college to expand its counseling services to the community in general, particularly to those individuals who in one way or another have some identification with it. As people work fewer hours per week, as they constantly face the danger of displacement by the consequences of technology, as some of them encounter the prospect of more or less permanent unemployment, it seems reasonable to believe that both their need for current, reliable occupational information and an easing of their tensions through a continuous personal assessment of themselves will increase. They will seek an identification with an institution or with staff members in institutions. In a sense, their security figure is likely to shift from an employer to a community agency. Thus the community college may be called upon to set up complete guidance clinics in which people can obtain vocational, educational, and personal assistance. Tests will be used but hopefully not to the exclusion of other means. It may be as common for people to come to the community college for counseling as it is for them to come for regular class instruction. Obviously, the college alone cannot perform all the guidance services needed in a community and other agencies will also be involved. It will be desirable that a high degree of coordination and referral arrangements with other agencies be affected.

In all of its formal and informal activities the community college will need to broaden its horizons. First, it will realize that technology and innovation have a place in its own operation and that the process of education can be improved by the use of modern methods and by scientific experimentation with its own educational processes. Second, in broadening the base for post-high-school education, it will do well to keep in mind a recent statement by Frank Bowles, director of the educational program for the Ford Foundation.

This impressionistic description of our educational evolution over the next few years makes a point that is not always clear. Democratization of education is not just the provision of more of the same. It is the process of increasing the capacity of an educational system by adding opportunities for study, to accommodate students who have heretofore been unable to find programs to suit their needs. It is not just educational improvement. It is social change. It has gone on in American education for a long time and given us reason to be proud of tolerance of innovation and freedom of opportunity.[6]

Finally, the community colleges, like all educational institutions, must realize that in serving older youth and adults in the years ahead something more is needed than helping people to gain academic or vocational competence or assisting them in a worthy use of their leisure time. There is a danger that the technology that will surround them may also consume them unless they can develop attitudes which enable them to rely heavily on the intrinsic values of human existence. Thus in addition to preparing people for making a living, the college—more than ever before—will need to be concerned with preparing people to gain perspective on man's continuous process of development.

3. *There will be increasing diversity among non-baccalaureate institutions beyond the high school.* While it is expected that the community college, by whatever name, will continue to be the dominant agency to serve as the local post-high-school education center, the great variety of functions to be performed, together with the different attitudes found among the states, will undoubtedly result in the utilization of other types of agencies. Among those that will likely grow in number and influence are specialized vocational schools or technical institutes. The great need for educational facilities at this level and the probable need for highly specialized occupational programs that serve fairly large geographical areas will lead to the establishment of occupational training centers in certain areas. It is probable that, eventually, many of these specialized schools will feel the pressure to increase their academic offerings and thus will become community colleges in essence.

The future of university extension centers is uncertain. In general, they are not comprehensive in nature and are not likely to become so. Thus they are most viable only in those states that are committed to a dual system of institutions at this level. It is possible, of course, for such units to become comprehensive educational centers in their respective communities. At present, however, there is a trend toward the establishment of community colleges in the states that have made extensive use of the extension idea. Whether the two types of institutions can and will exist side by side remains to be seen. A problem for extension centers is the influence exerted by the faculty in the parent university in the direction of regular university work and away from vocational and other less conventional programs.

Another unit to be considered is the adult education center which will be found in increasing numbers. It will likely not offer formal college courses for credit, but it will certainly be engaged in non-credit and many other kinds of informal activities. Whether as an independent institution, or one attached to a public school system, or—for that matter—

[6] Frank Bowles, Address at conference on Higher Education (Association for Higher Education, March, 1966).

to a community college, the adult center will likely take its place among those institutions whose principal services are directed to adults who already possess at least a high school diploma.

Diversity will occur, too, in the length of programs—even those of a formal nature. Many community colleges will move or attempt to move, to at least a three-year program—and possibly one covering four years. However, this extension will tend to be limited to non-transfer programs. Herein will lie a problem due to the pressure for these institutions to become degree-granting colleges. Obviously, no state could afford to permit all of its community-college-type institutions to become conventional colleges, nor would the basic functions of these colleges in serving the varied community needs be preserved if this were the case. Each state will have to so structure its organization for higher education that the local education centers will be protected by public policy and that *public baccalaureate colleges will be established by design when and where they are needed*, quite independently of existing education centers of the type here discussed.

Variety will also ensue in terms of control and support of community colleges and similar institutions. Although some states are likely to continue the practice of dividing the support between the local community and the state—and in many respects also dividing the control—it is likely that many states will move in the direction of state systems of community colleges and/or vocational schools. At least this will be true unless a revision of the tax structure makes it easier for local governments to meet the financial demands on them. Even then, the need for uniform services of the nature offered by the local education centers is so great that public policy may dictate that their establishment cannot be left to local initiative. It is possible that state systems of such institutions will provide the initiative and support for the formal aspects of local programs, such as preparation for pre-employment and transfer, but leave to the community the possibility of augmenting support for the informal programs. If this should be done, there will have to be concern that the latter aspect of the program, so badly needed in the years ahead, will not be neglected.

So far the discussion of this topic has related to the country as a whole and not to the mountain area states specifically. It is recognized that some of the mountain and inter-mountain states have peculiar problems in population distribution and that many of their communities are too small for centers such as have been discussed here. The most that can be expected is that each state will face the problem of adequate and equitable educational regions and programs. However, population and industrial growth of these states has been projected and in many ways the problems they face in education beyond high school are little different from those of other states.

IMPLICATIONS FOR THE PRESENT

As stated at the outset, 1980 is only fourteen years hence. It is likely that some of the drastic social and technological changes will not occur in any kind of straight-line progression but instead will be accentuated according to prevailing conditions or scientific break throughs. Thus it is urgent that state planning agencies begin now to consider this relatively new, dynamic and urgently important level of training.

Quite aside from the general problem of how state planning can best be affected, there are certain other problems that are inherent in education at the immediate post-high-school level. One of these applies particularly to the community college, namely the reluctance of its staff to subscribe to the philosophy that its role as well as its program should be vastly different from that of the degree-granting college. Various studies have revealed a tendency for the faculty, and frequently the administrators, of community colleges to be primarily interested in the standard transfer program, to discount the remedial function, to ignore the exceedingly wide range of students' aptitudes and interests, to be less interested in occupational education, and to subscribe to the notion that since the community college is increasingly recognized as a part of higher education, it should emulate the prestige colleges. Obviously, if such a tendency continues unabated it will destroy the concept of this type of college as a community education center. Should this be the case, it would only accentuate further the diversity of institutions needed to serve the many groups of people which have been the concern of this paper.

As indicated earlier, the direction in this regard is not entirely clear at this point. Faculty attitudes cannot be legislated nor can they be ignored in the administration of a college. Also, if specialized vocational schools are established, and if they subsequently find that they must become comprehensive institutions, they too may fall victim to the pressure to adopt the standards of the university and the cycle is again complete. It appears that a *new concept regarding the organization of the educational system must be developed—a concept that definitely identifies the mid-level institution and the notion of an advanced community center more clearly than has been done to date.* Once such a concept is legitimatized, the community-oriented school, regardless of what it is called, can rest on its own identification with a specially recruited and prepared staff that is contented and anxious to perform those services that are significant in their own right.

Though it appears at first to be difficult, such an evolution of an educational institution may take place more rapidly than might be expected. The social pressures to organize institutions of the kind described may congeal rapidly over the next few years. Also, over time, the manpower situation itself may influence potential teachers into considering this unique type of institution as one worthy of considering.

There will also be the recurring problems of enabling legislation, methods of financial support, and the appropriate pattern of control. *A new look needs to be taken at these matters NOW* so that the stage is set not merely for today or next year but for the decade and more ahead. The need for orderly development is too great to lean on a patch quilt design or a play-by-ear procedure in looking toward the future.

The economics of education at this level will undoubtedly become an issue. Some authorities have already raised the question as to whether society can afford near-universal education immediately beyond the high school. There are, however, many points to be considered in this connection.

In the first place, there is the grave social problem of how to accommodate the vast army of youths who, upon high school graduation, are not likely to enter employment immediately. Surely there will need to be an adequate program concerned with their further educational and personal development as well as with the worthy use of their time during these crucial years, or the country will face a degree of unrest among the members of this age group which will be difficult to comprehend. Moreover, many economists have effectively pointed out that the national gross product of a country bears a close relationship to the level of education attained by the citizens of that country. From a practical point of view, one may predict that, in the long run, society will find a way to support what it considers important.

On the other hand, it will behoove planning agencies to organize programs that are as economical as possible and that, in general, avoid undue overlap and duplication. In this connection, there is a potential danger of duplication and excessive cost when states organize both community colleges and area vocational schools, both of which may be attempting similar programs. It is urgent, therefore, that planning agencies consider the role of these two types of institutions and determine whether, in a given state, both are needed or whether the comprehensive community college may well be the most appropriate medium for rendering the multiplicity of programs needed in the average community.

Still another factor to be considered in planning is the effect of tuition charges at this level of education. It is to be recalled that many students who attend community colleges and similar institutions are from homes on the lower end of the economic scale. To many such students almost any fee is exorbitant and may result in their inability to partake of the educational opportunity. Ideally, there should be no charge to the student for educational services on this level but, if there is, great care should be taken to keep the cost to him at a minimum.

Planning is already under way in each state. A question must be raised, however, as to whether community colleges, for example, are being considered simply as an expedient means of bringing relief to the four-year colleges. The problem is infinitely larger.

Obviously, state departments of education share a responsibility in planning for this level of education. But since higher institutions are also involved, and local communities drastically affected, it follows that *there must be cooperative effort in planning as well as universal concern for the problem*. Expediency, log rolling, and protection of the status quo are possible barriers to planning and execution. Hopefully, the dreams of countless men and women, young and old, in 1980—in 1975—in 1970—and even now—will prevail over the barriers.

CHAPTER 8

Adult and Continuing Education

FRED HARVEY HARRINGTON*

As recently as ten years ago, there was little mention of adult and continuing education in the public pronouncements of educators and office-holders with responsibilities in education. But the last decade has brought a striking change. Over and over again one hears statements such as: "I believe in continuing education"; "As we plan, we must not forget the adults"; and "In our changing society every one must keep on learning for his entire lifetime."

Why this change? Simply because political and educational leaders are coming to realize that it is not enough to educate the young—that our nation cannot prosper if we do not teach grown-ups as well. There have always been a few persons who have made this point. Now there are many; and we can say with confidence that adult and continuing education are coming into their own. We can say further that *educational planners can no longer afford to neglect this field.* They must give it their attention as they assess the needs and opportunities of the next two decades.

PLANNING FOR ADULT AND CONTINUING EDUCATION

The trend is unmistakable, and it is strong at every educational level. Some of the most dramatic new developments are in elementary and secondary education, largely because of the recent nationwide decisions to do something about poverty and dropouts. But higher education is also deeply involved in the current efforts to prevent the waste of American manpower. And community colleges and universities are providing a large and growing amount of continuing professional and liberal education.

Business firms and trade associations are also in the act, as are labor unions and churches and every sort of voluntary organization and commercial agency. Both off and on the nation's campuses there is informal and formal instruction for grownups (credit or non-credit—take your choice). There is adult education for work and for leisure. There are home study courses and courses taught overseas. There is educational radio and educational television. There are lecture and concert series. There is on-the-job training. There are conferences and institutes and workshops and study groups dealing with the issues of the day—with the special problems of druggists and engineers, potato chip manufacturers, journalists, motel

* President of the University of Wisconsin; Member of the National Advisory Council on Extension and Continuing Education set up under the Higher Education Act of 1965; Currently preparing a special study on The Role of Adult Education in the University, under a Carnegie Corporation grant, in collaboration with Dr. Donald R. McNeil, Chancellor of University Extension at the University of Wisconsin.

owners, foremen, policemen, morticians and housewives. There are training and retraining courses, refresher courses and updating courses, courses for cultural improvement and artistic understanding, courses for fun and for community action. There are offerings for the ill and for the aged; for those interested in physical fitness or in making money. There is adult education for highly educated and illiterate citizens of the developing nations, many administered abroad; others handled here.

How can those charting the future of education possibly take hold of this vast, sprawling, confusing and untidy area? This can best be done by:

1. Recognizing that the field exists and is important;

2. Finding out what is being done, and what should be done;

3. Checking to see who is handling adult and continuing education, and who should handle it; and

4. Discovering how the cost is being met, and how it should be met.

These points are elaborated under the headings which follow.

ADULT AND CONTINUING EDUCATION ARE IMPORTANT

Now of course everybody knows that there is such a thing as the education of adults. Yet one can read educational planning report after educational planning report without encountering any mention of adult or continuing education. Many state and local school boards have never had a substantial discussion of the subject. Many colleges and universities have never considered the topic in faculty meetings or in their governing board discussions. Where there has been consideration, the tendency has been to treat adults and continuing education with a few words, as an incidental rather than as a fundamental matter.

The reason is obvious enough. Educators have been overwhelmed with numbers. The head count of Americans of school and college age has soared, and young people are staying in the classroom for more years than before. The resulting problems of space, teacher supply and finance have all been enormous. On top of that there have been revolutions in method, an astonishing increase in subjects to be taught, demands that standards be moved up, new concerns about student health and recreation, traffic safety, work with the handicapped, ties with the community and so on. The research revolution and the growth in international responsibilities have had a major impact on all aspects of education and have also changed the schools.

With so much to do, how can one find time to talk about adult and continuing education? It has not been completely forgotten; but too often it has been handled on the side. Space has been provided for the young—and used in off-hours for adults. Teachers have been trained and hired to teach "regular students"—and have handled adults as extras, not as part of the standard assignment, but as overload for a little additional pay (very little, as a rule). Or the grownups have been taught by pickup staff hurriedly recruited from the community. An observer could certainly draw the conclusion that educating adults has been rated as useful but not vitally important.

The situation is changing, interest is picking up. One could, therefore, neglect the long past and concentrate on the day that is dawning in adult and continuing education. But a brief historic review may be worthwhile, even so.

Those interested in the history of adult education in the United States point to the educational value of the lyceum lecture circuit and its successor, the Chautauqua movement. State and county fairs are other nineteenth century examples that fall into the same classification, as are the institutes and short courses set up for mechanics and farmers.

Then, at the turn of the century, came the progressive movement. This was a movement filled with optimism and the expectation of reform—with belief in the idea of progress and the perfectibility of man. Much of the high promise of this early twentieth century movement centered around education, for children and for adults. It was then that the public schools began to feature Americanization classes, designed to supply adult immigrants with literacy in English and at least a minimum of civic understanding. Night school provided further steps up the economic and social ladder in the growing cities.

Meantime colleges and universities and private agencies started offering correspondence courses, with William Rainey Harper of the University of Chicago—an old Chautauqua man—leading the way. Then, too, those were the days of the public library movement, a prime adult education effort.

About this time, state legislators began voting funds for vocational and agricultural education in a cautious sort of way. And the federal government entered the picture during the World War I period. The Smith-Lever Act of 1914 enabled Land Grant colleges, like my own University of Wisconsin, to work with state and local governments to build an agricultural extension organization that could transmit the results of research to farmers for practical use. Professor Cyril Houle, whom we all admire, has called agricultural extension the most important adult education experiment in American history. Certainly it had a great deal to do with improving farm methods, increasing production and making possible the transition to commercial agriculture of the profitable sort.

Soon afterwards, in 1917, Congress passed the Smith-Hughes Act. This made federal money available for vocational education, benefiting adults as well as younger citizens.

Meanwhile the even broader field of general extension was launched at many universities, with legislative and student fee support. It undertook a great variety of off-campus services to adults—so many as to enable one of my distinguished predecessors to boast that "the boundaries of the campus are the boundaries of the state." (Charles R. Van Hise, President of the University of Wisconsin 1903-18).

By this time a few writers were beginning to give adult education a theoretical framework. No one did it better than the authors of the 1919 report of the British Adult Education Commission, who said:

> Adult education must not be regarded as a luxury for a few exceptional persons here and there. . . . Rather adult education is a permanent national necessity, an inseparable aspect of citizenship, and therefore should be both universal and lifelong.

These were brave words for 1919; and the generation that followed brought the desired result neither to Britain nor to America. The years between the world wars did see the coming of educational radio; the establishment of schools for workers in a few American universities; an increase in academic and recreational offerings for adults in the public schools; something of a boom in commercial home study courses ("Would you like to earn $100 more a week with a few evenings' study?"); the rise of liberal-education-for-adults in the new suburbs, with talks about the Great Books, the League of Nations and Meaningful Use of the New Leisure. So much happened that one of the foundations (Carnegie) was able to underwrite a whole shelf-full of books about adult education in the republic; and adult educators formed their first national association.

This was quite a showing—but was disappointing, really, in light of the great hopes of the progressive era and the British statement of purpose of 1919. It was not until World War II that Americans began to raise their sights. Then, gradually, more and more were heard to say that, in our rapidly changing society, lifelong learning is a necessity. New knowledge, new machines, new political and social theories outdate the old. One must keep on growing for individual development and for the national good. This is the case at every level, from the grade-school graduate to the professional who has completed his advanced training in a graduate field.

In other words, *every one who stops learning is a dropout these days.*

Continuing education is a must, then, if we are to keep up with the world of work as it changes. It is no less important in terms of human satisfaction. Industrialization has brought leisure as well as change; and adults need to know how to make constructive use of their spare time. Again, education is essential—for those who want to travel, or dabble in literature or the arts, or understand today's problems at home and in foreign countries, or simply to avoid the boredom and decay that can come with leisure or retirement.

This makes a good package—the lifetime learning requirements of work and leisure. But even that does not complete the picture. The education of adults has another aspect, the salvage side. In its spectacular progress our prosperous republic has left some citizens behind. In fact, there are millions: the poor, the ill, the handicapped, the school dropouts, the untrained, semi-trained and ill-trained; the technologically unemployed who have skills but cannot use them in an automated economy; the victims of prejudice; the culturally deprived; the widowed and abandoned mothers; the neglected aged.

Welfare is important here; but so is adult education. You may decide that the education or reeducation of these adults is worth what it costs because it reduces the relief rolls. (It does). You may decide that the investment in education will pay off because it will provide the labor market with needed skilled employees, and will result in increased tax payments. (It will). You may conclude that the training of these individuals is necessary to prevent riots and other civil disorders. (This is very likely true). Or you may want to identify in yourself and in the body politic the element of compassion, and say that these adult education programs can be justified because they rescue human beings from despair and add to the store of individual dignity and the value of democracy.

Take your choice, or several choices—adult education to increase individual and national efficiency, to make better use of available time, to improve the lot of disadvantaged Americans. It all points to the need to plan and the need to act.

WHAT IS BEING DONE AND WHAT SHOULD BE DONE

When adult educators from other countries visit the United States, they are swept off their feet by the great variety of offerings available for adult students at school, college and informal levels. A few of the more perceptive make a second point: that *there are too few opportunities for the lower income Americans who most need help.*

One must beware of jumping to conclusions in the area of lifelong learning. The fact that there is so little available for disadvantaged adults should not lead one to conclude that there is too much available for the well-to-do. Such is not the case. There is an acute shortage at every point, made worse by the financial support situation which will be discussed later. Much needs to be done to increase the quantity and to improve the quality of what some call "higher adult education"—work at and above the university level. But right at this moment the national interest suggests that government and educational officials should give their particular attention to salvage, upgrading, refresher and retraining operations connected with the school dropouts.

A *New York Times* story of September 4, 1966 shows what can be done and is being done, though in a small way:

"A career?" the dishwasher asked, "I don't know. I never exactly thought about a career . . . Besides, what can I do?"

Five months later this minority-group American, and several like him, had completed a federally-financed training program, and could boast of having nine different kitchen skills. All these upgraded individuals had increased their take-home pay, and some were on their way toward supervisory jobs. Two of the group were enrolling in food service management evening classes in a New York City community college. Two others, who had been dropouts, were going to night school to complete work for their high school diplomas. And the skills developed were in such demand that hospitals were clamoring for similar training programs.

The non-profit organization handling this particular project is called "Skill Advancement, Incorporated." It was set up by an institution of higher

learning—Cornell University—and two special-purpose groups—the Urban
League of Greater New York and the Puerto Rican Forum. Financing—
a full half-million dollars—came from the United States Department of
Labor.

This is impressive—but it is a "demonstration project," limited to
1,500 workers. Much, much more is required even in this one metropolitan
area. Skill Advancement itself made that point, hinting at the possibilities
in a 600-page report entitled *Breaking the Barriers of Occupational Isolation: A Report on Upgrading Low-Skill Low-Wage Workers*.

This is a single example of the new effort. It would be easy to supply
many more. Sometimes funds are provided by the "Poverty organization"
in Washington—the Office of Economic Opportunity. Sometimes the United
States Department of Health, Education and Welfare pays the bill. Again,
the private foundations, large and small, come into the picture—Ford,
Rockefeller, the Carnegie Corporation, the Danforth Foundation, the
Stern Family Fund, the Johnson Foundation, and many more. Sometimes
state and local governments or school districts and colleges and universities
will take a hand.

Generally the major effort is in the cities in these days of urban crisis.
But much is going on in small towns, too, and in the country. The national
Job Corps, which works through universities and schools and private companies, has camps for the urban and for the rural disadvantaged. Results
to date have been better with the rural enrollees. There is reason for
optimism, too, in what has been done for special rural groups, such as the
reservation Indians and the depressed hill people of Appalachia. University
agricultural or cooperative extension, already mentioned, has lately shown
increasing interest in the rural poor.

But the big point, the overwhelmingly big point, is that *all the effort to
date is just beginning to scratch the surface*. We can already see that this
sort of adult education will pay dividends: But it will take time. (There is
confusion already because of the many efforts to get started in a hurry).
It will take money, lots of money. (There has been waste in these programs,
and it must be reduced. Funds available must be spent efficiently. But
even when we have a higher level of efficiency—and it is coming—the investment will be very substantial. It will average several thousand dollars
for each salvaged or retrained individual). It will take imagination, understanding and great effort. (When we persuade counsellors and vocational
specialists to work on anti-poverty assignments, there are that many fewer
trained teachers available for the regular schools. When we urge minority
groups to take the adult education route, we must expect resistance from
minority group leaders who prefer to concentrate on other objectives, say
open housing or political power).

Even so, it is very much worth doing. And all those who are planning
the educational future must address themselves to this area.

It is not necessary, really, to separate grown-ups from the young.
One should see the two groups together. Suppose we improve the schools,
and help all competent young people to secure the training they deserve

and need. Clearly, then, there will be less salvage and upgrading work required in subsequent decades.

In a number of states, students who drop out of school—some are actually pushed out—before reaching a designated age or grade level, are expected to continue their education on a part time basis. The responsibility for this type of education—sometimes called "continuation education"—has not been taken seriously in many school systems. It should be—not only for the benefit of the students but as a means of helping to avoid more serious problems including attempts at salvage at a later time.

There will still be plenty to do. New inventions will continue to eliminate old skills and call for the retraining of adults. Those who have learned will have to learn more as technological improvements make life increasingly complicated. Women who drop out of employment to raise families will need refresher work in practical nursing, teaching, social work—or whatever—to resume their careers. There will be those who picked or were pushed into the type of work they do not like, or into jobs beneath their potential. There will be need, as there is now, for adult and continuing education for political understanding, cultural improvement and meaningful recreation. But the desperate aspect of the adult education business should let up a little if we do our job in the present generation.

How well is it being done? It is hard to report with any degree of exactitude. Statistics are generally unavailable or, when available, are wretchedly inaccurate or misleading.

Nor is there any agreement on definitions. Here are a couple of examples:

—A housewife returns to high school or college and takes a diploma or degree along with her children or grandchildren. We see this in the papers all the time. It is good human interest material. Surely it is adult education. But in attendance statistics the housewife is almost certainly classified with the young students.

—More than a quarter of the college undergraduates and nearly all the graduate students have passed their twenty-first birthdays. Is teaching them adult education? Probably not. Anyway, it would not be so counted. Nor will 40-year-old teachers coming back for summer school be classified as adult students. "Evening school" on the other hand is generally considered adult education. So 18-year-old high school graduates or dropouts enrolling in night classes to continue their education while working on full- or part-time jobs are often included in the adult education count.

We could go on and on. Is on-the-job training in a factory adult education? It may be an hour long; it may take a full year. Is the casual watching of an educational television series adult education? Is the reading of a book in one's professional field adult education?

Perhaps it does not matter particularly; in any case we cannot resolve the semantic tangle overnight. The new National Advisory Council on Extension and Continuing Education has been asked to try its hand at definitions, but gives evidence of shying away from this thankless job.

Here is probably the best suggestion: Don't worry about the definitions—but be sure you know what you are discussing at any particular point. Make a distinction between youth work and the education of grown-ups. Permit an overlap; but do not neglect either field. Then make some effort through your school statistics or institutional studies office to find out roughly: What are the adult education enrollments in your district or university or region? How many adults are being taught? How many are being neglected? Are the offerings largely recreational? Are they mainly professional and vocational? Are they predominately in the liberal education field? What portion of your educational budget is going into the adult education area? How much of the effort is to help Negroes and other minority groups? How much is for upgrading and how much for refresher and retraining work? If your specialty is training teachers, how much are you doing to prepare people for careers in helping adults? What evidence have you about the results of what you are doing, or not doing?

You will not find it easy to get satisfactory answers. But asking the questions on the basis of such information as you can assemble is likely to change your planning goals—at least a little.

Although there are no really adequate statistics in the lifelong learning field, we are fortunate in having one good recent survey, conducted by Professor Peter Rossi's National Opinion Research Center (NORC) at the University of Chicago, with a grant from the Carnegie Corporation. The results of this investigation are summarized in an excellent volume by John W. C. Johnstone and R. J. Rivera, *Volunteers for Learning: the Educational Pursuits of Adults* (Aldine Publishing House, Chicago, 1965).

Using tested sampling techniques in four cities, Johnstone and Rivera concluded that about one in every five adults is involved in adult education activities each year, approximately 25,000,000 in all. The study disproved the often-asserted view that adults return to the classroom to earn credit and complete diploma or degree work. Instead, the preference is for non-credit offerings of a vocational or recreational nature (learn-for-work, learn-for-leisure). There is more continuing than remedial education. Adult students are more likely to be young than old (their median age is 36). They are more likely to be well-to-do than poor; more likely to be well-educated than poorly educated. College-educated executives, housewives and professional people earning over $7,000 annually become involved in adult education programs six times as often as $4,000 blue-collar workers with grade school educations. Citizens with lower incomes tend not to know about educational opportunities for adults, and generally do not see the value of such work. When they do become interested it is nearly always on the practical, vocational level; they show little interest in cultural and recreational programs.

Looking to the future, these survey authors predict a substantial increase in the education of adults. They base their conclusion on trends in schooling. Since the college-going fraction of the population is rising, and the grade-school-only percentage declining, a larger and larger part of the total population will be in the reasonably-well-educated bracket—which is the group most attracted to courses for adults.

These factually based projections—and other developments—suggest that educational planners should be alert. But measuring the assured market for adult learning should not blind us to the plain fact that *those who most need aid are not getting it.*

This is not merely a question of the poor—boosting the unemployed into employment, providing the undertrained with useful skills and all of that. It is also a question of what happens to the successful dropout, the citizen who stopped going to school but manages to hold a steady job involving some responsibility. The *Volunteers for Learning* study shows that 80 percent of all American adults took no educational work at all during the test year. Had they volunteered for learning they might have increased their earnings—or they might have become better citizens, by broadening their minds or by getting into a community improvement program.

I am not suggesting that there should be compulsory schooling for adults. I am saying only that those who are setting up future programs should think of the adult who is not now involved in any educational program.

Why is he not involved? The evidence shows that: (1) offerings for adults are very few in many sections of the country (Those who want to preserve our small towns should bear this in mind); (2) many citizens do not know about opportunities that are open to them (You can find advertisements for evening classes in any large-city newspaper, but we have been none too good in telling adults what is available and how it can help those who do not normally think of returning to the classroom); and (3) adult education tends to be expensive. (The planners will need to cut the cost if they want to broaden the base of learning among the adult population).

Perhaps it would be well to look at the 25,000,000 adult education experiences turned up in the NORC survey.

About a fifth of the work is recreational, and most of this appears to be of the learn-how-to-play-bridge type. Given the new leisure, such programs should be described as socially useful. They are not, however, really intellectual—nor are they going to increase income or improve community social development. This simply underscores the point made earlier: that adult education offerings are too few. The fun work is all right; but there should be more courses of the more serious type.

Since adult and continuing education is all odds and ends, we cannot expect much order in the listings. Still, *it does seem unfortunate that so many adult education experiences are brief and fragmentary and have no follow-up.* Educators should work on this.

The *great motivating force in lifelong learning is self-improvement.* One is not surprised, therefore, to find that a third of the total program is vocational or professional in orientation. The percentage is higher if we eliminate the adult education offerings of the churches.

On the whole it may be wise to retain this percentage, because training is needed everywhere and should be enlarged and improved. Yet it is also proper to note the present sad condition of liberal education for adults.

This term may seem way-out and impractical; but this classification includes courses which produce political and international understanding; and in many parts of the country community improvement depends on exposure to broad educational areas. (Race relations, urban history and sociology, the economics of poverty, the scientific and cultural background of regional economic growth—all of these are "liberal education for adults." So is the fine arts and humanities knowledge without which overall community improvement is impossible).

WHO PROVIDES AND WHO SHOULD PROVIDE ADULT EDUCATION?

Let me make four points:

First, The report, *Volunteers for Learning,* shows that American colleges and universities serve more adults than do the schools. This is curious. Only a minority of citizens enroll in higher education, let alone complete it. It follows that if lifelong learning is to be a broad reality, *most of the effort must be below the college level.*

True, many university adult offerings are open to persons who have not completed high school. The outstanding example is university agricultural extension, which has always worked mainly with the non-college population. University schools for workers fall into the same classification, as do many new university efforts in the community action field. Some colleges and universities, however, are unwilling to participate in this below-college-level activity. Others will do so only for the experimental or demonstration period. Still others point out, and wisely, that colleges and universities are alone in being able to mount much "higher adult education," including courses requiring a medical or engineering or PhD degree for admission. If they expand in this direction (and they should) they will have less time for below-college-level work. And some of their energies should be used on training teachers for adult courses in the schools.

Can the schools do more than they are doing in the adult field? For two decades they have been loaded down with the flood of post-World War II students. But the population lines are changing. There are increases still, but they are not as dramatic as they were in the 1950's. School administrators and superintendents may, then, be able to give a bit more time to the adults. New support patterns, particularly the availability of more federal dollars may also help. *While many local school systems are doing what they can, state boards and departments of education should face up to their responsibilities to provide programs of adult education that will meet the needs.*

Second, the NORC study indicates that very few adults use educational television for organized instruction. Correspondence courses, notoriously hard to carry through to completion, show up as far more popular than TV classes.

Why? Well, we all know that educational television has often been of inferior broadcast quality. It has been useful in the schools, where there are captive audiences. Adults, being volunteers, are likely to be attracted only if the medium is adequately supported and imaginatively programmed. With that backing, success is possible. We already know that correspondence courses and television work well together. It is also clear that *the outlook would be better if institutions were a bit more liberal in granting credit for off-campus instruction.* (The high schools and colleges have been backward in this). One need not, however, be credit-minded. If well done, educational television will be worth while without pay in credits. And it can be very useful if handled skillfully. As an example, it can educate adults and at the same time, achieve practical results in connection with community action programs.

None of this can be done without money. It is thus imperative that each state and locality decide how much it wants to put into television. The federal government and the private foundations can help—both have done a great deal. But state and local commitment is essential for success.

Third, the point about television opens up the whole matter of support. As of now, the chief innovating force in adult and continuing education is the federal government. The new approaches are coming mainly from Washington—in manpower training legislation, the heart-stroke-cancer program, the Higher Education Act of 1965, economic opportunity legislation, etc. There is room—and need—inside this federal legislation for state and local leadership (quite a bit, for example, under Title I of the 1965 Higher Education Act of 1965, which calls for state plans for extension and continuing education). The broad planning lines, though, are laid down by the national government.

If adult and continuing education are important (and we have decided that they are) *the states and regions of the nation should be deciding about lines of development.* So again we have a call to action, with the future lines of action depending on attention now.

Fourth, any examination of adult and continuing education demonstrates that little of the work is being handled by teachers trained for this specialty. The typical adult education instructor is one by accident—a person trained for another type of teaching, or not trained at all. Part-time instruction is common. Young teachers take on adult classes to make a little extra money. Or some one in business agrees to handle a class. Sometimes the result is excellent—adults may get a successful professional person who is willing to give a little of his time to continuing education. Often, however, the result is inferior teaching for people who deserve better.

Should we train a special group of adult educators? Certainly we do need more school and college officials who are experts in this field. This is necessary for successful planning for lifelong learning, and to improve the research on adult learning. (Much of what we have is poor). But adults need not be taught by teachers trained only for continuing education. The important thing is that teachers and others become interested in training adults—that they recognize it is important that adults be taught. And the money must be provided so that the job can be done.

Who Pays and Who Should Pay for Adult Education?

Too often the individual student is asked to absorb the whole cost. Now, if the education of adults is of benefit to society, and surely it is, the load should not be borne entirely by the student.

The standard American theory is that elementary and secondary education are so important to the nation that they must be provided free of cost to students attending public schools. In public higher education, the individual is expected to pay a part of the cost. But the state pays most (over three-quarters), because the educated citizen is an economic and political asset to the community. Even in private higher education the student is rarely asked to pay as much as half the cost of his education.

When we shift to adult education, the rules change. Presumably the thought is that adults can afford to pay. Actually, many adult students are worse off than younger undergraduates. They may be taking evening courses because they could not afford to go to college. The NORC study shows that adult students are relatively young, that is, that they have not gone very far up the economic ladder. Most of them have families to support, and they may be taking the work because their incomes are low. Yet, at present, they must pay, and will not have access to most of the scholarships, loan funds and work programs available to younger full-time students.

Generalization is difficult. Professionals taking continuing education courses in their specialties can afford to pay the fees. So can those enrolled in continuing education institutes for executives—though often their employers pick up the bill. Those less able to pay (teachers and nurses, for instance) may find institutions that adjust fees according to the ability of particular groups of students to meet the cost. And adult education is subsidized in many state universities and junior colleges and public schools. The state puts in a third of the cost at my institution.

There are also many zero-fee adult education ventures. Educational television and radio provide obvious examples. Adult education for the poor also fits in here, with all the federal programs so much in the news these days (and including the new Defense Department plan for upgrading citizens previously considered unfit for service). On-the-job training normally costs the student nothing; and the schools offer many courses free. But, despite this list, the central point remains: adult education generally costs the student a good deal. And *the cost is the main barrier to improvement in this area.*

Those who are concerned—and everyone should be—need to grapple with the cost question, and in doing so should come up with enough support that adult and continuing education will flourish. That is in the interest of us all.

CHAPTER 9

Colleges and Universities
and Their Relationships

Theodore L. Reller*
and
John E. Corbally, Jr.**

While the major emphasis of this eight-state project (Designing Education for the Future) is on the elementary and secondary, local and state levels, it is most appropriate that some attention be given to colleges and universities. This is true because: (1) The university, being at the apex of the formal educational system, exercises large influence over the other parts of the system and is influenced by them; (2) In the more complex society of the future all parts of the educational service will need to be better coordinated or inter-related than presently is the case; (3) The changes in education promised for the next couple of decades constitute such a challenge that various educational agencies need to coordinate their efforts to maximize potential benefits; (4) The educational results of various programs cannot reasonably be determined without reference to previous and subsequent educational experiences.

Further, consideration needs to be given to higher education when planning elementary and secondary programs. Heretofore these two large segments of the educational effort have been treated much too largely in isolation. At times they have been competitors for the tax dollar; too often spokesmen for one segment have revealed little understanding or even ignorance in their attacks on the other; too little have both parties realized their common responsibilities and the extent to which they inevitably share goal attainment.

Special Problems in Higher Education

In turning to the college and university, the problem of planning for 1980 should be regarded as even more difficult in some respects than in the case of elementary and secondary schools. Probably also the future in

* *Dean, School of Education, University of California, Berkeley;* Fulbright Lecturer, University of Amsterdam (1958-59); Professor of Education, University of Pennsylvania (1931-48); Director or staff member of numerous state and local school studies. Publications include: *Divisional Administration of English Education* (1959); and (co-author) *Administrative Relationships — A Casebook* (1960), *Comparative Educational Administration* (1962), and *Educational Organization and Administration* (1959, revised edition 1967).
**Vice President for Academic Affairs and Provost, The Ohio State University;* Chairman of the Executive Committee, Michigan-Ohio Regional Education Laboratory, Inc.; Ohio representative, Midwest Advisory Committee on Higher Education, Council of State Governments. Publications include *School Finance* (1962) and (co-author) *An Introduction to Educational Administration,* (1958), and *Educational Administration: The Secondary School* (1961, second edition 1965).

higher education will be more "surprising" in Boulding's[1] terms than in elementary and secondary. This assumption results from a number of factors such as: the greater variety of institutions and institutional forms; the multiplicity of goals; the recency with which higher education has come to be seriously regarded by the mass society; the "independence" of the higher educational institution; the more limited attention which has been given to the study of institutions of higher education; the age of the students —adults, but not so regarded by the society; the power of the modern university and its growing social significance.

It should be noted that in recent years there has been a growing recognition of the significance of higher education in the development of a society. This recognition became quite pronounced a few years ago in the newly developing societies. It was clear that unless they had developed human resources they could not effect essential advances. Leaders were desperately needed in many aspects of life. The industrial and economic development of the society was dependent upon the availability of trained engineers, economists and capable persons for business management. No less in demand were those who could offer leadership in the area of government. In addition, a field of study known as "the economics of education" was developed. More sophisticated "yardsticks" than had existed were designed to permit analysis both of the areas of education in which investment should be made by a society and of the extent to which such investments should reach. The simple concept that every society needs "elementary education for all" gave way to concepts involving societal needs for various kinds of educational programs at all levels from elementary to post-college.

The difficulties of the problem of education and development were further evident when an attempt was made to provide higher educational opportunities in the new societies. In some cases an institution much like the university of the economically developed countries was planned, but proved to relate extremely badly to the needs of the society. (In the United States the land grant college, perhaps our most unique or significant contribution in higher education, developed with the society.) In other instances students were sent to other countries for study—where too frequently they were prepared (and chose) to remain in the country to which they had been sent, rather than for service at home.

The economically advanced countries have had such substantial developed human resources that they have not been as conscious of the significance of higher education as a central element of their development as have been the less well developed countries. However, informed men have been increasingly aware of the growing dependence of the society upon education and especially upon the university. Kerr in commenting on this development speaks of the second great transformation of the American university. He states:

> The University is being called upon to educate previously unimagined numbers of students; to respond to the expanding claims of material service; to

[1] Kenneth E. Boulding, "Expecting the Unexpected: The Uncertain Future of Knowledge and Technology," in *Prospective Changes in Society by 1980*. (Denver, Colo.: Designing Education for the Future, 1966) Chap. 12.

merge its activities with industry as never before; to adapt to and rechannel new intellectual currents. . . .

So many of the hopes and fears of the American people are now related to our educational system and particularly to our universities—the hope for longer life, for getting into outer space, for a higher standard of living; our fears of Russian or Chinese supremacy, of the bomb and annihilation, of individual loss of purpose in the changing world. For all these reasons and others, the university has become a prime instrument of national purpose. This is new. This is the essence of the transformation engulfing our universities.[2]

While the problem of the economic and technological development of the society looms large, it is apparent that the problems involved in the ethical, social and political development are vastly larger and far more difficult. A consideration of the issues presented by Roger Shinn makes it apparent that the role of higher education in these areas is a large and critical one. He states:

Urbanization faces society with profound ethical decisions. In the United States, for example, urbanization has—in fact, if not by necessity—produced desperate and frustrated racial ghettoes.

The United States with its long traditions of freedom and justice, faces new ethical issues in seeking to make good its traditional values in history's vastest experiment in devising a large-scale, industrialized, pluralistic society.

The American society, therefore, is moving to an increasingly experimental ethic.

One of the urgent ethical issues of the years ahead will concern the responsibility of the rich nations toward the poor nations.[3]

Other areas he identifies are ethical factors or issuees related to affluence, alienation, the shift from an inherited code to making responsible decisions, and the structure of society.

Thus, only if one recognizes the significant opportunity or responsibility of the university in the field of social, political and ethical *development* can the role of the university be understood. If the university does not lead in these areas, what institution will?

THE EIGHT-STATE AREA AND HIGHER EDUCATION

Several papers included in *Prospective Changes in Society by 1980* make clear the unique opportunity which the eight-state area has in the field of higher education. Many of the severe problems of more highly industrialized and urbanized parts of the country have not yet reached serious proportions in this area. Population growth will probably not occur at such a rate that effective planning cannot reduce or avoid some of the more difficult problems. There is the opportunity to plan for urban development in such manner as to avoid the problems which cause men to wish to escape from the metropolitan area. Racial segregation, for example, has not reached such vast proportions that a solution to the problem appears to be impossible. Adequate planning should result in the avoidance of the problem in the tragic form that is found in New York or in Chicago.

As in the case of the development of the metropolitan areas, the

---

[2] Clark Kerr, *The Uses of the University* (New York: Harper and Row, Torchbook edition, 1966), pp. 86-87. (Originally published by Harvard University Press, 1964).

[3] "Human Responsibility in the Emerging Society," in *Prospective Changes in Society by 1980*, Chap. 15.

eight-state area should also be able to avoid many of the developmental problems in higher education faced by parts of the nation which became more heavily populated at an earlier date. There are clearly adequate material resources for accomplishing necessary planning and development in this educational field. Whether or not the people will recognize and accept their opportunity is the question before the area. Whether they will provide for and secure the talent which is essential for such advancement is another highly related issue.

It would be difficult to predict how this opportunity will be accepted. The area has certain traditions of initiative, openness, social sensitivity, human values, liberalism and change which bode well. However it also has traditions of clinging to the past, and of individualism in some forms which are socially self-defeating. The mere fact that the area is somewhat removed from some of the tensions of the major metropolitan centers may cause it to hope that they do not apply and can be avoided. On the other hand mobility of people and developments in communication may reduce the likelihood of disastrous inaction.

The natural resources and the natural environment of the region are a challenge. How they will be handled will depend upon the vision of the people, their general education (ethical, technological, political, social), the education of leaders in government and industry, and the development of research and planning for industrial and social needs. It is important therefore to turn attention to some of the issues in higher education, which confront the society and which may have special significance for this eight-state area.

SELECTED ISSUES IN HIGHER EDUCATION

What Should be Included in Higher Education? Some of the major current and emerging issues confronting higher education are discussed briefly under this topic. Decisions in this area should not be regarded as final or fixed for changes in the society and its needs will require careful consideration. Perhaps also some variation should be expected and encouraged since there are and will be features of the program that are extremely closely related to other aspects of education or even parts of other aspects. For example, if the college makes special arrangements to admit a number of outstanding secondary school youth to certain classes while they are still in high school, is this secondary or higher education?

Is the junior or community college a part of public education (secondary) or a part of higher education, or of both? Surely it must be closely related to each regardless of where it "belongs." Further the community college is properly and deeply involved in the adult education movement —a movement which may be expected to change and expand greatly in the coming decades. But how is adult education to be related to higher education? This problem grows larger when the possibilities of adult education through realistic social planning, for example, are considered. The university must be centrally involved in research and social planning but much adult education must be carried on through institutions other than those devoted to higher education. Policies need to be developed carefully to assure that the concept of higher education is not too limited and removed from the development area, that its activities are not too diffuse, and that they facilitate the coordination of the many agencies that will be inevitably involved in services which relate to higher education—now that it will increasingly have a central role.

What Should be the Purposes of Higher Education? In very broad terms the purposes of higher education are frequently listed as teaching, research and service. There is no question about the responsibility of higher education in the teaching area. It is widely agreed that a broad general education must be provided, for only on this basis can informed citizens and specialized leaders be formed. It is further recognized that the society in the decades ahead will be even more dependent than ours upon the preparation of a wide range of technologically and professionally competent people—men and women who will take leadership in the development and administration of essential social and governmental structures.

The role of many institutions of higher education in research and service is less clear, While it is clear that these three purposes need to be developed as a unit—each in relation to the others—it is far less clear how this should be done without neglecting one or another of them. Thus the close relationship between research and excellence in teaching in many situations is quite evident. Understanding this relationship, however, does not give assurance that some staff members in higher education may not become so involved in research that they neglect teaching. Similarly, in the United States especially, there has been a wide appreciation of the significance of the service function of the university. However the service function in some areas and institutions has been carried on in such manner as to impair, or at least not to advance, the research effort. At the same time one considers the broad, overall purposes of higher education, he must also recognize that it is unlikely—or at least unwise to assume—that each unit or institution within higher education can serve all these purposes with equal emphasis and with equal success. Institutional purposes as well as overall purposes of a system require careful study.

Who Should Plan for the Development of Higher Education? Higher education has developed with less coordinated planning than has been the case in elementary and secondary education. Even in elementary and secondary education, however, there has been remarkably little comprehensive research and planned development. The educational system has grown substantially through experience and as a result of pressures to meet growing needs rather than through careful analysis and planning. The resources that have been devoted to planning have been regrettably small—and have too frequently been available only for short intensive studies. Thus resources and expertness in planning have been extremely limited.

The needs of the society and those resulting from the growth which appears to be inevitable in higher education can be satisfactorily met only with a marked change in this regard. Provision therefore needs to be made by the states individually and cooperatively for the development of the planning staff and skills and resources to ensure a plan. Unless this is done large human resources will go undeveloped, important social needs will not be met, the society will expend substantial funds with little likelihood of maximum returns. There will be waste and duplication in effort. The increasing specialization which characterizes our society, and which has large implications for preparation and research programs, demands over-all planning for areas such as that under consideration. Within these regional plans the states can enjoy large freedom to initiate and test diverse programs. The state plans can and should stimulate long-range effective planning by institutions individually or in groups.

This area is fortunate in that it has had important experience through the Western Interstate Commission for Higher Education (WICHE)[4] in the study of and cooperation in meeting a considerable number of important problems in higher education. This base should enable the states to move forward rapidly in the development of planning procedures of a level of sophistication somewhat in accord with the demands of the next few decades. Unless this is done the opportunity to lead which now is in the hands of institutions of higher education will be largely lost. Such forward movement will be substantially dependent upon the development of a center for planning since no one of the states involved will alone have the resources (human and material) to develop high competency in this difficult area and to render the rather continuous analysis of the present and envisioning of the future which are imperative.

Such planning does not imply that there will not be large opportunity for each state to function on its own in planning and development. In fact, no state will probably function at a high level without the stimulation and assistance of such a center. Similarly private institutions as well as public will benefit.

What Plan for Coordination of Institutional Efforts and Programs Within a State Should be Adopted? The control of higher education has not been centralized in most of the states in this country. This is true of the public segment and understandably more so of the private. In part this is the result of the "independence" sought by faculties and of the traditional plan of having a strong board of trustees or regents for each institution. It has also been a result of the lack of consciousness of the great significance of higher education and of the relative availability of higher educational opportunities. With the growing awareness of the social and economic significance of higher education, of the difficulty of providing adequate places, and of the sharply increasing costs to the state, the question of planning and coordinating higher education activities is receiving increasing attention and action.

---

[4] The commission was created to administer the Western Regional Compact which has been adopted by 13 western states. It was formerly established in 1951 after ratification of the Compact by five states and began its program in 1953. It seeks to: increase educational opportunities for youth, assist colleges and universities in their academic programs and institutional management, aid in expanding supply of specialized manpower, aid colleges and universities in meeting changing educational and social needs, inform the public about higher education needs. It is financed by a small appropriation from each state and foundation grants. It has developed a staff, and created knowledge and understanding through various seminars, studies, student exchange activities and publications.

In many states in the past each segment of the public higher education enterprise acted rather independently and sought to achieve its goals through dealing directly with the legislature on financial and sometimes on other matters. Frequently this was accompanied by a measure of consultation and cooperation among the heads of major institutions with relatively little regard for the smaller institutions. The great increase in the number of institutions engaged in higher education, the need to plan for additional ones, the necessity of reaching some agreement on the spheres of activity of the respective institutions, the raising of normal schools to colleges and even to universities—all these developments have made it clear that continued independent action can only result in severe competition, unmet needs and chaos. Therefore, it is reasonable to expect the development of coordinating boards or bodies in all states. Such boards may begin with little power other than to seek cooperation and to review proposals for submission to the legislature. Gradually, however, it is to be expected that these boards will have substantial responsibility and will have the assistance of strong staffs which will play a large role in policy determination through the collection of essential data and development of proposals.

The coordinating boards will have less responsibility for private higher education than for public. However the role of the private institutions will need to be kept clearly in view, and these boards may indeed have direct administrative responsibility for private institutions insofar as they are recipients of federal grants for certain purposes.

The developments here described cause considerable concern among many people in the field of higher education. Two major reasons for this concern are (1) the fear of political control and (2) the fear that individual institutions may lose the opportunity to take initiative and to be free from petty bureaucratic controls which too often accompany a central organization. The first of these fears is probably exaggerated if the fear is that of political party interference and a spoils system. In part, higher education as well as elementary and secondary education have thought of themselves as being non-political. This has been true even of institutions which have been heavily involved politically in financing their programs. During recent years, however, there has been a growing awareness of the importance of the field of the politics of education and of a more sophisticated and understanding approach to political questions. This awareness is important since in the future the development of higher education is going to be more closely related to the legislature and to the governor's office than in the past. A recognition of these facts and of the desirable responsibilities of the various parties involved is essential for effective operation.

The problem of encouraging initiative, of fostering innovation, of removing barriers to change, of avoiding the conformity which results from detailed controls or the fear of detailed control is more difficult. The field of higher education is such a vast, developing, and complex one that it is not likely to be properly developed or conducted unless there is large opportunity for individual initiative and for experimentation. Not only must the opportunity for this exist, but active steps for encouraging and for facilitating such developments must be taken. The climate where this takes place may well be almost at the opposite end of the continuum from that central administration which engages in the checking on detailed compliance in accord with the stereotype of the bureaucrat. The problem thus is one of creating a strong central organization devoted to leadership which lives in accord with the recognition that it can only be strong if it is working with vigorous individualistic institutions.

What Should be the Role of the Student, Faculty, and Administrators in Policy Determination and Administration? In college and university administration, as in the case of many other public and private enterprises, the roles of the various parties that are centrally involved are being re-examined. It is to be expected that such re-examination will continue. It is related to the alienation and frustration in our society growing from the belief that we are not living in accord with either our value commitments or essential practices—and the recognition that we must do so if major disaster is to be avoided. It also is a result of changing conditions. For example, the university student body is becoming an older one—with much larger numbers of students in graduate and professional studies who enjoy full citizen rights and responsibilities in the society. The traditional programs of many colleges have not been designed for mature adults nor do such programs involve them in decision-making—rather the college has seen itself in *loco parentis.* Even "student government" has been a pseudo affair in many respects.

Again, the faculties of many colleges and universities have not had the opportunity to participate and/or have not been intensely interested in participating in many important policy matters. The interest of faculties is growing, and they are demanding a larger share of responsibility. In some instances these demands may in fact have been poorly thought through and may result more largely in interference with sound operations than in added contributions to policy determination. Some excesses and over-enthusiasm may be expected from faculty and students, and administration may at times be greatly undervalued. Basically, however, these movements should insure the disappearance of many indefensible practices of the past and eventual development of stronger institutions. In this area as in many others, however, many unresolved issues remain. These include: Can or should the college or university presidents and deans be more than mediators? Will faculty members, who increasingly use as their reference point colleagues in their own discipline in other institutions rather than in the institution with which they are connected, build a strong institution? How can the student movement contribute most significantly to college administration?

What Provisions Should be Made for General, Technical and Professional Education—and Units—Within the Institution of Higher Education? The field of higher education is an extremely broad one even when attention is centered on the teaching responsibility alone. The need for general education or liberal education remains large even though there has been little agreement regarding the manner (content, procedures) in which it may be best achieved. Meanwhile the enormous expansion of the technological world is a powerful magnet which draws students with a wide range of levels of ability. In an increasingly complex society, occupations grow into professions and new professions are created. But technologists and professionals also have responsibilities as citizens in a new world only beginning to emerge. Thus the struggle continues over general education and technical or professional education, over how to prepare the leader in technology for a world in which technological knowledge itself expands at a phenomenal rate. If technical or professional education is acquired at a relatively early age, is there time or—more important—motivation to secure a liberal education later?

Developments regarding these various programs of education have important implications for the structure of an institution of higher education. What size and types of units should be established? Are relatively small units within the large institution essential? Should these units be on professional school lines or should professional schools be closely interrelated? Where should knowledges and skills basic to various professions be obtained—in the respective professional colleges or in common, broad, and probably very large departments? What are the implications of various unit plans for research and development functions? To what extent is the tightly planned and directed program essential, or may "independent study" be realized? What are the implications of programmed instruction for the college and university in terms of its internal structure and units?

What Should be the Relations of Institutions of Higher Education to the Federal Government? The question of the relation of support of an institution of higher learning to its independence has long been an important one. Private donors have exercised or have attempted to exercise unreasonable controls at times. States have also seriously interfered with the freedom of the university to teach or do research in some instances. The public and private inadequacies or excesses have been resisted and eventually substantially overcome in part because of the different bases of support.

Since the Second World War, the federal government has increasingly become extremely influential in higher education. This has come about because many agencies of the federal government have had large resources for research purposes and have entered into contracts and made large grants to the universities for specific purposes. Public and private universities have thus become affiliated with the federal government. The federal government may have had no desire to direct the university in its teaching function. However, when substantial funds are available for certain schools or areas of study and none for others, the influence inevitably is very great. These funds have had a marked effect upon the attitudes and work of the faculty. They have emphasized organized research and have not especially valued individual research. They have sharply increased the opportunities of students for research and related experiences in certain fields, with some compensation, to the detriment of other areas of study.

In addition to the large influence of the federal government through financing research projects and grants, it has recently turned to grants to the states for higher education. These grants are available to public and private institutions and thus represent an important shift from the historic provisions through which public state universities and land grant colleges were initiated and assisted. These developments are closely related to the significant federal tax power and to the sharply increasing cost of higher education. It is to be expected therefore that these influences will increase in the next few decades. The question, therefore, of whether, or—perhaps better—what type of control or influence the federal government will exercise over the institutions of higher learning is an important one. In the eight-state area it may be especially important since it will be a region in which above average growth and development will occur.

What Should be the Relation of Higher Education to Research? Questions of the relation of higher education to research are especially important in the case of universities. One of the notable characteristics of our society is its dependence upon research. Only in recent decades has man been so consciously engaged in the modification of his environment and condition. Thus modern industry, agriculture, medicine, and in fact all phases of life are dependent upon research efforts. Research has become one of the important new occupations of this century. It employs hundreds of thousands of highly trained personnel and this number may be expected to increase considerably in the decades ahead.

Since research has been closely associated with teaching and, in the United States, has had a close relation to the university, there are important unresolved questions. What should be the relation of the university to the research development in our society? What part of the research effort should be integrated into the university? What shall be the status of the research institute and research personnel in the university? To what extent and in what manner should staff members of research agencies be utilized in the teaching function of the university? Are research services better or less well provided for through private industry, through non-profit corporations, or through public corporations related to institutions of higher education but not under their control, as in the case of the Educational Laboratories provided for in the Elementary and Secondary Education Act?

How can the higher education involvement in research best be related to other purposes of the institutions? The development and operation of universities in the last few decades has been most significantly influenced by the research movement. Many issues related to it are unsolved—in fact many have not even been carefully examined. This is a most important aspect of the planning of higher education in the decades immediately ahead.

What Should be the Relationship Between Higher Education and Service? Institutions of higher education in the United States have long had an important service function. Some of the land grant colleges have had a special commitment to service. In fact one of the most significant contributions of the United States to higher education has been the unique relationship which has existed between the land grant colleges and the development of agriculture and other aspects of the society. The service function has also been accepted and developed by many other universities. At no time has the demand for service by local, state, and the federal governments been greater. Private agencies and industries also seek research and consultant service.

When the necessary and probable development of the resources of most states in the next quarter century is considered, it is evident that the demand for services (other than teaching and development of leadership and technological personnel) will increase sharply. The organization of the institutions of higher education to meet this demand in a way which will strengthen rather than weaken their ability to discharge their primary function (teaching and human resource development) constitutes a major problem. In too many instances the need to organize and provide adequate staff to meet essential service demands has not been recognized. It is a matter which should be faced not by institutions alone but by states and through regional planning. Again the desirable close relation between teaching, research and service needs to be kept clearly in mind in this planning.

How Should Essential Innovations in Higher Education be Facilitated? The large and changing social demands upon higher education suggest the need of directly facing the problem of innovation. Otherwise the forces for the continuation of what has been will dominate. In large and established professions and institutions it is not enough to profess a belief in the desirability of change to meet present and developing needs. Steps must be taken to build a climate which is favorable to change and to support the efforts of those who encourage needed changes.

Certainly efforts along these lines should be closely related to the essential new levels of study and planning to which reference has been made. More than this is involved, however. First, the increasing knowledge regarding how change takes place must be considered. What are the characteristics of a proposed change which augur well or negatively for its adoption and use? What staff situations, changes, and relationships, stimulate adoption of changes? What is the role of those in leadership positions and how can various resources be used most effectively to the end of producing desirable change? What time factors related to change must be considered?

Change may indeed only occur in many situations when specific provision is made for stimulating and encouraging it, for providing assistance in overcoming barriers and strengthening positive forces. A recognition of the need for such a provision is found in the establishment of the Board of Educational Development and the appointment of a Vice-Chancellor for Educational Development at the University of California, Berkeley.[5] Such provisions of course do not guarantee success. However through such efforts much may be learned about obtaining innovations.

While the provision at Berkeley is within an institution, it should be noted that such organizations or instruments are not necessarily confined to a single institution. In fact in smaller institutions an institutional arrangement of this type could almost certainly not be justified or adequately supported. Even in the case of large institutions there may indeed be important

---

[5] University of California, Berkeley, Academic Senate. *Education at Berkeley* (Report of the Select Committee, 1966), pp. 107-120.

advantages (as well as some disadvantages) in having an agency which serves a number of colleges and universities. Such agencies could be developed as an arm of a high level planning and development agency. Whether within or outside the institution of higher education, such an agency may or may not relate in a vital manner to the institution and consequently may or may not be productive of innovation.

RELATIONSHIPS WITH OTHER EDUCATIONAL AGENCIES AND FORCES

This paper was prepared with the primary purpose of focusing attention upon the relations of colleges and universities with other educational institutions and agencies in the decades ahead. The review of issues in the colleges and universities had as its purpose the establishment of a background through which others could gain a better understanding of higher education and upon which proposals for relationships in the future could be formulated. Whether or not the design of education for the future will be well developed will be highly dependent upon the manner in which institutions of higher education discharge their responsibilities. No outstanding design will be developed or executed unless higher education prepares the essential staff, advances many creative approaches, prepares staff for and conducts relevant research, and takes leadership in identifying and attacking central problems confronting the society.

If these eight states are to benefit as they should from the experiences which others have had in many matters—and not have to build as if others had not done so before—it will be because higher education prepares men for creative action and constantly stimulates men and agencies in the attack on the problems. The most probable place in which to find the insights which will make sure that new ghettoes, for example, are not built in the future is in institutions of higher education. Unless these institutions develop men of commitment, concern, and action, who will insist upon the planning which will avoid mistakes, problems will occur. Unless they lead in the development of citizens who will understand and be able to work effectively in a very changed international world, the United States will have lost its opportunity to have a large impact upon that world in relatively few decades. As suggested earlier, therefore, this is the age of opportunity for the university. This opportunity in relation to value development, social sensitivity and needs, and in education is greater than it ever was in the sciences.

If higher educational institutions meet this opportunity, it will be in substantial part because they have had the cooperation and support of other educational forces in developing and carrying programs forward. Those concerned with elementary and secondary education must realize more fully the manner in which they can stimulate and assist higher educational institutions in meeting their responsibility. A few suggestions regarding procedures follow:

(1) A formal organization for coordinating the work of public schools and institutions of higher education should be developed in each state or substantial part thereof. The limitations of formal structures are appreciated. However, structures can be important channels through which

COLLEGE AND UNIVERSITY RELATIONSHIPS

understanding and cooperation can be developed—and at least a minimum structure should be available to identify problems and areas of mutual concern.

In this regard close and responsive relations need to be established with educational laboratories, state departments of education and with local school systems. Through such relationships very large mutual benefits are to be attained. If the educational research and planning needs of the states and local districts are to be met they will need to work closely with the universities. The staff and programs of the universities may benefit no less than the elementary and secondary schools if they are prepared to cooperate while keeping in mind their responsibilities for instruction, research and service—and achieving balance and mutual reinforcement among these goals.

(2) More studies of problems of education should be comprehensive, rather than limited, in the sense that they include elementary, secondary and higher education. Higher education has been studied too largely apart from secondary. If the purposes of education are to be clarified and their achievement estimated, parts of the system cannot be studied without considerable reference to other parts. If values are to be developed through educational institutions, they generally will need to be reflected throughout the years of schooling. The mass media already have, and promise to have, such an impact on education that the formal institutions of education will certainly have less and less influence on values unless they recognize their situation, improve their work and coordinate their efforts in an effective manner.

(3) New institutions need to be created which are not in the tight control of any existing institution. The new educational laboratories are a good illustration of the possibility in this regard. They hopefully will bring the needs and interests of elementary and secondary schools and the resources of universities and colleges together in the study, development and appraisal of educational programs. While coordination of efforts of this type may be needed, it must be recognized that the opportunity for the creation of new agencies is large.

(4) Institutions of higher learning need to involve other agencies in the development of comprehensive instructional programs to a greater extent than has been general. For example, members of professional groups need to be more closely associated with pre- and in-service programs. So also do other groups such as the faculty in basic and related disciplines and community leaders. The possible contributions and limitations of such groups must be recognized.

The pre- and in-service programs for the preparation of school personnel may well be taken as an illustrative case. The professional groups (teachers, administrators) have had too little relation to pre-service preparation programs. The people in the field too frequently believe the college or university is not interested in having them play an important role in such programs. Similarly many faculty members in colleges have had little interest in the preparation of teachers. The bitter but hopefully profitable conflicts over teacher education in the last decade are in substantial part the result of neglect of responsibility, commitment and coordination on the part of various parties involved in developing teacher education programs in accord with changing societal needs. Such programs are not likely to be effective if they are dominated by any one of the parties. The study of needs, the interplay of interested and committed forces, the critical evaluation of programs, and the development of creative new approaches— such steps, reasonably coordinated and supported by adequate resources offer genuine promise.

Developments regarding instructional programs may be varied and considerable in number. As indicated they may pertain to the pre- and in-service development of elementary and secondary school teachers. Staff also will be needed for teaching, counseling and administrative service in junior colleges, colleges and in the universities themselves—areas to which the universities have directed too little attention. Programs for the growing number of other professions and occupations requiring high ability, extended education and special competency will be required if the economic, social and governmental needs are to be met. The demands for personnel in the research area for example will be large. At least equally important will be programs for pre- and in-service preparation of administrative personnel such as school administrators, city managers and planners, state government personnel. In these complex and difficult areas reasonable success will not be achieved by legislatures acting without the assistance of the respective professions or by universities acting alone or guided largely by tradition.

(5) Colleges and universities need to take leadership in attacking highly significant social problems with the cooperation of public schools and other agencies. Institutions of higher learning have mobilized their resources to analyze scientific problems to a far greater extent than to analyze social problems. They will be enriched and have the opportunity to develop especially valuable associations with others by operating as partners in important social ventures. The sophisticated social planning that is essential, for example, is most likely to occur if universities accept responsibility for such activity and devote significant resources to it.

(6) Institutions of higher learning need to develop adequate staff to discharge their various responsibilities so that teaching is not penalized but rather is enriched through research and service projects. The provision and effective functioning of such a staff is dependent upon adequate financing and facilities. It is also related to provisions through which staff may, without penalty, be engaged in non-campus activities for periods of time. More planned rotation of personnel between public and private agencies, organizations and institutions of higher education may also be of value to both parties.

(7) Institutions of higher learning need to create within and among themselves organizations through which the utilization of their resources in projects of public value may be planned and facilitated. Such organizations would make possible the leadership proposed in (5) above. It would

also reduce the waste which occurs too frequently when no arrangement exists to plan the use of resources or to bring important needs and resources together.

(8)   All agencies or groups organized to coordinate various educational units or programs need to be alert to the possibility that coordination can—but should not—become a procedure which stifles rather than enhances individual initiative. Coordination should not seek the development of rigid, monolithic systems, but should stimulate the development of patterns and procedures through which a variety of unique, individual efforts contribute to meaningful progress toward carefully developed broad goals.

These views are not intended to suggest that planning for the future rests only upon the institutions of higher learning. They do suggest, however, that in this age of the university there are large responsibilities which rest upon it. Its teaching cannot be separated from the manner in which its graduates function as citizens. Its professionally trained men and women may be narrow professionals or creative innovators. Beyond the teaching function traditionally associated with higher education is the challenging field of continuing education and the area of research and development so greatly in need of its talents. Finally, the potential of higher education for leadership through the creation of new institutions and new vision should be recognized by the society and various groups in it so that it may be more fully realized. The quality of leadership of state departments of education and of schools and school systems is highly dependent upon use of the university—as is the quality of living in the society.

CHAPTER 10

Educational Research and Development:

The Next Decade

DAVID L. CLARK*

Five years ago, when the author was attempting to deal with the question which is the focus of this paper, the immediate future of educational research seemed to be clouded by the profession's failure to attend to the mechanisms necessary to mount a significant Research and Development (R and D) program. Specifically, it was noted that:

> In education . . . no mechanisms for the conduct and application of research similar to those which are in operation in health and agriculture exist, and few educators are directing their attention to the provision of such mechanisms. When professionals in the field of education discuss research goals, they cite invariably what needs to be known in the field, e.g., unraveling the mysteries of class size or pupil grouping. There is a prior question which is evaded, that is, what needs to be done to establish a research and development program in education which has the potential of adding to what we know about, and how we practice, education.[1]

With the passage of the Elementary and Secondary Education Act of 1965, the nature of the question has changed. An R and D program capable of moving educational research from the periphery of the profession to a central vehicle in the improvement of education has been provided. How the newly established mechanisms will be employed is now the primary determinant of where research in education is likely to go over the next ten to fifteen years.

A QUANTITATIVE PROJECTION

The simplest approach to the task at hand is a straight quantitative manpower projection of what is likely to occur in educational research in the foreseeable future. In a relatively stable field, such a projection would have little utility to the planner since it would merely reiterate conditions already well known to specialists in the area. However, with educational research in a state of revolutionary expansion and change, the implications of this change for the immediate future are not well known even among planners of research training programs. So, for what it is worth, without complicated definitions or assumptions, this paper will begin by painting

* Dean, School of Education, Indiana University; Associate Dean, College of Education, The Ohio State University (1962-65); Director, Cooperative Research Program, U. S. Office of Education (1958-61); Publications include (with Egan G. Guba) An Examination of Potential Change Roles in Education (1965), and Effecting Changes in Institutions of Higher Education (1966).

[1] David L. Clark, "Educational Research: A National Perspective," in Educational Research: New Perspectives, eds. Jack A. Culbertson and Stephen P. Hencley (Danville, Illinois: The Interstate Printers and Publishers, Inc., 1963), p. 8.

a gross, but reasonably accurate, quantitative picture of where we are and where we seem to be going in educational research.[2]

A BASE FOR PROJECTION

To find a stable footing for projection it is necessary to retreat a year or two before federal funds became available in large quantities to support research, development, and dissemination programs in education. The school year 1963-64 represented such a breakpoint and, fortuitously, a survey of educational researchers by Bargar, Guba, and Okorodudu,[3] on which fairly firm estimates can be based, is also available for that year. At that time, approximately 1500-2000 professionals could be classed as "hard-core" researchers; that is, they spent a significant portion of their professional time on Research and Development (R and D) activities of one sort or another. Another group, somewhat larger (about 2000 to 2500) could have been labeled "occasional-researchers;" that is, they would work from time-to-time on an R and D project and would be represented in the literature with a research-type report every five to ten years. The primary focus of their professional life was outside the R and D framework. A much larger group of from 4000-5000 could have been classified as "hangers-on". They maintained some communication with the research community through professional organization affiliation (e.g., American Educational Research Association), or at least through subscription to research-oriented publications, and viewed themselves as consumers of the product of research. They were not producers of research. Many of the members of this group were employed in public school settings and apparently lived in the hope or expectation that research and development should have some connection with a professional life.

Now this is a picture of educational research which most educationists can accommodate handily. It is not essentially different from that described by Griffiths in 1959[4] or Fattu in 1960.[5] The age-old stereotype of quantitative and qualitative deficiency in educational research was, for the most part, applicable. The standard complaint that this research was not substantially affecting educational practice was true. The number of people involved in the enterprise was minuscule—less than ½ of 1 percent of those who would be considered "educationists". The vital point to be established is that educational research, at this point in its historical development, was clearly inhabiting the periphery of the profession. It could literally have ceased functioning overnight without causing a ripple in the educational scene.

---

[2] The estimates and descriptions used in this introductory section are based upon studies being conducted in conjunction with O.E. Project X-022, "Roles for Researchers in Education," and should be considered tentative estimates. The co-investigators on this project are Dr. John E. Hopkins, Indiana University, and the author. The sources of data include a detailed analysis of all Office of Education R and D projects initiated in 1966, interviews with operational and policy level personnel within and outside the Office of Education, and a synthesis and analysis of all recent reports on researchers in education and doctoral students in education. A technical report of final estimates stating the explicit processes used to devise these estimates will be available in the fall of 1967.

[3] Robert Bargar, Egon Guba, and Conahann Okorodudu, *Development of a National Register of Educational Researchers* (Columbus, Ohio: The Ohio State University Research Foundation, December, 1965).

[4] Daniel E. Griffiths, *Research in Educational Administration: An Appraisal and a Plan* (New York: Bureau of Publications, Teachers College, Columbia University, 1959).

[5] Nicholas A. Fattu, "The Role of Research in Education—Present and Future," *Review of Educational Research*, XXX, No. 5 (December, 1960).

This is not to deny that the revolution had its beginning in those years. Fattu noted as early as 1960 that:

> The most important boost for educational research was the establishment of the Cooperative Research Program of the U. S. Office of Education and the various titles within the National Defense Education Act. When the history of educational research is reviewed with the perspective of the future, these federal programs will probably stand out as the significant turning points in educational research.[6]

Fattu, in retrospect, was certainly right and the impact of the programs was felt as early as 1963-64. Fifteen hundred hard-core researchers may not seem like much but this was a quantitative gain for education. The proportion of non-educationists represented in the educational research community was increasing, foreshadowing a broadened concern for educational research by discipline and cognate areas other than psychology. And a few massive development projects had begun to emerge under the sponsorship of the Course Content Improvement Section of the National Science Foundation (NSF), e.g., Physical Science Study Committee (PSSC), School Mathematics Study Group (SMSG), Chemical Materials Project (CHEM), etc.

However, the modest scale of gain is illustrated by the condition, at that time, of research training in education. Only 10 to 15 schools or colleges of education in the country had any planned programs in which an individual desiring to pursue a career in educational research could enroll. Only 1 of 20 Ed.D. or Ph.D. graduates in education entered the "hard-core" research group mentioned earlier. Ten years after receiving the doctorate, nearly 75 percent of the education graduates had published no research and only 12 percent had two or more research publications to their credit.[7] Despite the influx of federal funds to support educational research prior to 1964, Buswell, et al, in their study of 1954 and 1964 doctoral graduates in education concluded that:

> Perhaps the most striking finding was that there was little change in the characteristics of persons who had taken the doctorate in education in 1954 and 1964: most graduate students in education spent only part-time on their studies and took a long period to complete the requirements for the degree; too few had a broad undergraduate background in the liberal arts; and too many were too old when they finished.[8]

There seemed little evidence in the Buswell study that education graduate students in 1964 were any more likely to be actively engaged in educational research during their period of graduate studies than their colleagues from the class of 1954.

The typical hard-core researcher in 1963-64 was involved in (1) investigating an educationally oriented problem of "practical" derivation; (2) operating much as an individual entrepreneur on a small ($25,000 to $30,000) outside-funded project, (3) employing a psychological frame of reference, (4) devoting only a portion of his available time to his research.

---

[6] Ibid, p. 411.
[7] Guy T. Buswell, T. R. McConnell, Ann M. Heiss and Dorothy M. Knoell, Training for Educational Research (Berkeley, California: Center for the Study of Higher Education, 1966), p. 9.
[8] Ibid, p. iii.

TIME OUT FOR DEFINITIONS

This portion of the gross picture was presented prior to attempting any definitions of educational research, researcher, development, and the like because (1) no very useful or generally accepted definitions exist,[9] and (2) this picture itself may be useful in establishing some operational guidelines if not precise definitions.

Included under the term educational research will be activities normally designated as (1) conducting scientific inquiry relevant to education, (2) investigating educationally oriented problems, and (3) gathering operational and planning data. The first of these categories is meant to cover those individuals whose objective is to add to what is known in the social and behavioral sciences. The investigator may or may not see the content of his inquiry as relevant to the field of education but the results of any such inquiry form the knowledge base on which educational research and development is built. Personnel in the second category are attempting to add generalized knowledge to the field of education but the research problem is defined in educational terms; that is, the problem to be investigated is drawn from the operating context of education as a social process. In the third category are included the "social bookkeepers"; those whose purpose is to gather systematic and continuous data on individuals or events in this social process field.

To fill out the "D" of R and D are those who might be classed as developers. These individuals are divided into three categories—(1) the inventors, (2) the engineers, and (3) the product testers. The inventors are characterized by the effort to solve an operating problem within a system or to create a solution for a set of operating problems which would be applicable on an inter-system basis. The engineer is concerned with bringing together accumulated research, knowledge, and inventions into an organized form which can be used in creating an operating program or package, e.g., PSSC. The product tester assesses the efficacy of proposed solutions and programs either on an intra-system or cross-system basis; that is, he is concerned with how the innovation works in a single system or how generalizable it is for all systems.

There is a third "D" often attached to R and D—the process of diffusion (dissemination). Relatively little explicit attention will be directed toward the process of diffusion in this paper, but when it is referred to it will cover those whose task is to make practitioners aware of the existence of an innovation, to demonstrate the use of the innovation in educational systems, and to train practitioners in the use of the innovation.

Now to return to the picture of 1963-64 for illustration in relation to these definitions. The overwhelming percentage of individuals who could be identified with the educational research community at that time would have been covered by the definition of researcher given above (95.6%).[10] They were, for the most part, professors in institutions of higher

---

[9] The author is sorely tempted to dispense with the whole business by quoting Fattu in the First Annual Phi Delta Kappa Symposium on Educational Research that, "educational research appears to be what educational researchers do." (p. 14).

[10] These percentages are based on a re-analysis of the questionnaires returned in the Bargar, Guba, Okorodudu study cited earlier.

education—chiefly in departments of educational psychology or schools of education. Some public school and state education agency researchers were represented in this group but their number was surprisingly small. Using a very liberal definition of researcher there were probably not over 300 full time equivalent (F.T.E.) researchers in all the public school districts in the country.[11]

Developers were nearly non-existent (3.2 percent of the total). Most of this group were involved in the course content improvement projects of NSF. In the educationist community there was little or no activity which could be classed as development.

This latter figure may come as a shock to many dyed-in-the-wool researchers who lament an over-emphasis on what they call development or diffusion. In their consideration of the issue, anyone is thrown into the development category who consults with a school district, works on a school survey, joins the Association for Supervision and Curriculum Development (ASCD), exhorts practitioners to do better, does poor research, or, in some other way, acts differently than the researcher acts. Why research as a label should be reserved for a definable set of activities, while development encompasses any thing and every thing is hard to define. To paraphrase the earlier quotation from Fattu, "educational development appears to have been whatever educational researchers didn't do." Since it will be impossible to talk about educational research over the next decade without encompassing R and D it will be necessary to restrict the definition to inventors, designers, and product testers just as, at an earlier stage, the definition of research was specified—albeit clumsily.

TODAY IN EDUCATIONAL RESEARCH—A PERIOD OF TRANSITION

The Elementary and Secondary Education Act of 1965 was not the first, although it was the most dramatic and far-reaching evidence that the federal government intended to employ research and development in education as a device for improving educational practice. NSF had already had a most successful experience with its course content improvement effort and the United States Office of Education (Office of Education), through projects English and Social Studies, had moved modestly in this "development" direction. By definition, the Research and Development Centers of the Office of Education were obligated to attend to development and diffusion activities. Special subject area programs, for example, Adult and Vocational Education and Handicapped Children and Youth, had already established development components in their research programs.

But these "straws-in-the-wind" were just the beginning, as educationists learned quickly and sometimes painfully after July 1, 1965. The new Elementary and Secondary Education Act (ESEA) projects initiated in fiscal year '66 called for hard-core R and D personnel numbering over 6000.[12] There was a revolutionary change in the type of specialist required.

---

[11] Estimate based on analysis of data presented in Educational Research Service Circular #5, National Education Association, *Research Units in Local School Systems*, (Washington, D. C.: National Education Association, July, 1965), pp. 3-36.

[12] Remember that these personnel estimates are based on the definitions presented in the preceding section. They do not include the tens of thousands of supplementary service personnel required to implement Titles I and III—they are research, development, or diffusion specialists.

The percentage of researchers in the group fell from 95.6 to 49 while the percentage of development personnel climbed from 3.2 to 36, and that of diffusion or dissemination personnel from 1.2 to 15.

Where did they all come from? There was a distinct pattern of movement from the occasional-researcher and hanger-in categories into the hard-core group. Extensive recruitment was carried on outside the educationist community. Stop-gap measures were employed; poorly trained personnel were hastily recruited into leadership and staff positions; and many of the positions simply went begging despite the fact that they were called for in project budgets.

An R and D revolution was upon the field and one fact stands out as more important than all the others—research and development was moving into the mainstream of American education. The ambiguous role of research in education—the peripheral status of the educational researcher—seemed to be a thing of the past. The newly initiated effort involved public schools, state education agencies, inter-agency organizations, community health and welfare programs, as well as the traditional researcher in the college and university setting. A "tight little island" was no more. The educational research community was cracked open into an R and D component of the social process of education in this country. Not surprisingly, many of the initial efforts were low in quality. No field responds with systematic high quality production during a revolution.

This is a new cultural milieu for both educational practitioners and educational researchers in the United States. Neither will enjoy the marriage unqualifiedly for the first few years. Certainly, the marriage could have disastrous results for both sides, if, in the anxiety to bring research into education and education into research, there is not some basic understanding of the activities or functions which comprise the R and D process. It is perfectly true that research, at least of the sort that produces exciting new knowledge, cannot be organized to serve either development projects or practice. The probing of the unknown cannot be programmed or we would know what it is that we do not know. Research forms a basis for development but is not determined by the requirements of development. A cohesive and systematic effort to effect planned change in a social process field includes a mechanism for supporting research (on its own terms) as well as supporting development and diffusion programs.

There is no doubt that such a marriage can be performed successfully because it has already been working effectively in education. Listen for a moment to one of the most eminent educational researchers active today:

Fairly recently when lecturing at the University of London, I must confess to being rather baffled when another colleague of mine eagerly brought me in touch with some representatives of the London County Council. The purpose of bringing us together, I found out, was to convey to the politicians the idea that it might be a good thing to apply educational research techniques in evaluating the comprehensive secondary schools that had been set up in certain districts by the Council and that such evaluations ought to be the responsibility of the Council. I had not until then discovered that selling the idea that educational research could make a significant contribution both in framing educational policy and evaluating its products would in some quarters turn out to be a problem. We had taken it for self-evident that educational research would have to form part of the basis upon which important national policy decisions on educational matters are founded.[18]

TOMORROW IN EDUCATIONAL RESEARCH—A PERIOD OF EXPANSION

Of course, the full impact of ESEA has not yet been felt. The projects and programs which caused the quiet revolution of the past year were, for the most part, planning grants which are awaiting full implementation. Where is this type of activity likely to go over the next decade? That is too far ahead for the present data to be of any utility, but current efforts can illuminate the next five years, and the results are sufficiently dramatic that they provide an insight into the longer range future.

By the end of the school year 1971-72, the present R and D funding programs of the Office of Education alone would require 18,500 researchers, nearly 60,000 developers, and some 50,000 persons working directly on the process of dissemination or diffusion of research results. Translated into full time equivalents this would amount to:

Research Personnel .... 9,250 F.T.E. — 14.4%

Development Personnel ....30,000 F.T.E. — 46.7%

Diffusion Personnel ....25,000 F.T.E. — 38.9%

These figures represent only a projection of current Office of Education programs in terms of anticipated growth and expansion for the next five years. This estimate does not account for funding by private foundations, other governmental agencies or, more significantly, for the almost certain increase in local, state, and regional spending for R and D programs in education stimulated by the national programs.

These personnel demand estimates are so much larger than those which education has dealt with in the past that it may be useful to place them in perspective by contrasting them with projected supply estimates. Prior to ESEA, about 100 hard-core researchers (50 F.T.E.) were produced each year in education. If this level of input continued, some 250 to 500 new researchers would be available by the end of the school year 1971-72. But ESEA does have a training component which has already initiated some 150-200 projects. By 1972 this program, probably subsuming the old supply, will have produced something in the neighborhood of 3,750 F.T.E. researchers. This means that if all the effort of this training program were to be pumped into the production of researchers, the undersupply in five years would be 50 percent and this accounts not at all for the needed development and diffusion personnel.

Another way of dramatizing the extent of the revolution is to break out one program and examine it alone. The Research and Development Centers supported by Office of Education are expected to increase to approximately twenty-five over the next five years. If this is the case, and if their personnel and budgetary histories follow the pattern of growth established by the first four centers, there will be 2500 F.T.E. researchers work-

18 Torsten Husen, "The Contribution of Educational Research to Educational Change: The Case of Sweden (Address to the American Educational Research Association, February, 1965), pp. 1-2.

ing in such settings by 1972—double the total hard-core R and D population F.T.E. of just one year ago.

SUMMARY AND IMPLICATIONS

This has certainly been a uni-dimensional look to the future, employing, as the telescope, quantitative data derived from government support programs. The focus of the look ahead has been cast in terms of personnel supply and demand. In terms of a brief review, it would appear that:

1. A massive mechanism for R and D support in education has been created and is likely to grow and prosper.

2. *The primary effect of this situation is the establishment of research and development as a vehicle to promote change in education*—a movement of research from a position peripheral to the field of education to a position of centrality in the development of the field.

3. An immediate consequence of the change has been to "shakeup" the traditional milieu in which the researcher in education functioned. Expansion and alteration has occurred on several fronts:

a. The discipline base of the research activity is being broadened beyond the educationist and educational psychologist communities.

b. The number and type of people and institutions invovled in the R and D effort is changing. Developers and disseminators are no longer merely "hangers-on"; and the select group of higher education institutions which traditionally conducted the bulk of activity in the field are being joined by other agencies, e.g., school districts, state departments of public instruction, business and industry, inter-agency organizations (Regional Educational Laboratories), as well as by less prestigeful colleges and universities.

c. The nature of the R and D activity is being defined more broadly—in this paper such activities have been labeled invention, design, product testing, and dissemination and have been distinguished from the term research.

4. The startling requirements of rapid expansion are causing severe growing pains which will result in wasted money and time and internecine battles until the community can adjust to its newly acquired state of affluence.

PROBLEMS CONFRONTING EDUCATION IN ESTABLISHING
AN R AND D PROGRAM

In a recent article in the *Phi Delta Kappan,* Lee Cronbach, an influential spokesman for the educational research community, noted with alarm the emphasis of the Office of Education on development and dissemination activity stating:

While I can only praise in the highest terms the new commitment to education and the enthusiasm with which schools are searching for new practices, I am concerned lest the movement may cause the universities, and particularly their schools of education, to neglect their true and unique function. If those whose first calling is the study of education now put off the robe of the scholar and don the armor of the crusader, they will betray the public by leaving the scholar's badly needed work undone.[14]

Cronbach is not alone in expressing this concern; and the basis for his concern has significant historical roots in education. Some of the sharpest criticisms of the quality of research in education have focused on the derivation of problems to be studied in education from "practical" needs and requirements. Fred Kerlinger, recent author of a major text in educational research, struck at this concern sharply six years ago:

> I am not saying that practical research never has value. On the contrary, significant scientific hypotheses and discoveries are sometimes turned up in the course of research oriented toward the solution of practical problems. I am saying that major concern with practical ends impedes the advance of scientific discoveries and growth in education.[15]

Perhaps the most frustrating and irritating aspect of the issue from the viewpoint of the traditional researcher in the field is that this new danger rears its ugly head just when the quality of educational research seemed to be making some headway. Under the influence of funds made available through P.L. 531 (The Cooperative Research Program) serious scholars were beginning to turn their attention to education, and the standards of scholarly acceptability in the field were consistently on the upswing. Even the sharpest critics could see the improvement. Kerlinger, for example, noted that:

> It is evident, to me at least, that research in education is changing and changing for the better. Quite slowly but nonetheless plainly, the emphasis is shifting in some institutions from exclusive concern with practical ends to more preoccupation with fundamental approaches to educational problems.[16]

Most recent commentators on the quality of educational research activity have shared Kerlinger's optimism and the same commentators tend to share Cronbach's concern for the future.

ESTABLISHING DISTINCTION IN R AND D FUNCTIONS

In the first section of this paper, the position was assumed that the future of R and D in education is to a substantial extent predetermined by the programs already set up by the federal government. At least to this observer, that does appear to be the case. Cronbach's plea in the article earlier cited, to retain (if it ever existed) a distinct and particularized role for the university in research with the basic responsibility for development and dissemination resting in non-university settings seems to be an unworkable professional apartheid. But this is not to set aside lightly the concern being expressed by influential professionals in educational research. It is possible that one or more of them are speaking from the vantage point of

[14] Lee J. Cronbach, "The Role of the University in Improving Education," *Phi Delta Kappan*, XLVII, No. 10 (June, 1966), p. 539.

[15] Fred N. Kerlinger, "Practicality and Educational Research," *The School Review*, (Autumn, 1959), p. 290.

[16] *Ibid.*, p. 290.

entrenched interest in the power structure of educational research as it exists, but this surely does not account for the concern of the Cronbachs and Kerlingers who are mature viewers of the educational scene.

They seem to be reacting, instead, to the persistent over-simplification of basic issues by representatives of the Office of Education who, as Cronbach notes, represent, ". . . The colossus astride the educational scene", who issue "a bull-voiced challenge to educators to replace their old routines with revolutionary improvements".[17] In the natural anxiety of the public official to achieve results tomorrow it is not only possible but probable that action-oriented development, demonstration, and dissemination activities will hold the advantage over research in attracting money and attention from the federal government.

This could result in a major setback for the growth, quantitatively and qualitatively, of research and development in education. And is not this exactly what is shown by the reduction in the percentage of researchers in the R and D community from 95.6 percent in 1963 to 14 percent ten years later? Not at all, as an examination of absolute numbers reveals. The actual number of researchers will increase from fewer than 2000 in 1963-64 to more than 18,000 anticipated in 1971-72. As a matter of fact, it redresses the balance of research to development personnel in education to approximately what one finds in other fields, 1:3.

The danger would seem instead to lie in a failure to distinguish among these activities. Cronbach proposed a distinction based on institutional setting. This seems far too rigid, particularly at this early stage in the development of the field; and does seem to reflect a longing for the "good old days." *There is no earthly reason why a professional school in a university setting should not concern itself with improvement in practice* (invention, design, and product testing) directly. There is no law of nature which indicates that this function will eat up or even eat away at the institution's commitment to research. On the other side of the coin, non-university settings will not allow themselves to be cut off in this fashion from research as an activity.

There is even strong reason to insist that *an inter-communication network is vital to the success of R and D activity in education,* and that such a network would be seriously impeded by institutional isolation. But this does not mean that everyone should, could, or will do everything or that there is no distinction between the functions of research, development, and dissemination. As a matter of fact the distinction is critical and research which must be evaluated in terms of development criteria, that is, whether it affects practice, is unlikely to be scientifically productive. There seems to be no reason, however, not to establish and maintain appropriate distinctions without such artificial means as institutional exclusion. The accompanying is one effort to do this which Egon Guba and this author have employed in an earlier paper.

---

[17] *Op. Cit.,* Cronbach, p. 539.

*Schema of Functions Necessary to a Program of Planned Change in an
Institution or Social Process Field*[18]

		Function	*Purpose*
R			
E	1.	Conducting Scientific Inquiry	1. To advance knowledge
S	2.	Investigating Educationally	2. To advance knowledge about
E		Oriented Problems	the social process field
A			of education
R			
C	3.	Gathering Operational and	3. To provide a basis for
H		Planning Data	long range planning
D	4.	*Gathering* Operations and	4. To identify operational
E		Planning *Data*	problems
V	5.	*Inventing Solutions*	5. To solve operational
E		to Operating Problems	problems
L			
O	6.	*Engineering* Packages	6 To operationalize
P		and *Programs* for	solutions
M		Operational Use	
E	7.	*Testing* and Evaluating	7. To assess the effectiveness
N		Packages and *Programs*	and efficiency of the
T			packages and programs
	8.	*Informing* Target Systems	8. To make potential adopters
D		About Packages and	aware of the existence of
I		Programs	packages or programs
F	9.	*Demonstrating* the Effective-	9. To convince the adopter
F		ness of the Packages	of the efficacy of the
U		and Programs	packages or programs
S	10.	*Training* Target Systems in	10. To develop a level of
I		in the Use of the Packages	user competence with
O		and Programs	the packages or programs
N	11.	Servicing and *Nurturing*	11. To complete the institution-
		Installed Innovations	alization of the invention

DETERMINING RATHER THAN PREDICTING THE FUTURE OF EDUCATIONAL RESEARCH

This section is a plea to use what is now known to predetermine the
state of affairs in educational research ten to fifteen years from now. There
will be continuing political pressure applied to the educational research
community to abandon serious scientific investigation in exchange for work
directed to the solution of operating problems. This would be suicidal—
it would, in effect, establish the limit of educational improvement on the
basis of what is already known.

There will be counter pressures from within the educational research
community to ignore the functions of development and dissemination or
to cut off those engaged in these functions from serious intellectual dis-

---

[18] Adapted from David L. Clark and Egon G. Guba, "Effecting Change in Institutions of Higher
Education" (Address to the International Intervisitation Project of the University Council for
Educational Administration, October, 1966), p. 3.

course with "pure researchers". This, too, would be a suicidal move. There are no significant numbers of educational inventors, designers, product testers, or demonstrators available in the current personnel pool. The techniques of research necessary to carry out these functions are poorly developed, e.g., product testing, experimental design, etc. The content of preparation programs for such individuals is ill-defined or nonexistent. For the research community in education to attempt to remain intact without involvement in such messy problems will leave the field open to charlatans and hucksters. Attention will have to be paid to problems inherent in developing "development" in the field of education if there is to be any long range hope of establishing and maintaining useful distinctions in function.

The early history of ESEA does not show appropriate concern for these basic issues. Regional educational laboratories, despite their avowed intent to serve as development agencies, are floundering between overreliance on project type research and pedestrian extensions of current educational practices. The first round of Title III projects provides little in the way of innovation. They are ripe for the criticism of researchers who wish to view them as "boondoggles." The research training program of ESEA has nearly ignored training for any other than conventional researcher roles. This program has not, up to this point, seen its charge as extending significantly into the areas of development and dissemination. Most disturbing of all is the lack of attention which federal agents seem to be manifesting toward the future of educational research. Rich Dershimer has pointed out that:

> The emphasis today clearly is on diffusion and application . . . The new laboratory concept, the service centers being funded under Title III of the new Elementary and Secondary Education Act, and programs emerging from the Division of Elementary and Secondary Education in the Bureau of Research all emphasize the need for involving wide audiences from education in the research process so that results can be put to use in the classroom as quickly as possible.[19]

If he is correct in his assessment of the national educational scene, then there is, indeed, trouble in "River City." The emphasis in the Office of Education must be on nurturing and strengthening individually the several programs which support the various functions of research, development and diffusion.

SUMMARY AND IMPLICATIONS

The decade ahead holds almost equal portions of promise and danger for the establishment of a sound and successful R and D component in education. The promise arises from the support mechanisms now available to channel money into the development of a well-rounded program. The danger lies in the possibility of failing to use these monies for this balanced program of development, that is, in allowing the exigencies of the moment to overwhelm longer range progress in the field.

Educational research has had a tarnished history of low production both in terms of quality and quantity. It has not been complemented by any

---

[19] Richard Dershimer, *Educational Researcher* (AERA Newsletter, February, 1966), pp. 1-2.

significant attention to development or diffusion. The current direction of federal support is sufficiently broad based to accommodate progress on all fronts but a failure to distinguish among the diverse functions requisite to Research, Development and Dissemination could and might foster continued low quality production in research supplemented by equally inadequate development efforts. Inter-communication between the "R" and the "D" practitioners is imperative. Sensitive leadership from the scholarly community, attended to by governmental policy makers, is critical. The initiation of Regional Educational Laboratories blanketing the country and thousands of Title I and III projects is only an initiatory step; it does not spell success, it only indicates educationists can spend money quickly. What the laboratories *do* and what the projects *are* represent the measure of success. If such a measure were applied today the result would be discouraging. This must not be the case 2, 5, or 10 or more years from today.

LIKELY INNOVATIONS IN EDUCATIONAL RESEARCH

Quite apart from any concern for external pressures, which are influencing the field of research in education, there are conceptual, technical, and organizational innovations which are likely to affect educational research profoundly over the next decade. Had it not been for the passage of ESEA in 1965, this brief section on innovations might well have constituted the bulk of the presentation in this paper.

SUBSTANTIVE AND CONCEPTUAL REDIRECTION

The basic redirection of educational research over the next ten years will be best illustrated by the kinds of problems which are investigated. The earlier cited article by Kerlinger illustrated the peculiarly practical orientation which has traditionally afflicted research in this field. Hundreds of raw empirical investigations have been initiated over the past twenty-five years directed toward (a) defending the efficacy of small classes, or (b) simply relating class size to various measures of educational outcomes, or (c) establishing an ideal class size for educational policy makers. With as little understanding of the teaching-learning process as existed at the time of these studies, it would have been a startling scientific revelation had they amounted to anything—and they did not.

This groping and fumbling with a "sense of idea" in educational research will end because:

1.   There will be a revival of interest in the role of theory in the conduct of research and whole new theoretical fields will permeate the educational research community, e.g., information theory.

2.   The process of research will be studied in a broader context than simply design and analysis, that is, methodologists will concern themselves as much with problem identification as they have in the past with the design of experiments.

3.   The "heat will be taken off" the researcher for immediate practical results by the emergence of the inventor, the developer, and the systems engineer.

Theory Development. The notion that the use of theory in educational research will increase scientific payoff is hardly new but it has only been within the past several years that the influence of the idea has begun to permeate training programs and studies. Perhaps the most striking single example of this impact was the publication by the American Educational Research Association in 1963 of the *Handbook of Research in Teaching.* Contrasting this publication with earlier treatments of the same topic in the Association's *Review of Educational Research* even the casual observer cannot help but be impressed with the impact of theory on the field. Research in teacher education has undergone a revolution in which the product has assumed the form of the development of paradigms and systems for classifying and explaining teacher behavior.

Educational research in its purest state is multi-disciplinary. This allows or should allow it to be permeated by concept, theories, and techniques from other discipline areas. That this has not always been the case is testimony to the inadequacy of the field but the situation is changing. Again, a single striking example is afforded by the work of Maccia and Maccia on the construction of educational theory models using theoretical systems from other discipline areas.[20] The introduction of such systems will open avenues of investigation heretofore closed to educational investigators and will begin to create an additive dimension to the work in the field. Educational research will begin to exhibit areas of scientific inquiry which are recognizable as scholarly traditions.

Process of Research. Although marked deficiencies in the technical abilities of research workers in education can be easily substantiated, researchers in this field have been more technically sufficient than conceptually adequate; that is, they have often possessed the analytic tools to tackle problems which they could not comprehend. Abraham Kaplan has labeled this "the law of the instrument," . . . "Give a small boy a hammer, and he will find that everything he encounters needs pounding".[21] To some extent, this naievete can be attributed to substantive deficiences in the area being studied, but, in more cases, it seems to be due to training in research which equates methodology with the methods of research. Kaplan attempts to broaden this concept when he notes, "I mean by methodology the study— the description, the explanation, and the justification—of methods, and not the methods themselves".[22]

A new generation of research methodologists will arise in educational research whose concern is the description of the process of research. The fruits of their labor will be a content for the embryonic researcher which extends beyond consideration of the methods (or better, the techniques) of research. They will focus in on such problems as developing a "sense of idea" by describing and analyzing the full process of research and not simply that aspect of the process which relates to treating and analyzing data.

---

[20] See Elizabeth S. Maccia, George S. Maccia, and Robert E. Jewett, *Construction of Educational Theory Models* (Columbus, Ohio: The Ohio State University Research Foundation, 1963).

[21] Abraham Kaplan, *The Conduct of Inquiry* (San Francisco, California: Chandler Publishing Company, 1964), p. 28.

[22] *Ibid.,* p. 18.

Separation of Functions. The point has already been made that separation of functions may well enhance the position of the educational researcher as a scientist rather than an engineer. The practitioner has every right, indeed a responsibility, to insist that someone attend to the solution of practical problems. In the past, his attention has been directed toward the researcher since no developers of significance existed. In the future this need not be the case. While the researcher proceeds with his work directed toward better understanding the interaction of students and teachers on specified learning tasks, the inventor and engineer can be dealing with organizational adaptations of the formal learning setting, e.g., class size, individualized instruction, homogeneous grouping, team teaching, etc. While the researcher attends to problems of learning theory, the evaluator-developer can mount and carry out field trials of new curricula.

Granting that such specialization seems unlikely in the very immediate future, it is not so far off that it exceeds the limits of this ten-year projection. Until it occurs, the R and D program in education will suffer.

No specific attention has been directed in this section to the enumeration of emerging substantive areas of investigation in the field of education. For the very cogent reasons expressed by Kenneth Boulding in his paper, "Expecting the Unexpected" (in *Prospective Changes in Society by 1980*), one could justify the omission solely on the basis that we do not know what it is that we do not know. There will be topical areas of popularity to researchers as have arisen in the past five years in the study of creativity, teacher behavior, automated instruction, etc. Certain government support programs preordain a flurry of work in vocational education, adult education, higher education, the hardware of instruction, and the like. But such projections are either too gross to be useful or too specific to be defended. The R and D field in education is sufficiently underdeveloped to predict substantial knowledge gains across the board. The specific direction of these gains will and should be determined by early areas of breakthrough. The planner should be less concerned with the substantive area of gain than the maintenance of mechanisms which make such gains possible.

TECHNICAL ADVANCES

What can be said adequately in a few paragraphs to cover the technical advances which open new horizons to the researcher in education? The hardware available to the researcher allows him to tackle problems in minutes which were simply beyond the technical abilities of his predecessors. Statistical and analytic capabilities exist—and will be expanded—which open new problem-solving vistas. Storage and retrieval systems make possible the establishment of massive data banks for R and D purposes. The infusion of research techniques from other areas, e.g., operations research, allow for the development of unheard of specializations in education.

The most recent "methodological" issue of the *Review of Educational Research* (December, 1963) provoked the Editor, William Michael, to comment that, "One dare not think what the status of statistical methodology will be by the year 1972!" In the same issue, Frank Baker noted that in the brief three years preceding this issue, "The holder of the unofficial title of the most powerful computer on a college campus has changed many times during the period under review".[23] Perhaps from the point of view of the planner it suffices to say that technical capacities are advancing at a rate which will allow:

1. Researchers to attack and develop knowledge about problems which were considered unapproachable.

2. Social bookkeepers to collect, retain, and retrieve up-to-the minute data on people and events.

3. Developers to try out innovations in widespread field settings which will result in strong claims of generalizability.

4. Diffusion specialists to feed more new knowledge to more practitioners than has ever before been dreamed of.

Almost literally, technical advances have and will continue to outrun the researchers' ability to employ them effectively.

ORGANIZATIONAL INNOVATIONS

The primary and overriding organizational innovation in educational research and development is the inter-agency organization, best exemplified currently by the regional educational laboratories. Until the early 1960's the educational research community was characterized by a set of self-contained institutional settings which had little inter-communication. Most of the researchers were found in schools of education and departments of psychology working alone or in small teams. Some school districts and most state education agencies maintained research units for the purpose, chiefly, of gathering administrative data. A few private research organizations existed whose concern was predominantly in the field of education.

With the emergence of education as a national concern these compartments are no longer adequate to contain the change mechanism of the field. An observer of this phenomenon, Burton Clark, has noted that:

> At least in education, social forces are greatly increasing the importance of this area that is not bounded by the kind of structures that have usually been designated as organizations. Leadership is moving into the interagency compact, the limited alliance, the consortium, the grants committee, the federation.[24]

Professor Clark's observations were based on programs and activities prior to the ESEA of 1965 which has formalized these interorganizational arrangements with the establishment of the regional educational laboratories.

The significance of such developments cannot be ignored by planners participating in *Designing Education for the Future* which, in itself, represents one of these arrangements in operation. First, the existence of such bodies, parallel to but not a part of the local (and legally constituted) arrangement for education, reaffirms the national interest in education; and, more importantly from the point of view of this paper, affirms that this interest will assume its primary manifestation in terms of R and D activities.

[23] Frank B. Baker, "Use of Computers in Educational Research," *Review of Educational Research*, XXXIII, No. 5 (December, 1963), p. 566.
[24] Burton R. Clark, "Interorganizational Patterns in Education" *Administrative Science Quarterly*, 10, No. 2 (September, 1965), pp. 236-7.

The regional laboratories are not schools—they are, or should be, R and D centers. Creative federalism to the contrary, they will exist to place immediate and direct pressure on local educational agencies to improve their practice. If they fail in this mission they will be superseded by more effective interorganizational patterns to attain the same end.

The recent history of education in this regard has provided a clear blueprint for the future. The inter-agency organization called Physical Science Study Committee (PSSC), or Biological Science Curriculum Study (BSCS) or Earth Science Materials Project (ESMP) has existed parallel to the legally constituted agencies for education in this country, and has mounted effective pressures for change. More curricular innovation has occurred in response to these pressures since 1958 than in the previous fifty years of education in this country. This rate of change is expected to continue and the areas of change are expected to expand.

Educational R and D is coming of age. It is now central to the enterprise of educational practice, and the crude, fledgling regional laboratories are the first evidence of its organizational form. The look of the future in educational research will be composed of large, inter-agency centers housing large R and D operations. To participate effectively in such an R and D world, constituent agencies will have to build and maintain resident R and D staffs of their own similar in form, perhaps, to the R and D centers sponsored for the past few years by the Office of Education.

This latter point should not be left without emphasis. The inter-agency organization cannot be allowed to displace the R and D responsibilities of local agencies unless these agencies are willing to restrict their role to that of a passivet target system. To resist this possible consequence they must themselves manifest an active producing interest in educational research and development. This seems to have been the reason for the inclusion, for example, of Title V in the ESEA. In effect, this title gives the state education agency a chance to compete effectively for an appropriate leadership role in education. It can only do this, however, by meeting the R and D challenge thrust forth by such agencies as the regional laboratories. Leadership in education over the next decade will follow in the footsteps of those who produce new knowledge and devise and diffuse new applications of existing knowledge.

SUMMARY AND IMPLICATIONS

The next decade will surely see a new level of substantive and technical sophistication in educational research. The former will emphasize a more theoretical approach to the study of educational problems and a more adequate development of a "sense of idea" in problem identification. Research preparation will conceive a methodology as encompassing the whole process of research rather than being limited to a narrower range of techniques and tools.

The technical advances will be rapid and startling; influencing, but not limiting, what researchers can achieve. Limitations are more likely to arise from deficiencies in conceptual "software" to support technical advances in hardware.

The new organizational image of educational research will emphasize the inter-agency organization. Centers of research and development will emerge on a scale beyond anything presently in existence. And these centers will be in a position to influence and affect educational practice directly through constituent agencies and indirectly through the pressures of their quality production. To meet this challenge, local school districts, state education agencies, and colleges and universities will respond in kind with R and D components of increased size and potency.

EXEMPLARS OF THE NEW WORLD OF EDUCATIONAL R AND D

Another way to view the future of educational research is to predict the image of certain agencies in the field as they may look tomorrow. Briefly, with certain features highlighted for emphasis, four settings have been chosen for this purpose.

LOCAL SCHOOL DISTRICTS

Research and development will begin to assume the characteristics of operations research or quality control research in these settings. The object of the game will be to assess the processes and operations of the organization with sufficient precision that assessment can be made of the introduction of innovations into these operating systems. Objectives will be operationally defined, processes to attain the objective identified, and product measures constructed to fit local needs. This pattern of quality control research will become a part of the administrative process in even the smaller—but not the inadequate—districts as they strive to retain identity in the new world of educational change.

Larger districts will establish development and dissemination divisions for the purpose of local invention and engineering and to adapt more general programs to local needs. These districts will become critical field agencies for state education departments and regional laboratories in the field tryout of packaged programs. *The impact of these units on classroom teachers* (many of whom will be active participants in the processes of engineering and invention) *will be startling.* For the first time in the history of education someone will be working on and turning up with solutions to their problems. Exhortation will be replaced with help.

Needless to say, the local district will have an automated storage and retrieval system for its own use in solving educational problems and in educational planning. This system will also serve as the vital local link in a state and national system of educational information that can produce data on the operation of all schools nearly instantaneously.

STATE EDUCATION AGENCIES

The R and D program of state education agencies will probably emphasize (1) gathering administrative and planning data, (2) field testing innovations, (3) demonstrating and disseminating. Surely the state education agency will serve as a vital communications link between the federal government, regional laboratories, and the local district. It is likely that the

Office of Education will decentralize the administration of much of what is now included in Titles I and III so that the state agency, working directly with local districts, will administer completely the bulk of these monies.

Many state education agencies have already assumed leadership in establishing a national system of educational statistics. This trend will certainly continue and such agencies will represent storage and retrieval centers of major significance in educational planning.

Most state departments will set aside state monies to be used for innovation and will establish statewide, decentralized programs for the diffusion of educational inventions. These state hookups will tie in with all the regional educational laboratories in the country. They will be able to bring news of innovations to all teachers in the state through educational television and will be able to mount intra-state regional demonstrations at short notice. Key districts spotted throughout the state will serve as local dissemination and demonstration centers.

COLLEGES AND UNIVERSITIES

The traditional role of the college and university as the producer of new knowledge will be substantially enhanced. Fully functioning R and D centers will grow from the present ten to nearly fifty. A much larger segment of the professional staff in schools of education will be productive researchers and developers. University-wide involvement in educational R and D will be commonplace.

The role of development on the university campus will be reconceptualized and redirected toward invention and engineering rather than what is now termed field service. Through participation in regional educational laboratories, university personnel will accept the function of effecting change in schools as a responsibility correlative to research and teaching.

The graduate programs in these institutions will reflect the institution's changed character distinctly. A large proportion of the graduate enrollees in doctoral programs will be preparing themselves for productive research careers in education. Fifth and sixth year programs will concentrate on providing practitioners with sufficient background to participate in, and provide leadership to, programs of educational R and D.

The instructional program for teacher education students will be built upon a knowledge base sufficiently firm that the age-old question of the existence of content in teacher education will seem ridiculous.

REGIONAL EDUCATIONAL LABORATORIES

Some twenty to twenty-five agencies of this sort will be in operation within five years supported by local, state, and federal monies to the tune of 50-100 million dollars per year. The Regional Educational Laboratory will be a center for educational development with a smaller, but nonetheless significant, commitment to research. Invention and engineering teams will be at work constantly searching for solutions to educational problems. The staff of the laboratory will be flexible, using the talents of constituent agencies as they fit particular problem areas.

The laboratory will serve as a catalyst to educational change but will be more than this since its program emphases will determine the nature of the changes. Each lab will have sufficient resources to mount and carry out PSSC-type curricular projects alone, but will be more likely to concentrate on the development of better integrated instructional systems for its constituents.

SUMMARY AND IMPLICATIONS

The intent of this particular "flight of fancy" was simply to emphasize the integral role which R and D will play in education in the future. In a sense, *the educational research community will be the educational community,* and *the route to educational progress will self-evidently be research and development.*

CHAPTER 11

Leadership and Control of Education

LUVERN L. CUNNINGHAM*

The American school system has served the nation well for nearly two hundred years. The key to its genius has been the marvelous way that the public will has been served through a blending of insights from laymen and those who occupy professional and semi-professional positions in the schools.

For most of its history the nation's school system has been remarkably open and capable of responding to changing demands for education. The looseness of its formal governing structure has been its greatest strength during the country's expansionist period and the time when essentially local needs were primary. The reliance upon the states for developing and supporting their own systems of schools has proven to be an effective means for serving general requirements for diversity in approach to the solution of educational problems. The further decentralization of school government through several thousand local school systems or districts (at one time there were more than 125,000) has been an equally significant structural device for bringing the schools to the people. The national interest has been safeguarded by a series of federal interventions or expressions of interest in education sufficient to ensure the maintenance of national purposes when the recognition of need in the separate states failed to incorporate the larger needs of the country as a whole.

The total system, composed as it is of local, state, and national components, has demonstrated considerable capability for keeping pace with emerging educational demands. Currently, however, there are serious stresses within the system which cast some doubt on its continued capacity, as now organized, to cope with the important new expectations being defined for our schools.

This chapter is an assessment of the status of the national system of schools, its contemporary and anticipated internal stresses, and some conjectures about potential shifts in the control of American schools. Attention is directed also, to the lay and professional leadership requirements that will prevail in the years ahead.

* *Professor of Educational Administration and Director, Midwest Administration Center, Department of Education, University of Chicago;* Professor of Educational Administration, University of Minnesota (1962-64); Co-author of *The Organization and Control of American Schools;* Member of the Board of Trustees of the University Council for Educational Administration; Author of many publications in the areas of school government, urban educational problems, simulation in the training of administrators, and change in education.

THE PRESENT STRUCTURE OF EDUCATION

One federal government, the fifty states, a large number of inter-mediate structures including counties, and more than twenty thousand local school districts make up the formal structure of school government.[1] Thousands of laymen are involved in establishing educational policy through those governments; they serve as board members, legislators, con-gressmen, jurists and citizen committee representatives. Other thousands of persons serve the schools as employees, ranging in their services from teaching, administering and counseling to driving buses and operating cafeterias.

Local school districts range in size from New York City, which enrolls more than a million pupils, to the non-operating districts of the Midwest which have school boards but enroll no pupils. Within this size continuum there are numerous patterns of internal organization, each designed initially at least, to achieve particular, locally defined objectives. Some local dis-tricts are limited to serving only elementary school pupils; others provide programs from the pre-school years through four-year colleges.

The school boards of the nation exhibit equal range in their variation. Some school districts have only three board members. Many have five- or seven-member boards. Chicago on the other hand has eleven. Milwaukee fifteen, and New York City nine members.

School board members are elected to their positions in most districts, although about ten percent are appointed through several appointment procedures. Some school districts are dependent upon other local units of government for financial support, but most school districts enjoy consider-able autonomy and freedom from formal impingements from other types or levels of government in regard to finance matters as well as other policy issues. The operation of schools goes forward within an extraordinarily varied set of local governmental forms and procedures for lay and profes-sional involvements.

The intermediate forms of school government also evidence extensive variation. The intermediate services units are growing in importance in such states as Wisconsin, New York, and California, where new functions, clearly based on the identification of needs that extend beyond the capabil-ity of the local school districts for satisfaction are being defined for them. They are decreasing in importance in states such as Iowa and Nebraska where the county has been the intermediate unit.

The fifty states, although possessing some structural features that are common, are different in significant ways. Hawaii has chosen to govern its educational affairs centrally—there is but one school district and that is the state. Nebraska, at the other extreme, continues to have about three thousand local districts, each with its board of education. State educational government in Alaska assumes over-all management of the learning affairs of 53,000 pupils; New York on the other hand is responsible for nearly three and one-half million youngsters. Forty-eight of the states have some

---

[1] For a detailed description of contemporary school governmental structure see Roald F. Camp-bell, Luvern L. Cunningham and Roderick F. McPhee, *The Organization and Control of Ameri-can Schools*, (Columbus: Charles E. Merrill Books, Inc., 1965).

type of state board of education responsible in varying degrees for establishing policies vis-a-vis the elementary and secondary schools of the states. The Board of Regents of the State of New York is an exceedingly powerful public policy group; the State Board of Education in Minnesota, on the other hand, is much less influential and is relatively unknown as far as the average Minnesotan is concerned.

The federal government has reserved its participation to those educational problems which are national in scope and which may have been overlooked or neglected by the states in their separate pursuits of educational needs. The history of federal interest extends to the very beginnings of the nation and actually antedates the adoption of the Constitution. Federal interventions into education have been supported as essential to the general welfare since the Constitution is specific in its delegation of basic responsibility for education to the several states.

This system of governments, loosely woven in some instances, tightly bound in others, has responded to an extraordinarily difficult set of confrontations. It has successfully developed a system of mass education designed to provide free common schooling for every youngster in the nation. It has made available public-supported, post-high school institutions on a scale unapproached by any other nation in the world. It has been flexible enough to particularize educational offerings for the rural child, the vocationally oriented youngster, and the foreign born who have utilized the common school as the vehicle for social and economic entry into the American way of life. It has been an enterprise that has elevated and sustained human values; ways have been found to support educational programs for thousands of boys and girls with unique and special learning problems. In brief, it has probably been the most salient feature in the nation's development—feeding in talent capable of carrying the burdens of a self-starting, self-perpetuating social and economic order.

The control of American education historically has been diffuse. It has never for long rested with singular sets of interests. National interests have been served prominently from time to time; the states have responded differentially to their own needs but by and large effectively enough to carry the welfare of the states; the local units—prosperous in ideas and wealth in some cases, impoverished in others—have stood the test of time and continue to be useful vehicles for the expression of local public interests. Our system of educational government has by and large justified the faith of its sponsors.

STRESSES IN THE SYSTEM

Having acknowledged the exciting history of American education, and described briefly the structure within which educational progress has been achieved, it is imperative that several current tensions be noted within this time-honored framework of government. The fact that stresses and strains exist is to some extent an outgrowth of imperfections in the formal structures of government. To a larger extent these stresses are due to weaknesses in organization and the inability of educational leadership, both professionally and lay, to anticipate adequately the demands being made and about to be made upon the educational enterprise as a whole. These strains do not exist independently of one another; they in essence co-exist within the fabric of the society and the framework of the school and tend to feed upon one another.

TEACHERS SEARCH FOR POWER

Teachers are currently seeking improved opportunities for participation in the solution of American educational policy problems. Spurred on by such intellectuals as Myron Lieberman, teachers through associations and unions have launched into dramatic new attempts to control events which have substantial meaning for their own occupational lives.[2] The emergence of power is most apparent in collective actions in which teachers are placing demands on boards of education for improved salary and fringe benefits. These demands are spilling over rapidly, however, into other areas for policy action.

Teachers, either as individuals or as members of organizations, have been participating in or influencing policy matters extensively throughout the development of American schools. Associations and unions have taken stands on policy questions at local, state, and national levels for some time and in many cases teachers have possessed large scale influence, especially in the legislatures of the states. In Illinois, for example, the Director of Research for the Illinois Education Association has been an extraordinarily powerful influence on the Illinois School Problems Commission because he has become the most important single source of data about Illinois schools. Similarly, the Research Division of the National Education Association has been an important information source to the Congress. It is possible to document the influence of teachers on policy action, from participation on building level committees through the legislative lobbying activities of the American Federation of Teachers (A. F. of T.) and the National Education Association (NEA).

The current thrust for power on the part of the teaching profession is of a different order; the drive for negotiation privileges surpasses anything known in the past. Its origins are based on large scale frustration stemming from a feeling that teachers, as an important occupational group within society, have not been adequately recognized in terms of salaries and fringe benefits. The present mood of teachers is affected too by the bitter competition that developed between the NEA and A. F. of T., especially during the past decade. Another prominent factor is a growing tension between the teaching group and the administrative corps in education, apparently based partly on the inability of many administrators to involve teachers sufficiently in important decisions. Still another influence is the general press, within the public employment sector at large, leading toward organization of many types of public employees for collective bargaining purposes.

These and other factors contribute to the present unrest within the education community. There is sustained jockeying for power positions

---

[2] A prominent stimulus to aggressiveness on the part of teachers was the publication of Myron Lieberman, *The Future of Public Education*, (Chicago: The University of Chicago Press, 1960).

and many persons are experiencing for the first time participation in power struggles and power realignments. School districts that have experienced strikes, sanctions, boycotts, or other demonstrations of organized power on the part of teachers are somehow changed as a consequence of such exercises of force. The lives of teachers, administrators, and school board members who have taken part will never be quite the same again. As yet there is little evidence to suggest that such power plays are disfunctional or lead to undesirable outcomes; nor is it known that education will be strengthened as a consequence.

Teachers, through collective action, are seeking more and more opportunities to take part in significant decisions related to the basic interests of the educational enterprise. Their influence will be most far-reaching when such participation involves allocations relating to decisions. Teachers will be able to affect more directly the learning lives of students when they are a part of an allocation-decision team. The allocation of funds is one of these, human resources is another, and time is still another. Involvement in resource allocation includes the determination of the amount of available resources that go into teachers' salaries, fringe benefits, instructional materials, transportation, capital improvements and the like. Decisions related to the distribution of human resources have to do with class size, teacher-pupil ratio, the types of professionals to be involved in the learning process, and organizational decisions such as self-contained classroom or team teaching arrangements. The allocation of time, which in the long run may be as educationally significant as the two just cited, has to do with the length of the school year, day, and particular learning periods within the school day, the school week, or the school year. Previously these three areas for policy action have been largely within the purview of administrators and school board members. Sharing of these decisions may be viewed as a threat to the professional prerogatives of administrators and/or of laymen serving on policy-making bodies. It is predictable that these two groups will resist sharply invasions of some policy domains by any external group. Thus the extension to teachers of genuine participatory opportunities where they have not been involved will call for rather substantial accommodations on the part of many administrators and school board members. It represents a shift away from public authority over education toward professionally centered council.

CITIZEN UNREST

Most Americans, throughout the history of our educational system, have evidenced great confidence in their schools. Local communities have developed considerable pride in them and their performances. The school has become our most pervasive social institution; the one which has touched more lives than any other. Rich traditions have evolved and strong bonds have been formed between local societies and local educational systems. Similarly respect for education has been exhibited at state and national levels by legislative groups and our system of courts.

The faith that the public has generally held in the schools seems to be less strong at this point in the century than in the past. Whereas there has been a continuing recognition of the relationship between education and individual entry, acceptance and progress within the general society, the present conception of the need for education and "making it" in contemporary American life is much more advanced. The pressures of parents on their children to succeed in an academic sense are more severe than ever before. Similarly, the expectations for excellence in school systems themselves are more apparent than at any previous time. The schools must satisfy national purposes such as feeding young people into higher education, perfecting human capital to satisfy the demands of a business and industrial based economy, producing sufficient numbers of young men trained to meet the minimum aptitude expectations of the armed forces in order to satisfy the manpower demands, and refining persons sufficiently in the skills of democratic behavior so that they can assume citizenship responsibilities in adult life.

During and immediately following World War II, new and advanced concerns began to be registered about our schools. These were visible at all levels of educational government. Dissatisfactions with the quality of American schools, particularly in science and mathematics, were sharply in evidence in the Congressional hearings surrounding the establishment of the National Science Foundation. It is clear that the nation's leadership in science—the national science establishment—was unwilling to see generous federal funds poured into the nation's school system through existing structures of government. The U. S. Office of Education was seen as the handmaiden of the educationist; it was assumed that any allocation of resources through the established leadership structure within public education would accomplish little.

The persuasiveness of such arguments led ultimately to the creation of the National Science Foundation, a new structure designed to intervene into American education in ways which its architects believed would lead to qualitative changes in schools, especially in the disciplines of science and mathematics. The arguments advanced in support of the National Science Foundation received further recognition in 1958 when the federal government passed the National Defense Education Act. It is well known that this legislation was stimulated by scientific and technological advances within the Soviet Union. Further federal intervention into local school systems was defended on the grounds that our national competitive position dictated rapid and strategic expenditure of public funds to bolster the sagging public schools.

Educationists and noneducationists alike would agree in most cases that the curriculum changes developed through National Science Foundation sponsorship and the extensive in-service education programs developed for teachers as well as the provisions of the National Defense Education Act, have led to substantial improvements in our schools.

There have been many other examples of citizen dissatisfaction, registered on a large scale, with school systems. Attacks upon schools have issued from individuals and small ad hoc groups, as well as by highly organized associations and organizations national in scope and intent upon affecting school systems locally, regionally, and nationally.[3] The results of such attempts to modify educational policy, improve schools, or satisfy narrow and rather parochial interests, have been as varied as the pressures for change themselves. In some cases school superintendents have been fired, additions or deletions have been made to the curriculum, schools have been integrated and/or segregated, membership on boards of education has been changed, prayers have been abandoned, athletics have been emphasized or de-emphasized as the case may be, and principals have been removed or transferred.

The sustained press from the outside upon the schools has led to, in many instances, defensive behaviors on the part of teachers, administrators, and school board members. *There has been a gradual tightening of the boundaries of school organization, and the creation,* (probably unknown to school officials) *of an isolation of the school system itself from the constituency it was designed to serve.* The sensitivity of school officials in many places has reached the point where innocent requests for information are interpreted as real or imagined attacks upon schools. Many school personnel are extraordinarily cautious and communicate a hostility to the publics which they are professionally committed to serve. A separation of school systems from their constituencies has become rather advanced in many parts of the country, and particularly so in medium sized and larger cities.

Citizens—well intentioned for the most part—seem to be becoming increasingly restless and are seeking proper ways of intervening in the affairs of schools in the hope that the over-all quality of the schools can be strengthened. Citizen-initiated and sponsored school surveys have become increasingly popular in the past decade. Most large cities and several states have had them; major studies, with citizen involvement, are presently under way in many places. The PACE group in Cleveland, the We Milwaukeans education committee in Milwaukee, the HELP organization in Louisville, and the Citizens School Committee in Chicago are examples of short term and long term associations of individuals created to support the schools. The relationships between such organized groups and school systems are often strained. Lay citizens and school officials frequently have separated themselves into two camps and communications between them is often difficult. External observers of such situations often wonder at the fragileness of human association where two collectivities of well-educated and positively motivated individuals can co-exist and evidence ineptness in their relationships.

The present performance of the school systems of the nation apparently is not passing muster. The mobilization of persons seeking access to points of decision is indicative of large scale dissatisfaction. The protectionist behaviors of school officials is evidence likewise of uncertainties about the performance of the institutions for which they have assumed responsibility. As social problems apart from the schools tend to intensify, pressures on the schools will increase rather than decrease. It is imperative

---

[3] Comprehensive documentation for the effectiveness of external forces on the schools appears in Roald F. Campbell and Robert A. Bunnell, *Nationalizing Influences on Secondary Education,* (Chicago: The Midwest Administration Center, University of Chicago, 1963).

therefore that thoughtful leaders in America give time to the examination of the relationships between institutional sectors in the society and the influence of those interactions upon social affairs.

STUDENT UNREST

The general uneasiness manifest by the adult population vis-a-vis the schools is having its effect on the attitude and posture of the schools' student populations throughout the country. The most visible indicator of large scale client dissatisfaction has been registered at the higher education level.[4] There are, however, clear-cut signs that elementary, junior high and secondary school students are going to be heard as well. It can be expected that student demonstrations, strikes, boycotts, and other methods of protest will increase in the years to come. It is quite predictable since there is such intensive reinforcement for such behavior throughout the broader culture.

Many of today's students are not very sanguine about the contribution that education can make to their future. They are realists and acknowledge openly the intensified competition that exists for places in graduate schools. They think they know what it takes to "make it" in the business, professional, and occupational worlds. Present-day students have developed almost frightening sensitivities to the requirements for success in our bureaucratized world. They are increasingly sophisticated politically and are capable of attempting to usurp power if they are so motivated. The college administrator who has experienced the student protest capability of his student body is intensely aware of the new vitality of today's student movements. And in those places where secondary school demonstrations, sit-in strikes or boycotts have occurred, school administrators and board members can testify to this emergent demand to be heard.

The mobilization of student power will become more advanced. It will become a new feature in the policy life of American schools. Students apparently have a developing feeling of "being acted upon" rather than "acted with," and as they become more sophisticated in their uses of power, school officials will have to become equally expert in incorporating such new power appropriately into the decision processes of the school organization.[5]

Much of the student unrest is addressed to the need for participation in decisions which affect the educational lives of students directly. There is a companion unrest which has profound effects upon the school, but which exists apart from the school itself, essentially in the inner-city environment. The slum areas have been the spawning grounds for gangs for decades. Gangs are highly disciplined forms of organization which are functional in the sense that they bring some type of order and stability to the lives of young people. School officials in some inner-city schools have become somewhat adept at using the gang structures to support the disciplinary systems of the schools themselves.

[4] See Joseph Katz and Nevitt Sanford, "The New Student Power and Needed Educational Reforms," *Phi Delta Kappan*. XLVII, (April 1966) 397-401; also Martin Myerson, "The Ethos of the American College Student: Beyond the Protests," *Daedalus*, (Summer 1966) 713-39.

[5] A more comprehensive development of this point appears in Luvern L. Cunningham, "The Enviroment of Today's School Organization: Implications for Educational Leaders," *Proceedings Northwest Conference on Educational Leadership*, Seattle, Washington, July, 1966, (forthcoming).

Probably as a side effect to general unrest—racially based and otherwise—the gangs have become more visible within their own neighborhoods. Considerable publicity has been focused upon them in cities like Chicago, and this seems to have stimulated internal struggles for power within and among the gangs themselves. Whereas the arsenals of gangs a few years ago included zip guns, bicycle chains, knives and the like, many now possess expensive firearms and some even bring these into the schools.

Gang activities are spilling over more obviously into the affairs of the schools. Extortion within the school age population has run rampant through a few Chicago neighborhoods; older youngsters, sometimes armed, have been taking lunch and milk money from younger, unprotected children. Gang members have likewise posed as threats to teachers coming and going from the schools, thus requiring added police personnel to insure the safety of adults working in those neighborhoods. The gangs appear to be increasingly influenced by older leaders, hard core gang types, that, according to Chicago police officials, are solidifying the gangs into small, intense groupings who plan to stay together through their adult lives.[6]

Student unrest of the type just described does not mark a large percentage of the nation's schools, even of the inner-city schools. But it is present to some degree in most schools and symptomatic of latent features in the pre-adult society that could become manifest and much more widespread. Such behavior promises to effect the day-to-day operation of the schools in the immediate future more than it has in the past. And the presence of such disquiet intervenes in such subtle ways that it presents a difficult-to-define but nevertheless discernible constraint upon the schools.

STRESSES IN SOCIETY

Of the many current stresses in society, two that have direct implications for education will be discussed briefly.

SCIENCE, TECHNOLOGY AND THE SCHOOLS

There appears to have been an historical reciprocity between scientific advance and educational improvement. New technology is most apparent in the physical surrounding in which modern learning often goes forward. (See, for example, chapters 10, 13 and 16 in *Prospective Changes in Society by 1980*). Today's classrooms may possess several expensive and complex inventions designed to extend the effectiveness of teaching. Many of today's laboratories incorporate features equal to those found in the work stations of research scientists. Driver training classrooms utilize simulator devices much like those employed in the training of military and astro personnel. Libraries in a few schools are experimenting with information storage and retrieval systems patterned after similar developments in institutions of higher education. The thermal environment of the school itself has been the subject of research; some schools have year-round climate control capabilities that are equal to those found anywhere. And new concepts of space utilization are flowing in to the physical surroundings of modern education at an

---

[6] "Teen Gang Terrorism Triggers School Exodus," *Chicago American*. September 22, 1966.

increasing rate. Such developments represent one relationship between technology and education.

Another manifestation of this interaction is to be found in the improved preparation of American teachers. Obviously the number of top flight programs of teacher preparation is still limited. Nevertheless there have been some strong new components incorporated into teacher preparation design. For example. embryo teachers are getting new kinds of exposures to the range of problems they will encounter as practitioners through simulated teaching experiences. The richness of this exposure and its clinical nature represent advancements which in the judgment of their inventors bode well for teaching in the future. Ironical as it seems, technologies similar to those available to practicing elementary and secondary classroom teachers are now being employed in the preparation of teachers themselves. The National Science Foundation programs have become models for packaging short term intensive pre-service and in-service training. These institute-like efforts are addressed to strengthening the subject field capabilities of teachers. Since such programs have become generally available in the areas of science and mathematics they have provided the vehicle for feeding new science concepts into the classroom teaching of thousands of American teachers.

The schools themselves have contributed to scientific advance through their product. Few would deny that American secondary schools have produced much larger numbers of better prepared young men and women in the past decade. These able young persons have gone on to distinguish themselves in higher education and have contributed to scientific and technological advance themselves. There is a feedback relationship and upward spiraling effect in the interactions between scientific and technological progress, improved performance within the schools and new inputs into the nation's science capability. There is little historical documentation for this observation but practicing school personnel are aware of the phenomenon.

We appear now, however, to be reaching a point where our knowledge-creating capacity is improving at such a rate that it is no longer dependent totally on new inputs of resources from our public and private school systems. The perfection of artificial intelligence through computers and storage and retrieval systems, for example, has so successfully extended our knowledge-generating ability that a smaller number of minds are able to push our progress further than was possible in the immediate past. We may even be approaching some liberation of the scientific community's dependence upon the feeder service of the nation's educational system. It may become possible in the future—although of questionable desirability—for the schools of the nation to select an elite group of students, funnel them through accelerated or highly particularized educational experiences and permit them to carry the knowledge-producing responsibility for our society.

Such a conception obviously violates our traditional views about the function of education in a free nation. We have been opposed philosophically to elitism in any form, despite the fact that our schools have quietly incorporated some components of elitism into their performance. We have viewed the schools as the means for sustaining social balance, social responsibility and the vehicle for improving the life chances of all persons. We have prevailed against those themes which appeared to be leading us toward control in American education through narrow interests.

There appears to be genuine danger that the liberating potential inherent in knowledge advance may contain within itself the seeds of substantial constraint and encroachment upon the broader community. Should this observation be viable at all, its implications for curriculum and the in-school experience for large numbers of youngsters are difficult to comprehend. The Huxley-like developments which surround us call for penetrating and thoughtful analysis. Not only does artificial intelligence imply that the cognitive requirements for many people may be altered, but that the side effects of these advances are increasingly subject to scientific control themselves. Huxley's *soma* is remarkably close to our hallucinogens. Both have euphoria-inducing capacities.

Institutionalized escapism may be imperative if the social order of the future continues to be subject to pathologies such as those so visible currently. The society of the future may be forced to introduce mechanisms for utilizing living time in nonfriction-producing settings. Again such proposals, even such thinking, strike at such an extensive array of values that it is difficult to conceive thoughtful Americans contemplating such eventualities. Nevertheless, LSD is here, memory pills are apparently in advanced stages of development, and computer-assisted intelligence is a resource with few known limitations.

URBAN BREAKDOWN

More contemporary and less speculative are the observations to be made about urban breakdown. For present purposes, we will limit our commentary to questions of government, and more particularly those of educational government. We witness daily the struggle, for survival it seems, in our urban centers. The abrasiveness of life is increasing and our social actionists appear incapable of developing strategems which will lead to tension reduction.

The relationship between how we govern ourselves for educational purposes and social malaise are not at all clear. The standard metropolitan areas of the nation represent an interesting range of governmental patterns for educational purposes. Given the variation in formal structures, there are some common problems which mark most metropolitan governments: the large scale inequities in financial support of education that one finds within megalopolitan complexes;[7] many governmental structures perpetuate and encourage extremes; central cities offer limited political access for large numbers of people, whereas suburban fringes in most cases offer extensive opportunities for involvement in educational politics; the reciprocity between the core city and its fringes has been undervalued and not well known; structure itself produces dysfunction, particularly in the manage-

---

[7] Arthur E. Wise, "Is Denial of Equal Educational Opportunity Constitutional?" *Administrator's Notebook.* XIII, (February 1965).

ment of such problems as racial integration; and the inability to activate lay leadership in the interests of schools vis-a-vis metropolitan educational requirements.

The present structure of educational government mitigates against metropolitan planning and perpetuates the partial address of scarce resources to educational problems. This circumstance is wasteful and ineffective. Thoughtful concern needs to be registered in regard to governing urban education. There is serious doubt as to the capability of many states to assume much responsibility for urban centers. And since metropolitan developments do not honor state boundaries we may need to develop some interstate governments for education similar to those of port authorities and other interstate interests. In fact, we may need to experiment with several models of metropolitan educational governments in the hope that we can perfect a type that permits us to maximize multiple public values.

EMERGING STRUCTURAL FEATURES IN EDUCATIONAL GOVERNMENT

Problems such as those just described are producing changes in educational leadership and control, some overt and some covert. The actions of existing governments are testimony to the recognition of such problems as is the emergence of entirely new governments and quasi governments for education.

FEDERAL INTERVENTIONS

When national educational needs have been identified, and the ability of the several states to meet them has been in doubt, our national government has intervened to achieve some satisfaction of such needs. The most recent of these interventions has been directed at improving educational opportunities for disadvantaged and poverty stricken youth. The most prominent legislation has been the Elementary and Secondary Education Act of 1965. The five Titles of this law have influenced public school systems and their governing structures more dramatically than any single previous federal action.[8]

Title I, designed to improve the educational chances of disadvantaged youngsters, has made available generous funds for the achievement of that purpose. In excess of 22,000 projects were approved and funded through this legislation by mid-1966. The administration of this Title has strained the administrative capabilities of all levels of school government. Tense relationships have developed between and among units of government. In a few cases the stresses have bordered on breakdown. The large city school systems that had developed habits of working directly with federal agencies of government have had to channel Title I programs through the state. These changes have been painful, especially for large city school systems. State governments on the other hand have seen Title I, as well as other Titles, as providing opportunities to reestablish their "appropriate" position within the states. Thus Title I is leading to reallocations of power and control within the several states and among the levels of government.

---

[8] An appraisal of current federal educational activity is available in William W. Wayson, "The Political Revolution in Education, 1965," *Phi Delta Kappan,* XLVII, (March 1966), 333-39.

The important control feature within *Title II* has been the new juxtaposition of nonpublic schools vis-a-vis public schools in the distribution of public resources. Nonpublic schools have available to them limited, but at the same time, new public funds. The vitality of the longtime resistance of public school people to the allocation of public monies to nonpublic units seems to have been reduced. Public school leaders seem to have been so preoccupied with their own problems that they have either given up or lost their zeal for the "separation of church and state" argument.

Title III permitted originally the establishment of new institutions titled Supplementary Centers. The legislation, now altered, encouraged the creation of physical facilities which would incorporate new educational services for public and nonpublic schools. Such service units may cross existing district boundary lines, and although the precise nature of their governments was hazy in the original legislation, the law is open enough to permit a variation of local governing structures. The potential of Title III for educational improvement is unknown but it is a new feature in educational organization and one which has rather sharp implications for educational control. The authors of Public Law 89-10 saw Title III as providing catalyst input—as a means of disturbing the rigidity of traditonal educational structure, and as a stimulus to creative thinking relative to educational improvement on the part of a larger number of people. In mid-1966 over 800 supplementary center grants had been made. Some of the proposals are exciting and bode well for strengthening education; others represent sterile thinking and already antiquated designs. The future of Title III rests rather directly on the inventive capabilities of the professional educational leaders as well as of interested laymen who become involved.

Another new structural feature is provided for in *Title IV* of the Elementary and Secondary Education Act. This is the regional educational laboratory. The language of the legislation creating these new "institutions" is deliberately vague. Eighteen months after the passage of this law, twenty laboratories were being developed. They exhibit several conceptions of what a regional laboratory might be and face the common problem of establishing their own integrity with existing educational governments. Organizationally they are unique because they have few formal and obligatory ties with the constituency they serve. Each laboratory has a board of directors and a governing structure which ties it loosely to its region. The responsibility of the laboratories is fantastically unclear and diffuse. The U. S. Office of Education argues that it wishes only to provide general guidelines for the performance of the laboratories. The administrators of laboratories are torn between allegiances to the Office of Education and to their own boards of directors. The laboratories are expected to serve public schools and nonpublic schools, relate to all agencies with interests in education, be available as service agencies to state departments and to local school districts, place high priority on the dissemination of research findings to consuming publics, survey the region for educational problems that are not now known or are the subject of serious attempts at resolution, stimulate the growth of supplementary centers, and allocate certain kinds of project support funds to applying agents or agencies within the geography served by the laboratory. These are high risk ventures, surrounded at the same time with unusual potential and educational excitement. They are likewise new interventions into the ongoing educational processes of the nation which have influence—and likewise control—potential.

Title V of Public Law 89-10 is designed to strengthen state departments of education. Funds are made available for extending services of these agencies and more importantly, to provide the means for self study and reorganization. There has been national concern about state department inadequacy. Weaknesses in this level of government have become even more visible through the imposition of new administrative expectations for the management of other Titles of this law. Several states have found promising ways of using resources available through Title V. Other states have partly dissipated the potential through extending already weak and nonproductive services. Obviously states have to experiment and test their own inventiveness to extract the potential of this feature of the legislation.

One of the most imaginative projects supported under Title V is *Designing Education for the Future,* under whose auspices this volume has been developed. The purposes of the project, covering eight Rocky Mountain area states, are noteworthy. It is the only regional attempt that has ever been made to anticipate the changes that are likely to occur in society and to assess the implications of such changes for education, especially education in that region. The project is serving as a substantial stimulus to the thinking of professionals and laymen interested in education; it represents the kind of pre-policy reflection that has not been present in the past. Each of the eight states should be in a better position to move forward with individual state planning as a consequence.

If the aspirations of the architects of Public Law 89-10 are fulfilled, we can expect that state government for education will be stronger, more creative, and more capable of leading the states to adequate resolution of the difficult problems ahead.

COMPACT FOR EDUCATION

A recent innovation is the interstate educational compact, a loose confederation of states suggested by James Conant in 1964. The compact is similar to interstate commissions that have been established for other purposes. It is too early to generalize about the future of the compact plan except to observe that it has formed rapidly, developed its internal mechanisms for governance, and employed a full-time executive staff. The dispatch with which the confederation has been mobilized testifies to the commitment of its sponsors.

The compact, regardless of the purposes for which it was established or the vagueness of its authority, will have meaning for education. In its short history it has succeeded in enlisting support from many state leaders. Office holders such as governors and legislators, as well as prominent laymen, are involved in establishing compact policies. The increased interest in education that several governors have taken may be partially due to the influence of compact activities. The confederation may survive on the basis of the catalyst function for a time but sooner or later more visible results will be expected.

The influence that the compact will have on educational policy at the moment is conjectural. Although the designers of the organization disavow an anti-federal posture, the confederation has the potential for mobilizing opinion and offering positions on federal proposals. The confederation also offers a forum for the review of educational issues not available in the past and involves a new mix of persons in the review of educational problems. Discourse at this level may activate important new sources of support for education within each of the member states which can be drawn upon by the long established educational leadership structures.

The compact undoubtedly has pressure potential and will be perceived by some, as already has been the case, as an unnecessary political force directed at the schools. Rather than viewing the confederation as a threat or as an intervener between the states and federal authority, school leaders might well exploit the compact as *an added resource in the solution of the extraordinarily difficult problems on their doorstep*. The constitutional responsibility of the states is not in doubt; the compact may offer a means through which that responsibility can more effectively be accepted. In any event, the compact is in operation and has implications for the control of education.

POVERTY PROGRAMS

The mid-1960's has been a period of multiple federal interventions into educational problems. In addition to the Elementary and Secondary Education Act described earlier, other and more direct attacks on poverty were developed. The most prominent was authorized by the Economic Opportunity Act; this law in effect *created a new educational system and a new set of agencies for its administration and supervision*.

The Economic Opportunity Act, addressed as it was to the war on poverty, has succeeded in opening up new control problems for school officials. That precisely probably was, at least partly, what the designers of the Office of Economic Opportunity had in mind when they placed the responsibility for the educational features of poverty programs in the hands of anti-poverty functionaries rather than with public educational officials.[9] Placing the administrative burden for programs such as Head Start outside the domain of traditional educational government has served as still another evidence of the general lack of confidence in established educational leadership.

The anti-poverty efforts have been criticized severely by school people and as well as by citizens who have objected to the wasteful way that some poverty funds have been used. Nevertheless, the record of use of compensatory education monies available to school systems under other legislation may not be superior to that of the Office of Economic Opportunity. The basic issue is probably not one of waste or efficiency, but rather the issue

---

[9] See Donald A. Erickson, "The Poverty War's Multi-Organizational Mix: Congressional Blunder or Well-Timed Strategy?" Chicago: Midwest Administration Center, University of Chicago, Summer 1966, (mimeographed).

of finding ways that the learning of disadvantaged or poverty-affected children can be expedited. The pervasive nature of the problem is such that multiple efforts are in order and those that prove productive should be adopted on a large scale and with dispatch.

It is hardly in order to expend energy at this time on ironing out the location of administrative responsibility. This is not to say to school officials that the existence of supplementary educational structures should go unnoticed. The existence of such structures is a direct response to the inability of established institutions to keep pace with educational demand. The primary obligation is to make positive gains by using new resources now.

LEADERSHIP, CONTROL AND THE FUTURE

The preceding observations on stresses within the nation's school system, the society at large and the recent modifications on the posture of the federal government toward education have implications for the future. A few of these are developed briefly in the final portion of this chapter.

TEACHERS AND CONTROL

The emergence of teachers as determined power wielders is a new element in the control of education. The modest reaching for professional status that has marked the teaching occupation in the past will be affected sharply by the more exciting thrust for influence over educational policy, rules and regulations. The current militancy will spread in the years ahead. Few thoughtful observers will deny that teachers deserve a genuine participatory role in affecting the over-all direction that education should take. They would believe also that teachers ought to have a part in deciding the means for achieving educational goals and the development of the conditions which will expedite their achievement.

We can expect even greater press for participation in more and more areas of educational decision from teachers as well as from other professional groups. Principals, guidance personnel, social workers, psychologists and others currently engaged in establishing professional identities can be expected to push for participation in educational policy decisions as well as for collective bargaining privileges on salary and fringe benefit matters.

What may not be expected, but is bound to emerge, are elevated expectations for the performance of professional personnel, especially teachers, since they are the advance guard in the present power display. As teachers gain a larger voice in policy affairs and as their compensation is improved, the public inevitably will be expecting improved services. The performance "monkey" will be squarely on the backs of teachers. Questions as to "Why Johnny can't read?" will not be directed as much to school boards, or administrators, as to teachers. The responses teachers are able to give to performance questions will feed back directly into public acceptance or rejection of further participation in policy areas as well as compensation levels. Time will determine whether teachers can carry the responsibilities which accompany their new authority.

The roles of all participants in educational policy making will come under scrutiny. The clarification of roles, which has always been an aspiration, will continue to be needed as the number and influence of policy makers are modified. School administrators and school boards may be required to adjust their attitudes towards teacher participation and in fact develop new leadership skills to enable them to carry out successfully altered responsibilities.

CLIENT UNREST

Citizen and student disquiet will not abate unless and until our schools can provide more adequately for the satisfaction of present and future educational needs. Despite the reluctance of school officials in some cases to acknowledge the deterioration in relationships between the schools and their clients, breakdowns in those relationships exist. Tensions which are severe in some communities at present are not going to lessen without substantial effort on the part of school officials and lay citizens to establish communication and engage in the process of restoring confidence in the schools. This need is quite advanced as far as citizens are concerned and is emerging in regard to students.

School officials, sensitive from years of attack, have developed defense mechanisms which become almost automatic. Some attention needs to be given to the refinement of new ways of relating schools to their constituencies. This observation holds for the student constituency as well as for the public at large. The task appears to be one of invention since many established techniques and procedures seem inadequate.

PROCESSING CONFLICT

Pluralism in America is intensifying and our present social abrasiveness will probably continue in the years ahead. Frustrations associated with attempts to accommodate heterogeneous sets of interest will persist. Since conflict and tension will be the order of the day, school officials must develop conflict-processing skills.

The arenas for conflict are both internal and external to the school organization. Disequilibrium is likely to arise internally from student and staff origins and from a wide range of potential external sources. One attitude that will lend support to the conflict processer is that some tension is functional to the purposes of an organization, in this case a school system. A second supportive attitude is that conflict is bound to mark educational organizational life and that leadership skills can be refined to help reduce the dysfunction of stress to a school system.

Preparation of the school administrators of the future will include the academic exploration of conflict as a phenomenon as well as skill training in conflict processing. New techniques currently in embryo will be refined; leadership capacities will be sharpened through simulation, sensitivity training and field experiences. Emphasis on group process, already prominent in leader training, will be extended through in-service designs that will incorporate all members of school organizations into training sequences.

EXTENDING POLITICAL ACCESS

The large school districts in the United States, served for policy purposes locally by one board of education, are remarkably closed political systems. Individuals, neighborhood groups, even communities within the large district find it difficult if not impossible to reach boards of education or central office administrative personnel. There is often a queuing up of requests for "hearings" on neighborhood or individual educational problems. Space does not permit an adequate review of a fraction of the suggestions or complaints addressed to school officials. When the general issues facing the schools are many and severe, there is little hope that better opportunities can be found for examining specific problems.

Easy solutions to this problem are elusive. Two suggestions, however, are available. The first of these is to explore the establishment of special citizen-school task forces either on a special purpose or continuing basis. Membership on such groups would include both laymen and professional educators and their charge would be to review special problem areas, hear lay citizen points of view and report to the board of education. Task forces on such areas as race relations, teacher shortages, finance problems, or facility needs might be named.

The second suggestion is to create *a new pattern of educational government for large school districts,* indeed for entire metropolitan areas. Such new patterns would be designed with the specific objective in mind of extending political access to larger numbers of people. Metropolitan educational government might include a combination of structures, each one of which is intended to extend particular advantages to the urban community. A combination of a single metropolitan educational district overlaying an entire metro area and a number of small semi-independent underlay districts with their boards of education is being adopted currently in the Louisville, Kentucky, metropolitan center.[10] This pattern extends political access to two local levels and increases the capacity of the system to manage its problems by multiplying the number of boards of education responsible for operating the schools of the area. Acceptance of this design means breaking up a large city into smaller districts, an action for which there is no modern precedent.

LOCAL SCHOOL BOARDS

The external forces impinging upon the schools will be directed with increasing intensity on the men and women serving on local boards. The price of board membership, which is now high in terms of time and personal sacrifice, will be no less in the immediate future. Cries for the abolition of local boards will be heard and pressure for centralization of control will increase. *As new demands for education arise, the quality of lay leadership will need to improve.*

Local boards, which have served the nation's schools admirably throughout our history, can and should continue. There is a generally

---

[10] For a description of this proposed new government read Luvern L. Cunningham, Archie Dykes, James Kincheloe and Vincent Ostrom, *The Merger Issue.* (Louisville, Kentucky: The Louisville and Jefferson County Public Schools, August 1966).

recognized need to reduce the number of school districts in the nation, but each reduction in districts carries with it the companion reduction in the numbers of laymen thinking about and acting in an official capacity on the problems of schools. It is in the public interest to retain as many avenues of responsible public access as possible.

There is a need to study school board action much more definitively than we have in the past. Ways must be found to process difficult problems more rapidly and to avoid the current queuing up of educational matters that seem to immobilize some boards of education. Similarly new views of the roles and relationships of school superintendents and board members must be explored in order to "loosen up" the top management of the nation's schools.

THE SUPERINTENDENT AND STAFF

The superintendency will continue to be a tough and demanding post, but it need not be an impossible position. A "crying towel" attitude has developed on the part of some American superintendents but, although justified in a few instances, does not appear to be an appropriate posture for a leadership group. American superintendents have some maturing to do, and the same holds for school board members in some communities.

The superintendency will continue to require tough-minded men, with substantial energy reserves, capable of reasoning through complex internal and external problems. One of the first order modifications called for is a redefinition of the staff function in central office administration. New staff roles must be developed to aid the superintendent. Most of these may need to be filled by social scientists. Such staff people would be analysts, not decision-makers. They would be skillful in assessment and in the preparation of staff documents; they would be back-up men, not front men. An economist, an anthropologist, a communications specialist, and a systems analyst represent the staff types that ought to be available to the school executive of the future.

As this paper has indicated, the *developments ahead call for advanced thinking on the part of educational leaders*. The reflections which are needed cannot be made in the intense surroundings of the work-a-day world of the superintendent. Organizational and administrative arrangements will have to be made to allow adequately for long range planning and policy speculations. This is an imperative for the superintendency.

Similarly the universities, professional organizations, state departments and school districts have an enormous task ahead in the revitalizing of pre-service and in-service education for men in, and preparing for, the superintendency. The haphazard, catch-as-catch-can approaches of the past will not do. Rich new conceptions of preparation are in order; a national task force manned by thoughtful practitioners and academicians should be commissioned immediately to take on this assignment.

THE OBLIGATION OF THE STATES

The responsibility for education will continue to rest with the states, although it appears that there will be a contest over this obligation involving the large cities and the federal government. The contest will become severe unless the states can improve in their ability to satisfy educational need.

Current efforts to strengthen state departments bode well for the future, but the process of improvement has only begun. State boards of education need to be examined rather carefully and their functions assessed. The vitality of state board of education leadership varies but on the whole has not evidenced the boldness and farsightedness that seems to be in order. State departments, starved in most states by state legislatures, must be restored to positions of prominence and be modified to fulfill new and advanced responsibilities. Changes are needed especially in areas such as research and long range planning. The states have lagged badly in educational problem identification and anticipation of needs. Considerable growth in this capacity is in order.

MAINTAINING PERSPECTIVE

The present and future of American education rests heavily on the shoulders of its present complement of lay and professional leaders. People now in leadership positions will make many of the crucial decisions that lie ahead. The burdens of leadership, never slight, will tax severely their capabilities.

One consequence of the competing and varied demands placed on the nation's schools is the difficulty in maintaining perspective. When time, energy and resources are scarce there is an appeal in capitulation to one set of demands to the exclusion of others. The attractiveness of such behavior is extended when outcomes of one policy alternative are difficult to distinguish from those anticipated from other choices. Moreover, when requirements for action inundate school organizations the simple need to survive elicits non-rational responses. At a time when new objectives are being stipulated for schools, when social unrest is extensive, when new demands for sharing in school control are being presented, it is imperative that educational leaders maintain perspective and avoid hasty, non-reflective actions.

There is little doubt that changes in the environment of the schools will be reflected in the leadership and control of American education. The citizen of the future will have more to say about schools, and so will teachers and students. Demands for participation will lead to alterations in the structures through which schools have been governed and administered. The traditional leader roles of school board members and administrators will be modified but they will survive. The challenges are substantial but so is the nation's capacity to respond.

CHAPTER 12

Educational Personnel Policies and Practices

In a Period of Transition

Claude W. Fawcett*

A major revolution in the preparation, assignment, and administration of both professional and classified personnel in public schools by 1980 may be anticipated on the basis of prospective changes in society and in the economy. "Coming events cast their shadows before," as Thomas Campbell suggests. Joseph W. Garbarino commented in *Prospective Changes in Society by 1980* (chapter 9):**

> Perhaps the most important characteristic of the 1980 industrial relations system is that group bargaining will be much more pervasive than it now is. Administrative and managerial authority will be limited in all types of organizations. The 'consent of the governed' principle will be extended to employer-employee relations and bargaining out of decisions will be generalized over most of our organizations.
>
> Operation of this employee relations system will require a high degree of administrative skill and these skills will be in short supply. Successful industrial democracy, like successful political democracy, requires that both governed and governors work at their jobs.

The same influences that are bringing about the development of this anticipated employee relations system are at work in the public school systems. Being governmental organizations, school systems have special adaptations they must make, but public policy for schools is created by the very individuals who are experiencing, even developing, the growing industrial democracy. It is unlikely that they will fail to participate in the movement in public schools. Alternatives of choice concerning how adaptations best can be made are not entirely clear at this moment, but an examination of trends both in events and thought can give some insight concerning the probable emerging choices.

FACTORS AFFECTING PERSONNEL ADMINISTRATION

Major pressures now being exerted on personnel administration in public schools are provided by at least seven factors: (1) metropolitanization and reorganization; (2) assumption of greater leadership by state and federal governments; (3) transiency in the population; (4) technological change; (5) speed of transportation; (6) professionalization in all school occupations; and (7) the nature of research.

* *Professor of Education and Educational Placement Officer, University of California, Los Angeles;* Educational Director, National Association of Manufacturers, Western Division (1951-59); Assistant Dean, University College, University of Southern California (1949-51); Assistant Superintendent of Schools, East Grand Rapids, Michigan (1949-51); Publications include *School Personnel Administration* (1964).

** All similar references are to chapters in *Prospective Changes in Society by 1980*.

METROPOLITANIZATION AND REORGANIZATION

The most obvious effect of metropolitanization and reorganization on public school systems is to increase their geographic and population size. Other factors contributing to the growth in size of school districts are: (1) a demand for better-trained specialists for unique functions; (2) a search for a more adequate tax base for fiscal support; and (3) a growing appreciation of the need to provide a full educational opportunity to all students. William C. Wheaton reported (chapter 8) that the Intermountain States had fourteen average or smaller-sized metropolitan areas which he predicted would include 60 to 70 percent of the region's population in 1980. It is reasonable to expect that larger districts in both metropolitan and non-metropolitan areas are likely to be the rule, rather than an exception, by 1980.

The effect of size on personnel employed by school districts can already be observed in trends in present metropolitan centers. As districts grow, there is a tendency to develop specialization and division of labor. The teacher becomes, in addition, a consumer of information about students provided by counselors, social workers, doctors, dentists, and other specialists. Classified workers are often assigned to narrow specialties (e.g., food service, insurance, transportation, building design, computer operation, etc.). Urban areas tend to develop neighborhoods, or satellite communities, composed of homogeneous populations of an ethnic, economic or religious nature. The teacher needs to develop leadership skills essential for the population area he serves. Communication within large districts tends to break down, not only with the board of education but with the population of the district. The reaction of employees to this failure in communication processes is often to form employee associations for collective communication. The problems of developing the more complete and complicated skills of a specialized assignment, retaining some sense of broad understanding of the total program of the schools so the specialty becomes meaningful, and developing and maintaining communication not only with students but with the community, seem to be the emerging and most pressing problems of the teacher in a large school district.

LEADERSHIP BY STATE AND FEDERAL GOVERNMENTS

The federal government has made itself much more available to citizens for the solution of educational problems. The adoption of an American version of the Keynesian economic doctrine has been developed by successive Congresses to the point that it has included a policy of investment in education for the purpose of achieving national economic growth. Recent legislation emphasizing education for underprivileged groups has extended this economic purpose to designate the school as a conscious agency for social change. The events of the post-World War II international struggle for political balance between Russia and the United States have led to the tacit adoption of public education as an agency for the achievement of national purposes including defense. The classic purposes of public education to teach children the right and wrong of personal actions in society, to develop citizenship skills, and to provide an opportunity for social mobility have been augmented by both national and state purposes. A teacher tends, under these circumstances, to become to an increasing extent an agent of the state with relatively fixed goals requiring greater expertise to accomplish societal demands. The growth of specificity in results to be achieved by public school instruction may well lead to professional demands for definite assignments, evaluation in terms of known successful skills, and provision of opportunities for self-evaluation and intrinsic motivation not now entirely clear in terms of the more general purposes of education.

The increasing activity of the federal government in public education and the growing problems of local school government attendant upon geographic and population size may well spell an end to the lingering provincialism in teachers' participation in school government affairs. The total education program in the United States has been a partnership between local, state, and national governments, at least since the Northwest Ordinance of 1787. Each government has at different times assumed different roles and provided different shares of the cost. In this period of history, the federal Elementary-Secondary Education Act, the Higher Education Act, and the Vocational Education Act presage a major shift in acceptance of responsibility by the federal government. The roles of both state and local governments in education have been changed thereby. This augmentation of the role of the federal government in education has come at a time when major increases in the size and complexity of the local school governmental units have made the consultative-consensus procedures of local school boards difficult to maintain. Citizens and groups of citizens interested in educational problems have long accepted in practice, if not in theory, the partnership concept of tripartite educational governments. If their desires concerning education can not be satisfied in one government, they have been quick to submit them as proposals to other governments in the partnership. However, as Grant McConnell pointed out (chapter 7), "One of the essential checks upon public government is that it is required to operate according to law." It is easy to predict that the period to 1980 will find major governmental attention being given to a more accurate legal definition of the relative roles of local, state, and national governments in the educational process. The professional and classified staffs of public schools will necessarily be involved in this definition at all levels because the governmental actions of each partner define their responsibilities and their opportunities for service.

POPULATION TRANSIENCY

Transiency in the population forces educational personnel to be more precise concerning educational goals for students, and more cooperative in developing educational programs. The U. S. Bureau of the Census reports that: of the 185,312,000 people in the United States in March 1964, 36,327,000 (about one-fifth) changed residences during the prior year. Two-thirds of those who moved did so within the county in which they resided. A little more than a sixth moved to another county within the state. A little less than a sixth moved from one state to another. In thirteen or more years of public schooling it can be predicted that the average young person will have received instruction from approximately seventy teachers in at least three different school districts. The combined effort of all teachers in the different districts must somehow add up to the minimum skills, attitudes, and knowledge essential to complete participation in the society. This requires of teachers and districts an intercommunication system and a concentration on common educational objectives that would not have been considered worth serious thought in a stable, rural school district even twenty years ago.

TECHNOLOGICAL CHANGE

The most compelling pressures brought to bear on educational personnel have been the result of technological change. The occupations available to people with few skills and little knowledge are disappearing from the employment picture. The U. S. Bureau of the Census reports that employed persons increased by ten and one-half millions in the fifteen-year period between 1950 and 1965. The increase is accounted for by: (1) four and one-half millions more professional, technical, and kindred workers; (2) two millions fewer farmers and farm managers; (3) one million more nonfarm managers, officials and proprietors; (4) three and one-third millions more clerical and kindred workers; (5) one million more sales workers; (6) one million more craftsmen, foremen, etc.; (7) one million more operatives; (8) one-half million more household workers; (9) two millions more service workers; and (10) over one and one-half millions fewer farm laborers and foremen. The number of laborers other than farm laborers remained about the same. *The occupations on the increase are those that will require even more education in the future;* the ones that are on the decrease are those requiring few skills and lesser knowledge. As technological change proceeds, young people will be required to stay in school longer and develop a more advanced set of skills if they are to be economically effective in our society. The burden of teaching a diverse student body and teaching each member sufficiently well that he can become culturally and economically effective falls upon the teacher. This will be the greatest challenge to the profession that it has ever faced.

NATURE OF RESEARCH

This major responsibility has been placed on teachers at a time when their relationship to knowledge is an anomaly. The production of knowledge has become a profitable investment. E. Duerr Reeves, executive vice-president of the Esso Engineering and Research Company, has estimated that research alone could bring about a 5-percent yearly increase in plant capacity through the removal of bottlenecks.[1] These savings are in addition, according to Reeves, to the value to the company of new product development, which he considered to be of equal value with bottleneck removal and a 25-percent saving on the costs for new plant facilities. This kind of reasoning has led to the establishment of large subsidiary research organizations, the development of profit-making independent research corpora-

---

[1] E. Duerr Reeves, "Industrial Research," *Stanford Research Institute Journal*, Vol. 2, No. 2, (August, 1958).

tions, and the displacement of the university's formerly predominant role of supplying new knowledge. Knowledge produced by proprietary research organizations comes out labeled either "proprietary" or "classified" (when done for the government for defense purposes). In either case it is not immediately available to the teacher. The time lag for getting a new discovery into a textbook may be as much as fifteen to twenty years, depending upon the complexity of the discovery. Since he can no longer depend exclusively on the textbook, or even current journals, for up-to-date knowledge, the teacher must improve his skills for ferreting out current knowledge. This almost certainly means the development of close associations with developers of knowledge in his specialized field. Although this is far from being a new professional challenge, the developments of the past few years portend an intensification of the problem to the degree that by 1980, it will offer a severe challenge to the profession.

TRANSPORTATION AND COMMUNICATION

The challenges to the teacher to participate in national and state governmental activities in education, to develop cooperative programs of concern to both governments, to associate with the producers of knowledge, and to develop the skills of teaching essential in a technological society, are ameliorated by advancements both in transportation and communication. The former assists because it provides ready opportunities for educational personnel to participate in conferences and activities of responsible professional groups any place in the country or the world. The latter assists because so much information is given to the world through publications, radio, television, and other communication devices. As the teachers' problems intensify during the next decade and a half, it may be incumbent upon employers to recognize, through their personnel policies, the essential support they must give to teachers by encouraging and making it possible for them to avail themselves of opportunities to participate in professional and study activities.

PROFESSIONALIZATION

Optimism concerning the ability of the teaching profession to react to prospective changes in society is justified. They have already reacted to prior social change in a variety of ways including demands for specialization in certification. Separate kinds of teaching and administrative employees, for example, had successfully persuaded the legislature of the state of California to adopt specialized requirements until the state prescribed forty-seven different credentials and nineteen special certificates in 1961. The Fisher bill passed in that year was designed to reduce this number to five, but special requirements within each of the five soon produced about the same differentiation that existed under the prior system. Teachers are completing more formal educational requirements to qualify for specialties. The average number of years of collegiate preparation in California, for example, was only two in 1920. In 1965 the average number of years of collegiate preparation was 4.9. (The Fisher bill requires five for the standard license.) Schools of education are slowly beginning to react to demands for specialization; research concerning the content of skills, attitudes, and knowledge required for teaching occupations is beginning to be produced. It is reasonable to predict that the content of teacher training by 1980 will concentrate more on the professional skills, attitudes, and knowledge required for specified responsibilities.

Specialization has taken a somewhat different turn in the classified sector of educational employment. Computer specialists, insurance supervisors, food-service managers, architects, real estate purchasers, transportation dispatchers, electricians, plumbers, carpenters, and other specialists are hard to find among people with teaching licenses. There is a strong movement to relieve these specialists from the need to possess state licenses except in their own specialties. Undoubtedly, in a few years the classified sector of educational employment will be subject only to qualification through the personnel system of the school district.

SUMMARY

The dim outline of professional response by 1980 to societal change can be discerned. An educational employee is quite likely to be serving in a much larger school district than is common now. He will be faced with all the problems of large-group participation. He will have to participate freely in the educational programs of national, state, and local governments. He will need to cope with more precise national, state, and local purposes of instruction. He will need to accept personal responsibility for keeping abreast of new knowledge. He will have to develop precise skills for teaching many who are now neglected or considered substantially uneducable. He will need to give much attention to the professionalization of his own work. He will need to participate in the affairs of the profession on a state and national basis. Most of all, he will need to accept full personal responsibility for participation in an organizational democracy. *A major concern of eduactional governments should be to develop and maintain personnel policies and practices that will free educational personnel to make appropriate responses to societal change.*

MANAGEMENT THEORIES AND PERSONNEL ADMINISTRATION

The manner in which educational governments can plan and execute appropriate personnel policies and practices is no clearer than the dim outlines of the professional responses that will be required. Some assistance can be obtained in studying the problem by examining management theories and ascertaining the manner in which the most promising might be utilized in, or adapted to, personnel practices. This field of inquiry has moved from Max Weber's brilliant analysis of the contribution of organization to the betterment of individuals who work in it, through Frederick Taylor's scientific management ideas of improving the organization, and the ideas of consultative management of Kurt Lewin, to the more recent concepts of Philip Selznick of the University of California, Chris Argyris of Yale University, and Douglas McGregor of the Massachusetts Institute of Technology. The last three have pursued the problem of an employee's relations to an organization by using the tools of sociology and social psychology.

Selznick has been primarily interested in the role of organizational goals in assisting individuals in them to identify their own hopes and desires with the goals of the organization. He has inquired concerning the role of goal-striving in the processes of change. He sums up his main arguments in the title of a small volume of great merit.[2]

Argyris has been concerned about the fundamental conflict that exists between personal hopes and desires and the necessities of the organization. In his extensive research in this area he proposes seven processes as essential if management is to work successfully at the problem. They are: (1) precise assignments of responsibility, (2) evaluation and reward, (3) authority binding on all in the organization, (4) perpetuation of the organization, (5) communication, (6) identification, and (7) pacing of the work of the organization. In these processes of management, if conducted within the framework of the persistent problem of reconciling personal hopes and desires with organizational needs, lies some hope of assisting an individual to work productively.[3]

Douglas McGregor's contribution to management theory includes his endorsement of goal setting as one of the important functions of management and the means by which it retains and exercises its authority. He proposes the principle of collegial collaboration between superior and subordinate, the idea that subordinates are capable of self-control and self-development, and the idea that integration of organizational and personal goals is essential for achieving the broad goals of the organization.[4]

Persistent themes permeating the writings of the three men are: (1) the need to establish clear goals for the organization (Argyris emphasizes the need to break them down to specific goals for each employee's assignment); (2) the need to utilize intrinsic motivation for changes in employee behavior; and (3) the need to work together as colleagues to achieve cooperatively the goals of the organization.

These ideas seem exceptionally well-suited for use by educational governments during the next decade and a half. Educational personnel will be seeking more accurate definition of organizational goals. Increased specialization will require more accurate definition of each employee's role in the organization. Increasing professionalization means more acceptance of personal responsibility for self-development. Democracy in administration of educational governments suggests *collegiality*.

COLLEGIAL PERSONNEL POLICIES AND PRACTICES

Collegiality can be achieved in school administration, however, only if personnel policies and practices reflect the intent at each key process of securing, developing, and retaining personnel within the organization. An examination of possible practice in each of these essential procedures may shed some light on alternatives in the development of democracy in educational government.

[2] Philip Selznick, *Leadership in Administration* (Evanston, Illinois: Row, Peterson, and Company, 1957).

[3] Chris Argyris, *Personality and Organization* (New York: Harper & Brothers, 1957).

[4] Douglas McGregor, *The Human Side of Enterprise* (New York: McGraw-Hill Book Company, Inc., 1960).

DESIGN OF WORK ASSIGNMENTS

Mutual appreciation of each employee's contribution to the total effort of an organization will require that each subscribe to the goals of the organization, know precisely what his contribution to their accomplishment should be and is, and understand the part that each other person contributes in cooperation with him to the total effort. An accurate knowledge of the difficulty of the skills, attitudes, and knowledge essential to optimum acceptance of responsibility may well heighten the mutual appreciation of the common effort required to reach common goals.

Accurate description of each person's contribution to the common achievement of organizational goals may well require the development of unique and different personnel procedures. Most school systems have relied largely on an age-grade system of description in the elementary and a subject system in the secondary school. In a functional collegial system, goals of the thirteen or more years of schooling would be described for different kinds of students with different capabilities and motivations in terms of skills to be achieved, attitudes to be developed, and knowledge to be gained and utilized. The goals should be described not only in terms of maximum levels of accomplishment, but in terms of the sequential order of their development. In the light of the available knowledge of student growth and development, subgoals for each of the thirteen or more years of schooling need to be determined. Only then may goals of the organization become usable for the tailoring of co-ordinated assignments to individual employees within the organization. This procedure is essential to mutual appreciation of each employee's effort to accomplish the goals of the organization.

The process requires an accurate knowledge of the inherent problems in its operation. *Goals of public education change as society changes; they change as research provides more data concerning their content; they change as the capabilities of students and teachers change.* Each of these influences requires not only a complete re-examination of the over-all goals, but the manner in which they are to be accomplished through subgoals. The introduction of new personnel with different capabilities—either through development of staff in the organization or new employees—requires re-examination of accomplishment, goals and schedules. All employees need to participate and to be fully informed in the redesign and development of goal patterns within the organization if collegiality is to be maintained. The great danger in this process is that goal patterns may become fixed and obsolete because of inattention, bureaucratic and inflexible procedures for change, or failure to invite employee participation and sharing in dynamic revision.

Mutual respect for individual effort can be seriously impaired in the assignments of subgoals to persons for their professional accomplishment. Assignments to individuals need to be made with the full knowledge of the reasonable effort required to accomplish the subgoal with the type of students under the teacher's jurisdiction. If the anticipated result is to be achieved, total assignments must add up to a reasonable work load. If assignments of responsibility are unequal, or unrealistic in terms of the capability of the teacher, it is difficult to maintain the level of accomplishment which commands the mutual respect for results which is essential to collegiality.

It is unlikely that mutual respect for accomplishment can readily be maintained if assignments and expectations for individuals remain fixed over any long period of time. Workers change their potential for accomplishment in many ways. They become ill; they lose or increase their energy level; they encounter distractions in their personal and professional lives; they develop new skills and insights; they change their attitudes; they learn more. As a result, they are qualified to perform more duties, fewer duties, or different duties. They are more valuable to the organization or they may be less valuable. Changes in assignments or responsibilities are needed at each important change in the individual. If they are not made, it is difficult to maintain a level of accomplishment that can command the respect of colleagues.

The greatest hazard to collegiality may very well be encountered if the assignments of subgoals omit recognition of the contributions to goal accomplishment of administrators and other service employees. Collegiality with these classes of employees is dependent upon the clarity of the statement of subgoals assigned to them, and the completeness of understanding of all concerning the contribution to be made. Mutual respect grows not only out of the quality of the effort expended and the results achieved, but out of the importance to the total effort of the accomplishment.

SELECTION OF PERSONNEL

Selection of a colleague poses problems of his "fit" within the group of workers in the organization. This "fit" has several dimensions. His potential for identifying his hopes, desires, and ambitions with the goals of the organization should be ascertained. His potential for accepting the responsibilities assigned to him should be assessed in terms of his skills, attitudes, and utilization of knowledge. The kind of place he can occupy within the cooperative group—determined largely by the level of his skill, the nature of his attitudes, and his persistent habits in the use of knowledge—should be established. The selection of a new employee involves not only the addition of a person, but an examination of his potential impact on the cooperative endeavors of all persons within the organization. This kind of selection requires new techniques and complete information concerning potential employees.

Information gathered may have to be stated in terms of characteristic patterns of behavior. The types of behavior pertinent to selection decisions may be illustrated in terms of the information that can be used in deciding about the selection of a person for teaching. Information about potentiality for identifying hopes and desires with the goals of the organization may be obtained by studying persistent patterns of behavior in relation to young people. A corporation that is providing personnel services to business and industrial firms, describes *attitudes as characteristic patterns of organizational behavior* and states that they can best be described by the words income, security, approval, perfection, competition, attachments to great causes, authority, creativity, and investigation.[5] In this context *Income* is defined as behavior tending to demonstrate the degree of importance an individual places on level of income; *security,* as persistent patterns of reaction to reassure and confirm security in the organization; *approval,* as the search for applause or overt recognition of the quality of performance; *competition,* as behavior under a competitive situation; *attachment to great causes,* as composed of characteristic idealistic reactions to important problems; *authority,* as having two behavioral dimensions—reactions to authority and characteristic exercise thereof within a group; *creativity,* as composed of unique and pertinent behavior in the face of problematic, even traditional situations; and *investigation,* as curiosity concerning problems to be solved in the organization. Utilization of this information for predictive purposes concerning attachment to organizational goals will require accurate descriptions of employee behavior that is pertinent to them in each organization with differing goals. Norms will necessarily have a local definition.

The place of a person in the working group and his potential for mutual appreciation are defined in part by the skills he possesses and the success he achieves in the assignment made to him. Teaching behavior can be described under the following headings conveniently identified as skills.[6]

1. Interpersonal Skills With:
   A. Parents
   B. Fellow Employees
   C. Pupils
   D. Administrators

2. Classroom Management Skills
   A. Securing student adoption of appropriate goals of learning.
   B. Identifying appropriate procedures for efficient student learning.
   C. Confirming, reinforcing, and redirecting students' learning behavior.
   D. Securing classroom decisions that are self-directing for the members of the class.
   E. Maintaining current knowledge of teaching and learning.
   F. Record-keeping.
   G. Coordination of classroom learning with learning directed by other institutions and groups.
   H. Maintaining a cosmopolitan learning system that involves each student in the group.
   I. Communication with each student in the group.
   J. Application of appropriate time sequences, materials, and effort best calculated to assist students to reach acceptable goals.

3. Teaching-Learning Skills
   A. Maintenance of a learning climate within the classroom.
   B. Effective use of learning devices and materials.
   C. Maintenance of appropriate learning sequences.
   D. Analysis of students' learning difficulties.

It has been possible, to date, to identify 172 different behaviors of teachers classified under the categories listed above. It is not yet entirely clear just

[5] *Step-By-Step Selection Program.* New York: The McMurry Corporation. This manual is used by members of the company to gather information concerning potential administrative employees in the organization. For a statement of the rationale, see Robert N. McMurry, "Validating the Patterned Interview," *Personnel,* Vol. 23, pp. 263-272.

[6] Claude W. Fawcett, *The Skills of Teaching* (Los Angeles: University of California Teacher Education Project, 1965).

how valuable some of them are to goal accomplishment with different kinds of students. It is possible, however, to begin to gather data concerning these and other behaviors with the intent of developing norms that apply to specific teaching situations.

Securing information concerning the potential employee's knowledge has been characteristically a process of accumulating transcripts of grades from institutions. These data are seldom useful for the type of evaluation required in a goal-oriented organization or institution. *The crux of the problem* in a goal-oriented institution is *the manner in which the individual uses his knowledge and ability as tools for bringing about changes in student skill, attitude, or knowledge.* This procedure is somewhat closer to an examination of teaching methods used—if method is defined not just as a process, but as a process that involves knowledge, its sequencing and its selection in the goal achievement process. Data concerning the characteristic patterns of the use of knowledge in instruction can be used to identify, in part, the kind of role a potential employee can assume in a sequence of instruction covering thirteen or more years of public school instruction.

Utilization of these data in an institution committed to collegiality requires a kind of analytic procedure that should provide pertinent information relating to the following kinds of questions:

1. In the total pattern of goal accomplishment in the organization, what kinds of responsibilities can be assumed by the potential employee?

2. How must assignments of responsibility to other employees be adjusted so the total work of the organization can be properly completed, if this new person is added to the cooperative group?

3. To what extent do the attitudinal behavioral patterns of the potential employee offer promise that he may identify with the goals of the organization, and thus promise mutual appreciation of the efforts of others in the organization?

4. Do the skill patterns and use of knowledge data concerning the new employee offer promise of development soon enough to allow flexibility of assignment required by turnover in the staff due to deaths, resignations, terminations, and retirements?

ORIENTATION

A new employee, if he is to be a colleague, requires a great deal of information quickly about various aspects of the institution he is joining. He needs to find out as soon as possible the institutional goals and language. An accurate assessment would include some knowledge concerning the criteria used by the community and the board of education in making decisions concerning school affairs. This may well include, under the governmental tripartite cooperative system of school operation, a precise knowledge of the values used in state and national governments as they apply in the local school district. Institutional definition will need to show the precise decisions made concerning goals of instruction since they are, at any time, a product of compromise and adjustment of differences among citizens under professional leadership. The new employee will need to know the procedures by which goals are to be reached in the institution. He will need to know assignments, not only for himself but for all others within the organization with whom he participates in a cooperative endeavor. His goals, in relation to those of the school and school system are identifiable if these data are available to him, and he has some chance of examining them in relation to his own hopes, desires, and ambitions.

An effective colleague needs to be familiar with the characteristic interpersonal behaviorial patterns of those with whom he works. Mutual respect is often possible only if this kind of behavior is identifiable. One aspect of the problem is the group behavior of members in the organization. Schutz identifies this by the name *Fundamental Interpersonal Orientation*.[7] He identifies the three dimensions as acceptance, leadership, and affection. Although understanding of group behavior is indispensable, mutual respect is also dependent upon understanding of fellow workers' characteristic attitudes toward work, the difficulty of the skills displayed in work, and the utilization of knowledge in the teaching process. These are appreciated most when there is precise knowledge of their relation to cooperative goal accomplishment.

Since mutual respect is based on an appreciation of contributions to goal accomplishment, it is imperative that the new employee direct his activities precisely to the cooperative task for which he is responsible. The new employee, if he is a teacher, must have accurate and complete information about not only the thirteen-or-more-year plan and his specific place in it, but the precise skills, attitudes, and knowledge possessed by the students he is to teach. The record system, such diagnostic testing as is necessary, and other information to be gained only by consultation with students, need to be available at the beginning of instruction.

Schooling, however, is but one of the educational influences brought to bear upon students. The teacher, if he is to gain the respect of colleagues and students, must be able to provide instruction in the context of the effects of other educational influences.

Orientation, thus conceived, requires the planning of work assignments so the time for these four types of orientation can be provided.

EVALUATION

Collegiality, as described by McGregor, includes confidence in members of the cooperative group to direct their own self-improvement of skills, attitudes, and knowledge. Help provided through evaluation of personnel should make it a process for the improvement of performance through *reinforcement of behavior by approval of skillful acts performed by the teacher or other employee*. The process should provide assistance in redirection of behavior toward commonly held and commonly valued goals of performance, especially when actions tend not to produce the results essential to goal accomplishment.

This kind of personnel evaluation requires prior identification of requirements and expectations before there is any attempt at evaluation of the skills, attitudes, and knowledge most essential for accomplishing the subgoals of the assignment. If self-direction in performance improvement is the intent, then all the acceptable skills, attitudes, and knowledge for each assignment should be described. The employee should be assisted not only to

---

[7] William C. Schutz, FIRO: *A Three-Dimensional Theory of Personal Behavior* (New York: Holt, Rinehart & Winston, 1958).

know which of these he possesses, but the order of importance to the institution of those he does not possess. He should, furthermore, be provided ample opportunity in in-service programs to secure assistance in developing the next most valuable skill or skills he needs, the more appropriate attitudes, and the most useful ways of handling knowledge in the development of student behavior. Institutional support is essential for assisting employees to make maximum use of self-improvement motivations.

The emphasis on self-direction in the improvement of performance suggests several characteristics of a sound personnel evaluation program. They are:

1. The evaluation should be done proximate to the performance to be reinforced or redirected.
2. Time for evaluation should be identified by some critical incident system recognized by administrators and employees alike.
3. Emphasis on performance suggests that a single act or sequence of acts related to a skill, attitude, or knowledge should be the major emphasis in evaluation.
4. Since confirmation of behavior in this type of evaluation relies upon intrinsic instead of extrinsic motivation, the evaluative process should provide some definite recognition by the individual of the value to the organization of his accomplishment.
5. Proper institutional support suggests that the in-service training and recommendation for redirection of behavior be full and immediately available.
6. Evaluation should be done by a person in whom the individual has some confidence.[8]

If institutional support is to be given equitably in the self-direction of performance improvement, it is imperative that no successful, significant, pertinent act of an employee go unnoticed. Since the system of critical incidents must be related to self-improvement efforts of the employee, it would seem important that they be related to the new skill that an employee is attempting to perfect, the different attitude he is trying to develop or the use of knowledge he is experimenting with. Because the employee's recognition of success is all important to his own motivations, the evaluator should be willing to assist him in developing criteria for success. These may be put in terms of behavior of students on a test, behavior in the classroom, or behavior in study or work outside the classroom. The process is substantially the identification of evidence of success or lack of it to guide his experimentation with his own behavior.

COMPENSATION

In the collegial system, *mutual respect is difficult to maintain unless there is organizational justice*—particularly in respect to compensation. Roscoe Pound stated the general problem as follows:

Men wish to be free, but they want much besides. Thus we come to the idea of a maximum satisfaction of human wants or expectations. What we have to do in social control, and so in law, is to reconcile and adjust these desires or wants and expectations, so far as we can, so as to secure as much of the totality of them as we can.[9]

---

[8] For a more complete explanation of evaluation of personnel see Claude W. Fawcett, *School Personal Administration* (New York: The MacMillan Company, 1964), Chapter VI, pp. 55-66.
[9] Roscoe Pound, *Justice According to Law* (New Haven: Yale University Press, 1951), p. 31.

Pound was discussing the problem of government, but French points out that the problem applies to institutions in terms of compensation.[10]

The single salary schedule now used by more than eight of every ten school systems in this country, was ingeniously designed to meet the organizational needs of school districts at the time it was first formally proposed by the National Education Association in 1923. Now districts have developed problems in wage and salary administration for which policies need to be re-examined in the interest of equity. Seniority considerations have forced new teachers to assume positions that are more difficult, or those for which more substantial training is required.

The professional life of males in the teaching profession is about one-half of that of women. This is largely due to the fact that many teachers work and are paid only 180 days per year, while most others in the national work force are employed for 240 days per year. Emphasis on adequate beginning salaries causes many school districts to pay higher salaries to beginning young female college graduates than they can obtain in most other professions requiring comparable education. The growing market for college graduates in other occupations (e.g., mathematics, physical and life sciences, and English) has forced school districts into stiff competition with other employers for personnel. Despite growing specialization and division of labor, and the increasing requirements for quality of performance, there is little differentation of salaries in most school systems to encourage the learning of more difficult skills, attitudes, and knowledge.

Equity in compensation suggests that not only should an attempt be made to take into account the needs, wants, and desires of employees, but the needs, wants, and desires of the public within the educational government. The whole salary system necessarily is a set of compromises between the willingness of the public to pay for services it desires for accomplishment, and the availability of qualified persons to perform the services.

In modern wage theory addressed to the problem of organizational justice in compensation, one of the most helpful ideas is the concept of job evaluation.[11] Using this technique, *a salary schedule based on an estimate of the value of each position to the accomplishment of the goals of the organization can be established for each different kind of position.* Factors taken into account might well be the scarcity of the skills required, the amount of time required to meet the responsibilities assigned, the crucial contribution to the total goal accomplishment, the desirability of the position, the competition for personnel qualified to perform the duties by other employers, the difficulty of developing the appropriate skills, and the amenities of the community. This might mean, depending upon the factors listed above, that three elementary teachers in different schools might be assigned such different tasks that the value of their assignment to the total

---

[10] For a fuller statement of the problem see Wendell French, *The Personnel Management Process: Human Resources Administration* (Boston: Houghton Mifflin Company, 1964), Chapter IX, pp. 402-422.

[11] Three of the most helpful references on this subject are: (1) David W. Belcher, *Wage and Salary Administration* (Englewood Cliffs: Prentice-Hall, 1962, 2d ed), Chapters 7-10; (2) Adolph Langsner and Herbert G. Zollitsch, *Wage and Salary Administration* (Cincinnati: South-Western Publishing Company, 1961), Chapters 6-9; and (3) John A. Patton and C. L. Littlefield, *Job Evaluation.* (Homewood, Illinois: Richard D. Irwin, 1957), Chapters 6-9.

goal accomplishment of the district would be substantially different. This almost certainly would mean that a group leader in a team-teaching assignment would have a job of different value than other members of the team. If the responsibilities assigned to an administrator involved different and scarcer skills, his position would inevitably be valued higher in terms of goal accomplishment of the organization. The crux of the problem is the difficulty of the assignment made to the position, the scarcity of people willing to accept the responsibilities, and the value of the performance to the cooperative work in the organization.

A simple consideration of justice would suggest that an employee taking on new responsibilities should be afforded a reasonable time for developing the skills, attitudes, and knowledge most pertinent to adequate performance in the assignment. This would suggest that any schedule of salary for a position, or group of related positions, would incorporate an automatic progression for a period at least as long as the average time required to reach an adequate level of proficiency. Five years is often given as a reasonable time in the teaching profession.

Justice would also suggest that individuals who develop superior skills, attitudes, and knowledge for an assignment should either be reassigned to more difficult positions in which they can utilize them—and consequently receive more compensation—or that they receive pay at higher levels in the same position. This latter consideration is often referred to as merit pay. In that kind of collegial personnel system envisioned in this discussion, preference must necessarily be given to a redesign of working positions for the assumption of greater responsibility. This conforms more nearly to the concept of intrinsic reward for self-improvement in the interest of goal accomplishment.

TERMINATION

Essential organizational justice for support of collegiality extends to termination. In a period of rapid societal change—such as during the decade and a half to 1980—considerable attention must be given to this problem. As goals of organizations change, assignments to many individuals change. Some people cannot or are unwilling to develop the essential skills, attitudes, and knowledge to accept such changes. Most new employees start to work with minimum skill with the expectation that others will be developed rapidly. Some people improve—some do not. Individuals change during periods of employment because of illness, age, family problems, changes in professional interests, and accident. When the usual organizational processes of evaluation, redirection, and in-service training are insufficient to cause them to perform adequately for goal achievement, their employment must be terminated.

The public school teacher, however, occupies a particularly vulnerable position because of the nature of public education. Sumption and Engstrom describe it in the following statement:

> The school from the kindergarten to the graduate college has the magnificent goal of helping to achieve and maintain a free society of free people. To do this, the right of unlimited inquiry is essential. The school should foster

the spirit of intellectual freedom, the right to doubt, and the privilege of utilizing all available resources in the search for truth.[12]

The acceptance of this responsibility by a public school teacher in the next decade and a half in a rapidly-changing, industrialized society means major controversy. The maelstrom of disagreement in a mobile population with diverse values might well unseat a public employee if rigid safeguards for continued employment are not maintained.

Government response to exigencies resulting from this and related situations has led to the establishment of tenure laws in thirty-seven states.[13] These laws tend generally to identify the following as essential to justice in termination:

1. The school district has a trial or probationary period during which it should have a chance to determine the professional potential of an employee.
2. The board of education is obliged to specify the causes for termination.
3. The employee is entitled to prompt service of a notice of intention to dismiss giving specific causes for the contemplated action.
4. He is entitled to have this notice served long enough in advance of a possible hearing date so that he can arrange for an adequate defense.
5. He is entitled to request a public hearing on the charges brought against him.
6. He is entitled to a hearing in the court system.
7. He has the rights of appeal, due process, and judgment available to any other citizen in those courts.
8. If the charges are not supported to the satisfaction of the courts, he is entitled to relief from all costs, including his attorney's fees.

Classified employees are not normally so embroiled in public controversy. Most termination rules provide essentially the same steps, but access to courts is not normally specified in the regulations.

In a collegial institution such as is envisioned above, it is simple justice that retirement systems be used to encourage competent employees to continue in service and to orient themselves to new occupations and new activities beyond the organization. It is possible to anticipate some of the emerging needs in retirement in the next decade and a half:

1. The culture in which we live promotes transfers from one state to another. A method of transferring annuity credits from one to another should be developed.
2. It is imperative that the retirement amount be sufficient to provide ample incentive for reorientation.
3. Active participation by the employee not only in contributing to retirement and developing his own investments, but in planning for other activities, seems essential.
4. Disability retirement should be possible at any age and should be sufficient to provide for the reorientation which seems desirable.

EMPLOYEE ASSOCIATIONS

Personnel practice in a collegial institution might seem, at first consideration, to exclude the need for employee associations, except for promotion of professional purposes. Donald Wollett, Chairman of the American

---

[12] Merle R. Sumption and Yvonne Engstrom, *School-Community Relations* (New York: McGraw-Hill Book Company, Inc., 1966), p. 152.
[13] National Education Association, Research Division, School Law Summaries, *Tenure and Contracts* (Washington, D. C.: The Association, 1960), p. 3.

Bar Association committee on laws relating to government employment, has summed up the situation in government employment as follows:

1. A governmental employee association has grave difficulty in securing a firm commitment from a public official who is bound by actions of elected representatives who may themselves be recalled or defeated in the next election because of an unpopular decision.
2. Insistence by public employees on benefits or changes in working conditions when income may be fixed by legal restrictions causes employee associations to communicate an apparent willingness to place selfish considerations over public good.
3. The eventual resolution of the apparent impasse caused by these two conditions seems not to rest in legal procedures, but in the acceptance by employee associations of the responsibility to develop a complete communication system in terms of the public interest as it is supported or defeated by current personnel procedures.[14]

Wollett's comments suggest that some of the current conflicts and trends—which seem to be pushing organizations for educational employees into behavior more typical of industrial relations activity—may be misguided and eventually work to the detriment of such associations. He seems to imply the need for the creation of a special model for public school and other government employees. Instead of emphasis on collective bargaining, the prime concern might be on collective communication. This would imply definition of the role of professional employee associations as one of collegial cooperation for the public good rather than one primarily of economic combat.

The next decade and a half may very well see the development of a unique association among educational employees. It is clear that it can hardly be a copy of the industrial or business employee association that tradition and law have established as an integral combatant in a check and balance system with owners and the public to provide economic decisions of great importance to the society. The educational employee association appears to have more promise as an adjunct of the equity system in educational government. Operating as such it may become a key communication device with the public on such items as the following:

1. Feasibility of educational goals.
2. Equity in employment including compensation and termination.
3. Development of teaching skills, attitudes, and knowledge.
4. Criteria for specialists (perhaps even the designation of specialists).
5. Adequate school support.
6. Relative obligations of the members of the tripartite school government system.

SOME IMPORTANT IMPLICATIONS

District Size. The evidence shows that small school districts are inefficient and are not meeting educational needs. Many developments including the movement to metropolitan areas indicate that, by 1980, school districts and schools, especially rural and suburban areas, will be much larger in size. Metropolitan areas are also increasing in size.

[14] Donald W. Wollett, "The Public Employee at the Bargaining Table: Promise or Illusion?," *Journal of the College and University Personnel Association*, Vol. 17, No. 2 (February, 1966), pp. 20-27.

Implications:

1. Staff organization and operation will need to be adapted to the requirements of large school districts, but bureaucracy and red tape should be kept to a minimum.

2. Staff planning and assignment should be dynamic and flexible, providing maximum opportunity for each employee to satisfy his own hopes, desires, and ambitions by identification with the goals of the organization.

Educational Government. Educational government has been a tripartite partnership since 1787. Assumptions of new responsibilities by the federal government and increases in the size of school districts will require a re-examination of the roles of state and local governments.

Implications:

1. Direct professional attention should be paid to the nature of the partnership and laws relating to the powers of each should be designed to assure a unified pattern.

2. State programs for the training of teachers and administrators should concentrate not only on the training of specialists, but on the component teaching skills, attitudes, and knowledge essential for cooperation in deciding upon and reaching educational goals.

3. State certification policies should be designed to assure that teachers and administrators have minimum qualifications for assuming their appropriate responsibilities, and that properly organized districts have ample opportunity to determine their own personnel requirements in terms of their own needs.

Educational Goals. Technological change, metropolitanization, the availability of new knowledge, and transiency in the population are bringing about new concepts of the role of public education in society.

Implications:

1. New federal goals of education (i.e., economic growth, national defense, and social change) should be incorporated with classic goals (i.e., the right and wrong of social behavior, citizenship, and social mobility) to provide a unified goal structure for the guidance of the public and of school district employees.

2. School planning should translate these broad goals into specific outcomes of thirteen or more years of schooling, stated in terms of the expected skills, attitudes, and knowledge of students.

3. An effective planning procedure should be developed in every school district to establish rational sequential subgoals of instruction for thirteen or more years of public school education.

4. The planning mechanism should be sensitive not only to goal flexibility due to social change, but also to subgoal flexibility as more knowledge concerning how to achieve goals becomes available.

Educational Democracy. During the next few years, prospective changes in society and in education will inevitably involve every person engaged in education as well as the public. The method of involvement will reflect our current social commitment to industrial and governmental democracy.

Implications:

1. Developments relating to the search for a rationale for educational democracy indicate that schools should be institutionalized (goal-oriented as suggested by Selznick); that the relations between employees should be collegial (McGregor); and that personnel practices should be oriented toward assisting individuals to identify their hopes and desires with the goals of the organization (Argyris).

2. Assignments for employees (administrative, teaching, classified) should be based on or made in terms of specific subgoals stated in terms of behavioral changes required of students.

3. Individuals selected for employment should "fit" the cooperative working group in terms of compatible attitudes, skills, and the use of knowledge. New members of the working group should be able not only to appreciate the value of the work of others in the cooperative endeavor, but also to earn their respect and appreciation.

4. The school system should provide information to new employees in such form that they are able to understand the dimensions of the cooperative effort, and their unique role in the accomplishment of common goals.

5. Evaluation of employees should be geared to a confidence in their ability to direct their own self-improvement. Evaluation should be primarily directed toward reinforcement of desirable behavior.

6. Since collegiality is substantially impossible without organizational justice, inequities in compensation systems should be eliminated by the development of more flexible wage and salary systems.

7. Development of employee associations in government employment should enable them to become a major communication source for assisting citizens to make rational educational government decisions about the educational program and its support.

CHAPTER 13

Local Organization and Administration
Of Education

HENRY M. BRICKELL*

Not long ago the Superintendent of Schools in Manhasset (N. Y.) asked me to draw up some guidelines for our architect to use in designing a new elementary school building. "Describe the elementary school of the future," he said. After working on the paper for a few hours, I went back across the hall and said to the Superintendent, "About that elementary school of the future; what year did you have in mind?" It had not taken long to figure out that the elementary school program we wanted to put into the new building would change continually through the foreseeable future. It would not be fixed in some permanent shape, but would be always in the process of adapting to current social demands as well as to the growth in human knowledge to be transmitted, and adjusting to the emergence of better ideas about how to teach.

Specifying the year 1980 as a target simplifies the problem, but being handed some twenty-five thousand school systems to deal with—rather than just one—complicates it all over again. Schools in this country change along an extremely broken front; the school system I left a few weeks ago spends $1,600 per pupil and today enjoys a per pupil input of human and material resources most school districts will not have achieved even by 1980. Thus the projections in this paper will have to be modal; by 1980 some districts will be well beyond the condition predicted here, while others probably will be striving to achieve a 1960-calibre program.

It is difficult to choose between projecting *what will be* and prescribing *what ought to be.* I have made the choice rather reluctantly, projecting what I think will occur except where I believe it to be undesirable: in the latter cases, I say or imply what I wish would happen.

I recognize that the factors tending to hold education steady may be stronger than any forces now on the horizon which could change it appreciably during the next decade and a half. However, education constitutes what Kenneth Boulding has called an *evolutionary system* (Chapter 12).* In such systems, "time's arrow points up" toward the development of more complex, and sometimes unpredictable, forms. In evolutionary systems, a "system-break" may occur—a rather sudden (and often difficult-to-ex-

* *Professor of Education and Associate Dean for Research and Development, School of Education, Indiana University. Formerly Assistant Superintendent of Schools, Manhasset, New York. Publications include* Organizing New York for Educational Change.

---

* All references in parentheses are to chapters in the first conference report, *Prospective Changes in Society by 1980* (Denver, Colorado: Designing Education for the Future, July, 1966).

215

plain) decline, or a marked acceleration in the growth of knowledge or productivity such as occurred in American agriculture some thirty years ago. Forces now seem to be operating that could bring about such a "system-break" in education by 1980 or soon thereafter. Should such a break occur, some of the assumptions I have listed later in this introduction will need to be revised—and I shall be glad to revise them.

This paper is concerned with organizing and managing the various functions and services which the other speakers at this conference think education will be performing by 1980. It is difficult to write about organizing something without attempting to determine what that something will be—which has led me directly into the territory of some of the other speakers. Without knowing what they would predict, I have made the following assumptions as a basis for much of the discussion in subsequent sections of this paper:

> Changes in the major structural components of the local educational system —that is, in the choice of who teaches what to whom, at what time, in what place, with what methods and materials—will continue to be slow—probably too slow to meet some of the emerging needs.

> In 1980, full-time students in elementary and secondary education will still be selected by age, roughly the ages 4 to 17. By then, at least as many children will be receiving pre-kindergarten instruction as are now receiving kindergarten instruction, namely, about half the eligible age group. Probably some 5 year olds will still not be going to kindergarten.

> Students will be gathered into central locations and will be instructed primarily in school buildings. They will be taught by a staff of full-time and part-time professionals and a rapidly growing group of full-time and part-time sub-professionals.

> Instruction will be conducted basically from September through June, but by 1980 we will see an appreciable increase in summer instruction. School will operate Monday through Friday, with a larger use of Saturday for special experiences that cannot be conveniently scheduled through the week. The hours of instruction will remain about the same as at present, with special activities spilling over into afternoon and evening hours.

> Students will be grouped by age (the typical school in 1980 probably will retain the current grade designations), then be sub-divided by the subject being studied, and further sub-divided by ability and past achievement in these subjects.

> In the beginning years of school, one teacher will be responsible for teaching most subjects to a given group of children, but by the upper elementary years partial specialization will be the mode. This pattern is fully visible today in well-supported school systems where art, music, physical education, science, and in some cases mathematics, are taught by specialists—and even in a number of less well-supported schools where teachers exchange pupils for part of the day in order to teach their specialty subjects.

> Although the typical instructional groups will be 25 to 35 in size, there will be appreciable variations around that figure with groups reaching up to several hundred and down to one.

> The subject content will be contained largely in books, on film and in similar forms rather, in many cases, than in the teachers' heads. The information room in the school building will contain chiefly books but will have an appreciable collection of other materials.

> Very probably (I regret to assume), if one opens the door of a typical 1980 classroom and walks inside, the teacher will be standing up front talking.

This, then, is what I assume to be the basic shape of the local school to be administered in 1980. I hope some of these assumptions will not be consistent with the facts.

This paper gives attention to the following topics from among many which could have been chosen: an improved concentric pattern for local administrative units, the allocation of functions and the distribution of resources among them, the management of community relations and the role of laymen in decision-making, the management of personnel, and the management of instructional decision-making.

First, however, let me dispose briefly of two topics not dealt with fully in the paper:

School Business Management. Here I foresee by 1980 a more mechanized, more efficient accounting system without any appreciable change in the organization of the accounts. The ideas of program budgeting and cost accounting will still not be well developed and the typical school will still have only a primitive notion of what it is spending to produce a given amount of learning.

With respect to cleaning and maintenance, I expect added machinery to substitute for added manpower as schools are used more intensively. The transportation system will grow in size without changing in character; I expect that television will be used to bring the world in, and that school buses will not be used any more often than now to take the children out to see it. By 1980 we will have more central kitchens, more contract feeding services, and a far wider use of vending machines.

Non-instructional personnel will be appreciably more organized—perhaps more unionized—than today and school boards will be negotiating contracts with them as well as with teachers.

Administrative Use of Information. School men will be far better informed than they are today. The typical school will be collecting and processing far more information than it is today, either by using scaled-down computers or by sharing time on large ones. It will be possible to call up all sorts of summary information on pupils, on teachers, on budgets, and on buses.

However, we will still have such a vague notion of what is connected to what—of cause and effect relationships in education—that administrative decision-making will be scarcely any better than it is today. Improvement there will not come with the arrival of new data-handling equipment, but must await the emergence of better theories of school management and empirical proof that certain processes are associated with certain outcomes.

AN IMPROVED CONCENTRIC PATTERN FOR ADMINISTRATIVE UNITS

No one knows the optimum number of pupils for a single administrative unit—whether the administrative unit under study is a classroom, a school building, or a school system. Years of experience have generated such rules of thumb as these: a classroom should contain 25 pupils, or few enough that the teacher can teach each child occasionally rather than teach the whole class continually; a graduating class should contain at least 100, or enough that the high school can have a qualified teacher for every subject. For entire school districts, no widely-accepted rules of thumb seem to have emerged, except of course that the district should contain enough normal pupils to have classrooms of 25, graduating classes of 100, and enough handicapped and talented children to make it feasible to educate them at a reasonable unit cost.

Even in the past there have been problems with such rules of thumb. For one thing, both expert opinion and apparently successful practice have often differed from them. Private high school classes of 8 and 10 pupils have been advocated by distinguished headmasters and gladly paid for by affluent parents. City schools have operated elementary classes of 40 and 45 and have avoided scandal—at least until a needier population moved in and found their deficiencies unmet by standard city schooling. Many high school principals prefer a graduating class of 200 to 300, but graduating classes in some high-prestige suburban Chicago high schools climbed to over 1,000 before parents could be convinced that a second high school should be opened.

Moreover, recently it has been rather persuasively argued that the optimum size of a pupil group for effective instruction—or at least for efficient instruction—depends on what the pupils are to be taught. Some learning, the argument runs, occurs best when the student is taught all by himself; other learning occurs best in small discussion groups; still other kinds of learning take place better—or at least as well—when the student assembles with a large group to hear a superb presentation, which can be brought to him at a very low unit cost.

I would like to extend this line of reasoning about class size to the question of school size and school district size. Let me propose that there is no one optimum size for them any more than there is any one optimum size for a classroom group. Instead, these are probably optimum sizes for each of the many functions the school district has to perform. One size is probably best for educating blind children at a reasonable per pupil cost, another is probably best for underwriting a television production studio, another for genuine faculty involvement in policy-making, another for purchasing supplies and equipment economically, another for conducting in-service training, another for surrounding the schools with a fully-informed public, and so on for every function one can imagine. (I am speaking here of expenditure items but it ought to be equally clear that the optimum size of a school district for collecting revenue through local taxes would depend both on the functions it had to perform and on the distribution of taxable property in its section of the state.)

We have been attempting for a long time to establish minimum acceptable sizes for school districts, albeit without noticeable attention to any maximum size limit. We set a minimum by identifying some appropriate group of educational functions, determining the smallest number of pupils for whom those functions could be performed at a reasonable per pupil cost, and outlining a geographic area which we hope will contain the minimum number of pupils along with sufficient taxable property to finance their schooling. Then we set out to execute the plan despite changing school functions, a pupil population moving in all directions from the size predicted, and continually shifting property valuations. (We may later revise the plan to combine districts found to be still too small, although apparently never to divide those found to have grown too big.)

ALLOCATION OF FUNCTIONS

One consequence of seeking an acceptable minimum size and allocating all functions to every district above the minimum is that we immediately have to invent ways to escape the shortcomings of the sizes we have created. We arrange for too-small districts to use combined resources through such intermediate units as county offices. These regional supervisory and service units perform such functions as conducting surveys, operating classes for handicapped children, running film libraries, interpreting state regulations, sponsoring in-service training, offering consulting services of specialists, and so on. At the other end of the size scale we may arrange for too-large city districts to be sub-divided through such devices as subordinate school boards, area superintendents, neighborhood advisory committees, budget planning with public participation organized around individual school buildings, high schools with designated feeder elementary schools, and so on.

The unsuccessful struggle to find the perfect minimum size has been going on for many years. But the problem is going to get worse. Smith (Chapter 10), said that by 1980 a person "could have at his disposal a private telecommunications center which would incorporate a television and tape recording system, a two-way picturephone, a high speed electronic printer, and a combined computer and display unit." Under these circumstances a student might undertake a large part of his schooling at home. One function of the school district might then be to produce appropriate programs, transmit them, and monitor student responses. Every old argument for a school district of any given size collapses before such a prospect.

Or take William Knox's statement (Chapter 13) that "There appears, then, the possibility that a reasonable number of direct access computers will suffice to store and process in 'real-time' all the significant information now in the world's libraries." Judgments about the best size for a school turn in part on what it costs to put an information storage and retrieval room (commonly called a library) into the building. What Knox is telling us is that every library in the world may soon be put into the smallest school building for the price of a computer terminal. This means that by 1980 we may be able to forget the cost of an information room as a factor influencing school size.

Or take the suggestion by Philip Hauser and Martin Taitel (Chapter 3) that during the sixties and seventies grade school enrollment may go up an average of only one percent per year. Emphasis will shift, they suggest, from problems of *quantity* to those of *quality*—to the relocation, improvement and replacement of physical facilities, the improvement of personnel, and the innovation of better techniques and materials. Will the school district which has been best sized to grow in the past be sized best to improve in the future? Contrast predicted enrollment growth of the grade school with that of the colleges, which Hauser and Taitel place at 61 percent between 1965 and 1980—coming on top of the fifteen explosive growth years just behind us. Those writers point, of course, to the growing demand for community colleges. Will the school districts designed to conduct elementary and high schools be the best size to conduct community colleges—or should they transfer the ones they have to other administrative units?

One can go through every paper in *Prospective Changes in Society by 1980*, raising such questions. Having done just that, I now feel more strongly than before that we are not going to be able to find one ideal size for the 1980 school or school district.

I believe that what we need for 1980 and beyond is not simply bigger administrative units but instead a series of units arranged in concentric circles around each group of students, with *functions being passed back and forth among the units as circumstances change.* Let me emphasize the *back* since all we have learned how to do in most states is to pass functions *forth* to larger units, seldom giving them back again no matter how much the smaller unit grows in population, or wealth, or competency. I do want to point out that both California and New York have successfully handed on to growing local districts various functions which were previously performed by intermediate units when the local districts were smaller.

The smallest administrative unit is the classroom—or, in light of what we learned from the first publication, let us say that the smallest unit is the one which manages the interaction of one learner with an information source. The largest administrative unit is the entire nation. In between are the department, the school, the school district, multiple-district service agencies, the state, and multiple-state endeavors such as the Western States Small Schools Project, or the new Compact.

DISTRIBUTION OF RESOURCES

The walls between these units ought to be relatively thin and, to underscore the point once again, functions ought to be passed from unit to unit in either direction according to the job to be done and the resources available to the unit to do the job. It has occurred to me that the "resources available" test is not a very good one since larger units usually command more power to gather resources than smaller ones. This is one reason functions are passed upward to larger units and are seldom returned. To prevent the irrevocable flow upward, it seems to me that we *ought to associate the financing* with the *function and pass the funds back and forth along with the responsibility for doing the work.* What this means is that the cost of a specific function could be allocated in some proportion to local, area, state, regional and federal administrative units and that each of these would continue to pay its established share regardless of which administrative unit performed the work at a given time. What it also means, if we follow the matter through, is that students, teachers, supplies, equipment and whole buildings would have to be passed from one jurisdiction to another with relative ease. The flow should, of course, be reversible with equal ease.

It is essential that every ring of units be given equally effective taxing power so that functions will not gravitate to a level simply because it has the readiest source of funds. *Some form of tax sharing may be necessary so that revenues can be efficiently collected by the unit best situated to do so but made available to other units to finance their spending programs.* I believe that this nation is well served by a broken-front line of progress and by the imaginative diversity that can mean. Consequently, I rest easy with the idea of some administrative units on a given level being wealthier or better motivated than others, once all are enabled to operate at an acceptable minimum.

AN EXISTING PATTERN STRENGTHENED

You will recognize that the idea of concentric rings of administrative units is not revolutionary. Such a system has existed in part for many years and is even now being expanded. Teachers do some jobs in their own classrooms but hand others over to the remedial reading specialist employed by the school to handle problem cases. Principals find some new teachers on their own but depend on the superintendent's office to find most of the candidates. School districts operate classes for the handicapped if there are enough of them; otherwise they pool such children with neighboring school districts and have intermediate agencies operate the classes. Intermediate agencies of course look to the state to establish minimum standards for many school activities. The states expect the federal government to gather national school data and to support research and development in education.

Similarly, the new network of federally-financed school improvement agencies consisting of university-based Research and Development Centers, multi-state Regional Educational Laboratories, and multi-district supplementary education centers can be expected eventually to sort out activities along a research-to-practice continuum and begin to concentrate their efforts at selected stages. Local administrative units can be pictured as being located on the practice end of this continuum, in some cases handing existing local functions over to the new agencies and in other cases being handed new functions by those agencies.

Nevertheless, moving fully to the pattern recommended here would require many states to modify or scrap their present plans for school district reorganization and to map out instead a set of successively larger administrative units—smaller ones ringed by some larger ones—so that whatever the educational functions emerging from our changing society, there would be a unit of appropriate size to handle them. Undoubtedly an analysis would show that huge metropolitan school districts would have to be subdivided into administrative units of assorted sizes and that tiny rural districts would have to be combined and then ringed with administrative units of assorted sizes.

Without attempting to specify the size of various units, I have listed an illustrative set of functions for them below. The first function goes to the smallest unit; the latter ones to larger units.

Selecting learning experiences for students

Reporting pupil progress to parents

Diagnosing severe learning problems

Enlisting active parent participation in the education of children

Operating an elementary school

Operating a high school

Operating a community college

Operating classes for handicapped pupils

Purchasing instructional materials and equipment

Transporting pupils to school

Educating the staff in pedagogical method
Educating the staff in subject content
Maintaining an area film rental service
Providing high-speed, large-capacity data handling services
Establishing a cadre of external change agents
Demonstrating model instructional programs to encourage adoption
Evaluating instructional materials and equipment
Designing instructional materials and equipment
Producing and marketing instructional materials and equipment

As I sense the prevailing climate of opinion among those who think ahead about education, many read papers like those of William Wheaton on urban development (Chapter 8) and Paul Cherington on transportation (Chapter 11) and conclude that since we will become a few giant metropolitan areas, we ought to become a few giant school districts. While the proposition is understandably attractive to some, there seems much to be said for a multi-layer pattern of organization with the greater number of leadership positions it would create, its multiplication of staging areas for innovation, the opportunity to free a management staff for fresh duty by moving its former functions up or down one or two layers, the ease of adding a whole ring of novel-function agencies when necessary, and a better chance of getting some healthy inter-agency competition now and then.

THE MANAGEMENT OF COMMUNITY RELATIONS AND THE ROLE OF LAYMEN

During the economic cataclysm of the 1930's, our society underwent severe stresses that permanently changed many of its institutions of government. Schools did not escape. The high schools, suddenly asked to retain or re-absorb millions of young men and women no longer needed in the job market, found themselves with a non-college-bound group for whom most of them had no curriculum. There began an agonizing attempt at re-designing a school never meant to educate such students, coupled with an effort to hold the students inside while the remodeling was going on. Thirty years later, the high schools are still struggling to accommodate themselves to these students, so great was the change demanded of them.

Although the public had given the problem to the high schools in the 1930's, the professional staff at that time had to articulate the need for a new curriculum and try to elicit public support for it. Perhaps because the people were staring down a long gray road stretching to a leaden horizon they were not in an expansionist mood. Perhaps because everything else seemed to be adrift, the people wanted to hold education steady. Perhaps because the progressive movement in education had led to a few well-publicized excesses, professional leadership was under suspicion. Whatever the reason, attempted experimentation in the schools during those years aroused negative public reaction in some instances.

The recollection of those years lasted a long time in the professional mind. Not much happened during the educational neglect of the World

War II years to change professional feeling that the public was reluctant to accept change in education. And then after the war came the attacks on schools: We were trying to erect crystal palaces instead of schoolhouses; we were neglecting basic education in favor of teaching fly-casting; we systematically ignored the gifted; we were generally un-American and specifically favored the United Nations; and we had not taught Johnny Flesch how to read.

Then in the mid-1950's there came a great change. The waves of criticism pounded upon the educational shore still—but there was a difference in their sound. It was 1954. In that year the Supreme Court called upon the schools to take the first serious step in a century to move the races of the nation toward a long-delayed social integration. The order was a criticism of our past failures but it contained the confidence that we were important and the hope that we could serve a great purpose.

Three years later came Sputnik and with it a not-too-different criticism: once again we had failed the nation—yet we were worth rejuvenating and sending forth another time. The post-Sputnik years have seen us occupying center stage, uneasy under the spotlight, gratified by the applause, but fearful about our ability to reform as expected. Pricked by the foundations, kicked by the legislatures, enticed into a harness by the blandishments of the Congress, we are about ready to move. But we are wondering how many fast new steps the local public will accept—and will pay for. While we pause, wondering, we are dubbed "The Establishment." We are pictured as a tired old regime, opposed to change, backing down the road to the future.

How can it be so? How can the "wild" progressives of yesteryear— the identical men in some cases—have become the defenders of the old order today? What seems to have happened is that the public—the part that organizes itself around schools, in any case—has moved out beyond us so far that our goals of the 30's lag behind their aspirations of the 60's. What group of educators seriously proposed in the 30's that we should build a society so productive that if every man, woman, and child in the nation climbed into automobiles at once no one would have to ride in a back seat; that a basic income ought to be guaranteed to every family regardless of whether anyone in the house works; that the ideal of an equal-opportunity school where every child has a chance to learn should be abandoned in favor of a variable-process school where every child has the obligation to learn; that attendance areas ought to be manipulated to produce racial balance in the schools; that parochial school children ought to use public school equipment and materials and perhaps attend some classes there; or that every high school graduate should go on to some form of higher education? Yet these are the kinds of aspirations that guide our society and even now have either been achieved or are within reach.

Even in 1961, when I had an occasion to make a thorough study of change in schools throughout New York State, I could not find the public to be an anchor holding back professional experimentation. And today the people seem more ready for change than they were then. By 1980, the climate for innovation will be still better. The average citizen will have been educated a bit beyond high school, millions will have had personal experiences with new types of programs in their own schooling, the absolute necessity of being educated will have borne in on just about everybody, and an education will be regarded as the best legacy to leave one's young (as well as the only one most fathers can assemble). Moreover, new patterns of school finance will have been put into operation to ease the direct cost of new programs to the local taxpayer. In fact, an appreciable number of the innovations available will be designed to cost the same or less than current programs.

The factors mentioned will, at the same time, make the public more interested in and more intelligent about education. Communicating with laymen from the platform and in print and in person will consume at least as much of administrative time as it now requires. More school systems will be large enough to afford staff specialists to operate information programs.

Self-appointed and Board-appointed citizens committees will continue to rise and fall on the local scene. One difference will be advanced competency on the part of members. A more important difference will be the appearance on these committees of men who can claim expertness in educational media and methods because they are employed by public agencies or private companies to manage or conduct the internal or external education and training programs which speakers at the first conference predicted would suffuse our society. In other words, by 1980—for better or worse—the general public won't be so general any more.

Organized citizens' interest will continue to be expressed at the level of the local administrative unit, but it will also have been organized to exert influence on the new units ringing the locality. By then it will have become clear to citizens that one powerful way to shape programs in the local schools will be to guide what the external change-agencies choose to work on. What is at present predominantly professional control of the research and development agencies, such as the Regional Educational Laboratories and the Elementary and Secondary Education Act, Title III supplementary centers—which have been newly created by Federal funding—will in time yield to lay control as these agencies become fully institutionalized and establish working relationships with existing school systems.

The next two decades or so will witness a fundamental re-examination of lay governance of what will become increasingly professional, better staffed, and better-managed school systems. Some professional educators will urge that the enterprise has become too complex, too specialized, too technical for lay control. During the same two decades, there will be a less fundamental, less urgent but nonetheless serious re-examination of the substantial independence of school government from municipal government and its relative independence from other branches of state government. Some students of government and some practicing politicians will argue that the schools have become too big, too expensive, too central a public function for semi-separate government.

When the dust settles—and it will not have settled completely by 1980—the laymen will still be in charge and education will still be appreciably independent of other government endeavors. But there will be differences. For one thing, lay members of governing boards (down below 100,000 in number compared to about 500,000 in the 1920's) will be better educated and more intelligent than many of those now serving. They will be just as inquisitive and demanding as those of today but somewhat less picayune. Most important, they will be *far more interested in the substance and method of the instructural program than they are now. They will withdraw somewhat more than now to the policy level,* but when they do, *they will become considerably tougher-minded about what constitutes real evidence of accomplishment.* They will understand the difference between process (instruction) measures and product (learning) measures and will seek cause and effect relationships between them. They will be starting to talk about cost-per-learning-increment for assorted grades and subjects and types of pupils, and they will want to know comparable costs of alternative methods of instruction to which the school might change.

For another thing, the settling dust will reveal a *wholly-new pattern of interagency cooperation between schools and other public institutions.* Combined programs, jointly-appointed personnel, shared buildings, contracted services, common professional libraries, jointly-funded research studies, multi-agency project development teams, consolidated data-handling centers, and other such arrangements will link schools to welfare and health departments, to transportation and traffic bureaus, to hospitals and nursing homes, to municipal centers for the aged, to park and recreation divisions, and to planning authorities. Linkages will come about because of legislative concern for efficiency and avoidance of duplication, because of client demand for integrated services, and because of professional recognition of contiguous or overlapping areas of knowledge and expertise. Linkages will be accompanied by the mushrooming of educational components in the programs of every other government agency.

What should the states do now to prepare for all this? Most of it will happen through natural events and need not—probably could not—be directed. But there are two things a state should do, and rather soon. One is to see that the laws permit a broad range of inter-agency cooperative endeavors, including the pooling of funds for projects where the ultimate benefits cannot be allocated clearly among agencies and the project costs thus could not be. To give one example: an employee transferred temporarily to another agency should be assured of the same personnel benefits as if he had not moved.

The other thing a state should do through its education department is to make sure that universities, professional associations, or something like a state-subsidized Institute for Government Study, mount programs and train lay board members and school administrators to deal with each other. Both groups will have a lot to learn.

THE MANAGEMENT OF PERSONNEL

For about three decades, to manage personnel in public schools has meant to manage groups. Personnel have been clustered in a few large blocks and described by such position titles as classroom teacher, principal, supervisor, and guidance counselor. Members of a given group have been treated quite similarly with respect to responsibilities, recognition, compensation, fringe benefits, and training opportunities. Specialization of roles and differentiation of titles have been remarkably limited for an enterprise with two million employees and 40 million clients scattered in 25,000 agencies.

Consistent—in many cases blindly uniform—treatment of personnel came about partly because earlier abuses by school boards and administrators under an individual contract system eventually led professional workers in education to organize and press for uniform treatment under tenure and with identical salary schedules. The pressure succeeded partly because other factors worked toward the same outcome. Among those factors were these: the teaching act had not been carefully enough analyzed to allow for subdivision of the work; the simple tools available at the primitive level of technological development existing in education could be mastered by every worker; professional organizations did not develop devices to recognize levels of competence above the certification floor set by each state; teachers became readily replaceable and interchangeable in a system which had to be designed to operate successfully with a highly transient body of employees; strong connections between pupil ability and pupil achievement and weak connections between teaching and pupil achievement made the evaluation of a teacher's effectiveness difficult; and there were certain attractive administrative simplicities in the equal treatment of all personnel within a category.

The establishment of block treatment set the stage for an effective appeal by labor unions for the allegiance of teachers. The force of that appeal has been strengthened in the present decade as unions have begun devoting substantial resources to organizing teachers. The custom of block treatment, however, had set the stage equally well for the quick and effective reaction of the National Education Association (NEA) in offering its members the substitution of not-so-different negotiations and sanctions for the union offer of bargaining and strikes. Both the traditional union and the new NEA styles will lead to further rigidities in the pattern of block treatment of personnel as teachers' organizations successfully negotiate contracts with boards of education during the next few years.

We can fully expect that, by 1980, both local teachers' organizations and boards of education will employ full-time or part-time negotiators to present their cases at the bargaining table. We also can expect appreciable growth in arbitration machinery and in the number of arbitrators employed to settle disputes. The administration of policies and regulations determined under personnel contracts, and the handling of an unbroken string of grievances arising under them, will absorb so much administrative time that specialist positions will be created in school systems to manage this function. I confess to being more than a little distressed by this prospect but I am at a loss to see how the great forces moving us in this direction can be successfully resisted.

It can be expected that the multitude of changes detailed in this and in other papers will lead both to the elaborate subdivision of the position presently entitled "classroom teacher" and to the concomitant creation of a wide range of special management jobs. The process will have begun but will be neither clearly conceived nor well advanced in the typical school district by 1980.

The present role of teacher will gradually evolve into a cluster of roles encompassing such discrete functions as team leader, formulator of detailed objectives, instructional sequence planner, script writer, presenter of information, evaluator of pupil responses, and designer of supplementary pupil experiences. The new administrative and supervisory specialties will include position titles such as Specialist in Outside Developments, Supervisor of Professional Training, Director of Equipment Acquisition and Maintenance, Chief of Materials Production, Program Assessor, Coordinator of Temporary Personnel Assignments, Professional Librarian, and Travel Officer. We can anticipate that an Assistant Superintendent for Development and Training will cap off the pyramid of such positions in the central office of the school system. We can also expect specialists in development and training to appear in principals' offices at the school building level. In some cases, newcomers will take over administrative routine to free the principals for development and training work, but in most cases the principal will continue as before, leaving the new functions to new specialists. I expect that the new role will be titled "Specialist in Development and Training" more often than it is titled "Assistant Principal". I also expect that there will be appreciable tension between the two positions as the principal relies on his traditional authority in his dealings with teachers and the specialist relies on his access to borrowed central office authority and his ability to control assorted monetary and prestige awards in his efforts to cause changes in teacher behavior.

We can expect, even by 1980, an enormous expansion in sub-professional or para-professional full-time and part-time workers. Some will be attached to teachers as general aides, while others will serve as instructional machine operators, playground supervisors, information room clerks, data assistants, equipment maintenance technicians, travel aides, and so on. Assistant teaching will become one of the great service occupations of our nation in the final quarter of this century. (We can anticipate junior college curricula emerging to prepare such people.) There will, of course, be a matching expansion in the number of administrative officers at both system office and building office levels to recruit, allocate, train, compensate, supervise, and evaluate the growing army of education aides.

I believe the implications of all this for state action are quite clear, and I see no reason to expect them to be different in the mountain area states than elsewhere. Each state will be pressed into making laws governing the negotiations of teachers' organizations with their employing boards. I hope that the legislatures will lean toward requiring boards to give teachers a significant voice in an orderly, visible pattern of local policy making, with the policies recorded not in contract documents but in a more accessible location and one where they will be easier to change. I hope also that the legislatures will refuse to erect intricate, mechanistic, multi-phase schemes for negotiations and appeals that will drive teachers and school boards to send mercenaries to do battle in a legal jungle, speaking to each other thenceforth in pre-recorded messages transmitted through mouthpieces.

With regard to the coming multiplication of professional and semi-professional functions and job titles, any state which wishes to certificate either full-time or part-time personnel in either type of position will have to move very rapidly to avoid being squarely in the way of desirable change by local schools. A major restudy of certification requirements will probably be necessary immediately, along with the creation of a *well-staffed* agency or continuing commission to monitor the spate of changes ahead—especially in semi-professional employment. A periodic reassessment of the field will not be often enough; it will have to be continuous.

I would strongly recommend broadly-sketched position categories until clear-cut functions become firmly identified with particular positions. I would urge the use of all sorts of temporary and interim approvals to permit schools to employ whomever they want. The decade or two just ahead will give public schools their best chance in the past half century to attract lively, creative people of the sort who have too-often avoided school teaching in the past. I say: Swing open the doors. The place can be made neat again after they come in.

THE MANAGEMENT OF INSTRUCTIONAL DECISION-MAKING

By 1980, we may expect lay governing boards and administrative staffs to be making somewhat more rational decisions about modifications in instructional programs than is the case today. Orderly control of any process requires several steps: (See *Figure a, page 229*).

Orderly control of instructional change of course requires a similar series of steps : (See *Figure b, page 230*).

A sequence of steps like this forms a simple "control loop". A loop of this kind is absolutely essential for making instructional decisions systematically. Let us look at each of the major steps in some detail.

SETTING EDUCATIONAL OBJECTIVES

General goals are set for any institution by the external social system which controls and supports it. Thus *every school district needs a sensing device* to accomplish for it what the first publication accomplished for the eight states sponsoring this project: that is, to determine which coming events in the external environment have implications for the local program. It is not necessary for sensing devices to be replicated in every school district; one located in a central unit such as a state education department could serve many localities. However, every community needs to be firmly connected to such a mechanism. Otherwise, novel instructional programs will arrive as mandates from the state or subsidies from the federal government before sluggish local boards recognize that students need to be taught something new.

The key audience for the intelligence coming to the local district from a need-sensing device is the board of education and others who influence major policy decisions. *The board is officially responsible for setting local*

Figure a

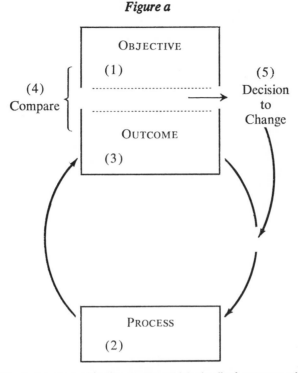

(1) The choice of an objective against which the final outcome will be judged.
(2) The selection of a process to produce the outcome.
(3) The measurement or description of the resulting outcome.
(4) The comparison of the outcome with the objective.
(5) If the outcome falls short of the objective, a decision to select another process.

school objectives beyond those specified by state law. In practice this is not done by the board *a priori,* but is done and redone with accumulating experience. And it is not done unilaterally. It is instead the result of interaction with the community and with the professional staff.

When objectives are casually selected and vaguely conceived, it follows that decisions about whether to shift to some newly-available instructional program will be made on grounds other than its probable effect on student learning. The popularity of an innovation, its cost, parental pressure, faculty lassitude, administrative enthusiasm, prospects of personal gain and other motivations to change (or to remain the same) are always available and they will be controlling. Instructional change in such circumstances is likely to be random.

Setting educational objectives is not a simple process. What a person needs to know in order to succeed under given social conditions is not apparent from a casual inspection of those conditions. Thus *every school district needs an arrangement for deriving school objectives from projected social changes*—that is, to do for local districts what this second conference

Figure b

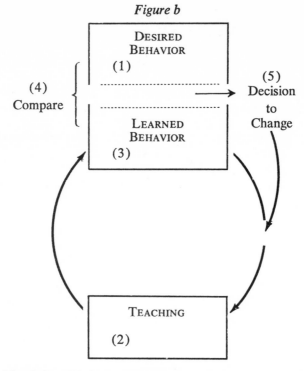

(1) The choice of desired pupil behavior against which learned pupil behavior will be judged.
(2) The selection of teaching activities to produce the desired behavior.
(3) The measurement or description of what pupils actually learned.
(4) The comparison of their learned behavior with the desired behavior.
(5) If the learned behavior falls short of the desired behavior, a decision to select a better set of instructional experiences.

is in part attempting to do for the eight sponsoring states. To make up an example, the city of Denver needs an arrangement for reexamining its present high school curriculum while it holds before itself the statement of Gerhard Colm (Chapter 5):

> If we are entering an age in which only few workers are needed in the production process, and in which for most people non-remunerative work must give a meaning to their lives, people must obtain purchasing power regardless of whether they do remunerative work or not. The emphasis would no longer be on the need to work but on the need to develop a society based on no-work.

A large district may have the resources and the time for thinking through such a statement and deriving instructional goals, but a great many local school systems will need outside help. To be useful, goals must be written as careful descriptions of what students should be able to do at selected points in their school and after-school careers. Unless broad goals are subdivided and made explicit by skilled professionals, they have no value in guiding instruction.

CHOOSING AND OPERATING INSTRUCTIONAL PROGRAMS

When an instructional goal has been established, the school must then choose a teaching program which it believes will lead to the desired behavior in students. Where is the program to come from? By 1980 it will be widely recognized that it takes a great deal of money to design reliably effective curricula with their associated equipment and materials. This should be fully apparent to us today inasmuch as virtually all major curriculum innovations for the past ten years have been lavishly financed, in most cases by the federal government. It will become increasingly evident by 1980 that many of the administrative units which can successfully operate schools are too small or too poor in resources, or simply do not regard it as their primary business to develop new instructional programs. They will operate largely as adopters or adapters of programs designed (and hopefully tested) by outside agencies.

I regard it as urgent that by 1980 the more resourceful administrative units such as cities, subdivisions of states, entire states, or clusters of states become aggressively engaged in curriculum development so that all schools will have a diversity of high-quality programs to choose from and we will not have drifted into nationwide curricular uniformity by default. Very large geographic areas are just being placed under the umbrellas of the new regional educational laboratories, which are being charged, among other duties, with the responsibility for designing outstanding new programs.

To return to the local school system which stands at the point of choosing an instructional arrangement, it must decide whether to modify a program it is currently using, or to create a wholly new one on its own initiative, or to adopt or adapt an outside program. Whichever it chooses, many steps lie between the final decision and the actual coming to life of the new scheme in the appropriate classrooms. The staff must be made aware of the decision, if this has not already been done, and must be told that the innovation enjoys strong administrative endorsement. In the best of circumstances, the staff will become genuinely involved in the decision as to how the program will be implemented. In addition, general public acceptance of the program must be aroused.

Beyond this, it may be necessary to amend the school testing program, to eliminate restrictive regulations which would interfere with the new plan to modify physical facilities, or to adjust time schedules. Probably it will be necessary to order and distribute new materials and equipment. Initial staff training is essential; continuing staff training probably will be needed for some time after the program has been introduced. It may be desirable to try the program in local pilot settings before introducing it throughout the entire system.

The new enterprise will be conducted with whatever degree of skill local personnel can bring to it. The result of an adoption may be a pale, fragmentary, or inaccurate copy of the original. On the other hand, it may be a full-scale, faithful likeness. Or it may even be something which, in the hands of skilled local teachers, becomes better than its designers ever dreamed it could be.

ASSESSING LEARNING

A student's learning can be assessed by administering paper and pencil tests, by interviewing the student, by observing his performance in contrived situations designed to test his skills or in real situations such as employment on a job.

Who should judge and measure actual learning? Good teachers do it frequently during the very act of teaching. They may check student progress from moment to moment as well as from week to week or month to month. A student's parents evaluate his learning immediately and his employers and adult associates evaluate it ultimately. While he is still in school, other students make highly influential judgments. In all likelihood, the most important judgment is that made by the student himself.

Because the school system is responsible for the design of a long requence of experiences which will develop as much of the student's talent as possible before he graduates, it must watch his progress from year to year. One teacher cannot be responsible for anything but a small segment of a student's learning. The school is made up of more than the teachers who individually staff it; as an institution it has responsibilities to the student beyond those of any teacher. It is chiefly for this reason that the school cannot leave even highly competent individual teachers to choose, unguided, the instructional programs they will use with their students. The school needs to maintain cumulative student records, open to all teachers who deal with the student. It also needs to make the long-term assessment of his progress the special responsibility of such personnel as guidance counselors.

COMPARING THE OUTCOME WITH THE OBJECTIVES

The educated—or schooled—student eventually enters his society (or more exactly, takes on new roles in his society) and displays his abilities along with other graduates. His performance is measured against what is necessary to succeed in the new roles he has taken on—worker, voter, father, user of leisure time, or student at a more advanced level. It must be recognized that some time has elapsed since the community first set the goals toward which the student's education was directed. As a consequence, he may launch into the rapidly-flowing stream of events which constitutes the society, only to find that he is not able to navigate. The society for which he was preparing may have become unable to absorb him in one or more roles. In short, the *school may succeed but the graduate may fail.* To repeat an earlier point, school boards need good sensing mechanisms to guide their choice of goals.

The quality of the graduate's performance eventually leads citizens, through the board of education and other channels of influence, to request the schools: (1) to continue striving toward the objectives previously set, or (2) to modify them in order to turn out students who can be more successful, or (3) to abandon the previous objectives completely and to choose ones which will help future waves of students enter a now-different society. It is absolutely essential for the preservation of local prerogative in education and distinctiveness in local programs that local educational in-

stitutions—which are at present so variously capable of sensing and responding to the demands from the external environment—be made sensitive
and responsive. This means in essence that they must be led to see what is
happening and to see what this means for their programs. Equally important, they must be financed well enough to gather instructional resources
when they are the logical agency for a job and they must be organized so
that they can pass selected functions up or down to other agencies which
can do that job better. Otherwise the people will not take their demands to
local school boards and school officials: instead the people will take them
directly to their state capitals or to Washington. Instructional decisions will
then be made at those levels and the local schools will tend to become instruments for achieving only those goals which can be forcefully presented
at the highest levels of government through the regular political system. If
that is allowed to happen in the next two or three decades, this century will
close with the loss of the most flexible and domination-proof mass education plan man has been able to devise.

SEARCHING FOR BETTER PROGRAMS

Whenever a school system finds an unacceptable gap between what its
students are learning and what it has chosen for them to learn, it then
searches among the alternative instructional programs available for teaching
the same behaviors. The alternatives include those programs it has abandoned in previous years, those now being used by its neighbors, those
being deliberately demonstrated around the nation to encourage adoption,
and those being marketed by commercial companies.

Suppose the search reveals nothing that promises to teach better what
the school is now teaching poorly. At this point we can visualize a request
going out from the school system, calling for the development of one or
more instructional programs to achieve its goals. If many such calls for
assistance arise from school systems, we can expect that the outside
agencies responsible for the development of programs will respond.

There is at present no adequate method for local school systems to collect and pool their instructional problems so that these can be transmitted
to some central agency. When the Elementary and Secondary Education
Act of 1965 provided in Title III for the creation of supplementary education centers, some state officials envisioned those regional centers as ideally
situated to survey the needs of school systems in their service areas. They
expected the centers to collect and consolidate instructional problems and
to transmit the more urgent and widespread of them to a development
agency. It remains to be seen whether the Title III centers will take on this
function and develop methods and instruments to perform it well.

Clearly, any state wanting to guide its school districts into the final
quarter of this lively century must design some way of surveying local needs
and articulating requests for help on problems which are widely shared. Certainly from the viewpoint of any agency interested in developing new instructional programs, it must have some sort of "market survey" to help it
set priorities among the almost infinite number of instructional problems it
might try to solve.

When a novel alternative does become available, the school in 1980 may be expected to be somewhat less casual than now in switching from an existing instructional plan to a new one because of vague claims made for the innovation by those who developed it or those who sell it or even those who use it. We can expect the school to search for and to study with extreme care the reports of field experiments which yield evidence on the strengths and weaknesses of the innovation.

The school should ascertain as accurately as possible, for example, whether the pupils for whom it intends to use the program are like those who used it successfully during the field experiment and whether the proper circumstances for the program can be duplicated locally. If data on the characteristics of the innovation or its cost or its limitations or—as always, most important—its probability of success are not available, the school should insist that they be provided before it will seriously consider adoption.

It is reasonable to believe that *unless the consumers of educational programs become more critical, the producers will not be obligated to become more careful.* Today it is only an ideal, but there would be a gain for the entire educational system if by 1980 the local schools would begin insisting upon sound information about the programs urged upon them by federal projects, national curriculum development groups, commercial publishers, state education departments, enthusiastic professors, neighboring school systems, other schools in their own city, half-informed parents, and teachers on their own faculties.

THE ROLE OF THE STATE IN IMPROVING LOCAL INSTRUCTIONAL DECISION-MAKING

Many of us talk today about a long continuum stretching from the research laboratory all the way out to the operating classrooms. We think of that continuum as consisting of a series of interlocked activities called basic research, development, evaluation, and dissemination. It has been my view that the state education department ought to be the direct sponsor of program development. By this I do not mean the writing of curriculum guides but rather the creation of complete instructional packages. This department also should be the direct sponsor of program evaluation. By this, I do not mean the convening of a committee to pass judgment on the latest textbook but rather rigorous field experimentation with new programs to find what they will teach to which children under what conditions. I believe that the state education department should leave basic research and program dissemination to other agencies. Basic research belongs to the universities and dissemination belongs in intermediate units which are closer to the receiving schools. While a function need not be assigned exclusively to one type of agency, those named seem best equipped for the work indicated. What may happen is that interagency organizations will take over most research, development, evaluation, and dissemination functions—using existing agencies for selected parts of the job.

But let us look at the local school which is the target of all this effort. How can the state assist it to get more rational control over all the outside help pressing in upon it? I have said that local schools need to use some sort of control loop to guide their decisions. State departments should help localities build such loops.

Suppose, for example, that the states suddenly stopped mandating specified amounts of instruction in assorted subjects and instead started mandating specified amounts of learning. After all, it is learning we are after, not the mere conduct of instruction. If a state department were to require learning instead of requiring teaching, it could drop its teacher certification apparatus completely, or at the very least treat teacher education programs like other schools—that is, specify what their graduates have to be able to do rather than what they have to be taught. What a change there would be—and what a scramble! Local schools would suddenly be free of state restrictions on how to instruct and they could choose any promising program. But because the school had to *produce learning instead of simply producing teaching,* we can imagine that the schools would examine alternative programs with a wholly new eye. Local demand for pretested and proven new programs would rise to a level unknown before. Program developers would, for the first time, face a tough, sophisticated market.

Think of the side effects. Program developers would have a set of performance specifications around which to design their instructional packages. States would have a rational base and a practical use for statewide testing. The need-sensing mechanism discussed earlier would have a place to send its reports.

Then the states would have to make sure every locality was capable of producing the mandated learning. Think what a new base this would give for organizing local school districts and for setting minimum levels for state finance.

In fact, think what such a shift as this would mean within the state education department, an agency utterly trapped in its 19th Century habit of regulating things. No other agency, public or non-public, is so trapped by its past. It is the picture of frozen power.

Unless the states can find some new way to apply their authority, other agencies will be created by the people to make their schools ready for 1980 and the years beyond.

Supplementary Statement

KEITH GOLDHAMMER*

Social agencies come into being to serve human needs. It is not likely that they are carefully designed. They seem to get started, to develop and expand, to acquire particular stable characteristics, to become institutional-

* *Associate Dean, School of Education, University of Oregon;* Professor of Education, University of Oregon (1961-); Associate Director, Center for the Advanced Study of Educational Administration, University of Oregon (1964-). Publications include: *The American School Board,* 1964; *Superintending American Schools* (*A Sociological Analysis*), in progress; and numerous articles in professional journals.

ized, to accrete functions in order further to justify their existence, and to persist. The longer they persist, the more instituionalized they become. The more firmly they become institutionalized, the more they resist pressures of outside agencies to change, to adjust, to accommodate to the newer and ever shifting demands of the broader society whose purposes they presumably serve.

Perhaps this is too pessimistic a view of a social agency such as public education. Perhaps, one will argue, the times demand change. and educational institutions will have to be responsive to that change. No doubt they will be. But most demands for change are primarily for minor changes—and powerful control mechanisms exist both within and without schools to guarantee that the normal organizational processes will maintain equilibrium and that dynamic changes will occur only under exigent conditions. It would be advantageous if educational organizations could be constantly self-adjustive to their environment and the needs of the society of which they are a part. It seems more likely, however, that most will change because they are forced to follow certain directions rather than because they are truly adaptive mechanisms.

IMPACT OF SOCIETY ON ORGANIZATION AND ADMINISTRATION

Brickell projects some characteristics of local school organization and administration in the not too distant future. This writer cannot add to his insight. Perhaps, however, it would be well to examine some characteristics of our society that are forcing educators and the relevant publics to look at the present structures and processes of local school administration in order to see in what directions the public schools may be impelled.

Can we possibly predict what types of changes might be legitimated for the schools of 1980 and beyond? One of the first characteristics of our age that comes to mind when we explore this question is that this is an age of mass communications dominated by commercial enterprises for the purpose of selling their products. Those suggested innovations which have the possibility of "stimulating economic activity" will certainly find acceptance in leading newspapers and journals which cater to the tastes and interests of present and potential advertisers. Couple this characteristic with the fact that this is an age of increasing technological advance, and there is some strong indication of what the future may portend.

The schools, obviously, must do their share to maintain the industrial machine by adapting structures, processes, and programs to the utilization of the technological products of industry. We can expect that powerful influences will endeavor to convince educators that the school of tomorrow can be run by computers. Scheduling will be computerized (and made sufficiently flexible to guarantee either maximum adaptability of the schedule to the needs of the child or maximum complexity of the process of schedule formation, even beyond the capability of human manipulation). Learning will be largely mechanized. Teaching will become a more highly integrated machine operation. As Brickell points out, the school administrator will have at his command the products of rather elaborate and technically astonishing data storage and retrieval systems so that he can obtain all of the information he wants on any subject pertinent to school operations. Industry, of course, has gone a long way in helping to work out the technologies involved. No one, as yet, has really helped the school administrator know what he should do with the machines after he does the socially acceptable thing of investing the taxpayer's money in them.

Because they are salable, technological innovations will be strongly endorsed, and school boards and administrators will be pressured to "join the club." We can expect that advertising and technology will lead to rather massive efforts to "individualize" the schools, using programmed learning, teaching machines, and computer processes as the primary technologies both of administration and teaching. Already, efforts are being made to encourage educators to draw up the models for the completely individualized and programmed schools and to define the roles of the teachers and the administrators when they will be plugging pupils into computers and *vice versa.* Lest we forget, in the 1930's educators tried to "sell" a "humanized" concept of individualization of instruction, including lower teacher-pupil ratios, adaptation of learning processes to the needs of children and communities, and provision of a range of special services required to help children overcome their learning disabilities. There were few, if any, gadgets to sell. Taxpayers at that time refused to invest as much in the human side of school enterprise as they will be called upon to invest in the mechanical.

A third characteristic of our age is that our *society is in a rebellion against paternalism.* This is manifested in all segments of society and takes on various forms and colorations. The growing student unrest, the augmenting taxpayer's revolt, the new militancy of teachers, the fluctuating tide of administrator acceptance by the public (love them today and hate them tomorrow)—all are symptomatic of the fact that people are not happy to be subordinated to the will of others. The administrator who feels that he is the "boss" of the school, or the school board that exercises proprietary authority over the schools, is bound to arouse displeasure among various groups and produce tensions within the community and the school, which have high potential for arousing increasing hostility and conflict.

Coordinated with the antagonism against paternalism is the increasing level of education of the publics with which the school administrator must deal. The level of educational attainment of the general public is much higher than at any other time in our history. It can truly be said that American society is the most highly educated society in the history of the world. We cannot expect a highly educated society—particularly when its members have been educated in a school system that taught the principles of democracy (the social Darwinian concepts of free enterprise, success through hard work, and the independence of the human spirit)—to be a docile society. The parents of today were reared in a spirit of search for human dignity, resistance to irrational authority, and concern for the principle of "to thine ownself be true." Inevitably, they reared their children more permissively than they had been reared. The spirit of independence and individuality dominated their art and literature—and they bought their children television sets and books in which defiance and "taking the law into one's own hands" for noble purposes were extolled.

The case of the school teacher is not much different. Thirty years ago the typical teacher was female, a product of a teacher's college, and was hoping someday to have a bachelor's degree through attendance at summer school. Today there are more men teachers with families to support. More teachers have master's degrees today than had bachelor's degrees thirty years ago, and more teachers are products of liberal arts colleges and departments. They are a different and more independent breed, and they want to have a voice in affairs which affect educational programs and their own welfare. The wise administrator realizes that here is a source of professional competence and knowledge that needs and demands to be incorporated into the decision-making process.

THE CHANGING ROLE OF ADMINISTRATION

There is no longer a single center of authority within the school system. The absolute powers of both the school board and the superintendent have long been "withering away." In all probability they will never completely disappear, but their functions are changing. Organizations need central, coordinating switchboards. And our instruments of traditional governance on the local level are inevitably becoming increasingly that. One reason is that the *publics relevant to the schools today need leadership rather than domination; they crave participation rather than obedience; they seek involvement rather than alienation.*

To a considerable extent, the schools are the victims of their own accomplishments. Better than anyone realized, it now appears, they taught a spirit of democratic participation. In a vast segment of our society, instruction caught hold, and the schools are now the center of a ferment for democratic participation in local governance.

It must be recognized that there are other pressures, as well, which force the school board and administration to become coordinating centers rather than autocratic governors of the schools. The concentric pattern of administrative units which Brickell envisages calls for several departures from the traditional patterns of school governance. Perhaps we will preserve smaller schools in sparsely inhabited sections of the country, but the educational needs of the children in these areas will not differ from the needs of their peers in larger communities. Educational programs and special services will have to be made available which would be beyond the ability of the local, isolated, rural community to provide. Attendance units will have to be preserved, but administrative units, to assure equity in the educational opportunities of children, must be enlarged. One would hope that adequate citizen and professional advisory, planning, and development opportunities will be provided, but coordinating and resource allocating centers, which will serve much larger geographic areas, will be essential. General policy-making for such areas will be more remote from and less capable of being scrutinized by the local citizen who has only casual association with school affairs.

There are both assets and liabilities associated with the larger administrative units. More essential educational services can be extended to more students. Programs which require special facilities and which serve the needs of only small segments of the school population can be available to larger numbers. Centralization should result in many efficiencies and economics of operation. But the larger the school organization becomes, the greater is its tendency to bureaucratize procedures and apply general rules for program and material allocations rather than remain responsive to localized needs. The more remote the government is from the people, the more frustrated the people are in being effectively heard and individually served. The fear of bureaucracy and its indifference to local requirements arises. Public relations become more difficult; operations become more political. The public is inclined to become less responsive to organizational needs. Somehow, the public school administrators must work out the means for maintaining public concern and support for the educational enterprise as they develop mechanisms for total organizational responsiveness to the human needs, values and aspirations of the many subcommunities and neighborhoods the centralized school district will serve.

ALTERED FEDERAL-STATE-LOCAL RELATIONS

In addition to the larger administrative unit for the schools, it is inevitable that the state and federal governments play more extensive roles in the management and direction of local education. There are at least two compelling reasons for this trend.

First, no state or locality has the ability to raise money equal to that of the federal government. It is not likely that this factor will change. We cannot in a highly industrialized age revert to a Jeffersonian agrarianism. The alternatives to our form of capitalistic democracy involve greater concentration of power in a central government and other restrictions upon human freedom and integrity, which are—to say the least—far less attractive to those who have been reared in American culture. Because of the taxing power of the federal government, it is to the advantage of public education that federal funds be employed to help local governments improve and extend their services.

Since the federal government cannot reasonably or efficiently deal with every locality in the nation, it is inevitable that it deal through an administrative intermediary. At the present time, this is most obviously the state departments of education. In the interest of maintaining local control over education, state departments of education have been kept professionally weak. There are few in the country today that can effectively mobilize energies for performing the leadership and coordinating functions which are necessary to maximize the benefits from current federal programs which fall within their jurisdiction. To a considerable extent, state departments will have to be strengthened, and they will have to share some of the authority and responsibility which have been traditionally allocated to local school districts.

A second factor in the greater involvement of the federal and state levels in education is that we cannot maintain a healthy society unless we utilize our educational investment effectively for the solution of our most pressing social problems. Some of these problems have become so vast for particular areas that they can no longer be solved within the geographical limitations of the area. For example, the large metropolitan centers have problems of poverty, of economic distress, of minority ghettos, and of clogged transportation which defy solution within their boundaries. People cannot be dispersed, however, unless suitable economic opportunities exist in other localties. The concentration of industry within a few centers is no longer as essential as it was in the days of the horse-drawn carriage and slow processes of communication. The dispersion of industry to enable people who live in concentrated areas to move to other less congested centers probably cannot take place without federal subventions. Schools may be prepared for influxes of individuals who have never lived outside of metropolitan complexes—and they cannot be prepared without massive sums of outside money, which must be injected before the time their tax rolls are increased by additional industrial sources. The problems of urbanization, in other words, are not the exclusive problems of the metropolitan centers. They are the problems of the total society, and the total society must be prepared to shoulder responsibility for their solution.

This means, of course, that less densely populated areas, such as the Rocky Mountain states, the Southwestern states, and the Pacific Coast states, will have to share some of their resources and their opportunities with others. This imposition can be made only if it is associated with some form of federal financing. Within states, programs must also be developed to improve the quality of education for meeting their total needs. State legislatures cannot require expanded school services unless they provide the means for financing them.

Taking all of these factors together, one must conclude that *the schools cannot continue to do business as usual* without encountering some grave difficulties. The pattern of decision-making is altered. Policy-making within the schools, and between the schools' instruments of administration and the public, will become matters of mediation and negotiation, of coordination and allocation, of planning and evaluation. The school board and local administration will be called upon to effect policy through the implementation of mandated state programs and permissive federal programs—but the problems will be such that there will really be no alternative for the school district but to accept federal subventions in order more effectively to provide for educational needs. In return for some loss of independent and discretionary decision-making, the local authorities will be the recipients of larger federal and state subventions.

Schools will not be cast aside or left to sink or swim in this process. The federal government is now creating instrumentalities which have high promise for giving the kinds of services school districts need to implement new programs, adapt to new requirements, and utilize knowledge effectively for the improvement of education. Regional Educational Laboratories and Research and Development Centers are such agencies. They are now in their earliest development stages. They are pioneering in education and may never live to outgrow their swaddling clothes. If they do, and if schools learn to use their resources effectively, the schools will have powerful allies in in-service education of teachers and administrators, in the development of educational technologies, and in the formulation of administrative strategies.

REORIENTATION OF ROLES OF THE SUPERINTENDENT

Special attention needs to be given to a point briefly indicated above. No competent observer could fail to recognize how fickle the public is about school administrators, teachers, board members, or other persons engaged in the administration or operation of the public schools. Because of public attitudes, school administrators, in particular, rest uneasily in their positions. School board members are rarely threatened with physical dislocation because of the loss of the sources of economic support, and teachers are increasingly protected by tenure. But the degree to which the superintendent of schools is an itinerant has not changed greatly in the past fifty years.

In view of this fact and the reasons for it, considerable attention must be given to the roles of the school administrator in the operation of the public schools. But values and educational aspirations in our society are quite diffuse. They are likely either to remain so or to become even more heterogeneous. Values and aspirations in society are mediated on the local level, rather than on the state and national levels. It will not be the federal goverment's fault, in the minds of those who feel aggrieved, that vocational education is not offered adequately in the local schools or that son George didn't make the college of his choice. We suspect that the scapegoat will still be the local school superintendent. Denied much policy-making—and some decision-making authority—he will still share responsibility with the school board for the inadequacies—but he will be the target.

As Brickell suggests, there will be new administrative and supervisory roles in the local schools. Whether or not they will have the exotic titles he suggests remains to be seen. The point is a reflection of the fact that even the superintendency in the smaller schools has become a constellation of specialized responsibilities toward education. It is unlikely that one man can have the necessary range of specializations needed for even smaller, but still feasibly sized, school districts. Regardless of the extent to which the public still wants the superintendent to be the scapegoat, the superintendent will need a team of specialists to advise him, to provide special technical information, and to operate highly technical operations within the school organization.

Many today expect the superintendent to play an increasing role in instructional leadership or in strictly managerial responsibilities. Neither seems to be entirely plausible. Instructional leadership will have to be close to the point of contact between learners and teachers. Program development and innovation will have to be done by specialists within technical areas, not by generalists who have only little time to give to instructional and program development tasks. It is also a matter of some urgency that both the innovators and the program leaders be somewhat insulated from popular attack—protected from the whims of transient moods—in order to perform their roles as expertly as possible.

This suggests some re-orientation of the roles of the superintendent. First, he cannot avoid becoming the primary link between the school district and other agencies of the community. He may not have the opportunities for face-to-face contact with parents as do teachers and principals, but he will have to represent the school district before other agencies whose programs affect school operations. Brickell suggests that the battle to make the school organization financially dependent upon the metropolitan governing body will be re-opened with renewed vigor. Recent endeavors of Mayor Lindsay of New York to enter arenas within the schools other than purely financial, indicate that at least in that city, education is not far removed from politics. City governments and city officials frequently remind us that it is a myth to assume that education is ever far removed from politics. We can, in part, agree. But the schools have attempted to maintain a responsiveness to the publics whose children attend and whose taxes support the schools; whereas cities have usually hired managers who are expected to take a relaxed attitude toward public relations. If schools have to operate in this arena, it will be the responsibility of the school superintendent to be their representative, for none less than the man in the pivotal position will be able to obtain a favorable treatment for the schools. If subordinate to city government, the schools will need a voice directly to the people, as never before, and the superintendent of schools will be responsible for mobilizing public sentiment for public education at the same time that he interprets the schools' needs among all of the demands placed upon local governmental agencies.

If Brickell's fears do not materialize, the structural governance of the schools need not change greatly. He suggests that the board will become more heavily oriented toward policy and further removed from day-by-day operations. The distinction between policy and administration has never been a very good one. It was a tidy little academic abstraction which some administrators seemed to like because it enabled them to slap the wrists of board members when the latter appeared to be meddling. The laws of most states undeniably involve the schools boards in administration. His unique positions within the school organization and responsibilities to and for the board, undeniably involve the superintendent in policy formation. No effective board actually adopts policies without careful study and formulation by the superintendent and members of his staff of the position to be considered. As boards increase in their ability to deal effectively with educational problems, their demands for expert assistance from superintendents increase. This, too, is a part of the political role of the superintendent, because he inevitably will remain the chief interpreter of the school programs both to the board and to the public. He will utilize resources more abundantly to assist him in meeting his responsibilities, but he will be the man who helps the board understand alternatives for action and the consequences which can be expected from the acceptance of any of them.

The superintendent will also have to play a mediating role within the school organization. In this role, he approaches instructional leadership most closely, for it is he who will have to allocate resources and decide upon critical points of strategy and directions in which to move; it is he who will have to provide balance among the various parts of the organization.

If the superintendent's roles are centered around those of politician and mediator, it is apparent that some other roles must be created and adjusted in order to get the jobs of the schools done. A wise public will provide more supportive and technically expert resources within the school organization than are presently available in most school systems. The schools have been slow to adapt and slow to improve, largely because there has been a dearth of personnel to perform the essential staff functions in preparing for change. Administrators have been provided sparingly, and their central functions appear to be "running a tight ship," "not rocking the boat," and "keeping the costs down." Some administrators have spent more time trying to figure out how to avoid ordering instructional supplies rather than in finding out how to use them most advantageously for the child's educational development. Educationally trained administrators have been bogged down with managerial chores and routines for which they are not particularly trained, which make little use of their professional training, and which prevent them, in many cases, from exercising what is hopefully termed "instructional leadership." Perhaps, by 1980, we will have come to realize that education is more important than economy. Perhaps we will have found a wholesome means of separating the educational and the managerial tasks and have freed the educator to educate.

CHANGING ROLES OF TEACHERS

One last point remains to be made. In the emerging structure of education, the role of the teacher, too, must change. Because of the teachers' demands for recognition, attention has been concentrated upon their roles in educational policy-making within the school system. Little thought has been given to the modification of their instructional roles for better use of their educational competencies. Some schools have been experimenting with teacher aides to relieve the teachers of clerical chores. Some schools are experimenting with team teaching, in which a master teacher serves as team captain and several assistants serve with him as team members performing specialized duties. Some schools are experimenting with the reduction of the number of class periods for teachers, to give them more time for preparation and individual instruction. All of these are wholesome developments, but more must done.

Teacher shortages will become more pronounced during the next decade. Manpower needs of the general society will drain off much of the teaching staff to other enterprises. The expansion of educational programs will also create the need for more teachers, as well as for teachers more highly trained in specialized fields. The inevitable result will be critical shortages in teacher supply.

The well-prepared teacher will be used as the director of a team, and less well-prepared individuals as assistants in special types of activities performed under the leadership of the master teacher. Not all of the teacher's time will be spent in the classroom. To achieve higher levels of instructional performance, probably the master teacher will spend no more than half of the school day in the classroom, and the remaining time will be devoted to the development of instructional materials, the formulation of lesson plans with associates, the coordination of the activities of the other members of the instructional team, and participation in curriculum development activities. This diversification of the role will call for new certification requirements and new teacher preparation programs, and may result not only in improved instruction but also in making teaching much more exciting and much more likely to attract and retain competent people.

IN SUMMARY

Some of the changes that appear to be on the horizon for the administration and organization of local schools may seem to be pronounced departures from the present general pattern. This is not necessarily the case. Most of the changes have been coming about gradually, and trends—both in public education and in the society-at-large—have already started the transition. They probably will effect no drastic revolutions in education. Changes could be accelerated by the public and by professional educators who want to achieve greater adaptability of the public schools to meet the challenges of contemporary and emerging society. It seems more likely that there will be slow evolutionary progress, and that new adaptations will be essential by the time adjustments to present conditions are achieved.

CHAPTER 14

State Organization and Responsibilities For Education

R. L. JOHNS*

State organization and responsibilities for education cannot be studied without also considering local and federal organization and responsibilities for education. The literature dealing with one or more aspects of federal, state, and local educational organization and administration in the United States includes hundred of books and thousands of monographs and periodical articles. Obviously it would be impossible to review this body of literature in a paper of this length. Furthermore, such a review is not likely to provide a rational basis for developing state organization patterns and policies adequate for meeting the educational responsibilities of the states in the future. Much of the literature deals with present and past practice. Recommendations developed from present and past practice may be more suitable for preserving the status quo than for meeting future needs. Therefore an attempt will be made in this paper to present certain broad concepts and theoretical formulations which will provide a rational basis for designing state organizations adequate for meeting state educational responsibilities in the future. The term "state organizations" is used deliberately because it is assumed that it is not possible to design any one state plan of organization which is ideal for elementary, secondary, and higher education in all 50 states. However, it does seem reasonable to assume that all satisfactory state organization plans have some common characteristics which can be identified from an adequate theoretical framework.

LEGAL BASIS FOR STATE
ORGANIZATIONS AND RESPONSIBILITIES

Let us first examine the legal basis for state educational organization and control. It is not assumed that the present constitutional and statutory basis of state educational organization is what it should be in all instances. Constitutions and laws can be changed. However, an examination of the present legal basis will reveal some of the constraints that will either have to be changed or lived with.

* *Professor of Educational Administration, University of Florida;* Main area of specialization: public school finance and theory of educational administration and organization; Consultant for numerous state-wide educational studies; Consultant to National Citizens Commission for the Public Schools (1950-53); Consultant to Committee for the White House Conference on Education (1955); Co-author of the following books: *Educational Organization and Administration; Financing the Public Schools; Educational Administration; Problems and Issues in Public School Finance;* Author of numerous periodical articles and monographs.

The Tenth Amendment to the Constitution of the United States provides: "The powers not delegated to the United States by the Constitution, nor prohibited by it to the States, are reserved to the States respectively or to the people." Since education was not mentioned in the Constitution, it has generally been assumed that the basic responsibility for public education lies with the states. However Clause 1 of Section 8 of Article I of the Constitution provides that: "The Congress shall have the power to lay and collect taxes, duties, imposts and excises, to pay the debts and provide for the common defense and general welfare of the United States. . . ." Although this clause of the Constitution deals with many other important matters, it is commonly known as the "general welfare clause."

Numerous court decisions on many matters through the years have given Congress the power to take action on practically any matter when Congress decides that it affects the public welfare, provided it does not act arbitrarily. Education, especially in recent years, has been deemed by Congress to be an important factor affecting not only the general welfare but also the common defense. Proof of this fact is seen in the federal budget for fiscal 1967 which provides approximately $8,400,000,000 in appropriations for education, training, and related programs. Most of these funds are allocated to the states or local educational institutions and agencies. However, a substantial part of this appropriation is expended directly by the federal government for schools, colleges, and educational programs operated by the federal government. These educational activities of the federal government have not been successfully challenged in the courts nor are they likely to be so challenged. The Supreme Court in an opinion dealing with the Social Security Act declared: "Nor is the concept of general welfare static. Needs that were narrow or parochial a century ago may be interwoven in our day with the well-being of the Nation. What is critical or urgent changes with the times."*

It has long been recognized that the states do not have the power to pass any law or to adopt any constitutional provision which denies any citizen the rights guaranteed to him in the United States Constitution. It has not been generally recognized, however, that the federal government has the power—if it deems it essential for the general welfare—to establish a complete federal system of elementary, secondary, and higher education. If the states should abolish their systems of public education—an action which some of the Southern states threatened to take following the 1954 decision of the Supreme Court abolishing school segregation by race—the federal government would no doubt establish a federal system of public education. This point is emphasized because it is sometimes assumed that the states have the exclusive right to operate public schools. Legally the states have the responsibility and the authority to establish and operate schools and colleges. The federal government, under the general welfare clause, also has the legal authority to operate schools and colleges. The extent to which the federal government will exercise that power depends to a large degree upon the extent to which the states discharge their responsibilities for providing educational opportunities.

* Helvering v. Davis, 301 Cr. S619, 57 SUP. CT. 904.

It has been argued that some states fail to discharge their educational responsibilities because of limited economic resources. This may well be true. However, this situation can readily be corrected by federal grants-in-aid. Some states may be unwilling to assume their educational responsibilities even though they have sufficient economic resources or may receive sufficient federal aid to supplement their resources. What should be the federal policy in that event? The states have long ago decided that no school district has the right to provide a grossly inferior educational program. All states have established certain standards which must be met by all districts. Will the general welfare of the nation permit any state to provide as inferior an educational program as it desires? This is a rational question and it will be raised much more in the future than it has in the past. The federal government at present does not have the direct legal power to require the states to meet desirable minimum educational standards. However, the federal government does have the power to attach conditions for participating in federal grants for education, that are in effect educational standards. The use of that type of power has greatly been extended since 1958. The federal government also has the power to operate educational programs itself if it is deemed to be for the general welfare. This practice has also been considerably extended since 1958 especially in the area of adult education. The evidence is clear that *the importance of the role of the states in education in the future will be determined by how effectively the states discharge their educational responsibilities* and not by any outworn legal theory of "states' rights." For example, the "states' rights" theory was used to justify segregation by race in the public schools. Court decisions have so riddled the "states' rights" theory insofar as it applies to education that the issue is no longer one of states' rights but of states' responsibilities.

Let us now consider the basic legal powers and responsibilities of local school districts. A local school district has no legal powers and responsibilities except those given to it by the state. School districts are created by the state, therefore there is no inherent power of local school government. The state can create local school districts or not create them as is the case in Hawaii. If a state creates school districts, it has the responsibility to create a local school district organization that is functional. There has been considerable improvement in local school district organization in recent years. However, most school districts in the United States are still too small to be efficient. Despite recent progress, 85 to 90 percent of the school districts in the United States should be reorganized and enlarged. The state itself cannot provide the services and leadership needed if it is handicapped by an inefficient local school organization. In many states of the nation, the most urgently needed educational change is for the state to accept its responsibility for creating a functional local school organization. This is not likely to be accomplished by wishful thinking. It will require strong educational leadership and courageous action on the part of the legislature and the governor of a state.

Summarizing: When one looks at the legal status of the states with respect to public education in relation to the federal government and to local districts, it is apparent that the states hold a strategic position of responsibility. The states have plenary powers with respect to education so long as provisions of the United States Constitution are not violated. However, the states do not have the exclusive right to provide public education and experience has shown that *the federal government can and will intervene in providing public education when the states fail to discharge their responsibilities. The states cannot blame their educational shortcomings on the failure of local school districts because the states created those districts and are responsible for them.*

SOCIAL SYSTEMS AND EDUCATIONAL ORGANIZATIONS

We have established that there are no serious *legal constraints* on the states which would prevent them from organizing to meet their educational responsibilities. Are there some *social phenomena* which may help or hinder a state in meeting its responsibilities for education? During the past fifteen years, behavioral scientists have developed some theoretical concepts which are quite helpful in assisting a state to evaluate its organizational arrangements and operational procedures for public education. One of the most useful of these concepts is general systems theory. Systems theory provides an important linkage among all the sciences. According to Hearn (12, p. 38):*

> General systems theorists believe that it is possible to represent all forms of animate and inanimate matter as systems; that in all forms from atomic particles through atoms, molecules, crystals, viruses, cells, organs, individuals, groups, societies, planets, solar systems, even the galaxies, may be regarded as systems.

A system can be defined as an aggregation of components which interact with each other. A system may be open or closed (12). The components of an open system interact with their environment but the components of a closed system do not interact with their environment. Also systems may be dead or living. In this paper we are interested only in open, living, social systems. A social system is a group of individuals who are associated with each other for the purpose of achieving common purposes. The school system is a complex social system, comprised of an aggregation of sub-systems and supra-systems interacting with each other and also with numerous other social systems in the total society. Our society can be described as a complex of social systems in interaction. How can we understand these complex interrelationships and how should we deal with them? Fortunately, systems theory throws some light on this problem.

Let us first examine the sub-system and supra-systems of formal school organization. Using an adaptation of Parson's formulation of formal school organization (22) the school social system can be broken down into the following components:

(1)   the *client system,* comprised of pupils and students
(2)   the *technical system*—the teachers and other workers at the operational level

---

* Each number in parentheses refers to a correspondingly numbered reference at the end of this part of the chapter.

(3) the *managerial system*—the superintendents, commissioners, college presidents, and their assistants at the local, state, and federal levels

(4) the *institutional system,* local and state boards established for the governance and coordination of schools, colleges, and other types of educational institutions, agencies, and programs.

It is readily apparent that each of these broad categories is comprised of a large number of sub-systems. For example, each individual school is a sub-system of a local school system and the individual school itself is comprised of a client system, a technical system, and a managerial system controlled by the institutional system.

Let us now examine some of the characteristics of a social system such as a school, a state department of education, or a college. Every social system has a boundary. The individuals within the boundary of a social system are the components of the system. Anything beyond the boundary of a system constitutes the environment of the system. The individuals within a social system interact with each other more often and more readily than they interact with persons in the environment of the system. *It takes more energy and effort to pass information across the boundary of a system than to exchange information within the system.* It also takes energy and effort to get information from the environment through the boundary of a system to the components of that system.

Every social system, if it survives, must come to terms with its environment. That is, it must exchange matter, information or service with the components of its environment to the extent necessary to meet the needs both of the environment and of the system. That is, the social system must meet the needs of its environment if the environment supports it. How does the social system know that it is meeting the needs of its environment? It gains that information through what behavioral scientists call "feedback." Lonsdale (14, p. 173) defines feedback as follows:

> As applied to organization, feedback is the process through which the organization learns: it is the input from the environment to the system telling it how it is doing as a result of its output to the environment.

If a system fails to learn from its environment, it will eventually fail to survive or forces in the environment will make changes in the system. On the other hand, the components of the environment cannot provide the school system with intelligent feedback unless the output-input of the system includes an appropriate interchange of information.

These are rapidly changing times and educational social systems are receiving more feedback from the environment than ever before. Local school systems, state departments of education, and colleges and universities are receiving numerous urgent and valid signals from their environments calling for change. Why do these systems not change immediately in order to meet the needs of the times? Again the behavioral scientists have provided us some findings from research which throw light on this problem. According to Chin (6, pp. 201-14) any system tends to achieve a balance among the many forces operating upon the system and within it. *Each system tries to keep itself in equilibrium.* Any factor, either from without or within a system, which calls for change disturbs the equilibrium of a system.

When the equilibrium of a social system is disturbed, that equilibrium must eventually be restored or the system will perish. When a system restores its equilibrium, it will be either stationary or dynamic. When a system returns to a fixed point or level after being disturbed it is said to have a "stationary equilibrium" (6). Such a system restores its equilibrium without changing itself or its output.

When a system "shifts to a new position of balance after disturbance," (6) it is said to have attained a "dynamic equilibrium" or "steady state". Such a system adjusts to disturbances by either changing itself or its output. A system in a steady state can receive feedback from its environment which disturbs it but it will meet the challenge by making the necessary adjustments in itself or its output. *Only those social systems that have attained dynamic equilibrium and achieved a steady state can expect to survive in a rapidly changing world.*

If this is true then, it would seem that the problem of creating and maintaining functional educational organizations would be a simple one. All that seems to be necessary under this theory would be to create educational systems, that is, state departments of education, colleges and universities and local school systems, that would all be in dynamic equilibrium or a steady state. But the problem is not a simple one. All social systems, like all human beings, have some perverse characteristics. Man created social systems and he seems to have created them in his own image. How does a human react when he receives feedback from his environment which disturbs him? How does a state department of education, or a higher institution of learning, or a local school system, react when it receives criticism? Behavioral scientists have noted a number of reactions from social systems that have been disturbed by such feedback as a criticism. The social system may employ a number of alternate strategies in order to restore its equilibrium after a disturbance. Not infrequently a social system reacts as follows when it receives criticism: first, it ignores it; second, it denies it; and third, it attacks the source of the criticism. If these defensive maneuvers fail, it may pretend to change but not actually do so and then restore its balance by returning to a stationary equilibrium. If the system cannot "get by" with this strategy it may at last decide to change and attain a dynamic equilibrium or steady state. But the system will not go all out for the steady state strategy. It may change just as little as necessary and with a minimum of effort and cost. If these reactions of social systems seem imaginary, consider the reaction of the automobile industry to Ralph Nader when he wrote *Unsafe at Any Speed*. First, the industry ignored the criticism; second, denied it; and third, attempted to attack the source of the criticism. When these strategies did not work, the automobile industry agreed to change. It remains to be seen how much change will be made. It will be safe to predict however that the companies will change as little as possible and with a minimum expenditure of money and energy.

Thus it is seen *the problem of establishing and maintaining educational organizations that are functional is not a simple one*. The social system must change in order to survive in its environment. But the system cannot adjust to an unlimited amount of change at one point in time. "These times, which require a rate of change greater than ever before, present an unparalleled challenge to the educational administrator to provide leadership for making desirable innovations and at the same time maintain a dynamic equilibrium" (19).

I have brought to your attention only a few of the theoretical formulations from the behavioral sciences which are applicable to the scientific study of educational organization and administration. In the remainder of this paper these and other pertinent concepts are applied to a discussion of state organization for administering the public schools.

STATE ORGANIZATION FOR EDUCATION

We have 50 different state plans for the organization of elementary, secondary, and higher education. While there are many similarities in these plans, no two states have identical organizational plans. I shall not attempt to describe and evaluate all of the many plans for the organization of education at the state level. Those interested in the details of the structure of state organization for the elementary and secondary schools or for higher education, should consult recent monographs published by the United States Office of Education.* The main focus of this paper is on the role and function of state educational organization. However, the legal structure of state organization is too important to be ignored. Therefore, in this paper some important trends in state organization will be described and appraised.

THE CENTRAL EDUCATION AGENCY

Let us first look at the central education agency for the elementary and secondary schools. While it is true in several states that this agency has some responsibility for higher education, its primary purpose in all states is to provide leadership and services for elementary and secondary schools.

Each state has a chief state school officer and a state department of education and 48 of the 50 states have state boards of education. These three components make up what is termed in professional literature as the "central education agency." In all states the professional members of the staff of the state department of education are appointed by the chief state school officer (in many states with—but in some states without—the approval of the state board of education). All professional staff members are technically and legally assistants to the chief state school officer. The chief state school officer and his staff are all components of the same social system. Therefore, in this paper, the term "state department of education," will be used to mean the chief state school officer and his professional staff.

The Components of the Central Education Agency. The states differ widely in the methods by which the members of the several components of the central education agency are selected. The chief state school officer is appointed by the state board of education in 23 states, appointed by the Governor in 5 states and elected directly by the people in 22 states (30).

The methods used in selecting state school board members varies still more widely. Eight states elect state school board members by popular

* See, Robert F. Will, *State Education: Structure and Organization* (1964); and S. V. Mortorana and Ernest V. Hollis, *State Boards Responsible for Higher Education* (1960).

vote; in three states, representatives of the people select the state board members; in 32 states, the Governor appoints the majority of the members (in most cases, subject to the concurrence of one house of the legislature); in four states, the majority of the members serve ex-officio; and in one state, the chief state school officer appoints the board. Two states (Illinois and Wisconsin) do not have a state board of education.

Why have the states created a central education agency? These agencies in all states exercise some executive, legislative, and judicial powers. This practice seems to conflict with our traditional belief in the separation of executive, legislative, and judicial powers. In most states, the central education agency, to a considerable degree, is independent of the executive branch of government. This is no accident. State legislatures have always been loath to extend the power of the executive branch of government, and especially so in a politically sensitive area of government where considerable discretion must be exercised in administering the law. If a law can be drawn with provisions so specific that there is but little administrative discretion left to the executive branch, legislatures usually have little objection to the Governor or his political appointees administering it. But if a function of government is so complex that the legislature cannot prescribe in detail all important policies necessary for the operation of that function, it usually creates some type of board either to approve or advise on administrative law or rule making. This is particularly true of education. Although two of the fifty states do not have a state board of education, each of these states has boards for certain educational institutions, agencies, and services. Therefore, all 50 states have some type of state created educational boards. This policy is not surprising. The American people have always been reluctant to give any one person too much power. It is believed that when a wide degree of discretion must be exercised in so important and sensitive an area of government as education, the judgment of more than one person should be involved in the decision making process.

A number of political scientists oppose that point of view. They believe in the efficacy of the strong executive and argue that the heads of all departments of state government, including the chief state school officer, should be appointed by the Governor. Political scientists generally do not believe that the chief state school officer should be responsible to a board. However, they do accept the use of boards for special quasi-legislative or judicial and advisory purposes (28, p. 9). The recommendations of political scientists generally follow the monocratic, bureaucratic, hierarchical model advocated by the great German scholar Max Weber.

Educational leaders who are students of state educational administration commonly hold that the central education agency should consist of a policy forming board which appoints as its executive the chief state school officer who is assisted by a professional staff in a state department of education. Under this model the executive and legislative functions of government are separated because the board performs exclusively policy making or legislative functions and the chief state school officer and his assistants perform the professional administrative functions. The judicial functions are shared by the chief state school officer and the board but there is a right of appeal to the board. In practice, a neat division between legislative and executive functions is not always possible. Furthermore, it is not always possible to differentiate between administrative and judicial decision making. Experience has shown, however, that these theoretical differences in governmental functions need not create great difficulty in a central education agency which has a cooperative climate.

Robert F. Will of the United States Office of Education has summarized the recommendations of many students of state education administration substantially as follows:

> 1. *All members of the state board of education be elected by the people or representatives of the people on a nonpartisan ballot, or chosen in some appropriate manner which will assure that only people with outstanding ability and competence are selected for the board.* It is hoped that the procedure used will be consistent with our democratic traditions and will remove education from the partisan political arena.
>
> 2. *The board truly represent the people of the state in educational matters.* This is intended to preclude any special interest representation on the board.
>
> 3. *No member of the board be gainfully employed by or administratively connected with any school or school system in the state.* This excludes from membership any person who is subject to state board rules and regulations by virtue of his employment or administrative connection with an educational institution or system.
>
> 4. *No salary be paid to board members.* This discourages the commission-type operation in which members devote full time or a large block of time to their duties. The commission-type operation invariably places board members in the position of administering both legislative and executive functions. There is firm agreement that board members should be compensated for actual expenses incurred incident to the performance of board duties.
>
> 5. *The state board be empowered to select a chief executive officer—the chief state school officer.* This establishes the board as the head of the agency. The employees engaged to conduct the executive functions of the agency are subject to state law and the administrative rules, regulations, and policy determinations of the board (30, pp. 8-9).

The evidence indicates that there has been a long-time trend toward adoption by the states of the model of state organization generally recommended by students of state educational organization. For example, in 1900 the chief state school officer was appointed by the board in only three states; this number had increased to 23 by 1963.

If a state department of education is to function effectively it needs to have the highest possible quality of educational leadership. Experience has shown that it is difficult—and in some cases impossible—to get the top educational leadership of a state to "run" for an elective office, such as chief state school officer. While it is true that educational leaders of high quality have sometimes been elected to the position of chief state school officer, it is also true that these men have usually not been maintained in that office for a long period of time. In some states operating on the elective basis, the state superintendent cannot even succeed himself in office. The evidence is conclusive that there is a much higher probability of attracting and holding outstanding educational leaders in the office of chief state school officer by the appointive method than by the elective method.

The emerging role of the states in education demands a more functional structure of state organization than now exists in most states. Although there has been some progress in improving state organization structures for education in recent years, the progress has been entirely too slow. Too many states have been in a state of "static equilibrium" as defined in the first part of this paper. How long will the environment tolerate a weak, poorly organized, poorly staffed central education agency? If a social system such as a state department of education does not satisfy the needs of its environment, other social systems will supplant it.

Higher Education. It is not the purpose of this paper to treat state organization for higher education. However, one cannot deal with state organization for the public schools and ignore entirely the state organization for higher education. In some states the state board of education is the operating board for one or more institutions of higher learning. In such states, a section of the state department of education usually is established to service all or a part of the higher institutions.

The organization for higher education varies greatly in the United States. In some states, a single board for all higher institutions has been established. In other states a state coordinating board has been established with varying degrees of authority over the boards of individual higher institutions. In still other states, each institution has its own board of control and no formal method has been established for coordinating these institutions with each other. The whole matter of state organization of higher education is deserving of intensive study. It would seem reasonable to assume that some method of coordinating higher institutions either through a single operating board or by a coordinating board should be provided.

Community Junior Colleges. The arrangements for the operation and administration of community junior colleges also are deserving of mention. The methods of operating these institutions also vary greatly. In some states, junior colleges are operated by local school districts or special local junior college districts created for that purpose. In other states, junior colleges are under the control of the state board of education. In still other states, junior colleges are operated in effect as subdivisions of higher institutions. The available evidence indicates that the community junior college is more likely to emphasize all of the functions of a comprehensive junior college if it is controlled directly by a local school district of adequate size, or by an adequate size special junior college district. This facilitates coordination with the secondary school program at the local level. States operating junior colleges under local boards usually provide junior college leadership services through the state department of education and this further facilitates coordination of the junior colleges both with high schools and higher institutions.

THE EMERGING ROLE OF THE STATE DEPARTMENT OF EDUCATION

Let us now examine the emerging role of that part of the central education agency known as the state department of education.

The usual procedure in papers of this kind is to develop a thesis, examine the evidence and present the conclusions supported by the data. I am going to modify this process by presenting the conclusions first, and then present the evidence in support of those conclusions. Here are my conclusions:

1. *International and national conditions make it more imperative than ever before that all 50 state departments of education provide aggressive and competent professional and political leadership for educational decision making.*

2. *Few, if any, state departments of education are now adequately staffed to provide the leadership and administrative functions required of them.*

3. *There is a need for improving the administrative, supervisory, and leadership services for education at all levels—federal, state, and local— but at this particular time, the most critical need is to provide more adequately for these services at the state level.*

SOME CONDITIONS AFFECTING THE ROLE

Let us first look at some of the conditions which are changing the role of the state department of education. My entire paper could be devoted to this portion of the problem before us. However, I will only summarize the evidence.

Changing Role of Education. The role of education itself has changed throughout the civilized world. Education has had different purposes in different countries at different times. Some of those purposes have been political indoctrination, preparation for the next world, increasing the earning capacity of the individual, perpetuation of the special privileges of the ruling class, preservation of the status quo, bringing about uniformity in the population, etc. In the past in many countries of the world, education above the elementary level was considered either a luxury or a special benefit for which the recipient or his parents should pay. Prior to World War II, that was the prevailing attitude toward post-secondary education even in the United States.

Today every advanced country in the world recognizes that education is the key to economic growth and even to national survival in this world of change. This change in attitude toward education in the United States is well expressed in the National Defense Education Act of 1958 which reads in part:

> . . . that the security of the Nation requires the fullest development of the mental resources and technical skills of its young men and women. The present emergency demands that additional and more adequate educational opportunities be made available. The defense of this Nation depends upon the mastery of modern techniques developed from complex scientific principles. It depends as well upon the discovery and development of new principles, new techniques, and new knowledge.

It is true that this act had limited purposes (subsequently extended) and that it was triggered by the launching of Sputnik I by the Russians. However, the forces that eventually produced this Act and many other subsequent acts, had been in operation for a long time.

Substantial Categorical Federal Grants. Kurth, a member of the staff of the College of Education of the University of Florida, recently made a

study of the Acts of Congress during the period 1862 to 1965 that related
to elementary, secondary and higher education (13). He analyzed the 47
most important of these acts and major amendments thereto, and found that
while only 17 were passed prior to 1958, 30 were enacted by Congress
between 1958 and 1965.

The numerous federal acts supported by federal appropriations are
causing a major shift in the locus of decision making from local and state
levels to the federal level. When either the state or the federal government
distributes substantial sums of money to local school systems and *attaches
conditions to those grants for participation,* it has decision making power.
The federal government, particularly through the use of categorical grants
and so-called "guide lines" which in effect are rigorous controls, has greatly
increased its decision making role in education. For example, during the
year 1965-66, the federal government supplied eight percent of the revenue
receipts of the public schools of the nation and the states 39 percent. However, *most local school systems spent far more staff time in complying with
federal regulations to obtain eight percent of their funds than they spent in
complying with state regulations to obtain 39 percent of their funds.* The
federal government now allocates sufficient funds to the public schools, to
institutions of higher learning, and to research in both the public and private
economy, to exercise substantial control over all of these institutions and
agencies.

I would not have you believe that I oppose federal aid for education.
I have been a supporter of such aid for many years and I still advocate
federal aid for public elementary, secondary, and higher education. However, I do not advocate that the main locus of educational decision making
be shifted from state and local levels to the federal level.

Current Federal Policy. If the philosophy of certain non-educational
federal officials prevails, we are likely to have far more federal control over
education than at present. Two political scientists, Professors Masters and
Pettit of Pennsylvania State University, directed attention in a recent article
to the possibility of a substantial increase in federal controls through program budgeting (16). They expressed concern about the following statement of Federal Budget Director Charles L. Schultze in a budget hearing
before the 89th Congress:

> Federal programs have an "output"; they result in something being
> accomplished in a given timespan—providing a given type of military
> capability, or helping to educate a specific number of children each year,
> or providing a particular set of recreational opportunities, and so on.
> Currently, budgetary decisions are too often made in terms of the level of
> support for an organizational unit, or the quantity of inputs purchased.
> In order to make intelligent budget choices, however, we really want to
> be able to analyze the output of a program and compare what we get for
> what we have to pay. We want to compare output with cost. To do this,
> we need to be quite specific about program objectives.*

Masters and Pettis stated that, "The implications for an extended
form of federal control (be it desirable or undesirable) are apparent: 'we

* See the testimony of Budget Director Charles L. Schultze in: Joint Committee on the Organization
of Congress, *Organization of Congress,* Hearings before the Committee, 89th, 1st 1965, part 12,
pp. 1775 ff.

really want to . . . compare what we get for what we have to pay . . . we need to be quite specific about program objectives' " (16, p. 86). Who is the "we" referred to by Schultze? I am sure that the "we" he referred to is not located at the state or local level.

Decision Making and the Political Process. I have already pointed out that federal aid for education has increased greatly in recent years and it will undoubtedly increase still more in the future. State aid for the public schools has also greatly increased. State aid for public schools increased from $3,800,000,000 in 1955-56 to $9,700,000,000 in 1965-66. State support will certainly increase rapidly in the future. What do these trends mean? When school funds are provided at the federal level, important educational policy decisions are made by the political process. When school funds are provided at the state level, important educational policy decisions are made by the political process.

Earlier, I stated a conclusion that both the educational and political leadership potential of state departments of education should be strengthened. How can the 25,000 local school systems effectively participate in political decision making on educational matters at the federal level? How can these same 25,000 local school systems effectively participate in political decision making on educational matters at the 50 state levels? *Only strong state departments of education can provide the needed linkage between local school systems and political decision making at the state and federal levels.* It is true that professional associations provide some linkage but usually professional associations or teachers' unions are considered by the lay public to be private lobbies. They perform desirable functions, but they do not constitute an official part of the government which has the ultimate power to make decisions.

Local school boards have broad authority to make decisions on educational policy at the local level. However, school board associations do not have much power in most states to influence state decisions on educational policy. The National Association of School Boards has had very little influence on federal educational policy. This Association has officially opposed federal aid for schools for several years and therefore has not been in a position to assist in shaping federal legislation affecting education. An individual local school system has but little power in dealing with Congress or a federal agency unless that school system is as large as Chicago and the mayor of the city is a political ally of the President.

Education needs a strong, official state department of education to represent it at the state level and to assist local school boards in dealing with the federal level.

James E. Russell (18, p. 77), Secretary of the Educational Policies Commission, pointed out that it was relatively easy to make education an independent branch of government at the local level with wide powers of self-management, including fiscal powers. Local school districts frequently even have their own separate geography. However, the separation of educational government at the state and federal levels from other governmental structures is much more difficult to maintain even if it were desirable to do so. Russell suggests that the separation of educational government from political processes at the federal level is a myth. The same thing is true at the state level.

Professors of educational administration have probably been more responsible than any other group for spreading the myth that education "should be kept out of politics". But the term "public education" itself in a democracy means that basic public educational policies are decided by the people through political processes. It is true that *public education should be protected from the vicissitudes of partisan politics* but all important educational policies must ultimately be legitimized through political processes.

The political scientists, Masters and Pettit, previously referred to in this paper, commented as follows concerning this point:

> Unquestionably most Americans still perceive that there is, or ought to be, a wall of separation between the educational system and politics. In recent years, however, scholars from several disciplines have begun to visualize the process of educational policy making in terms of the many political factors that are involved. Whether we define it in terms of "who gets what, when, how," or more abstractly as the "authoritative allocation of values for a society," the mantle of politics impinges upon every societal activity that involves the distribution of costs and benefits. Thus, when we speak of educational policy making, we are speaking of a dimension of the political process.
>
> We are concerned with the values, attitudes, and actions of governmental decision makers, with political resources and their use, with political symbols and their manipulation. Moreover, in an effort to determine what factors operate to shape various sets of alternatives and what factors lead to the selection of one alternative over another, we are concerned also with the political context (16, p. 81).

Meaningful educational policies cannot be determined without considering purposes, and purposes are determined by values. Perhaps the greatest single problem facing the civilized world today is the determination of what values shall take precedence in these changing times. The priority of values in a democratic society is determined by political processes. To insist that education should keep out of politics is to assume that educators are not concerned with values.

Kimbrough made the following statement in a paper presented at a conference on "Strategies for Planned Curriculum Innovation" held at Teachers College, Columbia University, in July, 1966:

> Viewing the school system as insulated or isolated from the political environment contributes to the impermanency of planned changes. Of even greater concern, however, is that this view sometimes leads to changes which are not in the best interests of education.

The National Compact for Education. A National Compact for Education has recently been established. This compact was originally advocated by Dr. James B. Conant but its acceptance was primarily due to the enthusiastic support generally given to it by the governors of the 50 states. Its chief promoter has been Terry Sanford, former Governor of North Carolina. One of the major purposes of this Compact is to provide the machinery by which the states may have more influence on educational policy decisions made at the federal level. This could be a desirable purpose. However, unless the leadership, authority, and influence of chief state school officers and state departments are firmly established, the state governors through the National Compact may attempt to influence federal policy decisions on education without consulting state departments of education. This would almost certainly bring education into partisan politics. Furthermore, it would deprive the Congress of the expert assistance it needs in formulating educational policy at the federal level.

Demand for State Educational Leadership. Major attention has been given in this paper to showing why strong (effective) state departments of education are needed in order that education might participate effectively in educational decision making at the state and federal levels. State departments of education cannot provide the linkage with the federal and state levels needed by local school systems unless they are staffed with highly trained and highly competent personnel.

In that connection Daniel J. Elazar, Associate Professor of political science, stated the following in chapter 6 of *Prospective Changes in Society by 1980:*

> Increase in expertise will inevitably strengthen the administrative branches vis-a-vis the legislature unless the legislatures follow through with programs presently under discussion to acquire experts of their own. At the same time, increased expertise at the state and local levels will not only improve the quality of their governmental services but will put the states and localities in a better position to negotiate with their federal counterparts. Not only will these professionals share the same professional values and long-range aspirations, with a consequent easing of communications, but they will also enable their governments to negotiate from positions of greater strength.

State departments of education have many other important functions which require top quality professional personnel if adequate services are provided. Important administrative duties are required of state department personnel in all states. Those tasks are so well known that it is not necessary to enumerate them in this paper.

The most important relevant new development emerging from these times is the rapidly increasing demand for educational leadership from state department of education personnel. There are a number of areas in which leadership is being sought. The demands of local school boards for consultant help in developing the types of educational programs required for receiving federal grants are numerous indeed. But probably the most important leadership function now being requested of the state department of education is that it provide a linkage between innovators and local school systems. State department of education personnel are now expected to serve as "change agents" in spreading desirable innovations, developed not only by universities but also by innovative local school systems throughout the nation.

Research and Development Activities. Some state departments of education are greatly expanding their research and development activities. For example, the New York State Department of Education has established a Center for Innovation in Education. Some state departments of education have inaugurated research projects and others have established departments of research. Most of the research projects now being engaged in by state departments of education could be classified as applied research and development. The universities give a relatively greater emphasis to basic research. Perhaps this is a proper division of labor. However, it requires highly competent personnel to use basic research in applied research.

The larger school systems are also establishing research and development services. For example, the Dade County (Miami) school system in Florida recently announced that it is establishing a research and development center funded at $300,000 annually.

DEVELOPING EFFECTIVE STATE AGENCIES FOR EDUCATION

What does all of this mean? It seems obvious that, if state departments of education are to provide the linkage services needed among universities, local school systems, state government and the federal government, those departments must be staffed with personnel equal in training and competency to the top-quality personnel provided in the universities, the U. S. Office of Education, and the larger local school systems. Very few state departments of education are in a favorable position to compete for top-quality personnel. In some states the controlling factor is the limitation on salaries and in other states it is the political "spoils system" coupled with low salaries. Recently, at a meeting of the Board of Trustees of the University Council for Educational Administration, a professor from one of the major universities of the nation reported that one of his doctoral graduates sought employment at the state department of education of the state in which the university was located. He was told that he could have the job if he contributed a fixed percent of his salary for political purposes. In a number of states, many of the top state department personnel are changed when the party in power changes. Obviously, a state department of education cannot be staffed with high quality personnel under these conditions.

If a state department of education is to compete with the major universities and the larger school systems for top-quality personnel in 1966, it must be able to pay salaries considerably in excess of $20,000 annually for its key personnel. Furthermore, departments of education must be able to pay a beginning salary of at least $12,000 annually in order to attract promising, young, inexperienced doctoral graduates, and a considerably higher beginning salary to attract experienced principals and supervisors who have the competencies needed by state department personnel. Only a very few state departments of education are in so favorable a position. There is every indication that competition for top-quality educational leadership will be keener in the future than at the present time.

CHALLENGES OF THE NEW ROLE

Will the state central education agencies and particularly state departments meet the many challenges of their emerging role? Roald Campbell, Dean of the College of Education of the University of Chicago, presented a paper on "Process of Policy Making Within Structures of Educational Government . . ." at a seminar at the University of Illinois in 1959 (18, pp. 59-76). In that paper he directed attention to two problems affecting the formulation of educational policy. Those problems are: (1) some confusion about values and (2) the folklore of localism. The problem of particular interest to us as we study state educational organizations and responsibilities is the folklore of localism. Campbell commented as follows with respect to the long tradition of home rule:

> But the myth has outlived the fact. Free land is gone, the rural predominance has vanished, industrialization has taken over, cities have spawned, mass media bring immediately every world altercation to all eyes and ears, man circles the globe in hours, and competitors have planted a rocket on the moon. These technological changes have their social, economic, and political repercussions. Complete local government in today's world is an anachronism (18, p. 67).

He stated that this folklore of localism causes state and federal policy to take strange forms:

> Usually, at the state level, policy tends to be formulated in terms of minimums and the state agency's role in implementation becomes one of regulation or enforcement of these minimums. . . . At the federal level, conditions are even more deplorable. Seemingly in order to perpetuate the myth of localism, policy is fragmentary and diffused (18, p. 67-8).

Campbell glumly concluded: "The national government pretends not to make policy, the state governments will make no more than they must, and most local governments cannot make adequate policy" (18, p. 68). Seven years have elapsed since these observations were made. How valid are Campbell's observations in 1966? The basic problems he described are still with us. However, some trends are more clear today than seven years ago. Our knowledge of systems theory, described early in this paper, gives us some leads to the trend of events to come. A social system—such as a local school system or a state department of education—must meet the needs of the environment that supports it or other social systems will supply those needs. It was evident to the nation in the late 1950's that most local school systems did not have the financial capacity, or educational leadership, or aspiration to meet the needs of the times. It was also apparent that many states did not have the necessary financial ability or educational leadership or aspiration to meet the educational needs of the people. Obviously something had to be done by the federal government and something was done. Attention has already been directed to the fact that 30 federal laws or major amendments to existing laws were passed between 1958 and 1965. It is true that these acts all provide categorical aid instead of general aid and that they have given the federal government far more influence on educational decision making than it possessed prior to 1958.

What should be the respective financial roles of local school districts, the state and the federal government? The economy of the nation is such that proportionately greater financial support for the public schools must be provided by the federal government and state governments. In 1965-66 the federal government provided 8 percent of public school revenue receipts, the states 39 percent and local sources 53 percent. Considering the economy of the nation, equity to taxpayers and the desirability of equalizing educational opportunity up to a reasonably adequate level, it would make much better sense to provide 25 percent of school revenue from federal sources, 50 percent from state sources, and 25 percent from local sources.

It is not suggested that this is an ideal formula for allocating financial responsibility for the public schools in all states. These percentages should of course vary from state to state depending upon variations in wealth and other factors. However, it is suggested that for the nation as a whole, 25 percent of school revenue from the federal government, 50 percent from state sources, and 25 percent from local sources is much closer to a rational allocation of financial responsibility than the present practice.

It is not the purpose of this paper to present projections in school finance, but it is apparent that the proportion of the gross national product allocated to education will increase. In 1965-66 the revenue receipts for the public schools were approximately 3½ percent of the gross national product. Within twenty years, it is quite likely that as much as 6 percent of the gross national product may be invested in the public schools.

RECONSIDERATION OF ORGANIZATIONAL MODEL

What kind of social systems do we need at the local level, at the state level, and at the federal level for the organization and administration of the public schools? There are some who argue that local school districts have largely lost their usefulness and that they should either be abolished, or their numbers greatly reduced. For example, Professor Benson, an economist at the University of California in Berkeley, argues that the minimum size of school districts should be set at a total population of 250,000 except in areas where there is an extreme scattering of the population (4, p. 45). Benson's recommendation, if adopted, would reduce the total number of school districts in the United States from 25,000 to approximately 600. While the evidence available from research does not support a recommendation as extreme as Benson's, it does indicate that if local school districts are to be viable partners with the state and federal government in operating the public schools, the minimum size of a school district should not be less than 50,000 total population. The establishment of this minimum would reduce the total number of school districts from 25,000 to somewhere between 2,000 and 3,000.

Assuming that school districts are reorganized into school systems of sufficient size to have the potentiality of being efficient and capable operating units, then what should be the respective roles of local school districts, the state central education agencies and the federal government? Will we continue to wrangle over the relative merits of local, state, and federal control? Will the folklore of localism and states' rights prevent us from establishing educational organizations (or social systems) at the local, state, and federal levels adequate to meet the requirements of the times?

THE CONCEPT OF CREATIVE FEDERALISM

Considerable attention has been given recently to the concept known as "creative federalism." Opposition to the increase of state or federal control over education has been based on the traditional assumption that there is a fixed quantity of power and that if the power of one level of government is increased, automatically the power of other levels of government is decreased. It is similar to the assumption of the classical economist that there is a fixed volume of goods and services and that if more goods and services are allocated to one sector of the economy such as education, the amount of goods and services consumed by other sectors of the economy, especially the private sector, would be automatically reduced. This concept of the classical economists ignored the fact that in a dynamic economy, the total volume of goods and services is never fixed but constantly growing. Therefore the increase in the allocation of resources to investment sectors of the economy, such as education, will not reduce but actually increase the resources available to other sectors of the economy.

The concept of creative federalism is based on the assumption that the power to deal with educational problems is not a fixed quantity but that it is expanding very rapidly. The *increase in the power of one level of government to deal with a particular educational problem does not reduce the power of another level of government to deal with that problem.* For example, educators have known for many years that education was one of the important means by which economic and social deprivation can be reduced. But the power of the states and local school districts could not be effectively harnessed to deal with this problem until the federal government was given the power to assist in dealing with it. Therefore the increase in the educational power of the federal government to deal with social and economic deprivation actually increased the power of the state and local school districts to deal with this same problem. This is what is meant by the term creative federalism.

In my judgment, the concept of creative federalism of the national, state, and local governments is a valid one. It is a concept of partnership in which the federal, state, and local school districts operate as equals, each assuming the responsibility to perform the educational functions that can be most appropriately dealt with at that level. The model for educational organization that I suggest is not a Max Weber, monocratic, pyramidal, bureaucratic model with the federal government at the top of the hierarchy, the states in the middle, and local school districts at the bottom of the pyramid. I am suggesting that *what is needed is a social systems model with a strong, well-staffed, capable federal education agency interacting with strong, well-staffed, capable state education agencies in interaction with strong, well-staffed, capable local education agencies.* Furthermore, each of these social systems—the federal education agency, the state educational agencies, and the local education agencies—will be in continuous interaction with the decision making political power systems in their environments. I am not suggesting that local education agencies should not interact with the federal education agency. The federal agency needs the feedback from local school districts and one of the important functions of state education agencies is to provide the linkage necessary for the federal education agency to receive that feedback.

Organizing education as a series of social systems in interaction provides the structure necessary to maximize the opportunity for desirable change. A bureaucratic hierarchy maximizes the possibility of preserving the status quo. *We need organizational structures for education that will maximize the opportunities for desirable changes and innovations.* Despite this fact, the prevailing concept of organizing education at the present time is the hierarchical, bureaucratic concept. In some states, the state department of education performs only routine, bureaucratic functions. Recently the director of a study of the operations of one state department of education requested his staff to conceptualize the operation of education in that state without a department of education. This is a state in which the legislature has not provided for an effective state department of education. The staff of the department performs only routine administrative and control functions. Salaries are much lower than those paid the leadership personnel in the local school systems and the colleges and universities of that state. Not a single person with a doctor's degree is employed in that department.

After analyzing the operations of that state department of education, the survey staff concluded that it could be abolished without affecting unfavorably the operation of the public schools. State school funds in that state are distributed by simple formulas which could readily be used by the state treasurer's office. School statistics could readily be collected, processed, and published by a data processing center serving other departments of government. Teachers' certificates could be issued by a licensing bureau serving other state licensing functions. Since no educational leadership is provided by the state department of education, it would not be missed. Perhaps this is an over-simplification of the situation but it comes much closer to describing the role of the state department of education in that state (and in some others) than the emerging role of the state department of education that I have described in this paper.

In conclusion, I have no fear of the dangers of federal control of education if we develop strong state and local education agencies. Leading officials in the United States Office of Education supported the Elementary and Secondary Education Act of 1965. Title V of that act was deliberately designed to strengthen state departments of education. I know of no responsible educational official in the United States Office of Education who is seeking to take over the control of education in the nation. The federal government cannot possibly perform its educational functions efficiently without the help of regional, state, and local education agencies. The Department of Health, Education, and Welfare has already established nine regional offices, each of which performs some important educational functions. The United States Office of Education is now in the process of establishing 20 regional educational laboratories. Local school districts are here to stay. They will be reorganized and expanded in size but they are too inter-woven in the "warp and woof" of American life to be discontinued. The same thing is not true of state departments. If state departments of education do not accept their new and emerging roles, they are going to sink into bureaucratic impotency and their leadership functions and even their control functions, will largely be taken over by regional federal educational agencies which have already been established or will be established. The program of activities now being carried on by the eight mountain area states indicates that you do not desire that to be your fate.

Major Implications for State Education Agencies

When one looks at the legal status of the states with respect to public education and in relation to the federal government and to local school districts, it is apparent that the states hold a strategic position of responsibility. *The states have plenary powers with respect to education so long as provisions of the United States Constitution are not violated.* However, the states do not have the exclusive right to provide public education and experience has shown that the federal government can and will intervene in providing public education when the states fail to discharge their responsibilities. *The states cannot blame their educational shortcomings on the failure of local school districts because the states created those districts and are responsible for them.* The states should reorganize the present small local school districts into districts with minimum total population of 50,000, except in areas of extreme sparsity of population. It will require school districts of this size or larger in the future in order to provide at a reasonable cost the educational services which should be made available to all children.

Students of state educational administration generally recommend that:

1. All members of the state board of education should be elected by the people or representatives of the people on a nonpartisan ballot, or chosen in some appropriate manner which will assure that only people with outstanding ability and competence are selected for the board.

2. The board should truly represent the people of the state in educational matters.

3. No member of the board should be gainfully employed by or administratively connected with any school or school system in the state.

4. No salary should be paid to board members.

5. The state board should be empowered to select the chief state school officer, who should serve as their executive officer.

The available evidence indicates that:

1. International and national conditions make it more imperative than ever before that all 50 state departments of education provide aggressive and competent professional and political leadership for educational decision making;

2. Few, if any, state departments of education are now adequately staffed to provide the leadership and administrative functions required of them;

3. There is a need for improving the administrative, supervisory, and leadership services for education at all levels—federal, state, and local. *At this particular time, the most critical need is to provide more adequately for these services at the state level.*

The major functions of state departments of education in the future will be to provide both professional and political leadership for the inauguration and implementation of educational policies and programs. They must provide a linkage between local school systems and the federal government if local initiative in education is preserved. If the state departments of education do not provide adequate leadership, the locus of decision making will shift from local school districts and the states to the federal government.

Considerable attention has been given to the concept known as *creative federalism*. This concept is based on the assumption that the power to deal with educational problems is not a fixed quantity but that it is expanding rapidly. The increase in the power of one level of government to deal with a particular educational problem does not reduce the power of another level of government to deal with that problem. For example, educators have known for many years that education is one of the important means by which economic and social deprivation can be reduced. But the power of the states and local school districts could not be effectively harnessed to deal with this problem until the federal government was given the power to assist in resolving it. Therefore the increase in the educational power of the federal government to deal with social and economic deprivation actually increased the power of the states and local school districts to deal with this same problem. However, creative federalism cannot operate unless we establish strong well-staffed state education agencies, strong well-staffed local education agencies and a strong well-staffed federal education agency.

Finally, *local school systems are not likely to be abolished. They will be reorganized and expanded in size, but they are too inter-woven in the "warp and woof" of American life to be discontinued.* This is not true of state departments of education. If these departments do not accept their new and emerging roles, they are going to sink into bureaucratic impotency and their leadership functions—and even their control functions—will largely be taken over by regional federal education agencies which have already been established or will be established. This would be most unfortunate for the states and would negate the concept of creative federalism.

FOOTNOTE REFERENCES

1. AID TO ELEMENTARY AND SECONDARY EDUCATION. Part 1. *Hearings Before the General Subcommittee on Education of the Committee on Education and Labor, House of Representatives, Eighty-Ninth Congress, First Session on H.R. 2361 and H.R. 2362.* Washington: U. S. Government Printing Office, 1965.

2. AID TO ELEMENTARY AND SECONDARY EDUCATION. Part 2. *Hearings Before the General Subcommittee on Education of the Committee on Education and Labor, House of Representatives, Eighty-Ninth Congress, First Session on H.R. 2361 and H.R. 2362.* Washington: U. S. Government Printing Office, 1965.

3. BAILEY, STEPHEN K.; FROST, RICHARD T.; MARSH, PAUL E.; and WOOD, ROBERT C. *Schoolmen and Politics,* A Study of State Aid to Education in the Northeast. The Economics and Politics of Public Education (No. 1 in Series). Syracuse, New York: Syracuse University Press, 1962.

4. BENSON, CHARLES S., *The Cheerful Prospect.* Boston: Houghton Mifflin Co., 1965.

5. CALIFORNIA STATE DEPARTMENT OF EDUCATION. *The Emerging Requirements for Effective Leadership for California Education.* A Study to Provide a Basis for Planning the Services and Organization of the California State Department of Education. Submitted by Arthur D. Little, Inc., Sacramento, Calif.: The Department, 1964.

6. CHIN, ROBERT. "The Utility of Systems Models and Developmental Models for Practitioners" in the *Planning of Change,* Warren G. Bennis, Kenneth D. Bennes, and Robert Chin, eds. New York: Holt, Rinehart and Winston, 1961.

7. COMMITTEE FOR THE WHITE HOUSE CONFERENCE ON EDUCATION. *A Report to the President.* Neil McElroy, Chairman, Washington: U. S. Government Printing Office, April, 1956.

8. CONANT, JAMES BRYANT. *Shaping Educational Policy.* New York: McGraw-Hill Book Company, 1964.

9. COUNCIL OF CHIEF STATE SCHOOL OFFICERS. *The State Department of Education:* A Policy Statement of Guiding Principles for Its Legal Status, Its Functions and the Organization of Its Service Areas. Washington: The Council, 1963.

10. COUNCIL OF CHIEF STATE SCHOOL OFFICERS. *Guidelines for Development and Codification of Policy for State Departments of Education.* A Handbook for Identifying, Organizing, and Compiling the Policies that Direct and Control the Operations of State Departments of Education. Washington: The Council, 1965.
11. GRIFFITHS, DANIEL E. *Behavioral Science and Educational Administration.* The Sixth-third Yearbook of the National Society of Education. Chicago: University of Chicago Press, 1964.
12. HEARN, GORDON. *Theory Building in Social Work.* Toronto: University of Toronto Press, 1958.
13. KURTH, EDWIN L. *Federal Aid to Education.* Gainesville, Florida: Florida Educational Research and Development Council, University of Florida, 1966.
14. LONSDALE, RICHARD C. "Maintaining the Organization in Dynamic Equilibrium," Chapter VII in *Behavioral Science in Educational Administration,* Daniel E. Griffiths, ed., the Sixty-Third Yearbook of the National Society for the Study of Education, Part II. Chicago: University of Chicago Press, 1964.
15. MARTORANA, S. V. and ERNEST H. HOLLIS, *State Boards Responsible for Higher Education,* Washington, D.C.: U. S. Government Printing Office, 1960.
16. MASTERS, NICHOLAS A. and LAWRENCE K. PETTIT. "Some Changing Patterns in Educational Policy Making." *Educational Administration Quarterly,* Vol. 2, Number 2 Spring, 1966.
17. McCONNELL, T. R. *A General Pattern for American Higher Education.* New York: McGraw-Hill Book Co., 1962.
18. McLURE, WILLIAM B. and VAN MILLER, eds. *Government of Public Education for Adequate Policy Making.* Urbana, Ill.: Bureau of Educational Research, College of Education, University of Illinois, 1960.
19. MORPHET, EDGAR L., ROE L. JOHNS, and THEODORE L. RELLER. *Educational Organization and Administration.* Englewood Cliffs, N. J.: Prentice-Hall, Inc., 1967.
20. NEW YORK STATE REGENTS ADVISORY COMMITTEE ON EDUCATIONAL LEADERSHIP. *School Boards and School Board Membership.* Recommendations and Report of a Survey. New York: The Committee, December, 1965.
21. OHIO LEGISLATIVE SERVICE COMMISSION. *Organization and Methods of the Ohio Department of Education.* Staff Research Report No. 43. Columbus, Ohio: The Commission, 1960.
22. PARSONS, TALCOTT. "Some Ingredients of a General Theory of Formal Organization," Chapter III in *Administrative Theory in Education,* ed. Andrew W. Halpin, Chicago: Midwest Administration Center, University of Chicago, 1958.
23. SCHULTZE, CHARLES L. in: *Organization of Congress,* hearings before Joint Committee on the Organization of Congress, 89th, 1st. Washington: U. S. Government Printing Office, 1965.
24. SUBCOMMITTEE ON EDUCATION OF THE COMMITTEE ON LABOR AND PUBLIC WELFARE, UNITED STATES SENATE. White House Conference on Education. *A Milestone for Educational Progress,* Washington: U. S. Government Printing Office, 1965.
25. U. S. DEPARTMENT OF HEALTH, EDUCATION, AND WELFARE. Office of Education. *The Impact of Urbanization on Education.* Summary Report of a Conference, May 28-29, 1962. Washington: U. S. Government Printing Office, 1962.
26. WALKER, IRVIN E., PEARL PEERBOOM, ALMA DOWDY, EARL E. HUYCK, and EUGENIA SULLIVAN. *1965: Year of Legislative Achievements.* U. S. Department of Health, Education, and Welfare, Office of the Secretary. Washington: U. S. Government Printing Office, 1965.
27. WILL, ROBERT F., LOUISE R. MURPHY, and JAMES E. GIBBS, JR. *State School Administration: 1900-1957, Reports of Major Surveys and Studies.* Washington: U. S. Department of Health, Education, and Welfare, Office of Education.
28. ————. "Separation of Powers at the Administration Level." *School Life,* 43:24-27, January, 1961.
29. ————. "State Administrative Rulemaking." *School Life.* 44:19-21, April, 1962.
30. ————. In Cooperation with the Study Commission of the Council of Chief State School Officers. *State Education Structure and Organization,* With Particular Emphasis Upon Public Education at the Elementary and Secondary Levels. Washington: U. S. Government Printing Office, 1964.
31. WILSON, LOGAN, ed. *Emerging Patterns in American Higher Education.* Washington: American Council on Education, 1965.

SUPPLEMENTARY STATEMENT

ROALD F. CAMPBELL*

States are a part of the larger society and the concept of social systems used by R. L. Johns in the preceding paper is a useful one. The federal government can and will deal with education, but this new force need

* *Dean, Graduate School of Education and Chairman, Department of Education, University of Chicago;* Superintendent of Schools, Preston, Idaho (1933-42); Professor, University of Utah 1942-51); Professor, Ohio State University (1952-57); Reavis Professor of Educational Administration, University of Chicago (1961-present); Member of National Academy of Education; Co-editor *Administrative Behavior in Education* (1957); Co-author *Introduction to Educational Administration* (third edition 1966); Co-author *The Organization and Control of American Schools* (1965).

not detract from—indeed it may actually enhance—the role of the states. With the Johns statement as background, I would like to suggest a few steps many state education agencies need to take if they are to strengthen their operation.

CLARIFY THE MISSION

Despite the rhetoric sometimes employed, most state departments of education devote the major part of their energy to regulatory activities. Teachers must be certificated, state funds must be distributed, and textbooks must be adopted. These and other regulatory functions need to be carried out, but in many instances the operation is little more than a routine implementation of the law. The time has come when the leadership function, long bandied about and quite ambiguous in meaning, must be taken seriously.

Perhaps the meaning of leadership can be sharpened if it be contrasted with maintenance. To keep the organization going, to administer the law, to visit schools as usual, to convene the state board as is the custom are common maintenance activities. We shall always have maintenance functions with us and I do not disparage them. But if the state department is to exercise leadership *it must help create new law, work out unique arrangements with schools in the field,* and *convene productive meetings with people and agencies never before involved.* In short, the educational scene in the state will undergo some change ascribed, at least in part, to the leadership activities of the state agency for education. *Leaders must lead.*

To be more specific, most state departments have responded, after due course, to the pressures around them. These pressures may come from school districts, from the state legislature, and they are now coming increasingly from the federal government. In many instances the state does little with federal pressures except act as a broker between federal and local agencies. If the state is to lead it must do more than mediate, it must influence federal legislation and guidelines as well as the positions taken by local districts in their responses to federal provisions. The state department ought to be a responsible voice—at times a countervailing voice—and not merely a reluctant expediter of federal programs.

Recent federal legislation actually provides a new opportunity for state departments of education. In the relationship among agencies required for the implementation of provisions in Titles I, II and III of Public Law 89-10, the state department can provide some of the direction needed to help these agencies function in some kind of viable partnership. For instance, how many public schools establish productive relationships with non-public schools, with universities, with museums, and with other cultural institutions? The state department, in part because it is not charged with the immediate operation of schools, may give more perspective to such considerations and may identify and publicize successful models which are developed in the field.

Or, to consider the matter more broadly, a state department is in a good position to suggest the kind of relationships which ought to exist between school organizations and planning, housing and other agencies where many decisions having educational implications are being made. The problem of racial integration, for instance, can never be solved by the schools alone. Only as the problem is viewed in its total social context, and as the programs of many social agencies are brought into focus, can ghettos be eliminated and schools become attractive to whites and Negroes alike and to people of varying social class.

ADOPT A NEW APPROACH

In addition to clarifying its mission, the state department of education needs to develop a new approach. In the future, state departments should stress—far more than in the past—coordination and support. Perhaps what is meant by coordination and support can best be suggested by presentation of a few examples. One such illustration may be found in the use of demonstration centers. For instance, instead of employing a number of so-called specialists in education for the gifted, one state chose to set up centers where model programs for the education of the gifted could be developed and where these programs might be observed. The state invited proposals from schools and school systems and offered some financial support for the proposals found acceptable. Each center involved a number of its regular teachers in the establishment and operation of its program and, thus, the efforts of the state were multiplied by using the talent found in the local districts. State money was granted to the local district for the employment of a coordinator of the project and for compensation of released time of local staff necessary in the demonstration of the project to many visitors.

The research function—now largely neglected in most state departments—could be coordinated and supported in much the same way. With the employment of a few competent research people in the state department itself, the talents of gifted researchers in universities and other research centers might be enlisted on a contract basis. Some of the perplexities facing state repartments of education probably overlap the interests of these researchers. The discovery and nurture of this overlap may be one of the most important functions a state division of research can perform. With appropriate encouragement, the talents of individuals outside the organization can be enlisted toward achieving the ultimate purpose of the state department. In short, research divisions of state departments may become expert in sensing problems, in supporting researchers in many institutions in working on such problems, and in disseminating to the field useful information growing out of such research activity.

Even the planning function—almost completely non-existent in most state departments—might become a reality if the approach is to be one of coordination and support. Few state department personnel are trained to be planners and few state board of education members have the time or competence for such a task. One approach—used increasingly in recent years in higher education and in government—is the appointment of a group of able and influential citizens to an ad hoc committee or task force. Several states following this policy have developed master plans for higher education. *Every state needs a master plan for elementary and secondary edu-*

cation. If the state department can define the task and make it appear important, able citizens can be attracted for short periods of challenging service. Ordinarily, such citizens expect no pay. They do expect to have a small staff available to them, and, of course, they should be reimbursed for expenses incurred. Thus, the talents of many people can be enlisted in helping with the business of the state agency.

SEEK PUBLIC SUPPORT

Unlike schools and colleges, state departments of education have no students and no alumni. This lack of clientele makes public support for state departments difficult to achieve. At the same time it is apparent that state departments cannot perform a significant role in the improvement of education unless that role be understood and supported by the public. The use of leading citizens on task force assignments, as suggested above, may represent one step in the direction of securing more public support.

Another way for increasing public support would be to raise the status of the citizens who become members of the state board of education. Neither popular election of state board members nor their appointment by the governor appear to have worked very well. In a popular election it is obvious that the state board of education contestants do not lead the ticket. In regular elections the contests for the governorship, for the congress, and for other offices appear much more important to most voters and, thus, the merits of candidates for the state board receive little consideration. If state board members are elected in special elections, the turn-out is usually small and thus again relatively few people pay much attention to the educational issues involved.

These considerations cause me to favor a plan whereby state board members are appointed by the governor subject to the approval of the senate. But this procedure must be upgraded over the way it now operates in many states. The all too common practice is to appoint the most prestigious and able citizens to the board of regents of the state university, the second layer of citizens to governing boards of state colleges, and finally to reward a few of the politically faithful, almost unknown, and often quite inept, with appointments to the state board of education.

No state department of education can become distinguished unless some of the state's ablest citizens are willing to serve on its board. I can think of no single way by which a governor could do more to improve public education in his state than to seek out some of the best citizens of his state and convince them that they should accept a term or two on the state board of education. A state board with such membership would not only provide visibility for the education function but also would do much to merit public confidence.

A state board of education composed of able and astute citizens could represent effectively the educational needs of the state to the legislature and to the governor. This is seldom done now; board members apparently possess neither the information nor the stature to influence the political forces of the state. In our desire to keep schools out of *partisan* politics we have misperceived the political character of the process by which resources are allocated among the various state services. Schools will get their due share of state resources only when both professional and political voices are well represented in the decision-making process. While the chief state school officer has a place in this operation, his efforts can be greatly strengthened by appropriate activity on the part of state board members upon whom the epithet of special pleading is much harder to bestow.

With state boards composed of citizens of the type suggested here, the purpose and operation of the board would be much better represented among the electorate as well as in the legislature and the governor's office. Seven to nine such citizens can appear before many groups over the entire state and help to explain the ways in which the state is helping to improve all the schools. If there are demonstration centers, as suggested above, such practices can be disseminated and interpreted to citizens as well as to school people. If long-term planning is going forward, the procedures and projections of such activity can be given wide publicity.

A state board of this kind can make a significant difference in the decisions pertaining to education reached by a legislature and a governor. In turn, the legislators and governor must defend their decisions before the electorate. This very process means that the educational problems and state provisions for meeting those problems became an important part of the accountability to which most elected officials are subjected. When there is movement in any public service the politicians are required to explain that movement and this process seems central to better public relations.

UPGRADE PERSONNEL

I am convinced that state departments can be changed very little unless there is a substantial upgrading of personnel. I would start with securing abler citizens to serve on state boards, as emphasized above. If the appointment process is followed, the high expectations held for state board members can be made clear to the governor and to members of the senate. If the election process is followed, every effort can be extended to induce able citizens to accept nomination. In either case, organizations of people supporting education have an important job to do.

Despite some notable exceptions, we must also secure more competent people for the position as chief state school officer. In most states, the incumbent officers would not merit appointment to the office of superintendent of schools in the major city school districts of their states. The unattractiveness of the chief state school office appears to be, in part, a product of our long tradition of localism, particularly in education. But that tradition is no longer adequate; a growing number of important decisions are being made at the state level and we must have some of our ablest and wisest people serving at that level. Among other attractions to the office, we shall have to provide better salaries than are now paid to most chief state school officers.

If the chief state school officer is appointed by the state board of education and if the board itself can be improved as suggested above, the attraction of able people to the chief state school office would appear to be a relatively simple matter. If this officer is elected by popular vote, the problem may be more difficult. Even under these conditions, however, as a few states have demonstrated, strong people can be secured. The key to the matter rests in the nomination procedure more than in the election process. If those who insist upon competence in the chief state school office are vigilant in seeking and supporting good candidates, able people can be placed in the office.

Fully as important as seeking better state boards and better chief state school officers is a program for upgrading the staff of the entire state department of education. In some states, the number of staff members probably needs to be increased, but *more important than number is the quality of the people who serve in the department.* At present, most states use the public schools as almost their only source of staff members. Frequently these are the rural public schools for the reason that state department salaries are not competitive with salaries paid teachers and administrators in city and suburban school districts. With staff members coming from the rural schools, the rural orientation of most state departments is reinforced and the inadequacy of state departments to deal with urban and metropolitan problems is thus accentuated.

Obviously, salary levels and working conditions—including freedom from the political clearance that still is characteristic of practices in some states—must be improved so that able people in urban as well as rural settings can be attracted. It is also necessary that state departments seek personnel from agencies and institutions other than schools. For instance, a research director may come from a university, a planner may come from a planning agency, a staff member in finance may come from business, and a computer expert may come from one of the testing agencies. In any case, the pool from which talent is sought needs to be enlarged.

In Summary

I have accepted as appropriate the social systems approach presented by Johns. I think state departments are part of the larger social system and that they can perform important services for that system. As these services are perceived to be relevant to the total system, adequate resources will be provided for such services. Some immediate steps toward this end would appear to include more emphasis on the leadership role of state departments of education, increased use of the approaches involving coordination and support by state departments, deliberate attempts to increase public understanding and support, and finally the upgrading of all functionaries in state education agencies—board members, chief state school officers, and staff members of the department.

CHAPTER 15

Political Competence:

A Challenge to Education in a Changing Society

HENRY TOY, JR. *

The implications for education arising from the anticipated changes in society during the next few years—particularly as the inferences are associated with intergovernmental relations—could make a long list. However, it is appropriate, I think, to discuss them as elements of two basic questions: (1) How will we prepare students, and future voters to improve their understanding and attitudes toward government and politics? and (2) How will *we* conduct *ourselves* during this period of political decision making? All the evidence points clearly to the conclusion that these are two of the most important questions with which we must deal effectively during the next half generation.

The key message presented in the scholarly papers included in *Prospective Changes in Society by 1980,* as it relates to the subject we are now considering, is that the nation will be faced with the necessity of supplying more and better public services for more educated adults who will be vying for their special places in the sun; that these services and the handling of social unrest will cost much more in tax money and will create new administrative problems; and, that we should be prepared for some surprises during coming years.

However, partly because changes which are likely to take place in intergovernmental relations are so pertinent to the subject of this paper and partly because I am somewhat less sanguine in certain respects than Dr. Elazar** about "The American Partnership", I feel it is necessary for me to summarize my views about the direction in which intergovernmental relations is headed as a setting for my later comments.

CHANGING CONCEPTS

The concept that the states are the source of all government powers is, it seems, being modified. The *legal* concept has been that the people and the states were sovereign in that they created our federal government, granted it essential powers and delegated certain functions. Similarly, it was the states which accorded powers to local units of government. The supremacy of the states can now be questioned since, in just one generation, we have seen another power—that of money—moving to take command

---

* *President, Henry Toy, Jr. and Associates, Educational Consultants, New York City;* President, National Citizens Commission for the Public Schools and National Citizens Council for Better Schools. (1949-59); Phi Delta Kappa Lay Citizens Award (1960); Author of numerous articles and of chapters in several books on education and citizen activities.

** See *Prospective Changes in Society by 1980* (Denver, Colo.: Designing Education for the Future, 1966) Chap. 6. All similar references without footnotes are to chapters in that publication.

273

over legal theory. In this period, while the state and local share of the support of expenses for all local services increased twenty-three fold, the federal government's contributions, or share, increased eighty-six fold. Stated another way, the federal government's share had been less than one-fiftieth and now it is one-fifth. The states' portion remains relatively unchanged and this has its effect upon relationships.

Early in 1966, Senator Edmund S. Muskie, Chairman of the U. S. Senate's Subcommittee on Intergovernmental Relations, reported that, for all state and local purposes, "federal aid programs have now passed the 175 mark . . . for an anticipated Federal outlay of $14 billion this year . . . in contrast to a $4 billion Federal expenditure 10 years ago." In August of this year, Senator Edward M. Kennedy, when presenting a Resolution to authorize a computerized information system to provide state and local governments with information on federal programs, said: " . . . almost twice as much federal aid has been appropriated during the past five sessions of Congress as the total appropriated by all previous Congresses going back to 1789."[1]

Certainly Senator Muskie was aware of this when he reported further:

> These figures show the overwhelming part that State and local jurisdictions continue to play in our federal system, and they indicate the increased role which such jurisdiction must assume in the future. At the same time, these facts demonstrate the clear obligation the Federal Government has to help the States and their localities obtain maximum benefits from Federal aid and technical assistance to plan better and to service better their own expanding responsibilities.[2]

The numerous federal-aid programs to which Senator Muskie referred affect every major function of local government and have changed the lines of communication and administration among all levels of government. It is true in practically all areas—highways, public welfare, public health, education and so on. One brief example in education should illustrate. Appleton-Century-Crofts has just introduced a new service called "The Guide to Federal Assistance for Education." Included in this system are over 150 educational program folders containing instructions on how to obtain available federal funds. In those cases where administration takes place at other than the central federal agency level the user of "The Guide" is directed to a state folder for further "how to" information. It is interesting to note that *fewer than one-third of the program folders direct the applicant to a state administrative agency.* This gives some indication of the shift in autonomy.

THE CALL FOR REFORMS

It seems apparent that the "push" is on to get our house in order to make "Creative Federalism" work. The "push" is further evidence of the weakening legal concept of state sovereignty. The federal blueprint has been drawn and we should know by now what is expected. Failure to deliver could change our entire tradition.

---

[1] "Statement by Senator Edward M. Kennedy on a Bill to Authorize a Computerized Information System to Provide State and Local Governments with Information on Federal Programs," (Office of Senator Edward M. Kennedy, August 10, 1966).

[2] Statement of Senator Edmund S. Muskie before the Executive and Legislative Reorganization Subcommittee, House Committee on Government Operations, March 1, 1966, on S. 561, the proposed Intergovernmental Cooperation Act.

There are those in Congress who believe strongly that smooth intergovernmental relations will be dependent upon strong constructive action at the state level, particularly by the legislatures. Senator Muskie, for example, when speaking to The American Assembly, listed four general areas where state legislatures could take the initiative in modernizing and strengthening the government role of the states. *First,* he declared,

> "We must initiate the reforms that will convert our State legislatures into responsible and respected—as well as representative—deliberative bodies."

Second, he warned that state legislatures must strengthen the administrative organization and personnel management of their executive branches. The Senator added:

> This branch is a fragmented cluster of departments, boards, agencies, and commissions . . . In the popular mind, it is headed by the State's chief executive; in fact, it is headed by no one in particular.

Third, Senator Muskie urged that state legislatures modernize the executive machinery for preparing state budgets, and their own machinery for reviewing them. *Fourth,* the Maine Senator called for an across-the-board reform of state tax laws and financial procedures to be initiated by state legislatures. Having called for these actions, the Chairman of the Subcommittee on Intergovernmental Relations warned that, "The die is indeed cast, and many State executive and legislative leaders know it." He added: "The States must step into the breach. If they do not, they can claim only a junior partnership position in our federal system."[3]

Governor Warren E. Hearnes of Missouri must be one of those leaders who understand the situation because, when speaking this summer at the Midwestern Governors' Conference in Cincinnati, he said, "Whenever the States provide a vacuum through inaction, the Federal Government sooner or later will fill it."

Here is another similar example with an interesting twist. Late this summer when only one challenger to Frank D. O'Connor for the Democratic nomination for the New York governorship remained, the challenger, Howard J. Samuels, was offered, as a consolation, the opportunity to run on the same ticket with Mr. O'Connor as candidate for Lieutenant Governor. The major function of the Lieutenant Governor is to preside over the State Senate—not much of a reward for the up-state industrialist. But Mr. O'Connor offered, as an enticement, to turn over a whole broad portion of the Governor's job by suggesting that the Lieutenant Governor be put in charge of federal funds in the state.

Another example of federal intent is the Intergovernmental Cooperation Act of 1966. Among other things, this measure is intended to achieve the fullest cooperation and coordination of activities between levels of government, to improve the administration of grants-in-aid, to provide for periodic congressional review of grants-in-aid, and to permit provision of reimbursable technical services to state and local governments.

Then there is the proposed Intergovernmental Personnel Act of 1966

---

[3] Excerpts from address by Senator Edmund S. Muskie (D-Maine) Chairman, Subcommittee on Intergovernmental Relations, Senate Committee on Government Operations, "The State Legislatures in an Age of Creative Federalism," April 30, 1966.

which remained in committee when Congress adjourned. Its main purpose is to encourage state and local governments to improve the quality of their own public service. It proposes to do this by focusing on three problems in the personnel area: merit system, personnel administration, and in-service training programs. The call for planning also is manifest in the Public Works and Economic Development Act of 1965 and in the Demonstration Cities Act of 1966. The Economic Development Act is an excellent example of both intent and direction resulting from a feeling of need for decentralization through federal support to have regional planning and combined state financing. It will take a long time to happen but the tempo probably will accelerate when reapportionment is completed.

TOWARD REGIONALISM

Many members of Congress are beginning to recognize the jungle created by functional or categorical grants-in-aid. As time goes on they will become increasingly alerted to this problem and the trend could shift toward block grants to states and later to regions.

The Office of Regional Economic Development could very well be an early step in a series of moves which one day could lead to nine to twelve regional governments poised between the federal and state governments. To be sure such a possibility would be a long way off. At this stage, the average citizen has not given it much thought; but we can be reasonably certain that it is part of the active thinking of those planners in Washington who are concentrating on the idea of a more efficient system of government. There are many powerful forces that will actively object to such a proposal when it is made; but it *will* be made and, perhaps, even by 1980. However, the signs are all around us and we cannot dismiss the forceful catalyst: *need* —need for efficiency, need for dollar savings, and need to combat crises. We are mindful of water shortages, transportation problems for commuters, air pollution and water pollution. But these problems have not yet reached crisis proportions. If the concept of regional governments is to be avoided as a political issue, then it will be because these public necessities—water, air, and transportation—are cared for by some other means.

Whether or not the concept of regional governments is avoided as a political issue, our system of intergovernmental relations will continue to be a marvelous experiment in adapting the contradictory goals of:

1. Developing political union on the one hand and an active division of powers on the other;

2. Developing the desire and the strength at all levels to solve common problems through unity while maintaining diversity as opposed to uniformity;

3. Creating a powerful love of country while maintaining a devotion to state and local communities; and

4. Accommodating majority rule with protection of minority rights.

Education will continue to be in the center of this magnificent experiment.

Some Observations

Certain trends within the educational system with respect to relationships are observable. *These trends suggest a need on the part of all educators to develop a strong political competence.*

Inter-Agency Conflict

In the past two and one-half years I have spent a great deal of time in our nation's capital. I have visited with officials at all levels in dozens of agencies which administer programs involved with education. The first observation I would make as an outcome of these experiences is that inter-agency conflict is the order of the day. *When federal government personnel discuss new education programs, their first questions are* rarely about the concepts or the merits of the program; but rather, *with which agency power over the program will reside.* This is a natural but not wholly healthy situation and it is much too early to predict how well the United States Office of Education (USOE) will fare in this conflict and thus where to form one's alliances.

Intra-Agency Conflict

A second observation is the depressing feeling one gets from the struggles within the Office of Education itself. Almost overnight, upon becoming affluent, there was an infusion of new blood and considerable internal shake-up. The fact that this was done is not the issue; under the circumstances, it may have been the best thing to do. The manner in which it was accomplished and the way it was received is the difficulty. Associations of many years have been changed from friendly to antagonistic and the comfortable feelings that many professional organizations have had in their dealings with the Office are now ones of caution. These individuals and groups may have to change their activities or at least their political styles.

Money Versus Influence

A third observation relates to the attitude now held by so many of the earlier strongest proponents of federal aid. I recall how avid certain professional leaders were in their expressions, back in the fifties, that unless federal aid became a reality all would be lost. Today, many of these same individuals are most critical about what we have. Their concern is not that the extra dollars have become available but rather that the political influence has shifted. Some complain bitterly that not only have policy decisions about education been pre-empted by the federal government, but that these decisions are made too often by agencies without educational expertise. Two examples, both using poverty as the justification, will illustrate. First, the case of Head Start where the Office of Economic Opportunity, almost overnight, made the decision for schools across the country that formal education shall begin at age four instead of the traditional six. The second is that of the Defense Department announcing its intention for the military services to use advanced techniques to train up to 100,000 of the 600,000 who are, each year, rejected for physical or educational reasons.

LOSS OF INITIATIVE

During the past year it has been my good fortune to visit 18 of our state capitals and in so doing I have made a fourth observation. I was disappointed on these visits with a difference I seemed to note from my observations during almost annual visits to all state capitals from 1949 to 1959. In most—although not all—of these states, I seemed to detect a loss of initiative—a wait-and-see attitude. Admittedly this is a generalization, but I had the impression that too many states were withholding decision-making, fearing that it might not be in keeping with mandates to be issued from Washington. Perhaps this is why the Governors of 33 states and 3 territories were prompt in adhering to the Interstate Compact. None of us can tell for sure what the strongest motivation for joining might have been although, I suspect, fear of growing federal power with the prospect of lessening state control was at least one of the primary reasons.

Former Governor Terry Sanford of North Carolina, a strong advocate for strengthening the capacity of the states to meet educational needs, is one of the backers of the Interstate Compact which is supported by the states themselves on a pro-rata basis, with some aid from private foundations. In explaining what the Compact is and is not, Governor Sanford has said:

. . . It *will* be a partnership between the educational and political forces for the advancement of education.

. . . It *will not* be a policy-maker.

. . . It does *not* represent a drive for uniformity.

. . . It does *not* represent an effort to curtail or attack federal aid to education, or federal activity.

. . . It *will not* compete with, replace or make obsolete the current voluntary associations and national or regional organizations in the field of education.[4]

THE ROLE OF PHILANTHROPHY

The fifth observation is the changing attitude of philanthropists. "For the year 1965 the American Association of Fund-Raising Counsel estimates that total giving to philanthropic causes and institutions amounted to $11.3 billion."[5] Education received 17 percent or just under $2 billion. Foundations which had for many years provided the cutting edge for new ventures in education are now questioning their role. One of the first questions they ask about a proposal is whether it is something that should be supported by one of the new federal programs. A continuing dialogue has already begun between foundations and government in order to keep each other informed on changing developments. This has advantages, since one does not have to look far within the government to find those who believe that foundations were set up first to take advantage of tax laws and second to do good. With this kind of cynicism it does not take much imagination to conceive of government restrictions upon foundations or mandatory filing of spending plans to assure that foundation activities do no harm to governmental

---

[4] *The Peabody Reflector*, March-April, 1966, p. 66.
[5] *Giving USA, 1966 Edition*, American Association of Fund Raising Counsel, Inc., New York.

planning. Whether or not this happens, I think we can be sure that foundations will tend to become more cautious in their philanthropic awards.

Professional Grant Gathering

A sixth observation concerns the emergence of a new breed of professionals in the field of governmental grantsmanship. The larger institutions of higher education and even the larger public school systems now have
full-time trained personnel who are after the Washington dollar. The smaller and sometimes more needy are lost in the race. The result could very
well be that instead of equalizing opportunity there will be an increase in
the inequities.

Guided Initiative

My seventh observation is somewhat related to the sixth. It represents
a dichotomy. On the one hand, in order to lessen the inequities which can
result from the more aggressive approaches of those who seek out Washington help, the federal government has undertaken a concerted program to
strengthen regional offices thereby making its services more readily available to the grass roots. On the other hand, there are those programs whose
language would seem to call for initiative on the part of the grass roots but
where in actual administration it would be more accurate to say the initiative was planned or at least motivated from Washington. This is not meant
as negative criticism. Certainly it makes sense to take steps to avoid duplication of effort in order to gain the most from limited resources, just as
long as the effort does not result either in favoritism or in loss of diversity
by confusing unity with uniformity.

Growth of Consortiums

An eighth observation is that there is a definite desire on the part of
educators and governmental planners to share in solutions to common problems. What we are witnessing in this eight-state area is an excellent example
of two observations. First, the federal government's concern for strengthening state leadership resulted in the enactment of Section 505, Title V,
of Public Law 89-10. Second, your concern for getting the most from your
available resources brought about this eight-state project concerned with
Designing Education for the Future. Similarly, there are numerous cases
around the country where several colleges in close proximity are beginning
to pool their resources to improve the quality of all. For example, in the
District of Columbia, American, Catholic, George Washington, George-
town, and Howard Universities, two years ago, incorporated a Consortium
which could lead to the creation of a distinguished graduate study center
that none of the five has been able to provide by itself. It will take time to
achieve, because it will be necessary to untangle a lot of red tape on five
campuses and will have to deal with a fivefold supply of faculty skepticism.
One of the more obvious examples of federal encouragement for the creation of new types of institutions is Title IV of the Elementary and Secondary
Education Act. These new institutions, it is hoped, will result in the
sharing of resources and "know-how" to add a new dynamic force in behalf

of education, frequently on a regional basis. Ideally, these Laboratories should become excellent pilot experiments not only in the problems they are to attack but also in combining intergovernmental relations with the private sector. But there is considerable uncertainty if not suspicion on the part of many applicants as to where initiative really rests.

THE SCHOOL ADMINISTRATOR'S JOB

Ninth among my observations is one that I have had for many years but which has become keener in the past several months. The school administrator's job, especially one in a big city, is loaded with agitation, tension, and insecurity. He has to cope with a school board, competing governmental bodies, civil rights and religious groups, social reformers and, like any other government leader, must always be concerned with his public image lest he not be in the job tomorrow. The social revolution we are entering, which includes the federal trend toward concentrating on the procedures of government, will necessarily make his job more demanding and require even greater political statesmanship.

SUBSIDIZED RE-AWAKENING

A tenth and highly significant observation is that a number of new grants-in-aid programs have encouraged a type of social unrest that government leaders in the past have tried to avoid. There was a day when many power centers objected to the broadening of educational opportunities mainly because they felt that increased knowledge by the masses could make their positions less secure. Rarely would they say what they really meant. Instead, it would come out in such cliches as "What they don't know won't hurt them." What this really meant was "Let's not trouble trouble." One brief example will suffice.

Early this past summer eleven law students were given job opportunities under the Work-Study program in an area in New York City known as Clinton. These law students, working as community organizers, began to bring the people together to discuss their common problems to see if together they could find some solutions. The problem that was present for all of the people involved—the problem they understood best and felt most keenly—was poor housing conditions. Soon they were organized into tenants' associations.

Clinton is one small area of Manhattan where in 1965 there were 362 fires and no citizen demonstrations resulting from them. On June 30 of this year there was another fire, but this time the residents decided not to sit idly by while suffering their indignities. Aided by educated youth, who were there to show them which way to turn, they tried, without success, to get assistance during their crisis situation from local governmental agencies and from organizations in the private sector. All they got was excuses and frustration which, in turn, bred alienation on their part. Having already experienced other successes through their efforts, the frustration in this case is acting as a spur rather than a dampener and agency officials are beginning to feel the pressures of an aroused citizenry.

There is no telling what this may mean, since the program can be multiplied many hundreds of times throughout the country. On the one hand we have a group of heretofore helpless older people who have learned to act. On the other hand there is a group of youth whose formal education is being supplemented by active experience in the political arena made possible through federal assistance and who are emerging with a feeling of disrespect for local leadership. The impact that this will have upon these future leaders could result in drastic changes in the structure of government and in the balance of power.

AN IRREVERSIBLE TREND

My eleventh observation is that the trend is irreversible. Last Fall, when speaking to a combined meeting of the Oregon School Boards Association and the Oregon School Administrators Association, I warned against any attempt to try to decrease Federal participation. I said: "It is too late for that." Today I am more sure it is. *What is needed, therefore, is increased acceptance of responsibilities on the part of state and local leaders. This is the way to strengthen the partnership among all levels and bring about educational improvement.*

THE ROAD IS NEVER SMOOTH

Despite my position that the trend is irreversible, I am, nevertheless, aware that there are many powerful forces at work which will serve to impede the progress, or the retrogression, whichever suits your beliefs, although they will not alter the direction. Let us review just a few examples of these, mainly because of the implications they have for many other activities that will occur in the next few years.

A recent ruling by the State Supreme Court in New York could stimulate new challenges to the federal school aid programs enacted last year. Here was a case where the East Greenbush, New York, school board, a governmental entity, and the New York Civil Liberties Union, an association in the private sector, cooperated in a court case to test whether a state law violated both state and federal constitutional provisions regarding separation of Church and State. The issue was whether state funds could be used to provide books on loan to pupils in non-public schools. Justice Kane's ruling was that pupils are part of the school and that aid to pupils was the same as aid to the school and, therefore, in violation of both the establishment clause and the free exercise clause. The ruling will, of course, be appealed and, therefore, is far from final. It is significant, however, in its implications for many state and federal programs and its reminder that care must be taken not to permit expediency to push aside constitutional principles.

On the same day that Justice Kane issued his ruling, Governor Wallace of Alabama made a proposal to circumvent the desegregation guidelines of the U. S. Office of Education. His proposal was for the state to appropriate additional funds to make up for any loss of federal revenue by the refusal of the local schools to comply with the guidelines. Governor Wallace also asked the legislature to declare the federal guidelines null and void in

Alabama and to allow the Governor to take over the duties of local school boards in dealing with federal agencies. But the educational community was unified in its opposition to the Governor's proposal. It is not clear whether the opposition was caused by a concern over the loss of more than $41 million for education or about a change in the structure of intergovernmental relations. Despite the opposition, however, the legislature overwhelmingly and quickly gave the Governor what he asked for.

Almost at the same time this was taking place, six civil rights leaders were appearing on the TV program "Meet The Press." One of them, Whitney Young, Jr., head of the Urban League, explained what "black power" meant to him. He said: "The Urban League takes a position that power is something that one acquires through having sufficient economic means, educational resources and political know-how."[6] On the same program, Martin Luther King was demanding federal registrars at elections to remove an atmosphere of intimidation and economic reprisals.

Perhaps, most people in this region feel they will be untouched by some of these problems. But might I suggest an incident that occurred as recently as two months ago that might very well have its repercussions in less than a generation. The incident to which I refer is the National Education Association's release of a 40-page report on what was termed the "most acute educational problem" in the Southwest, an area which includes three of the states involved in this project. The problem referred to was the inadequate schooling received by 1,750,000 Mexican-American children. At the risk of encouraging procrastination in the correction of this problem, I would point out that this case is not unlike one mentioned earlier where the cliches "What they don't know won't hurt them" and "Let's not trouble trouble" were used.

EXPERTS IN AGREEMENT ON NEED FOR POLITICAL COMPETENCE

As a further setting for a discussion of what I believe to be a basic responsibility of the schools and the great challenge of the next half generation, I should like to emphasize certain statements in your first conference report.

Kenneth E. Boulding, in reporting on the uncertain future of knowledge and technology (chapter 12) said:

> Our research resources in particular are poorly allocated in the light of the importance for human welfare of the problems to which they are addressed. I have argued more particularly that the resources devoted to social systems are absurdly small in the light of practical importance of these systems, and that whereas a failure of knowledge to advance in the physical and biological sciences for the next twenty-five years would not present mankind with any serious problems, the failure of knowledge to advance in the social sciences could well be fatal.

T. A. Smith, in discussing the role of communications (chapter 10), observed that the promise of a total communications capability poses two distinct problems. The first—technical in nature—he predicted would be solved. The other, he said, ". . . is a thicket of non-technical problems that

---

[6] *The New York Times*, Monday, August 22, 1966, p. 36.

relate to the economic, social, and political consequences of instant point to point communication anywhere on earth." His prediction on the solution of this problem was much less certain and he concluded with the warning: "However it is employed, the communications capability of 1980 can change the course of the world."

Even the discussions on transportation carried this theme. Paul W. Cherington (chapter 11) cautioned that the extent and speed with which the technological and economic advances in transportation are made "will be heavily dependent upon a variety of social and political factors which are quite divorced from basic technological or economic trends."

Two medical doctors, Herman E. Hilleboe and Ray E. Trussell, presented the case of the medical sciences, 1980 (chapter 4). They concluded that:

> In the long run, the quality and extent of community health is largely determined by the knowledge and attitudes citizens possess and by the behavior they demonstrate.

In concluding his paper on natural resource trends and their implications (chapter 2) Joseph L. Fisher commented that "To a major extent the well-being of Western society in 1980 will depend on intelligent and informed voters and how they cast their ballots between now and then."

Roger L. Shinn, in discussing human responsibility (chapter 15) concluded with:

> In the decades ahead the American society will have many opportunities to experiment with answers to the question of how a pluralistic society incorporates values in its public education. To the extent that the public educational process itself generates certain values—respect for truth and cooperative inquiry, concern for opportunity for all persons, the appeal to evidence and rationality rather than prejudice—another asset is available. But in the momentous social changes through which we are living, the task will not be easy.

In discussing the industrial relations system (chapter 9), Joseph W. Garbarino made the interesting observation that one determinent of the success with which the employee relations system will be able to adapt to the world of 1980 will be the degree of resolution of the problem of combining two skills in one person or organizing their cooperation in the same institution. The skills he referred to are administration as a science and administration as a political process—giving implementation of a decision equal in importance to its content.

After identifying trends in the basic character of intergovernmental relations, Daniel J. Elazar (chapter 6) made this plea:

> The increasing complexity of American government means that better education in the political processes of this country—what we have called in the past Civics—is absolutely necessary. Schools at all levels must develop means to convey some sense of the functioning of the American system to their students, not along the simplistic lines of the past, or for reformist purposes as so frequently has been the case in recent years, but to give them an understanding of a very complex system of government so that they may function as intelligent citizens within it.

Grant McConnell opened his discussion of non-government organizations in American political life (chapter 7) with two quotes from Alexis de Tocqueville. One of these was:

> If each citizen did not learn, in proportion as he individually becomes feeble, and consequently more incapable of preserving his freedom single-handed, to combine with his fellow citizens for the purpose of defending it, it is clear that tyranny would unavoidably increase with equality.

In concluding his paper, Dr. McConnell raised, but did not answer, the question as to whether the pattern of associations which has worked so well for material goals will work as well for others.

These papers were prepared independently of each other. It is, therefore, all the more interesting that such a common thread seemed to run through the concerns of almost all of them. Before concluding this presentation of evidence of concerns of others, I should like to cite two more, because the authors have been, are, and will continue to be heard on matters which concern all of us.

Late this past summer the highly respected Committee for Economic Development published a statement by its Research and Policy Committee entitled "Modernizing Local Government." The concluding statement in the report read:

> Citizen information and understanding in public affairs, particularly at the local level, are all too low. Blame for this must be widely shared, among all those groups and institutions—including the family—that influence attitudes and modes of conduct in formative years and beyond. The importance of local and other governments in gaining and keeping an economic and cultural climate in which our basic institutions may flourish must be fully understood. Not only in school curricula from primary grades onward but in all community circles, citizen responsibility for policy-making and for service in official posts of trust and honor must be recognized as the foundation sustaining this Republic.[7]

And finally, we refer to one which appeared in the July-August edition of *American Education*. The article covered an interview with Francis Keppel, former Commissioner of Education. Among other questions he answered was: "Can you give us an evaluation of your nearly four years in Government?" The former Commissioner made three points. The first was that during these years the nation began to see education as a whole. "The second view that I take away with me," he said, "is how ignorant I was about the system of government we have." His final view was his concern that we have not achieved anything like a good system of communication, federal, state and local; public and private. He added: "I strongly believe in the balance of powers but if it is to work we need a continuing dialogue between the various parts."[8]

REASONS FOR BETTER CIVIC EDUCATION

The quotations above provide expert testimony for the proponents of improved education in the social sciences and particularly in the field of civic education. Why are so many thoughtful leaders from such a variety of specialties insisting that more attention must be given to this aspect of edu-

---

[7] *Modernizing Local Government to Secure a Balanced Federalism.* A Statement on National Policy by the Research and Policy Committee of the Committee for Economic Development, July 1966, p. 64.

[8] "An Interview with Francis Keppel," *American Education*, July-August 1966, p. 13.

cation? The reasons are many, I believe, and are inherent in some of our earlier discussions.

Education for citizenship in the schools has not kept pace in recent decades either with changes in American society or with research about the political process and political behavior. The school curriculum is generally antiquated in respect to the responsibilities and rights of individuals in a modern industrialized and urbanized society. Contemporary schooling is not as sound a foundation for American democracy as, by the American tradition, it should be—or as it can become.

We need to take a new and creative look at school programs for producing good citizens, and fortunately striking resources are at hand for doing so. In recent years the behavioral sciences have produced significant research data concerning political behavior and political socialization. These data need to be intermeshed with educational theory and practice. Moreover, the techniques are now at hand for additional research enterprises by political scientists, lawyers, sociologists, psychologists, and educationalists in direct focus on the problems and potentials of political learning. A coordinated research program, drawing on diverse disciplines and dealing with all educational levels could achieve major results in this area.

Certain general conditions in contemporary life also lend urgency to the need for a renaissance in civic education. In a sense, we are faced with the necessity of creating a new program of Americanization for the coming generation—Americanization not in terms of assimilating successive waves of immigrants, but of creating a unity around our ethnic and racial and economic and regional diversities. We must avoid the catastrophies of political and social alienation among minority groups, and, in a more positive sense, must reinvigorate the whole program of education for all members of the body politic. Education must be enabled to deal creatively with preparation of young people and with better orientation of older people, for effective membership in what political scientists are calling "the civic culture."

The need for a revitalized civic education is by no means local. It is not limited to one nation, but is a world-wide phenomenon. American citizenship has to be exercised within a framework of world-wide international relations. In the newly developing countries civic responsibility and democratic political behavior must be given priority consideration, both for the development of nationalities and for the stability of allies in a free world. The study of civic education needs to be pursued comparatively on an international scale—and the development of comparative education as rooted in the social sciences makes this possible. It must study the experience of other countries in the making of citizens, and must produce findings applicable in other societies which are committed to democracy.

The need for a revitalized program in civic education is not confined to the elementary and secondary schools. Experience under Title II-B of the Economic Opportunity Act has emphasized the need for a bold new look at materials and approaches to be used in training for citizenship while teaching adults to read. With changes in the immigration laws, there will be further need to concentrate on citizenship programs as the teaching of reading and writing in English as a second language gains momentum.

As most people are well aware, many organizations have become actively engaged in programs which tend to influence the teaching of citizenship in our schools. Such diverse groups as the American Bar Association, American Council of Learned Societies, American Jewish Committee, American Legion, Chamber of Commerce, and Education for Freedom, to name but a very few, have manifested their concerns by conducting studies, preparing materials, offering in-service programs for teachers and sponsoring "contests." Unfortunately, from a national educational point of view, there has been a disorganized multiplicity of efforts and a fragmentary approach to a problem requiring a total attack.

The problem is aggravated by federal grants-in-aid in one area and lack of federal assistance in another. The infusion of federal funds for one activity inevitably becomes a pump-priming device requiring additional state and local investment for the same activity. This, temporarily at least, reduces state and local ability to do things in other areas. Yet, frequently the success in the one creates the need for the other. We have already seen how a number of new federal programs will result in the need for more political sophistication if the balance of power and level of citizen respect are not increasingly to move away from the local to the federal level. Yet the federal administrative agencies have seen fit to use but minor portions of their appropriations for research or experimentation in civic education. And only in rare cases have foundations stepped in to fill this void, believing that it is an area which is covered by available federal funds.

SOME ENCOURAGING DEVELOPMENTS

One of these exceptions is The Danforth Foundation which has generously supported numerous activities in this area. Several years ago the Chief State School Officers in the nine Northeastern States joined together to sponsor a citizenship project of a scope that none could afford to pursue alone. The Danforth Foundation has provided financial assistance and the work is centered at the Lincoln Filene Center for Citizenship and Public Affairs at Tufts University. In addition to providing seed money for a local citizenship education project in the St. Louis area, Danforth also decided about two years ago to support the beginning efforts for a national group known as the Council on Civic Education. This group has sponsored a variety of research projects in the hope of providing essential information for use by educators as they increase their concern about this area of the school program.

While the Council at this time has not formulated specific recommendations for reform—it is much too soon for that—it is convinced that with the changes taking place in American society there is no area of the free public education system which deserves more attention than that of preparing youth to operate effectively in our political system. That is why the Council has supported the efforts of an interdisciplinary committee on civic education at the University of California at Los Angeles. The committee has written and is experimenting with a new unit for the elementary grades in the area of rights and responsibilities of an American citizen. The purpose of this unit is to help young people develop certain abilities rather than merely to be prepared to regurgitate certain facts. The general objectives for children through this unit are:

Ability to use a frame of reference for analysis and evaluation of the process of society. This structure includes the major concepts of power, liberty, conflict, justice, law, government, democracy, and value.

Ability to understand some of the essential values of American society:

Belief in the right to live in a relatively predictable society.

Belief in the right to have a voice in the control of social processes.

Belief in the right to create and utilize non-violent means of resolving conflicts in order to provide maximum protection for one's life, liberty, and property.

Belief in the right to expression of individuality.

Ability to understand the use of laws to contain individual, group, or governmental powers in order to preserve the essential values of American society.

Ability to understand the value of the expression of conflicting ideas and beliefs as an inherent concept in democracy, and the consequent need to tolerate the widest possible divergence in the expression of ideas and beliefs.

Ability to understand the need to balance the conflicting rights of individuals in reference to the essential values of the society.

Ability to understand the instrumental value of democratic processes providing for peaceful resolutions of conflicts in order to preserve the essential values of the society.

Ability to understand the need for procedural safeguards for individual rights when solving conflicts between individuals or between individuals and the State.

Ability to understand the imperfect nature of man and of the laws and of the consequent necessity for constant vigilance of the processes of society in order to protect the basic values.

Ability to analyze and evaluate the processes of society in order to predict the probable consequences of alternative courses of action upon the preservation of the basic values of our democratic tradition.

Ability to analyze laws in order to determine their functions and the reasons for them.

Ability to determine the values which laws preserve.

Ability to write laws designed to protect certain values.

Ability to apply relevant laws to conflict situations and to evaluate their effectiveness in regard to the preservation of essential values.

Ability to understand that there are no absolute answers to many of the questions of profound importance to man.

Ability to give a wide range of relevant responses to questions on significant issues.[9]

If all or even most Americans who pass through our schools possessed these abilities, we would have no reason to be concerned as we live through this period of transition. Whether we call this period of transition evolution or revolution, the fact is that people are beginning to think seriously about the dignity of man. The thinking and accompanying actions have taken us through several stages—stages which are fairly well identified by catchy phrases. First there was the stage of "equality of opportunity" which Dr. Elazar (chapter 6) has suggested is moving over into the stage of "equality of condition," particularly in the realm of public education. But "equality of condition" was preceded and aided by the period of "rising expecta-

---

[9] Unpublished Teaching Guide prepared by The Civic Education Committee of the University of California at Los Angeles, Summer 1966, pp. 1-3.

tions." Now we have begun to move into a period of "aspiring to self-determination". It is in this period that our system will face one of its fiercest tests—a test of our philosophical notion that

> . . . given whatever knowledge there is concerning man and processes of reality, and the freedom to choose between alternative courses of action, most men will choose wisely most of the time through the use of their own intelligence.[10]

Members of the Council on Civic Education are sure of one other point —any increase in activity or any departure from the traditional approach is going to be greeted with both cheers and jeers. This is part of the American way and is part of our system of checks and balances at work. It is the inevitable gauntlet any group must run in the race to progress. To back off in fear is to yield to mediocrity.

The schools need not live in awe of pressures from the private sector, however. They can operate in a partnership with the numerous organizations to assure a fuller understanding of what changes are needed and why more attention is essential in this part of the school program. Together we can investigate the needs and together we can fearlessly proclaim what it is we intend to do and why we intend to do it. It is our duty to prepare youth to live in the kind of society which thrives on pressures of public opinion from all quarters and, therefore, we must not ourselves retreat from these pressures. Our concern must not be for just getting through the school year comfortably. It is our duty to think ahead with less concern for immediate consequences and a fuller determination that our students will understand and appreciate the system in which they must live.

THE EDUCATORS' TRUST

Dr. Elazar (chapter 6) pointed out that we are presently moving into the last third of a generation where, between now and 1980, we will have the task as a nation of implementing the new programs established in recent years. He said that "while one cannot say what kind of new legislation will be enacted by 1980, we can assume that it will have to do with the reform of administrative and legislative procedures and will probably pay considerable attention to problems of intergovernmental relations as well." It is in connection with the probable proposed reforms that the implication for education—how we conduct ourselves during this period of political decision making—will face a severe test.

Earlier, I made reference to a number of "pushes" already under way to get our house in order. Inevitably these general programs will get around to a crusade to reduce the number of local governments and the number of overlapping layers of local government which now breed inefficiency and curtail progress. This crusade will find its leadership from the private sector —many and varied types of organizations—as well as from higher levels of government. This you may say is nothing new; that education has been doing this through reorganization of school districts for years. But you would be only partly right. While the efforts from a variety of quarters have resulted in a sizable reduction of independent school districts, na-

---

[10] The Civic Education Committee, UCLA, *loc. cit.*

tionally little or no gain has been made in local governments being structured in such a way as to secure unity in administrative operations to cope with the varied but interrelated problems of a political entity. It is in this regard that the next crusade probably will be directed. This will mean a challenge to Education's insistence upon separatism.

This is not the time nor the place for me to choose sides between the cause of separatism or the cause of viable, complete institutions of local self-government. It is, however, proper to raise the question of the effect reactions by educators will have upon students when this crusade becomes a political issue. Education has enjoyed, during the past decade and a half, a sort of "honeymoon" when Americans were preoccupied with the problems of public schools. Citizen interest, on the positive side, in other services has been much less intense. There will be a natural tendency to try to hold on to this favored position.

When the day comes that the lines are drawn on this issue, I am hopeful that Education will debate its cause on the philosophical and practical merits of the case while taking great care not to leave any impression that politics per se is evil. To do otherwise would have the effect of undoing all that teachers are trying to accomplish when they attempt by exhortation or otherwise to instill in their students a healthy respect for our form of government. We cannot at one moment encourage the young to grow up as responsible and active citizens and at the next moment have them hear us express fear of general politics and denounce the means by which democratic government is achieved. We must, instead, set the good example of rational persuasion and open-mindedness as we permit our system of checks and balances to remain at work. And if we do, then, and only then, can we rightfully accept the plaudits for helping to maintain the public schools as the cornerstone of democracy.

SUMMARY

The first of two major conclusions to emerge from this discussion is that local school systems and state education agencies should make a serious effort to relate their participation in federal programs to their own needs. From a long-range point of view, they cannot afford to take expedient action in order to get some federal funds, or merely await developments as a basis for determining their destiny. They need to proceed promptly and skillfully to devise better plans and better ways of implementing those plans. In other words, they should take their responsibilities for educational policy seriously and make adequate preparation to meet those responsibilities. To do less will be to invite a change in the relative importance of the parties within the federal-state-local partnership.

The second conclusion is that the evidence clearly supports the need for a larger proportion of the citizens of the nation to become better informed about the processes of government and to take a more active part in its operations. No single agency can be expected to accomplish this alone but the basic responsibility for improving the understanding and attitudes of future voters toward government and politics—and thus for helping to assure better government at all levels—inevitably must rest with the schools.

SUPPLEMENTARY STATEMENT

HAROLD TAYLOR*

Henry Toy, Jr., has provided illuminating comment on the impact of the new federal legislation on the idea and practice of state and regional governments and operations relating to education. His description of inter-agency conflict and cooperation in Washington, his remarks on the situation in the education departments of the states, and his account of the major trends in the national management of education, give content to generalizations which are usually made without the sort of specific reference we are fortunate in having from Toy's present research and writing.

My comments have to do with what is happening beneath the surface of the educational structure, that is to say, what the students, teachers and citizens interested in education are doing in the day-to-day part of the educational system.

I begin by making a basic distinction between the organization of education and the process and content of education itself. By the organization, I mean simply the administrative apparatus, the work of the agencies of government, the state departments of education, the administrative officers of the universities and schools, the meetings of educators, conferences attended by faculty members, and that whole part of education which deals with setting up structures, policies and programs. By the process and content of education, I mean what goes on in the classrooms and on the campuses, what students and teachers say to each other, what books they read, what influences are exerted on them both inside and outside their formal education, what are their hopes, fears, ideas, anxieties and aims when they work together.

FOCUS ON TEACHING AND LEARNING

All the apparatus of organization and the thousands of persons employed in the bureaus and offices of education exist to make possible the actual work of live teachers with real students—yet most of the educational discussion, both in the public sector and in professional and official circles, is about the organization of programs. There is relatively little direct discussion of the quality and content of education itself. This is, of course, perfectly natural, since the problems of a mass expansion in the school and college population, and the radical increase in the demands made by society on its educational system, are bound to require an intensive focus on the organization of the whole system—from the political problems of developing a broad tax base to the budgeting problems for constructing new buildings.

In a mass democracy with a mass culture which is itself expanding enormously, there must be what is in fact a mass education, and mass organizational problems. But here I wish to make another distinction. Simply because there are massive numbers of persons involved, with one out of four

* Vice Chairman, National Commission for Support of the Public Schools; Chairman, National Research Council on Peace Strategy; President, Sarah Lawrence College (1954-59); Editor, co-author of Essays in Teachings (1950); Author: On Education and Freedom (1954), Art and the Intellect (1960).

Americans presently enrolled in some form of educational institution, we need not assume that "mass education" is a necessary outcome of the organization and planning. The genius of the American school system has been its reliance on local and regional planning, and one of the greatest virtues of the American educational system lies in its varieties of style, which range from the work of progressive private schools to large suburban high schools, and from small church-related colleges to huge land-grant institutions with dozens of departments and a score of professional schools. The problem is to create situations within the schools and colleges in which the individual student can find his own identity and can establish ways of linking himself with others in some form of intellectual and social community. This is what the young dissidents who compose the major elements in the student reform movement are concerned about. It is the constant theme of their writing, discussion and educational proposals.

Toy has pointed out, for example, that "education for citizenship in the schools has not kept pace in recent decades either with changes in American society or with research about the political process and political behavior. The school curriculum is generally antiquated in respect to the responsibilities and rights of individuals in a modern industrialized and urbanized society".

THE NEW GENERATION OF STUDENTS

The students themselves are putting it in slightly different terms. They are saying, and with justice, that the curriculum of the high school and the undergraduate college is an impersonalized array of academic subjects taught from textbooks by professional practitioners who, in the colleges, are more concerned with the production and distribution of knowledge than with the ways students can learn to achieve a grasp of the knowledge available to them and to make it relevant to their lives. In this sense, the function of the schools and the colleges has been considered by educators to be the dissemination of knowledge to various consumers, among whom are the students. The general pattern of instruction follows the lecture-textbook-examination-academic credit-grading system which, by its very nature, sterilizes the content of the curriculum of its moral, political and personal values.

The heavy emphasis on the academic reform of the school curriculum has led many critics and educators—particularly the academic faculty of the universities—to attack the teaching of civics and to put it in about the same category as driver-education, as a "time-wasting affair". What the critics do not seem to understand is that unless the schools undertake to fill a gap—either in driving or democratic politics—which parents and the community have shown themselves unable to fill, we encourage an even larger toll of lives on the road and of ideas in the voting-booth. It is not enough to teach American history and the social sciences simply as academic subjects necessary for admission to and graduation from the colleges and universities. The purpose of such studies is not to produce little academic experts but to develop enlightened and aware citizens who are eager to take part in self-government.

The impulse of reform-minded students in tackling these problems, and of others in the mass society, is to act on their own, and to substitute through their own experience for the inadequacies of the school and college curriculum. They are attempting to make a specific return to various forms of small group democracy, to work with indigenous leadership in the particular situations in which they find themselves. The approach of students who are involved in the Student Non Violent Coordinating Committee, the Students for a Democratic Society, and the campus members of the National Student Association is to work in small groups of like-minded associates on particular reforms in the society and its educational system through their own efforts in their own communities. For example, the Economic and Educational Projects of the Students for a Democratic Society are designed for work within the deprived areas of the inner cities with the poor, the unemployed and the Negro to improve the conditions for living and to teach citizens to exercise their rights as citizens for good education, housing, and employment—rather than to form a mass political movement on the basis of an ideology. The students at San Francisco State College have, over the past three years, formed their own Experimental College within the larger structure of their campus, to attempt to meet intellectual and educational needs which they find lacking in the larger system. They did so, not by urging the abandonment of the present system or attacking the administration of the College, but by building their own plans and carrying them out, teaching their own courses to each other—in a sense, educating the faculty and the administration of the College to understand their point of view. They formed themselves into small groups and learned from each other how to make their own community.

This approach to education marks a distinct change in the attitude of the younger generation about their own responsibilities and the situation in America. They have formed a society of the young—inside the framework of the larger society—and have become, among other things, an eleven billion dollar market for the consumption of products, creating demands for new kinds of products. They have their own culture, their own tastes, ranging from the politics of Bobby Kennedy and Bob Dylan to the sound of the Beatles and the movies of Humphrey Bogart. They know more than any previous generation in sheer general information; they can't help knowing it, since a stream of images, reports and facts flows over them daily through television and the mass media. They see before their eyes the circumstances of war, the reality of the Negro, the injustices of the ghetto, the popular arts of a mass culture. The more informed and sophisticated among them are the intellectual equals of the older generation—having moved to a position of political literacy and social awareness which previous generations could never reach, since the knowledge contained in our contemporary mass culture was not available to previous generations through the instruments of mass communication. I can remember vividly my own boyhood when the outside world was represented by the murmurs and squawks of KDKA, Pittsburgh, the only station we could reach on a crystal radio set with headphones. In a real sense, the outside world was concealed from us by the absence of a communication system which could bring it before our eyes and ears.

With the help of the mass media, the new generation now forms a sector of society which is making new political and social demands that must be recognized. Many of the young are no longer willing to accept the authority of the older generation or the authority of its educational system. Mario Savio—as a political leader in the Berkeley protest movement—is a symbol as well as a factor in the response of a segment of the younger generation to contemporary culture. Stokeley Carmichael represents, within the civil rights movement, a similar refusal to accept society and its regulations in the terms which the society presents to the young. Five years ago, the ideas and opinions of such twenty-four-year-old students and civil rights workers could not have achieved national attention. The difference now is that young leaders like Savio and Carmichael have formed their own constituency and speak to the concerns of a sub-culture which in former years was invisible.

THE PROBLEM OF THE SUB-CULTURES

There are other sub-cultures which have been equally invisible and which have now begun to force their own entity into the social system. I mean of course, the Negro himself and the white poor. The strength of the idea of a political base for the Negro within his own race lies not simply in the slogans of the Black Power advocates, but in the sense of community now felt by groups of Negroes in the South and North who have learned to be proud of the fact that they are Negroes and are learning to act in concert. Dr. Robert Coles, whose work in psychiatry has developed so many valuable insights into the moral and psychological strengths of the Negro family, quotes in a recent article the remarks of the Negro grandmother of a child in Boston. She said:

> Before, we were in the closet, and under the rug, and you know the white people in this country, they have big homes, so they have a lot of closets to hide us, and rugs all over the place . . . Then just a few years ago, we started getting out of the closet . . .
> The way I see it, they can try shoving us back in the closet, but let them go ahead and see what that'll cost them. Or they can keep telling us we're their equal, and be satisfied with equality, and eat it three times a day, and use it to keep the rats around here from biting our kids and if it gets cold the landlord says no, there's no heat for you, then go down on our knees and thank the white man for telling us how equal we are, and for saying we can pull the voting machines just like him, and get the same crooks he does to boss over him.
> If they're smart, they'll leave us be out of the closet like everyone else, and they'll give us what's our right, after all they got from us since the country was started. They say we're lazy, but we've been working on their land and taking care of their dirty dishes and cleaning as long as they've been here. They grabbed us and put us to work, and they pushed the Indians all over the place, and shot them up, one tribe after the other, and now they call us lazy and the Indians lazy, and they call us bad and wild because we're stuffed in corners of the closet, and we can barely breathe, and we're trying to force the door open, and want to get out—not to go live with them whites, but to live, period.[9]

To come across language and ideas as vivid as this is to realize that the

9 *New Republic;* (November 12, 1966), pp. 20-21.

generalizations made by political scientists about the culture of the white middle class and its overwhelming role in the society are true. However, this untutored grandmother has slashed through all the generalizations and exposed the heart of the matter. It is here that the generation of white youth also finds its truth—in the lived-through experience of working with the poor, *Negro and white*—and by identifying with the problems of those who are trying to get out of the closet.

When the right-wing politicians begin to talk about the dangers of Negro rioting and the necessity for greater police control of the violent Negro, they are invoking the right of the white middle class to imprison the Negro and the poor within their own ghettoes. When the United States Commissioner of Education tries to apply the provisions of the Elementary and Secondary Education Act to the practical situations of schools in Southern states, he is challenged bitterly by the white power elite on the grounds that this is federal interference with the right of the states to confine the Negro to his ghetto and his non-educational system.

In this situation we have both the paradox of federal leadership in the face of regional opposition, and the paradox of an educational system deliberately designed to democratize the population, yet functioning as a support to white supremacy. Those who in the past opposed for so many years the possibility of federal aid to education, did so on the grounds that it would mean federal control. Now that we have the federal aid, we have found that too often the federal government is powerless to act because of regional control. We have also found that initiatives for the improvement of educational quality and equality more often come from Washington than they do from local communities. Toy has pointed this out in connection with Senator Muskie's accurate account of the inadequacies of state legislatures and state departments of education, and their inability to keep up with the social, economic and educational problems of the states. Commissioner James Allen has pointed to the same difficulties in connection with New York, California, Illinois, Michigan, Pennsylvania, Maryland and Texas—the states which include the largest cities in the country. Commissioner Allen, in an analysis of state policies, has shown that the school system in each case is organized to deal with rural problems and interests rather than with the enormously more difficult problems of the big cities and the slums. State departments of education, in dealing with the inflow of federal funds, are simply not ready for the kind of initiatives which they should have been taking all along.

REORIENTING TEACHER PREPARATION, TEACHING AND LEARNING

However, there are other ways in which the search for initiative in persons and agencies needs to be carried on—that is, within the educational institutions themselves. One of the discoveries I have made during a year of research on the problem of educating teachers in the field of world affairs, is that not only have the programs of education for teachers not changed significantly to take into account the changed position of the United States in world affairs and of world society itself, but also they have not adapted themselves to the radically new needs of a society which has now discovered its disadvantaged children in the urban and rural slums. The teacher education programs consist almost entirely of regular academic studies, in the undergraduate liberal arts curriculum, plus 15 to 20 percent of the student's time taken up in professional education courses (only a few of which have anything to do with the extreme social problems of the slums) plus some practice teaching, usually carried on in middle-income, upper middle-income city and suburban schools.

An illustration of what I mean by the initiative coming from the government lies in the fact that the National Teacher Corps was organized as a project outside the regular apparatus for educating teachers, and used direct experience in the society of the slums as the means through which the student-teacher could learn his art. Similarly, the Head Start program, which made a remarkable change in educational policy on a national basis, was initiated by persons in the government rather than by educators, and within a single year involved more than 600,000 four- to six-year-olds in educational programs outside the regular school system.

What I now see happening is the amalgamation of a new set of forces in the regions and communities for social and educational change. On the educational side, the growth of the student protest movement, which has now partially turned from direct involvement in the civil rights field toward a greater concern for educational reform, is supplying what in my judgment is the major initiative inside the educational institutions for reforming the system. On the government side, there are working educators in the U. S. Office of Education, the Peace Corps, the Office of Economic Opportunity, the Job Opportunity program, Head Start, and other agencies, who are interested in educational innovation and are responsible for administering funds for carrying it out. One of the problems which confronts them in their work is that when the programs of educational aid are announced, too few persons in the colleges, universities and schools have the initiative to create interesting and imaginative ideas for carrying out the tasks for which the legislation and funds have been provided. The attitude of too many educators is to ask the government officials what sort of projects they are interested in providing funds to carry out, rather than bombarding the government with a series of projects and ideas which could give leadership and encouragement to government thinking.

On the other hand, students in the colleges have been enterprising in developing projects of their own for work in the slums, and there are now approximately 250,000 students across the country who are presently engaged in some form of tutoring program for disadvantaged children. Many others have volunteered for work in Job Opportunity centers, Head Start and, of course, the Peace Corps. The new amalgamation of forces I am thinking of would involve the student reformer and tutor, interested teachers and faculty members of the universities—particularly in the colleges and schools of education—and the new group of persons at work in the community in poverty programs who are, in a sense, creating new vocations in the social welfare field. Students who have had experience in tutoring find themselves doing much more than helping children in arithmetic, spelling and reading. Very quickly the student becomes involved with the entire set of problems experienced by the families in the deprived areas. Although many of the students do not intend to enter the field of teaching, they are led by the experience of tutoring to fields within the helping professions where new talent is needed.

My plea is that we support the idea that young people, working in their own communities on community problems, including education, should be supported in their efforts by changes in the curriculum of the colleges where teachers are prepared, to make a direct relationship between experience in community-work and the academic studies in which the students are engaged in college. Too often the students find that there is no relevance between their courses in sociology, psychology, education, etc., and the actual experiences they undergo in their own lives—either as members of their communities or as volunteer workers in other communities. Colleges and schools of education that wish to take the initiative in welcoming returned Peace Corps volunteers into teacher education programs— taking special advantage of the community experience and teaching which the Peace Corps volunteers have had overseas—would be able to develop a new kind of teacher whose interests in social change and in educational reform coincide with the needs of modern American society.

The link between these forces and the federal government could be established by the development of federal subsidies for innovative programs sponsored by the colleges and schools of education and for recruiting student volunteers of all kinds directly into the work of teaching in the public schools. There is room for a great deal more experiment and innovation in the development of new kinds of school board activities through which boards could have the advantage of the research done by graduate students in education and undergraduate volunteers—particularly in the case of school board members in the inner cities who represent directly the poor and the under-educated.

One of the greatest problems which have risen to haunt Sargent Shriver and the members of his staff in the Office of Economic Opportunity, is that of developing indigenous leadership and genuine representation of the poor in settling the problems of poverty. Graduate students of education could make a significant contribution by acting as research staff for school boards and administrators in the inner cities who have neither the time nor the necessary proparation to carry out the research itself. The colleges and schools of education would then become partners of the citizens of the deprived areas rather than a distant source of teacher-candidates for middle-income communities.

It seems to me that the colleges and schools of education and the universities that are concerned with developing teachers have an open opportunity in the placement of students—as part of their education—to work as tutors, teacher aides, recreational leaders and counsellors to young people by attaching themselves to the schools directly and working with students slightly younger than themselves to create community action programs which could range from recreational supervision and leadership to the rehabilitation of slum dwellings. This would involve a radical shift in the entire attitude of the universities in the education of teachers. The preparation of the teacher must begin by his developing a sensitivity to the culture and the society in which he exists; the entire range of experience available within his society is the prime source of knowledge appropriate to his education. This, in my judgment, is the most effective way to educate the student to understand the American political process.

We also need to look at the education of teachers as a way in which the person who is to become a teacher can learn to teach by teaching someone else. This would argue for a radical shift in the way undergraduates are now taught in college—to take advantage of the primary fact that students can and will teach each other whether the program intends them to do so or not. Only when we remove the university faculty member from his role as lecturer, administrator of grades and transmitter of subjects—and think of him as a person who has had a wider range of knowledge and experience than the people he is teaching—can we consider him to be an educator and not simply a lecturer.

The teacher of the disadvantaged must be just such an educator—one who understands the necessity for adapting himself and his knowledge to the context and needs of the people he is teaching. This is, of course, true of all teachers and educators. Like the physician who diagnoses and prescribes in order to cure, the educator must discover the educational ailment and construct appropriate remedies. But in the case of the inner city problem, we see the effects of mass society in their most extreme form, and the natural sympathy of young Americans for those who are in trouble can be counted on as a source of motivation to enter the teaching profession, or the Peace Corps, or both.

The point is that not only has there been a marked shift in the political relationship between the federal and state governments with subsequent new responsibilities placed upon the states, but the visibility of the poor and the problems of massed populations in the cities (where 70 percent of the population now lives) made obsolete most of the conceptions of education which have dominated the field of teacher education. We are driven back to the necessity of solving our cities' educational problems by efforts made directly within the cities themselves. No matter how much money and how many plans exist in Washington or in state departments of education, there will be no real improvement in education in the cities until we call upon the profusion of new resources existing within the younger generation, and give youth the opportunity to learn by teaching and to teach those children who have most to learn.

CHAPTER 16

Financial Support of Education

JERRY MINER *

The post-war expansion of the educational system has been one of the most striking features of contemporary American society. This expansion is characterized not only by absolute increases in school enrollments and expenditures per pupil, but by rates of increase greater than those of population or of national income. Yet, reports of widespread shortages of teachers and classrooms are only one indication of inadequacies in the present system. *One of the most profound problems of social policy is how to expand and modify the educational system to interact with rapidly changing technology and values.* The financial aspects of this challenge to education are vital because *decisions regarding the magnitude and character of education affect the size, composition, distribution, and rate of growth of income and therefore, have profound influence on the economic welfare of the nation's citizens.*

The purpose of this paper is to explore the economic aspects of educational responses to emergent national and international developments. Another way of describing the paper would be to say that it constitutes an examination of the future of educational finance. Educational finance, however, has the connotation of dealing almost exclusively with school revenues from public sources. The intent here is to treat not only revenues for public schools but expenditures, fiscal relations between public education and other government functions, alternative sources of school revenues, and the internal efficiency of the educational system.

It is possible, of course, to speculate regarding the future and attempt to trace the implications of anticipated developments for educational policies and educational finance. The shortcoming of such an exercise is that its utility is limited by the arbitrariness of presumptions regarding the future, although there is no denying the value of projections made on the basis of reasonable assumptions. This paper will refer to projections of financial needs and resources for education, but its emphasis is on the application to problems of educational finance of recent developments and research results in the area of quantitative approaches to public sector decisions. The value of such an emphasis is that the development and use of effective tools of analysis provide assistance to policy-making whatever the future may bring. Indeed, *the establishment of arrangements and procedures that recognize and effectively respond to change is probably far more important than attempts to predict in detail these developments far in advance.*

* *Associate Professor of Economics, Syracuse University;* Senior Research Economist, UNESCO, Paris (1962-64); Publications include *Social and Economic Factors in Spending for Public Education* (1963) and "The Relationship Between Economic Planning and Educational Planning" in *World Yearbook of Education* (to be published 1967).

THE ECONOMICS OF EDUCATION, EDUCATIONAL FINANCE
AND PUBLIC FINANCE

Fifteen or twenty years ago the main concern of British and American public finance, including the finance of local public schools, was the study of taxation. This emphasis derived from the view that public expenditures yielded non-identifiable aggregate benefits while taxes constituted a burden on those specific individuals upon whom they came to rest. *The primary objective of public policy, at that time, was to devise a budgetary system which minimized the burden of financing public expenditures and ensured strict control over outlays.* This restrictive conception, however, never was fully accepted. As economists began to apply the principles of economic analysis to the entire budget rather than only to the tax side, there emerged an approach to public finance as an integral part of the economic system and a view of the public sector as no less amenable than the private sector to analysis in terms of its effects on allocation of resources, distribution of income, employment, and economic growth.

Partly as a result of this new concern for analyzing the expenditure side of government budgets, and also because—with an apparent solution to the problems of cyclical unemployment—economists renewed their investigation of the causes of economic growth, education became a focus for economic study. *A major aspect of what has come to be called the economics of education is the analysis and measurement of the economic benefits of different types and amounts of education.* But, the economics of education—as does the economics of any area—also deals with internal efficiency insofar as questions of least-cost operation are concerned, with the determinants of demand, and with effects on income distribution. Indeed, the economics of education encompasses all aspects of education which have economic implications. Public finance, on the other hand, is concerned primarily with that portion of education which falls within public budgets, but it includes social, political, and other non-economic as well as economic objectives for public educational outlays.

Whether one talks of the economics of education or of the principles of public finance, spending for education—as for all other economic activities, public or private—should be related to the general objectives of economic policy: efficiency, equity, full-employment, and growth.

Essentially the criteria for economic efficiency call for the comparison of the benefits achieved from a particular use of scarce resources with the benefits of alternative uses. Social economy is achieved when—given the distribution of income, consumer preferences, and techniques of production—the existing pattern of resource use is such that no transfer to alternative use would increase total satisfactions. The question of whether a particular commodity should be provided according to the market principle (quid pro quo) or the budget principle (available to all free of direct charge) is essentially a matter of whether the full benefits of a particular use of resources are reflected in the price that buyers are willing to pay sellers. If this is not the case because the character of the commodity is such that substantial benefits can be obtained without payment, then social economy indicates provision according to the budget principle. If public finance is called for, there is further need to determine such matters as the quantity and quality of service to be provided, necessary level of public expenditures, sources of revenue, and levels of government to be involved.

Efficient use of resources is not, however, the sole goal of the economy. Objectives of economic policy also include full employment, relative price stability, an equitable distribution of income, and an adequate rate of economic growth. A satisfactory conception of educational finance must encompass virtually all of these concerns. Educational finance, therefore, cannot be limited to considerations of how to raise revenues for public schools. *Determination of the proper level of finance for education depends on the valuation placed by society on specific educational programs.* Furthermore, benefits derived from the devotion of resources to education must be compared with benefits from alternative public and private use. Finally, educational finance cannot ignore the redistribution of income or the growth in labor productivity that occurs when tax proceeds are used to finance free public education, nor the differential tax burdens that result from alternative tax structures and inter-governmental fiscal arrangements. In addition, as part of its concern for economic efficiency, educational finance has to consider the effectiveness with which schools transform scarce resources into educational output.

To preserve perspective with regard to the "proper considerations" of educational finance, it is essential to note that they do not constitute a comprehensive framework but are only the fundamental economic concerns. It should not be surprising that educational finance is viewed as primarily falling within the rubric of economic analysis, especially since the economist's notion of preferences is wide enough to encompass love of learning, learning for its own sake, and any other humanistic motives for school attendance. He only insists that these preferences be compared with preferences for other uses of limited means for satisfying the infinity of human wants. It is, of course, likely that certain social, political, cultural, religious, and other arrangements will be more conducive than others to maximizing economic production. At the same time, society may be quite willing to accept lower levels of economic satisfaction in exchange for preferred institutional arrangements. Where these matters become issues of policy, the economist's role is to specify the cost of various institutional arrangements in terms of the value of the product given up.

Clearly, then, the economic criteria discussed in this section and used as a basis for evaluation and proposed modifications in the next, are not the sole standard for the practice of school finance. They deal with a crucial but only partial dimension of social welfare—the economic.

PRESENT AND FUTURE POLICY ISSUES OF
EDUCATIONAL FINANCE

The previous section developed the position that educational finance should be concerned with fundamental issues of economic policy as they pertain to education and also indicated that in educational finance, as in all areas of public policy, there are non-economic objectives of sufficient importance to offset economic considerations. Under these circumstances the relevance of technical economistic analysis is to ensure that decisions are made with full knowledge of alternatives. Discussion of policies regarding educational finance, therefore, requires careful distinction between technical economic considerations and those of wider social concern.

ISSUES OF PRINCIPLE

Public Finance and Public Operation of Schools. Economic justifications for public finance of education include spill-over of benefits to others than pupils,[1] desired interference with consumer preferences, and income redistribution. Richard A. Musgrave, in the most complete discussion of the principles that determine whether the budget or market principle should apply to the provision of particular commodities, distinguishes *social goods,* whose characteristics are such that persons cannot be excluded from benefitting whether or not they pay, from *merit goods* where the exclusion principle does apply but societal values indicate that minimum quantities be provided regardless of individual incomes and preferences.[2]

Clearly, education has characteristics of both social and merit goods and, therefore, public finance is indicated to meet these considerations. Somewhat less clear cut is justification of public finance of education to achieve income redistribution by its provision free of direct charge and financed through progressive or even proportionate taxation. Those who uphold the sanctity of consumer preferences in the economic realm argue for neutral income redistribution achieved through progressive taxation and unrestricted transfer payments to provide adequate incomes for the attainment of minimum living standards, but which leave actual decisions regarding the use of purchasing power in the hands of the individual family unit. Lack of knowledge, lack of concern, and other shortcomings on the part of parents in the area of decisions regarding education for their children— coupled with the life-determining consequences of such decisions—provide a powerful argument for income redistribution in kind rather than in unrestricted transfers.[3]

These considerations taken together make an overwhelming economic argument for a substantial degree of public finance of education. Present arrangements clearly reflect this conclusion since some eighty-five percent of educational outlays are derived from public sources. This high proportion, however, greatly understates the non-tax contribution to education made by students and their families since it omits earnings foregone as a result of attending school instead of working, as well as school-related personal expenditures.[4] These personal expenditures and foregone earnings

---

[1] Burton Weisbrod's enumeration of those receiving benefits from education other than students and their families include: neighbors, taxpayers, fellow-workers, employers, and society in general. See *External Benefits of Education* (Princeton, New Jersey: Industrial Relations Section, Princeton University; 1964), pp. 15-39.

[2] Richard A. Musgrave, *The Theory of Public Finance* (New York: McGraw-Hill Book Company, Inc., 1959).

[3] For a more detailed discussion of the economic rationale for public finance of education see J. Miner, *Social and Economic Factors in Spending for Public Education* (Syracuse, New York: Syracuse University Press, 1963).

[4] Rudolph C. Blitz in "The Nation's Education Outlay," *Economics of Higher Education* (Washington, D.C.: United States Department of Health, Education, and Welfare, 1962) estimates that in the United States in 1955-56 and 1956-57 earnings foregone were almost equal to direct costs for formal education.

along with tuition payments and other fees can be thought of as imperfect reflections of those benefits of education that accrue directly to students. Such a conception leads to the notion that public finance for education should encompass only those benefits which do not accrue to students, with financing of direct benefits left to individuals. This notion does not take account of the "merit good" and "income redistribution-in-kind" arguments, but it can be modified to do so by an arrangement of government transfer payments restricted only to use for education and grants to privately operated schools. The magnitude of transfer payments would be such as to allow for merit wants and redistribution as well as externalities, and the role of government would extend to regulation and supervision.

Advocacy of this approach stems primarily from non-economic considerations and derives from values placed on freedom of choice and decentralized decision-making, and a relative lack of concern for the reinforcement such a scheme would give to the social, cultural, and economic distinctions engendered by income differences.[5] At the same time, it is essential to note that, for the most part, arguments in favor of public operation of schools are not based on technical economic considerations. Such arguments stress the role of public schools in engendering a national rather than parochial outlook and in moderating class, ethnic, religious, and cultural differences. The major economic consideration regarding public or private operation is least-cost production. *Public operation of schools, then, is supported by the contention that with only one school system in an area, there is a far greater chance of attaining sufficient size to permit efficient division of labor, specialization, and physical facilities.*

Convincing empirical evidence that costs decrease as the size of individual schools or of entire school systems increases—with the exception of small schools and districts—is difficult to obtain. Most multi-variate studies of determinants of educational expenditures find no negative association between outlays and enrollment level. Such findings, however, do not bear directly on the question of decreasing costs which is concerned with the cost of providing units of output of stipulated quality. Higher outlays in larger schools probably reflect improved quality. Schmandt and Stephens contend that their study of the Milwaukee area "strongly suggests the existence of economics of scale in school district operations" when measures of service outputs are used in conjunction with average daily attendance.[6]

Acceptance of the merits of some public support for private schools is indicated by state and federal government grants to students for study at private institutions of higher learning. On the other hand, the strength of American values in favor of public operation of local public schools seems to preclude alternative schemes becoming genuine policy considerations in the future. There are indications, however, that without direct confrontation on this issue, an increasing amount of public funds will be used to support

---

[5] This viewpoint is most effectively presented in A. Peacock and J. Wiseman, *Education for Democrats.*

[6] Henry J. Schmandt and G. Ross Stephens, "Measuring Municipal Output," XIII *National Tax Journal* (December 1960), p. 375.

elementary and secondary non-public schools through publically provided transportation, books, and lunches for pupils and for training and other services for teachers.

Education and Economic Stabilization. The policy concern here is whether public educational outlays should be varied over the business cycle in an effort to contribute to overall economic stability. This idea generally is rejected mainly because it is thought that stabilization goals should be achieved without a prejudgment about which goods or services should be affected. The presence of underemployment, and thus indications for public policies that increase total spending, does not imply a presumption that there should be expansion of the public sector generally or of education in particular.[7] On the other hand, if inflation threatens there is no reason to presume public rather than private outlays should be curtailed. Contemporary analysis places the primary responsibility for stabilization policy on the tax and transfer mechanism of the federal government which has the duty to provide a full employment level of income out of which state, local, and even the federal government can meet the educational and other requirements of their citizens.

Stabilization objectives, then, are an area of policy which should not influence educational finance. Yet, programs of federal aid to education motivated by recognition of the nationwide extent of the benefits of certain educational programs—not by counter-cyclical objectives—none-the-less run the risk of variation in accordance with stabilization concerns. *With the increasing importance of federal programs of support for education it is essential that such programs be insulated from year to year fluctuations and insofar as possible be legislated in a manner so that they do not require annual obligational authorization by Congress.* They must, of course, be subject to review and modification, but in terms of effectiveness.

ISSUES OF MAGNITUDES

The social values of American society (which make for a mixed but predominantly publically operated educational system) and the basic economic considerations (which make for even more predominant public finance of that educational system) seem unlikely to undergo substantial change in the next few decades. Within this framework, however, the range for financial policies remains enormous.

Issues of economic policy generally are classified in accordance with whether they are concerned with the size of and relationship among aggregates or with the provision of particular products and methods of production. Applied to educational finance, *macro-policy issues* encompass the balance of total expenditures and resources, and, thus, involve such matters as projections of educational needs and revenues, relations between public education and the entire public sector, and educational outlays as a share

---

[7] Acceptance of Galbraith's contention that the public sector traditionally is neglected might lead to a judgment that it should always be expanded whenever possible. The implication of this view is that it would then be curtailed when contraction is called for. Instability of this sort seems highly undesirable.

of national income. *Micro-policy* on the other hand, deals with the mix of specific educational programs, the internal efficiency of schools, specific revenue sources, and inter-governmental relations involved in financing schools.

A major tool of macro-policy analysis is the technique of projection in which estimates of future needs and resources are balanced. Projections can encompass aggregates as large as overall national spending and production and details as small as the demand and supply of particular industries or commodities. However, since the major objective of projections is to test the capacity of the economy to fulfill certain sectoral needs and to examine the implications for productive capacity of a projected pattern of demands, the analysis of individual commodities is generally thought of as falling within micro-analysis, Application of these considerations to the public sector is reflected in projections of needs or requirements for particular functions or services, estimates of amounts to be provided by public authorities, and potential revenues. Further application is made in the combination of projections for the totality of public functions and governmental revenues to obtain global projections of the public sector. The methods, conclusions, and significance of recent projections of the education sector constitute the subject matter of the next section.

The reader should note that projections of expenditures for education do not evaluate particular educational programs and the efficiency by which specific educational outputs are derived from the use of scarce inputs. Moreover, projections of revenues for education do not explore the economic consequences of alternative revenue structures and thus do not provide normative guidelines for these aspects of financial policy. The application of contemporary developments in the analysis of public fiscal decision-making has opened new areas of micro-policy determination to rational methods of planning. Following the discussion of projections, the paper will turn to the application to educational finance of these techniques for the determination of the composition and structure of budgetary expenditures and revenues.

PROJECTIONS OF EXPENDITURES AND REVENUES FOR EDUCATION

One of the most useful methods for estimation of the fiscal consequences of anticipated future developments is projection of the expenditure implications of standards of performance or service level. For market produced commodities such projections indicate requirements for future capital and manpower while for the public sector they also reveal revenue needs. Consolidation of a series of projections can reveal the overall implications of standards for individual sectors and, when combined with information on the availability of resources, can show whether sufficient inputs will be available to meet the entire set of projections.

There have been a number of projections of educational needs and resources in the past few years, some of which have encompassed the entire public sector and others only education. Most include private as well as public outlays.[8] Methods, assumptions, and even data employed in these projections differ far too much for any attempt at reconciliation or detailed comparison here. Instead, emphasis is placed on two recent studies; one a highly detailed, state-by-state analysis by Selma Mushkin and Eugene P. McLoone, undertaken for the Council of State governments; the other a study for the Committee for Economic Development by Dick Netzer. Comparison of these two studies is especially rewarding because Netzer follows the traditional approach of the application of projections of overall rates of increase in expenditures per pupil to anticipated enrollments, while Mushkin and McLoone build up estimates of expenditures on a state-by-state basis by projections of such components of expenditure as pupil-teacher ratios, teacher salaries, extension of school programs, and initiation of new programs. Both studies integrate education into the entire state-local government sector, and neither considers private expenditures for education. A final important difference, however, is that Mushkin and McLoone project revenues for education separately from overall state-local revenues while Netzer makes no such separation.

EXPENDITURES FOR LOCAL SCHOOLS

Mushkin and McLoone's projection to 1970 yields an estimate of $35.9 billion of revenue requirements. (Total revenues in 1962 were $17.4 billion.) Most influential among the assumptions that underlie these figures are: (1) an increase in public school enrollments of 15.2 percent between 1962 and 1970; (2) only slight reductions in class size; (3) increases in instructional salaries in line with projected rises in non-farm wages and salaries plus some additional adjustments for states which have lagged during the past decade; (4) moderate expansion of pre-school, summer school, and adult education programs; (5) inclusion of expanded federal programs of health and nutritional services, and (6) new construction to take account of emerging needs and to alleviate classroom shortages. These and other assumptions are applied to each state individually, and the totals are obtained by summation.

Netzer develops three alternative projections based on different assumptions regarding changes in expenditures per pupil. For 1970, his benchmark estimate of general utility expenditures, which assumes no change in expenditure per pupil and includes $2.5 billion for capital outlay, comes to $22 billion. A second projection assumes increases in teacher salaries sufficient to meet competition for trained personnel and yields expenditures of $25.1 billion. Finally, in a third projection, called the "improvement model", Netzer assumes current expenditures to be 15 percent more than in the previous model to reflect improvement in

[8] Otto Eckstein, *Trends in Public Expenditures in the Next Decade*, (Washington: Committee for Economic Development, 1959); Gerhard Colm and Manuel Helzner, "Fiscal Needs and Resources Over the Next Decade at All Levels of Government," and Dick Netzer, "Financial Needs and Resources Over The Next Decade: State and Local Governments," in *Public Finances: Needs, Sources, and Utilization* (Princeton, Princeton University Press, 1961); Selma J. Mushkin and Eugene P. McLoone, *Local School Expenditures; 1970 Projections*, and *Public Spending for Higher Education*, 1970 (Chicago: *The Council of State Governments*, Nov. 1965, Feb. 1966); Selma J. Mushkin and Gabrielle C. Lupo, *Project '70: Projecting The State Local Sector*, Mimeo. (Washington: The George Washington University State-Local Finances Project, March 1966), Dick Netzer *State-Local Finance in The Next Decade*, mimeo. (Aug. 1965); Kenneth A. Simon and C. George Lind, "Expenditures," in *Projections of Educational Statistics to 1973-74*, (Washington: U.S. Department of Health, Education, and Welfare, 1964); *Financing the Public Schools, 1960-1970*, (Washington: National Education Association of the United States, 1962).

standards—but holds capital outlay constant at $2.5 billion—and arrives at $28.5 billion. Netzer extends his projections to 1974-75 and obtains estimates of $23.1, $29.9, and 36.8 billion respectively for the three models.

It is not the purpose of this paper to attempt to reconcile alternative projections developed by such different methods. A significant point is that the estimates of Mushkin and McLoone and of Netzer's "improvement model" which he considers to be most relevant—are within 10 percent of each other and are presented by their originators as reasonable estimations given prevalent trends of the near future.

There are a few other projections which should be mentioned. Kenneth A. Simon and C. George Lind of the United States Office of Education projected local school expenditures to 1973-74 on the basis, "that the 1953-54 to 1963-64 trend will continue through 1973-74, which means that no allowance was made for any expenditures needed to increase the rate of improvement in the quality of education beyond trend levels."[9] Their projections of total public expenditures come to $24.7 billion for 1969-70 and $28.1 billion for 1973-74. In contrast to these moderate assumptions regarding rate of improvement by the U. S. Office of Education, the National Education Association has estimated the necessary level of current expenditures to meet what they term "minimum standards of quality." Attainment of these standards will require current expenditures of $33.6 billion in 1970. This figure is arrived at by the application to projected enrollments of current expenditures of $720 per pupil—a figure derived by assuming a salary of $6000 for a beginning teacher in 1970 and fixed ratios of: (1) beginning salaries to average salaries; (2) cost of professional salaries to total current expenditures, and (3) pupils to professional staff.[10]

Using the expenditure levels for 1970 projected by Mushkin and McLoone as illustrative, attainment of their projections would mean—taking 1961-62 as the base—an increase in per pupil expenditures of 40.5 percent (from $381 to $536); in per capita expenditures, of 133 percent (from $79 to $183); and in the share of personal income devoted to local schools, of 21.4 percent (from 3.4 to 4.1 percent).

REVENUES FOR LOCAL SCHOOLS

Among the projections mentioned above, only Mushkin and McLoone estimate revenues available for local schools. They are able to do this only by assuming that, "taxes devoted to school finance represent the same share of state and local tax dollars in 1970 as in 1961-62," and that there are no increases in tax rates. On the basis of these and other assumptions (including a four percent rate of growth of gross national product and federal sources of finance in excess of $5 billion) Mushkin and McLoone estimate general receipts for local schools in 1970 to be between $32 and $33 billion.

The discrepancy of $3 to $4 billion between the revenue requirements of about $36 billion and the estimated general receipts for local schools,

9 Simon and Lind, op. cit., pp. 27-39.
10 Financing the Public Schools, op. cit., pp. 133-150.

amounts to some one billion in excess of estimated capital expenditures. Since capital expenditures usually are financed through borrowing, this one billion dollars represents needed additional tax receipts. A deficiency of this magnitude cannot be considered serious since the revenue estimate is based on the highly conservative assumption of no increase in tax rates.

The apparently optimistic situation for local schools requires further examination, first in the context of the entire educational system, and then in the context of the whole state and local government sector. Even within the limits of local schools, however, the overall balance of revenues and expenditures may conceal considerable variations among individual units. As a consequence of their state-by-state approach, Mushkin and McLoone are able to specify that—depending upon assumptions made regarding property tax revenues—there are some twenty-four to thirty states where projected revenues fall short of projected expenditures. Of the thirty, however, in only thirteen will revenues in 1970 be as much as ten percent below projected expenditures. Another product of the state-by-state analysis is the estimate that $500 million of additional funds will be required in 1970 to bring the twelve states with lowest current expenditures per pupil up to 80 percent of the projected national average.

Further geographic disaggregation is not presented by Mushkin and McLoone, but results of an ongoing study of "Policies and Policy-Making in Large City Educational Systems", at the Metropolitan Studies Center of Syracuse University, reveal that current expenditures per pupil in central cities in 1962 were about equal to the national average and were some $62 less than in corresponding suburbs. In only one of fourteen cities for which data were available did assessed property valuation per pupil keep up with values for the rest of the state in which they were located.[11] Similar findings for median family incomes in central cities in relation to those in the remainder of the state are virtually conclusive evidence that projections for central cities would reveal substantial discrepancies between revenue requirements and public receipts for local schools.[12]

EXPENDITURES FOR HIGHER EDUCATION

Assumptions for the projection of higher education are even more intricate than those for local schools mainly because institutions of higher education not only educate students, but engage in research, public service, and extension activities. Mushkin and McLoone again apply their assumptions to each state individually and reach a total expenditure of $12 billion for 1970. This figure is considerably higher than Netzer's estimate of $8.6 billion for the "improvement model" and approximates his estimate for 1974-75. Simon and Lind's projection for 1970 is $8.4 billion and for 1973-74, $10.4 billion. Without detailed analysis it is impossible to attempt to reconcile these figures, but it is significant that Mushkin

[11] Seymour Sacks and David C. Ranney, "Suburban Education: A Fiscal Analysis," and Alan K. Campbell and Philip Meranto, "The Metropolitan Education Dilemma: Matching Resources to Needs", *Urban Affairs Quarterly, Special Education Edition*, Vol. II (September 1966).

[12] This disparity arises when central city expenditures per pupil are presumed to be equal to those projected for the entire state. This presumption makes no allowance for the above average expenditures that are generally recommended for central cities to meet the higher cost of urban education and to provide education of a kind capable of dealing with the special characteristics found in large American cities.

and McLoone's estimate, while above that of Netzer and Simon and of Lind, implies a growth rate lower than that which prevailed from 1954-64. Given the manifold increases in responsibilities being placed on public colleges and universities it seems difficult to argue for lower projections.

REVENUES FOR HIGHER EDUCATION

Mushkin and McLoone project revenues for higher education mainly by assuming that previous shares of state tax revenues will continue to be allocated for this purpose in the future. Under this assumption, prospects are not especially encouraging since (on this basis) projected state and local revenues plus tuition and federal payments fall short even of instructional costs, to which must be added other current expenditures plus capital outlays. The authors do not specify the size of the gap between their projections of expenditures and receipts, but it appears to be about eight billion dollars. This substantial deficit is explicable in terms of the high rate-of-increase in enrollments and the far-below-cost tuition charged by public colleges and universities. In this regard, Campbell and Sacks in their forthcoming study of metropolitan finance calculate that the rate of growth of expenditure for local schools in the decade 1954-64 (127.6 per cent) just about matched that of total state-local expenditures while outlays for institutions of higher education increased by more than twice this rate of growth.[13]

PRIVATE OUTLAYS FOR EDUCATION

For a complete picture of educational spending, private outlays must be considered—although it should be noted that public payments to private institutions for research and other services and to students enrolled in private schools for fellowships and scholarships are included in projections of public expenditures. According to figures given by Simon and Lind, private expenditures for education are expected to remain at about 23 percent of public outlays. It must be kept in mind that revenues to meet these outlays come from private expenditures and, therefore, do not require governmental revenues. Their importance with regard to projections of public expenditures, however, is that private schools do meet a portion of the needs for education, leaving that much less to be provided publicly.

EDUCATION AND THE STATE-LOCAL GOVERNMENT SECTOR

The extension of projections of educational expenditures and revenues to include private outlays is less significant than the integration of such projections with the future total fiscal situation of state and local governments. Education is but one of many governmental functions, and state and local governments which have predominant responsibility for education face an enormous variety of demands for public services. Any meaningful projection of the education section must be consistent with that for the rest of the public sector.

The composite projection of state-local government presented in the

[13] Alan K. Campbell and Seymour Sacks, *Metropolitan America: Fiscal Patterns and Governmental Systems* (New York: The Free Press, 1967), forthcoming.

summary volume of Project '70—the overall study of which the Mushkin-McLoone studies are a portion—amounts to $121.8 billion of expenditures and between $102.2 and $107.9 billion of revenues.[14] This range in the revenue estimates is largely a result of alternative assumptions about federal aid. The low estimate of additional fund requirements falls well within state and local borrowing capacity while the higher estimate would require slightly increased revenues unless borrowing were to account for a greater share of state-local sources of funds than in the recent past. On the whole the projection of total public expenditures for public schools and higher education, of $44 billion in 1970, is quite consistent with projections for the remainder of the state-local fiscal picture. At the same time, this overall sanguine conclusion does not apply to all states nor to all areas within states even where statewide totals indicate no special fiscal imbalances.

Dick Netzer's overall figures are remarkably similar to those of Project '70. Total financial needs are projected to be $121.2 billion which is within $.6 billion of the corresponding figure obtained by Mushkin and Lupo. On the receipts side, excluding borrowing, Netzer's estimate of about $100 billion is some $2 billion less than the low revenue estimate, but almost $10 billion short of the high revenue estimate, of Project '70. The similarity of total receipts is a consequence of offsetting differences: Mushkin and Lupo project considerably higher revenues from state and local sales taxes and lower federal aid and program assisted receipts. Netzer concludes that, with $12 billion of borrowing, state and local governments still will face the need for almost $10 billion of additional tax revenues in 1970 while, as noted above, Mushkin and Lupo find that additional tax revenues are indicated only for their low revenue illustration. When Netzer extends the projection to 1974-75 he finds no increase in the gap between needs and revenues because of the responsiveness of revenues to the presumed rate of growth of gross national product.

SIGNIFICANCE OF THE PROJECTIONS

The salient point of significance of these projections for educational finance is that they reveal a feasible pattern for the expansion of the educational system for the next decade. This expansion encompasses increased outlays which make possible a number of developments (e.g. reduction in class size, extension of school programs, higher teacher salaries) which generally would be termed improvements. The studies indicate that, subject to modest tax rate increases, there are likely to be sufficient revenues to meet these educational expenditures and also to cover projections of requirements for other functions carried out by state and local governments. They do not, however, demonstrate that all states or areas within states will have the revenues to meet their needs in education or in other fields; in fact, *there is substantial evidence that many problem areas exist especially in low income states and in large central cities.*

It is frequently charged that projections of the kind discussed here often seriously underestimate future public expenditures and outlays. Netzer

---
[14] Mushkin and Lupo, *op. cit.*

compares previous projections of expenditures with actual experience for 1957-63 and finds a virtually uniform pattern of underestimation. As a check against this tendency Mushkin and Lupo apply their methods and assumptions to data for 1954 and find that projection of such data to 1964 gives expenditures in excess of actual expenditures in that year. They conclude, therefore, that their estimates for 1970 do not contain a conservative bias.

None of the projections discussed above attempts to project beyond 1974-75. Extension of projections beyond this period on the basis of unchanged assumptions runs strong risk of serious error not only because of the accumulation of gradual distortions but also because of the danger of what Boulding calls a "system break." *The fundamental shortcoming of projections as a tool of policy,* however, *is that they do not deal with questions of changes which should be undertaken in view of the objectives of society and the alterations taking place in the system within which education operates.* In other words, perhaps a "system break" is necessary to cope with societal changes—and educational programs substantially different from those presently provided should be the ones for which projections are made.

The function of projections is to reveal internal inconsistencies or, at best, indicate alternative "menus" which are mutually consistent. But, *consistency of projected expenditures and receipts is no indication of the appropriateness of standards of, or the nature and scale of, the programs employed in the projection.* With regard to education, a projection cannot determine the proper balance of expenditures between primary and secondary education, between vocational and academic training, the distribution of educational outlays between central cities and suburbs, nor the pupil-teacher ratio that maximizes subject matter achievements. Yet, knowledge of matters such as these is essential to efficient use of resources and to policies of educational finance that are responsive to a changing society. Such knowledge must be embodied in the programs which constitute the bases for projection lest such projections be nothing more than demonstrations of consistency.

The following two sections deal with recent developments in the microanalysis of public decisions. Contemporary techniques for the determination of those standards or service levels which yield the highest benefits to society and how these levels can be achieved at least cost, are examined for their relevance to educational finance.

INTERNAL EFFICIENCY OF EDUCATION

The concepts of optimum expenditures for education and the internal efficiency of schools are closely related, yet separable, matters. It is useful to think of the former as dealing with the link between outputs of education and the benefits which ensue; the latter as concerned with the link between inputs into education and the outputs that result. Ideally, the proper quantity and quality of a commodity should be provided by least-cost methods of production. In the public sector, however, the relation between outputs and benefits is difficult to determine primarily because outputs of public activities are not sold but provided free of charge. Attempts to estimate the benefits of public expenditures, then, require synthetic measures of the values of government activities to substitute for market determined prices which serve as measures of benefits of private goods. Investigation of least-cost methods of production, on the other hand, does not require measurement of ultimate benefits but of relationships between inputs and units of educational outputs. Thus, instead of the quantification of benefits, studies of the internal efficiency of schools require measurement of educational outputs.

Analysis of internal efficiency implies nothing about the appropriateness of educational outputs. Its concern is to specify how particular outputs vary in accordance with changes in inputs. In economic parlance, such a relation is called a production function, and when the prices of inputs are combined with knowledge of the production function the least costly methods of achieving a given level of output can be determined. This conception can be applied to useful or worthless educational outputs alike so, in and of itself, it is not a sufficient criterion for educational decision-making. But, as has already been indicated, educational priorities require consideration of both costs and benefits of educational outputs, and also the specification of the production function of alternative educational programs on the basis for their provision at lowest cost.

MEASUREMENT OF EDUCATIONAL OUTPUTS

In efforts to quantify the output of public agencies, a distinction is drawn between *programs* and *performance*. Measures of performance involve detailed work units related to specific end products, such as school meals served or number of pupil-miles of transportation provided. Programs refer to sets of performances which have common objectives such as improvement of achievement in subject matter areas or reduction of dropout rates.[15] Although there are many functions performed by schools which could be measured in terms of performance or activity units, there is general agreement that instructional activities are by far most important and that these cannot be subdivided meaningfully beyond the various subject matter disciplines of the curriculum. This does not mean, however, that measures of educational output must be limited to test scores on achievement tests since instruments and procedures for a great number of attitudinal measures now exist. Moreover data on other aspects of school performance such as retention rates easily can be obtained. Kershaw and McKean, in their now classic study, present as major dimensions of educational output: "learning in the standard subjects, improvement in the ability to reason, stimulus to intellectual curiosity, stimulus to 'creativity', development of social poise, reduction of emotional disturbance, and improvement of physical health".[16]

---

[15] See Jesse Burkhead, "The Theory and Application of Program Budgeting to Education," in *Trends in Financing Public Education* (Washington, D. C.: National Education Association, 1965), p. 185.

[16] J. A. Kershaw and R. N. McKean, *Systems Analysis and Education* (Santa Monica: The RAND Corporation, 1959), p. 8.

Despite the specification of these and other operational dimensions of educational output,[17] measurement of the full range of educational outputs clearly is out of this question. However, measurement of the total consequences of the operation of any organization is impossible; thus, there is no reason why educational organizations should be exempt from efforts to specify their outputs and to rationalize their internal arrangements.

MEASUREMENT OF EDUCATIONAL INPUTS

For the most part, the inputs or factors of production used in the educational system are not different from those used throughout the economy, and therefore, present no special problems. There is, however, one unique input into education, the student—whose foregone income while he attends school is a cost which is not reflected in budgetary expenditures. The main significance of student inputs in education for the study of internal efficiency of schools is not foregone earnings. It is the recognition that different students "embody" varying quantities of motivation, ability, and previous learning in order to avoid attribution to school inputs of levels of performance due to student characteristics.

Another unique feature of educational inputs is the application of a single salary schedule to instructors regardless of their specialty. While the salaries of most public employees are determined administratively, government salary schedules generally are responsive to relative scarcities and to demands from potential private employers. The single salary schedule—now almost universally adopted by local school systems throughout the United States—makes no allowance for variations in salary due to conditions in factor markets. As a result, school administrators cannot adjust salaries in specific subject areas such as mathematics and science in order to retain instructors of normal ability. Schools thus face the Hobson's choice of raising all salaries or using less well qualified personnel in those areas where demand is relatively high. This dilemma, expounded with clarity and much evidence by Kershaw and McKean,[18] seems to arise from the fear that educational productivity would be lessened if a multiple salary schedule were adopted due to problems of teacher morale. Systematic studies of school outputs can reveal the extent to which this notion is correct, and whether its effects are sufficient to offset the gains which would result from the more efficient use of educational resources which a multiple salary schedule would permit.

INPUT-OUTPUT RELATIONSHIP

One use of measures of inputs and outputs is in program budgeting in which the costs of specific programs are estimated on the basis of known methods of operation. When programs are specified in terms of measurable units of output, extremely useful comparisons of cost-effectiveness emerge, and policy can be based on knowledge of alternative achievements attainable from given outlays or of the incremental outlays necessary to provide

---

[17] Further discussion of measurement of the quality of education can be found in Warner Z. Hirsch, "Quality of Government Services," in Howard G. Schaller, Editor, *Public Expenditure Decisions in The Urban Community* (Washington, D. C.: Resources for The Future, Inc., 1962).
[18] J. A. Kershaw and R. N. McKean, *Teacher Shortages and Salary Schedules* (New York: McGraw-Hall Book Company, Inc., 1962).

a specified change in output. Unfortunately, the usual categories of educational program areas are so broad that useful program or performance classifications are impossible.[19] Uniform detailed program and performance classification and procedures for objective budgetary review would produce an enormous amount of invaluable data relating educational inputs to measures of performance.

Program budgeting is concerned with the costs of provision of specified service levels under the assumption that known and proven procedures will be employed. There is no assurance that alternative methods might not yield equal or greater performance at lower cost. Where comparable data exist, statistical methods can serve to estimate the extent to which measures of output increase per unit of increase of various inputs. In addition to the difficulty of obtaining accurate measures of variables, this kind of analysis is subject to many conceptual difficulties especially in the treatment of the effects of non-school variables on measures of educational performance.

The pioneer study in this area is the already mentioned *Systems Analysis in Education* by Kershaw and McKean. This work outlined persuasively and clearly the values of treating education as a system amenable to quantitative analysis, capable of evaluation in terms of efficiency, and responsive to policy decisions regarding inputs and administrative arrangements. The massive Project Talent study of the University of Pittsburgh[20] and the Quality Measurement Project of the New York State Department of Education[21] have obtained vast amounts of data on school inputs and outputs and several investigators recently have collected and analyzed similar information for Chicago, Atlanta, and Boston.[22]

Analysis of data have not yet revealed any generally consistent findings. Data, variables, and methods have differed, but almost all studies have had some success in the separation of school and non-school determinants of educational performance. Although the socioeconomic characteristics of pupils accounts for much of the explained variation in outputs among schools, most studies have found evidence that school characteristics such as overcrowding and average years of teaching experience also explain a portion of output. A further factor which makes research of this sort extremely complex is the finding in the Quality Measurement Project that the effect on educational outputs of school characteristics varies in accordance with sex, IQ, and socioeconomic level of the pupil. Difficult as this type of analysis may be, its necessity is underscored by

[19] For an attempt to organize the education activities of the Federal Government under program budget categories see Werner Z. Hirsch, "Education in the Program Budget," in *Program Budgeting* (Washington, D.C.: The RAND corporation, 1964-1965). Further discussion of program budgeting applied to education is found in Burkhead, *op. cit.*, Donald W. Hill, "Progress Report on Program Budgeting in Chicago"; and E. C. Stimber, "Progress Report on Programmed Budgeting in Memphis," *op. cit.*

[20] J. J. Dailey, J. C. Flanigan, I. Goldber, D. B. Orr, and M. F. Shaycroft, *Project Talent* (Pittsburgh: University of Pittsburgh, 1962) and Dailey, et al., *Project Talent* (Pittsburgh: University of Pittsburgh, 1964).

[21] N. Y. State Education Department, Division of Research, School Quality Workbook-*Achievement Norms for New York State Schools by Type of Community and Socio-Economic Level, The Quality Measurement Project* (New York: The University of the State of New York, 1963).

[22] Jesse Burkhead, *Input-Output Relationships in Large City High Schools* (Syracuse: Syracuse University Press, 1967) forthcoming. See also Martin Theodore Katzman, *Distribution and Production in a Big City Elementary School System*, mimeo, doctoral dissertation (Yale University, 1967).

Burkhead's comment, "unless some effort is made to gather and analyze such information, there are no economic or educational guidelines for the allocation of resources within public education."[23] Yet, even for the most pressing problems of contemporary education such efforts are not yet being made, as indicated by Weisbrod's complaint:

> One thing is clear. We are now essentially ignorant about the production function for dropout prevention, and we will remain so until there occurs a sharp increase in the number of prevention programs with experimental designs that shed light on the factors determining their success or failure. It is amazing how many attempts are being made around the nation to prevent dropouts, and how few are designed so as to premit assessment of their effectiveness.[24]

CRITERIA FOR EDUCATIONAL EXPENDITURES

After a discussion of efficient methods for the provision of specified educational programs, it is logical to turn to the question of what programs to provide. As has already been mentioned, the formal rule for achieving optimum levels of expenditure is that the benefits of the marginal resources employed for a particular purpose be just equal to the benefits which could be obtained from their most beneficial alternative use. While prices and costs in competitive markets do not always indicate society's valuation of additional units of commodities, such valuation does provide an operational basis for decisions regarding the allocation of resources for private good. For those commodities and services provided under the budget principle, the market provides neither prices to serve as measures of benefits nor profit maximization as an inducement to cost minimization. Under these circumstances, there is need for synthetic measures of the benefits of actual and potential public programs to compare with their costs in order to provide information essential for rational decisions. These synthetic measures are limited in scope since it is not possible to encompass the full range of consequences of the provision of public services in quantifiable, comparable units. Thus, such measures do not and should not be sole determinants of policy but, used imaginatively, they can indicate the relative magnitudes of certain kinds of benefits that result from various public programs. They, therefore, can be used to compare programs and to show what must be given up in terms of measurable benefits to attain goals in areas where benefits cannot be subject to measurement.

TECHNIQUES FOR SETTING PRIORITIES

Although there are still unresolved issues in the application of these notions to budget determination,[25] their use in a wide variety of areas, including education, is increasing rapidly.[26] The essential elements of the framework within which these quantitative aids to decision-making operate has been described as follows:

---

[23] Burkhead, "The Theory . . . ."*op. cit.*, p. 189.
[24] Burton A. Weisbrod, "Preventing High School Dropouts," in Robert Dorfman, Editor, *Measuring Benefits of Government Investments* (Washington: The Brookings Institution, 1963), p. 149.
[25] A systematic review of issues and problems is given in Otto Eckstein, "A Survey of the Theory of Public Expenditure Theory," in *Public Finances . . . , op. cit.*
[26] Presentation of a wide range of applications is found in Robert Dorfman, editor, *op. cit.*

A decision is a choice among feasible alternatives. The feasibility condition arises because of technical, legal, and organizational constraints upon choice or alternatives. Assuming that the behavior is purposive the choice involves a valuation of the consequences of the alternatives and a criterion to choose among them. In the evaluation, goals should be formulated and then, usually, translated from subjective values to objective indices, i.e. from psychic goals of welfare maximization to instrumental objectives such as housing standards, school facilities, traffic flows, etc.[27]

For the most part, in the actual determination of public expenditures, especially those—like education—for which state and local governments have primary responsibility, little heed is paid to this approach despite instances where it has been utilized with apparent success.

It is difficult to describe briefly the complex decision-making that ultimately results in overall educational budgets and allocations to specific programs. A list of factors surely would include legislation, state and school government administration, economic, demographic, and sociological characteristics, citizen attitudes, and a host of other elements. Yet, among this complex array, little if any concern in practice is given to systematic procedures for balancing the costs and consequences of particular educational programs. This is not to suggest that such analyses have not been undertaken, but that their use in the United States generally has been limited to scholarly studies of the contributions of education to past economic growth. When used to influence policy they have been mentioned as justifications for across-the-board additions to resources for education without regard for particular programs being advocated. Thus, the studies of Shultz, Denison, Becker, Weisbrod, Mincer and others have not yet found their rightful place in American educational finance. Their proper place is not confined to articles in proceedings of the Committee on Educational Finance of the NEA or similar reports, but must extend to use by those who prepare educational budgets.

It is not easy to spell out exactly how detailed quantifications of educational costs and benefits should be used in educational finance. Interestingly enough most of the efforts to make this approach a part of educational decision-making comes from those working on educational planning for underdeveloped countries where relatively rudimentary educational systems and a great shortage of resources generate enormous pressures to ensure that the education budget provides those educational services most essential to the achievement of national objectives.

In the quest for methods of setting educational priorities, there is still controversy regarding the distinction between consumption and investment aspects of education and, more importantly, with regard to the rate of return and the manpower approaches. The former suggest that the expected costs and benefits of alternative educational programs be estimated in terms of monetary units and that those that yield the highest internal rate of return be accorded priority. In contrast the manpower approach utilizes projections of the future structure of the economy to derive occupational requirements and, on the basis of assumed educational backgrounds for various occupations, provides an estimate of future needs for persons of

[27] Nathaniel Lichfield and Julius Margolis, "Benefit-Cost Analysis as a Tool in Urban Government Decision Making," in Howard G. Schaller, Editor, op. cit., p. 119.

various educational attainments. There are serious shortcomings in both of these approaches as exclusive indicators of educational priorities. Neither deals effectively with the non-economic benefits of education. Rate-of-return analysis of a single sector fails to make explicit vital complementarities that are crucial to the estimation of benefits. The manpower approach is virtually technocratic—being based on fixed relationships between the mix of economic outputs, occupational structure, and educational requirements—and ignores the effects of wage levels on the demand for skills and the costs of education.[28]

REQUISITES OF EDUCATIONAL PLANNING

Despite these and other shortcomings, *integration of new quantitative methods being developed for setting priorities in education into the mainstream of American educational finance is essential if education is to meet its future challenges.* Such an integration imposes substantial problems in an educational system as decentralized as that of the United States. Experience and impressions largely substantiated by studies of Weisbrod and Hirsch regarding geographic spillovers of education indicate that *educational planning and the setting of priorities requires consideration of areas far larger than traditional school districts.* This necessity derives not only from the spillovers of educational costs and benefits but because the effects of an educational program depend so much on conditions and developments in surrounding areas that effective policies of public expenditures require co-ordination among the entire range of public programs. Important and interesting as are these problems of appropriate governmental jurisdiction and administration, they are not peculiar to education and this is not the place to pursue them at length.

What is important for education and educational finance is that in a rapidly changing society and economy neither rules of thumb, repetition of past patterns, nor arbitrary intuitive changes will satisfy emerging needs. At a minimum, systematic and comprehensive analysis of costs and benefits of various educational programs by state and federal governments and dessemination of information regarding estimates of future demands for skills is required. At the same time, measures for inducing local schools to base decisions on such anlyses and information also are necessary. However, belief that such influence interferes with local autdomy and the miserly allocation of funds to educational research (estimated at less than one-tenth of one percent of expenditures during prior years) are strong hindrances to the implementation of these essential practices.

The essentials of sound educational planning go far beyond projections of school enrollments and per pupil expenditures. They extend to considerations of student performance standards, relevance of curriculum to future requirements for trained manpower and social aptitudes, compensatory education to offset deficiencies in home and neighborhood environment, and development of efficient educational techniques to accomplish

---

[28] For a review of these controversies see Jerry Miner, "The Relationship Between Economic and Educational Planning," in *The Yearbook of Education* (London: Evans Brothers Limited, 1967), forthcoming.

these ends. Such planning must, of course, be done with awareness of available resources and competing needs. All of these considerations, to a greater or lesser degree, transcend the technical and financial capacities of local school districts and their governing boards. *State, regional, and national bodies must supply information, leadership, and incentives for local schools to provide the education necessary to meet the challenges of the future.*

FINANCIAL ARRANGEMENTS

The organizing principle of this paper is that the proper conception of educational finance necessitates joint consideration of expenditures and revenues. In the previous two sections reflection of this joint consideration is implicit in the emphasis on comparison of the benefits that result from educational programs with their costs—the latter being interpreted as a measure of the value of foregone alternatives. Attractive and valuable as is such a framework for normative evaluation and even for policy recommendations, the practice of public finance is not based on voluntary exchange and is concerned with a great deal more than efficient allocation of scarce resources. As a consequence it is not justifiable to move directly from benefit-cost, rate of return, or manpower requirements analysis to policy conclusions even with regard only to economic considerations. The particular arrangements for the financing of public expenditures definitely matter because there are costs connected with taxation in general and there are different economic effects of tax dollars collected in different ways from different taxpayers.

In a sense, the objective of analysis of the effects of alternative revenue sources is the determination of the locus of tax burdens. Unfortunately the complex interactions that result from taxation make it not only impossible to ascertain the ultimate locus of a tax but even make this question meaningless. Instead, the study of actual and normative consequences of taxation stresses the effects of different taxes on such general matters as distribution of income, division of output between consumption and investment, and influence on the balance between work and leisure and on appropriate taxes for different levels of government.

PRESENT PATTERN OF FINANCIAL ARRANGEMENTS IN EDUCATION

The pattern of revenues traditionally used to finance local schools in the United States is a combination of local property taxes supplemented by grants-in-aid from general state government revenues. For public colleges and universities, state revenues provide the great majority of funds. Over the past decade, state-local revenues for public education have in the aggregate remained at about a 40-60 ratio, while the federal government's share has grown recently from 5 to 15 percent of total public spending for education, Throughout the period, the sources of state government revenues remained predominantly sales taxes and federal government grants. The impression of stability in state-local revenue sources is confirmed in the more extensive examination by Sacks and Campbell who conclude, "Over-all, the most remarkable aspect of state and local revenue sources over the past decade has been the stability of their proportional contribution. There have not been any dramatic developments in traditional revenue sources nor have there been any major new sources found."[29]

During this period, the division of state grants for local schools, according to purpose and method of distribution, has undergone only moderate change, mainly in favor of general-purpose equalizing grants. The magnitude of this type of grant—intended primarily to provide minimum expenditure levels in districts of low property valuations per student—increased from 40.6 percent of the amount of grant distributions in 1953-54 to 57.8 percent in 1962-63.[30]

Relative stability in patterns of state-local sources of funds and of grant distributions have been accompanied, of course, by large increases in absolute amounts of revenues and grants. Furthermore, average figures for the nation cannot portray the variety of relationships in individual states. This paper is not the proper vehicle for a detailed discussion, but it can be pointed out that the local share of total state-local revenues for public education, which averages about 60 percent, varied in 1964-65 from a low of 8.5 percent in Alaska and 23.6 percent for New Mexico to a high of 89.3 percent in Iowa.[31] Universal grants, which account for 91 percent of the total provided by the states, vary from 49.1 percent in Massachusetts to 100 percent in Idaho, Kentucky, Texas, and Wyoming.[32]

SIGNIFICANCE OF THE PATTERN

The emphasis on the property tax for the locally contributed share of school revenues has received heavy criticism. In the past, the attack was double barrelled involving both the inequity and the low responsiveness of this tax. Recent studies have confirmed the first hand experience of school finance administrators that in the past decade the responsiveness of the property tax was far greater than expected.[33] All of those who have projected local government revenues into the 1970's have used property tax elasticities substantially in excess of one.

If the sole issue were the future productivity of the property tax, it would suffice here to refer to the earlier discussion of projections and the contrast between the encouraging overall picture and the highly discouraging prospects for central cities and certain less affluent regions and areas. But, as with projections of expenditures, the question is not simply one of what the magnitudes will be if certain trends and assumptions are accepted, but importantly *whether the assumptions reflect what should happen.* For property taxes, a relevant issue is whether this highly inequitable, regressive, distorting yet productive tax should continue to play a major role in the finance of education. Despite the acknowledged validity of these defects there is an equally widely acknowledged characteristic of the property tax

[29] Campbell and Sacks, *op. cit.*, p. 15.
[30] *State Programs for Public School Support* (Washington, D.C.: U.S. Department of Health, Education, and Welfare, 1965), p. 112.
[31] *Financial Status of the Public School, 1965* (Washington, D. C.: National Education Association, 1965), p. 48.
[32] *State Programs for Public School Support, op. cit.* p. 98.
[33] See, for example, Jesse Burkhead, *Public School Finance, Economics and Politics* (Syracuse: Syracuse University Press, 1964), p. 186-189.

that accounts for its continued extensive use: it is amenable to local collection and administration. As a result, with the consent of the state, local governments—from municipalities to counties to sanitary, water, school, and other special districts—can achieve the autonomy that comes only with the power to levy taxes.

The issue of the property tax, then, appears to break down to the choice between an especially undesirable tax or the loss of fiscal autonomy. School administrators have almost without exception, opted for the tax, but public finance economists have not so readily accepted it as the lesser evil. In fact, there are reservations regarding both the independence of school districts and the finance by property taxation even of dependent school systems.

A great many alternatives to property taxation as a source for finance of local governments have been proposed. In the United States today, grants-in-aid account for some 30 percent of local government revenues and over 45 percent of revenues for local schools. Such grants-in-aid provide funds that reduce requirements for local tax revenues, but so long as the local government is to retain fiscal autonomy it must have legal taxation powers. The device of shared taxes gives to local governments a stipulated portion of revenues collected from within the local jurisdiction from a tax administered by the state. A variant—supplementary taxes—gives local governments leeway to determine individually the rate which they wish to apply for the local portion of a state tax. It is true that, even with a supplementary tax, the local government must accept the base and provisions of the state tax, but this does not seem an excessive surrender of sovereignty —especially since local property tax administration usually is closely supervised by the state.

Another proposal is to grant credit against federal personal income tax liabilities for state and local tax payments. While there is much to be said in favor of the uniformity in state-local taxation which such a policy would engender, the credit itself does not do away with the need for a locally administered tax. On the contrary it encourages state and local governments to levy those taxes for which credit is given or, if such taxes already are in effect, it provides an opportunity to increase revenues at the expense of the federal government. Since it is generally agreed that property taxes are the only major revenue source amenable to local administration and since such taxes would not qualify for tax credits, this proposal, in effect, encourages greater use of state sales and income taxation and thus would provide funds for state grants-in-aid but not for direct revenues to local governments.[34]

Failure of American local governments to adopt tax arrangements that would permit them to abandon heavy reliance on property taxation almost certainly can be attributed to their unwillingness to relinquish any of their hard-won powers of taxation. Until the past decade there was a basic unity to the municipality which was consistent with a desire for taxation

---

[34] The most extensive discussion of tax credits is James A. Maxwell, *Tax Credits and Intergovernmental Fiscal Relations* (Washington, D. C.: The Brookings Institution, 1962). For a more favorable evaluation of the property tax see Maxwell's *Financing State and Local Governments* (Washington, D.C.: The Brookings Institution, 1965). Chapter VI.

powers roughly commensurate with expenditure responsibilities. Today, with the movement of the locus of income and property to the suburbs, the unity of the city has been destroyed and the fiscal problems of metropolitan areas lie largely in efforts to undermine local fiscal autonomy. The independent school district, however, always was a separate entity. Economists and political scientists remain unconvinced that it is proper for decisions regarding one particular public function to be made outside the context within which support for all other local government functions is determined. The argument that fiscal autonomy is necessary for the proper functioning of the educational system is far from convincing since health and hospital services, police and fire protection, streets and roads, and sanitation—all function without such autonomy.

Arguments for fiscal independence are not limited to the necessity for fiscal autonomy to preserve the freedom of the schools but extend to the pragmatic contention that independent school systems obtain greater revenues. Even if correct, this would not necessarily be desirable from an economic standpoint if the additional revenues would have yielded higher returns in other public or private uses. Recent studies, however, by the author of this paper and by H. Thomas James, J. Alan Thomas and Harold J. Dyck have revealed that when account is taken of other determinants of school expenditures it cannot be demonstrated that fiscal independence is associated with higher levels of educational outlays.[35]

INTER-GOVERNMENTAL SOURCES OF REVENUE

The economic issues involved in inter-governmental relations are an extension of those relating to general governmental economic policies: given the objectives of efficiency, equity, stabilization, and growth, what is the most appropriate distribution of responsibilities for services and granting of powers of taxation? Very broadly, the answers given by economists who study these problems of fiscal federalism are that *the expenditure responsibilities and taxing powers of any particular level of government need not be commensurate;* that *local governments must play a major role in the provision and finance of government functions which primarily benefit local residents;* and that *services yielding benefits over a more extensive area may be administered by local governments but require wider sources of funds.* Also, since local governments cannot contribute to regional redistribution of income nor to stabilization objectives, funds to meet such concerns must come from state and federal sources.

The ultimate general pattern of governmental responsibility that follows from these economic concerns is that local governments administer the schools and contribute toward total educational outlays an amount determined by the local communities' demand for education. The funds for these outlays should come from local residents and business firms according to acceptable standards of equitable burden, although they may be raised by the state or even the federal tax system and returned to the point of collection. To this amount is added the demand for education emanating from

[35] H. Thomas James, et. al., op. cit., p. 98-100. See also Part III for a detailed discussion of fiscal and political independence of school systems.

benefits of education obtained by persons residing outside the locality. The funds for these outlays come from sources outside the local government. Finally, state and federal grants to local schools to redistribute income in the form of educational service, provide additional sources of funds for educational spending by local systems.

This ideal pattern of inter-governmental relations is a reasonably accurate qualitative picture of the prevailing situation in the United States. *Since all levels of government now are involved in the finance of public education, questions of policy revolve around the relative magnitude of involvement.* It seems clear that future social and economic developments will heighten still further the overall inter-dependence and great geographic mobility of American society. These features increase the extent of geographic spillovers of education and *indicate that a greater portion of support for local schools should come from state and federal tax sources.* Another element that militates for a movement in this direction is the continued failure of the property tax base to reflect even the local benefits of education, since political pressures have led to property tax concessions to attract new industry or the drawing of school district boundaries to reduce tax pressures on industrial and commercial property. Reliance on the far more equitable tax structures of the state and especially the federal government would relieve these undesirable conditions. An additional factor of growing importance is the demand being placed on education in central cities throughout the nation and in the rural south as the key to long run reduction of poverty and ghetto life. Only through regional redistribution can high-cost compensatory education programs be financed.

These arguments for greater state and federal finance of local schools imply, for the most part, general purpose grants, but prospective developments suggest that some strings be attached to state and federal grants. First of all, *care must be taken to ensure that funds given for education do not lead to equivalent reductions in local taxation for this purpose, except where equalization is intended.* Special provisions can prevent such reactions, but care must also be taken to avoid the distortion of the entire pattern of local expenditures that can come from higher levels of government offering matching funds at highly attractive rates. The study by Campbell and Sacks mentioned above indicates that state and federal aid generally does not lead to offsetting reductions in local taxes in suburban areas, although they do find that local taxes are higher when local governments have a greater share in the finance of local expenditures. They find evidence, however, that central cities tend to reduce local taxes in response to grants-in-aid. Such tax relief may be sound and reasonable policy in view of high urban taxes and costs of living, but educational outlays are not augmented by this reaction. In some situations, special-purpose grants —which cannot be used to substitute for regular expenditures—may be the only way of insuring increased educational expenditures.

A second reason for attaching strings to grants is that *local school systems may not know of or may not be sufficiently concerned with the educational requirements of future society.* General purpose grants so far have not led to massive injections of educational inputs into schools heavily populated by negroes and other low income groups. Program grants from both state and federal governments aimed at these and other specific areas of educational activities are a necessary complement to general purpose grants. There is probably no educational policy more effective than special purpose grants to speed the process of change by local schools.

In summary, the increasing expenditure requirements for all state-local government functions are likely to generate pressures for increased property tax rates unless there is a shift to greater reliance on state sources of revenue or a transfer of federal revenues to state and local governments. Objection to the former course is not primarily fear that the property tax base is insufficiently elastic to prevent large increases in rates, but arises largely from a concern that vastly superior tax sources are available only if some reduction in local autonomy is accepted. More specifically with regard to education, the nature of its benefits and its potential power for stimulation of economic and social mobility indicate an increased role in finance and control by levels of government which have wider responsibilities and outlooks than local school systems.

FINANCING HIGHER EDUCATION

Much of the major lines of the preceding discussion also apply to higher education. One important feature of higher education is that, because much of the benefit accrues directly to the student and because obligations with regard to equality of opportunity are seen by many as less important beyond high school, students are required to pay some portion of the costs. Since a substantial portion of the benefits of higher education accrue in the form of increased incomes for its graduates, students who can afford to do so stand ready to pay tuition roughly commensurate with costs so that private colleges and universities are financially viable. Public colleges and universities which charge lower tuition than private are largely financed from governmental revenues partly to redistribute income and partly because public institutions of higher education perform functions such as research and extension services whose benefits accrue largely in the form of external effects from which non-payers could not be excluded.

Here again it is relevant to point out that the local nature of benefits from junior and community colleges which emphasize training to meet local demands for technicians indicate the appropriateness of local and state sources of finance, and that the geographically wide-ranging benefits of colleges or universities indicate state and national government support.

Even where tuition is quite low, private expenses of completing a program of higher education are considerable, rising with length of study. Expectations that the present value of increased future after-tax income will exceed these costs, plus earning foregone along with non-pecuniary motives for acquisition of higher education, provide sufficient motive for almost 25 percent of the relevant age group to attend colleges and universities. For many qualified persons, however, the financial outlays required plus the income foregone during the period of study present a sufficient burden to prevent them from attendance. Although it would be actuarially sound for such persons to borrow to meet these needs, the private capital market is not receptive to loans without collateral and potential students are reluctant to incur long term obligations given the risk that they might not complete their studies. As a way out of this problem, Seymour Harris has championed the proposal that the federal government establish a program for lending money to students at low rates with repayments a function of future earnings. While such a scheme would not resolve the loss of potential students for reasons associated with earlier inadequate education, it would open possibilities to many, and appears to be a most useful complement to policies for strengthening local education and increasing retention rates in high schools.

CONCLUSION

This paper takes the view that the proper concern of educational finance extends to all those aspects of education which involve use of scarce resources. Within this context, adaptation of educational finance to prospective changes in society requires not only that decisions regarding overall allocation of resources to the education sector be consistent with alternative private and public uses but that specific educational programs be determined in light of their contribution to the objectives of society. Since many detailed educational decisions depend upon unknowable specific future developments, the emphasis here is on methods and arrangements for the introduction into educational planning of information relevant to the evaluation of alternative educational programs. Included among such methods are projections, systems analysis, cost-benefit analysis, manpower requirements studies, and program and performance budgeting.

All of these methods reflect the importance, in matters of educational finance, of considerations that transcend the boundaries, knowledge, and competencies of local school governments. The need for recognition of the wide scope of benefits and therefore of sources of finance for education is strongly reinforced by prospects of even greater future regional, social, and economic interdependence.

Perhaps the greatest challenge of the future for technologically advanced societies is to devise methods of policy formulation and institutional arrangements that can cope with the already enormous and steadily growing interdependence of social systems. Education, surely one of the most vital components of this social system, must not lag in expanding the frame within which its decisions are made.